Natural History
in America

Natural History
in America

From Mark Catesby to Rachel Carson

Wayne Hanley
Massachusetts Audubon Society

A Demeter Press Book

Quadrangle/The New York Times Book Co.

Library of Congress Cataloging in Publication Data

Hanley, Wayne, 1915-
  Natural history in America.

  "A Demeter Press book."
  1. Natural history—United States—History.
  2. Naturalists—United States—Biography.
  I. Title.
QH104.H28 1976   500.9'73'0922 [B]   76-9704
ISBN 0-8129-0643-8

Dedicated to Eleanor, for her forbearance

Contents

(Illustrations follow pages 84 and 180.)

Acknowledgments

The Massachusetts Audubon Society is grateful to the Museum of Comparative Zoology of Harvard University for permission to photograph some of the treasures in its library. Specifically the Society thanks Ann Blum, who searched the material used in illustrations, and A. H. Coleman and Paula Chandoha who copied the original art.

For making available first editions of various naturalists' work, the Society expresses its indebtedness to Edward D. Pearce, librarian, and Barbara Wiseman, reference librarian, both of the Boston Museum of Science; Ruth Hill, librarian, Museum of Comparative Zoology; and a cohort of here unnamed librarians, most now dead, whose patience and understanding opened access to the sometimes wonderful shelves over which they presided.

Gratitude goes to Dr. William H. Drury of the College of the Atlantic whose careful notes on the late M. L. Fernald's lectures at Harvard on the history of botany and botanists were made available; to Dr. Gordon DeWolfe, former taxonomist, and Dr. Stephen Spongberg, present taxonomist, Arnold Arboretum, who so willingly answered many questions; to James Baird, without whose encouragement this volume never would have been completed, and to Margaret McDaniel and Louise Maglione, librarians, whose orderliness made retrievable a small collection of valuable natural history volumes owned by the Society. Special thanks to Dr. Ernst Mayr, former head of the MCZ; Mrs. Aaron M. Bagg, Mr. and Mrs. Robert Shaw, and John H. Mitchell. An accolade to Virginia Jevon and Doris Ellis whose patience in the manuscript stages was sometimes Spartan.

For overlooking the compiler's transgressions, including diversion of working time, and providing many other acts of compassion, the compiler owes thanks to the Massachusetts Audubon Board of Directors and Allen H. Morgan, Executive Vice President.

In spite of a wealth of good advice, the compiler acknowledges in advance the probability that faulty interpretation, and occasional flagrant error, have crept into a text of so broad a spectrum. A few errors were copied from others; but most are original.

Introduction

This is not a profound volume.

It is essentially a collection of readable passages selected from the writings of great American naturalists. In their day, these paragraphs were profound. But their impacts already have been made. Man's view of the world already has been changed by them. If you are reading them for the first time and yet they seem familiar, it is because they have become part of your culture. Many of the ideas have pervaded the western pattern of thought; you know them subconsciously.

So, why bother with such a collection?

Since the compiler is as interested in the roots of modern natural history as he is in the flourishing branches of the present, he has devoted years to gaining access to the observations of the early practitioners.

As a pursuer of ancient tomes, the compiler knows how difficult they are to borrow, or even to read by permission while a librarian hovers nearby. Fewer than one hundred original copies of some of these works still exist—in some cases, fewer than one hundred copies were printed. Time, fires, accidents, and even wars, have taken a toll among the even rarer. These volumes are almost inaccessible to the general reader.

Since this anthology consists of fragments, the compiler has chosen segments that reveal the humanness of the author rather than his or her heft as an observer. Behind the selection process lies a wicked plot: to send you delving into the works of the old masters in search of more adventures in reading.

Anyone familiar with the originals will tell you that the beautiful plates reproduced in this volume do not do justice to the real thing. And, in many cases, that is true. There is no printing process today that can reproduce all the nuances of the delicate tones that hand colorists applied from their palettes. After more than two centuries the art in a well-preserved copy of Catesby retains vibrant colors that only an artist working by hand could apply to paper. The single exception may be the work of Louis Agassiz Fuertes, whose art was plied with the color press in mind.

Although there is no direct channel of transition, the continuity exists in the chronological order in which the chapters appear. It is in essence a history of natural history development in America through 200 years. Catesby and the Bartrams bring us from the early 1700s through the American Revolution. From Lewis and Clark through John Edwards Holbrook one sees American naturalists at work between the Revolution and the Civil War. Muir and Burroughs through Brewster, Hornaday, and Company finish the nineteenth century. Theodore Roosevelt ushers in the twentieth century, beginning the recent trends that lead through to Rachel Carson.

Natural History
in America

Chapter I

In the Beginning: Catesby

The Western Hemisphere was not completely unknown to Europeans when Mark Catesby began the biological exploration that resulted in his book. Many early visitors had sent back accounts of the New World, as well as collections of plants and such curious wildlife specimens as the rattlesnake, opossum, and hummingbird.

Although it is unfair to a few of the observers, one may regard most early natural history reports from America largely as promotional material designed to lure settlers to the new colonies. Wildlife lists in these reports were little more than suggested menus indicating that settlers would find plenty to eat. The rare exceptions were such things as rattlesnakes and alligators, which settlers were told to avoid. Most of the writers had but vague ideas of the relationships among animals or plants, and they saw the natural world generally encompassed by the book of Genesis. Some had no idea at all of relationships. For instance, John Lawson working on his *History of North Carolina* in the period between 1700 and 1712, wrote: "Tortois, vulgarly called Turtle: I have ranked these among the Insects because they lay eggs, and I did not know well where to put them. . . ." Although true, Lawson's comment exaggerates the level of ignorance in the field. There were naturalists in England and France, and others in America, who had a better grasp on the problems of classification than Lawson. Yet his remark illustrates the problems of colonial naturalists who worked in isolation and had little more than their own instincts to guide them. Taken in that light, Lawson seems less ludicrous. He at least was thinking. The turtle does have an external skeleton, as insects do, and like insects, the turtle depends upon environmental heat to activate its movements. Lawson disappeared in North Carolina in 1712 and supposedly was tortured to death by Indians. When Lawson's *History* was published in 1714, John Bartram was fifteen years old.

An exception to the general rule of incompetence or worse among early eighteenth-century naturalists was Mark Catesby. Catesby's

Natural History of Carolina, Florida and the Bahama Islands was unquestionably the most competent guide to the southeastern colonies of
its period, and its art was a model of accuracy until Alexander Wilson
began his paintings of the birds of North America. Catesby, however,
was an Englishman. He was merely a visitor to the colonies, although
he remained west of the Atlantic longer than most of his contemporary
naturalists. Thus both the period in which he worked and his nationality disqualify him as an American naturalist. His two-volume, large-
folio *Natural History,* which began appearing in parts in 1730, is
among the most ambitious undertakings associated with American
natural history. Each volume contained one hundred hand-colored
plates, and after completion of the original goal of two hundred plates
in 1743, Catesby in 1748 added an appendix containing twenty more
colored plates.

The scope of Catesby's work is given in its extended title, which
reads: "Containing the Figures of Birds, Beasts, Fishes, Serpents, Insects and Plants: Particularly the Forest-Trees, Shrubs, and other Plants,
not hitherto described, or very incorrectly figured by Authors:
Together with their descriptions in English and French. To which are
added, Observations on the Air, Soil and Waters: With remarks upon
Agriculture, Grain, Pulse, Roots, Etc." He could have added "comments upon Indians and other inhabitants with a bit about their cultural attributes," for he included rather extensive coverage in those
fields as well. In fact, his voluminous report on the southeastern
Indians and their ways is one of the more interesting sections of the
work. He treated the Indians as humans, rather than wildlife, an attitude not too prevalent in that day and one that later would fall from
style.

As a person Catesby seems almost never to have existed. Not even
the shadow of a personality remains except what is reflected in his
writing. There exists no known portrait of him. Even the date of his
birth, supposedly between 1679 and 1682, is unrecorded. His death has
been reported variously as having occurred either in 1749 or 1750, one
version recounting his death and burial at sea from the vessel *Portfield.*
While disappearance without a trace is the lot of many men, it seems
unusual in Catesby's case, because he was well known and honored in
life. He was a Fellow of the Royal Society, an honor that meant he
was accepted by members of that exclusive scientific group. He was a
friend of Sir Hans Sloane, president of the College of Physicians and
secretary of the Royal Society, and a friend and correspondent of
Peter Collinson, who also became a patron of John Bartram. It is
obvious from the list of men who sponsored his second journey to

America that he was a respected and trusted botanist. Yet the only conclusive record that he existed is his *Natural History* and his comments in it regarding his life.

Although nothing is known of Catesby's education, he relates in his book that he moved to London because he had been living too far from a center of science. He says that he spent seven years in Virginia, where a sister was the wife of the secretary to the governor. He arrived there in 1712. On this first visit to America, he seems to have roamed the countryside and even spent some time in Jamaica. He collected and took home to England botanical specimens, seeds, and several tubs of living plants, possibly trees.

Apparently his reports on Virginia and a few botanical drawings he had made there impressed fellow botanists in England. Catesby is vague on the point. At any rate, in 1722 a group of English botanists agreed to back him financially in a trip to the Carolinas. Among the backers was Col. Francis Nicholson, governor of South Carolina, who promised a small stipend for his support. Catesby spent three years roaming South Carolina and ventured across the Savannah River for a limited look at Georgia, which seems to be as close as he actually got to Florida. The fourth year he spent in the Bahamas, living mainly on Providence Island. In 1726 he returned to England, never to see America again.

It is important to note that Catesby, and Bartram after him, were supported by wealthy men who had an interest in botany. In that period, the wealthy were the equivalent of foundations or government agencies in supporting naturalists. In effect, they were men with a deep interest in a subject who were sending out servants to get information for them from the library. But in this era, the library was the world and the information was unrecorded. So they had to choose the servant wisely, for the information they received would depend totally on his wisdom and background.

When Catesby returned to England, he soon learned that his backers, who had been avid for botanical specimens and seeds, had no desire to enter the publishing business. Though interested in his paintings, they had no intention of investing in their publication. Meanwhile, Catesby lacked the funds to pay an engraver to produce plates. He finally solved the dilemma by learning to engrave copper plates himself.

In Catesby's day, and for more than a century later, the color printing process was unknown. Engravers made a copper plate, usually a reverse image of the painting, and then printed an uncolored line drawing of the art. The publisher or author then employed painters, known as colorists, to apply color to every copy of the plate. The colorist followed the colors as they appeared on the original art. To some extent, the operation was comparable to the sort of painting that bears a number in each area to indicate to the hobbyist the color to paint that area. Catesby comments in his introduction that he advanced the art of color plates by rejecting the common practice of the day of cross-hatching a bird's body to suggest feathering. Instead, he engraved individual feather marks, thus heightening the reality of his birds. As a result of the colorist process, each purchaser of Catesby's book had a sheaf of hand-colored plates. While the quality of coloring depended upon the skill of the colorist and the degree to which the author demanded perfection, the result usually was a strikingly beautiful volume. For his book, Catesby chose brilliant paint, which has resisted deterioration. More than two centuries later, the plates still are beautiful.

Catesby relates in the book that he had no training as a painter, that he did not understand perspective in art, and that his goal was a flat representation to be studied for its accuracy rather than its artistic merit. He thereby described his product very well.

Among Catesby's achievements was a classification of South Carolina soils as rich lands, oak and hickory land, pine barrens, and scrubby oak land, a sorting that hinted a vague understanding of ecosystems, for his classifications are still valid. He suffered, however, under the handicap common to all workers in natural history of that era: the lack of any standards or reference points upon which to base scientific descriptions of the organisms they discovered. Each naturalist chose whatever part or parts of a plant he considered significant and used these reference points (which often had significance only to him) in determining where the plant might fit in the natural scheme. Naturalists made frequent references to a Wise Creator who, it was assumed, shaped plants and animals as it suited His fancy during the creative week of Genesis. Although heresy among them ranged from hints to outright statements, one may doubt whether they recognized their thoughts as heretical to the theological assumption that once God finished his creative work, all things remained immutable. It was a time given more to cataloging than classifying, the tools for classification in any systemic fashion being missing and the philosophical climate being devoted to the idea that second-guessing God was unproductive.

Catesby chose South Carolina, he said, because of "its Productions being very little known, except that barely related to Commerce, such as Rice, Pitch and Tar." This made his *Natural History* a unique and valuable contribution, for he dealt with plants and animals in terms of their intrinsic interest rather than their commercial value.

The outstanding pictures by Catesby are of fishes. He states that he deferred painting fishes until he went to the Bahamas, "for as they afford but few Quadrupeds and Birds, I had more time to describe the fishes, and tho' I had been often told they were very remarkable, yet I was surprised to find how lavishly nature had adorned them with Marks and Colours most admirable."

He wrote of the barracuda:

This Fish grows to a large size: some of them I have seen ten feet in length, and some, I was told, are much longer; though the more common length is that of about six or eight feet. It is long in proportion to its thickness, and in shape resembles somewhat the European Pike. The eyes are large and bright: the mouth is very wide, having the under jaw longer than the upper: the upper jaw is armed with four large teeth, placed at the fore part of the under jaw; next the head are placed ten smaller teeth, being five on each side; and in the fore part of the same jaw grows one single large tooth. On the back grow two short fins, distant from one another, with six ribs in each fin; near the gills grow two more, at a like distance; lower on the belly was another pair, and a single one a little behind the anus; in all, seven fins. The tail wide and forked.

This Fish was covered with thin scales of a middling size; dark brown on the back, lightening gradually to the belly, which was white. It is a swift-swimming and very voracious fish, preying on most others; and some of the largest size have frequently attacked and devoured men, as they were washing in the sea. They are in great plenty in all the shallow seas of the Bahama islands, and in many other places between the Tropicks. The flesh has a very rank and disagreeable flavour both to the nose and palate, and is frequently poisonous, causing great sickness, and intolerable pain in the head, with loss of hair and nails: yet the hungry Bahamians frequently repast on their unwholesome carcasses.

Although Catesby promised to confine his natural history to organisms found "between the 30th and 45th degrees of latitude" (roughly the Bahamas to Boston), he strayed beyond the bounds to accommodate the "moose deer," a species which he admitted not seeing and which occurred above the 45th latitude; the Quickhatch, whose description roughly fits a wolverine and which he said came from Hudson's Bay; and the "white bear," or polar bear.

His mammal paintings are the least satisfactory. Many mammals are partly hidden behind vegetation and are not rendered to scale, the vegetation having been given prominence. In a few cases, such as his painting of the bison, the lack of perspective creates astonishing contrasts in scale. The bison rubbing against the trunk of a tree appears about the same size as a leaf of the tree jutting from a branch supposedly growing toward the observer. But lacking perspective, the composition appears grotesque.

He was unaware that the house mouse and the black rat were immigrants accidentally introduced to America, and placed them among "Beasts of which the same are in the old World," rather than under the heading "Beasts that were not in America till they were introduced there from Europe."

The opossum, being a marsupial that carries its young from embryo stage to independence in a pouch under the abdomen, was a curiosity to Europeans, who had no comparable animal. In his description, Catesby includes a few experiments that corrected general misconceptions regarding the opossum:

> Though contrary to the laws of Nature, nothing is more believed in America, than that these Creatures are bred at the teats of their dams: but as it is apparent from the dissection of one of them by Dr. Tyson, that their structure is formed for generation like that of other animals, they must necessarily be bred and excluded the usual way of other quadrupeds; yet that which has given cause to the contrary opinion is very wonderful; for I have many times seen the young ones just born, fixt and hanging to the teats of their dams when they were not bigger than mice; in this state all their members were apparent, yet not so distinct and perfectly formed, but that they looked more like a fetus than otherwise, and seemed inseparably fixed to the teats, from which no small force was required to pull their mouths; and then being held to the teat, would not fix to it again. By what method the dam after exclusion fixes them to her teats, is a secret yet unknown.

Catesby was astute in his observation that the young opossums looked like embryos—which, indeed, they are. The young he describes as appearing like mice would have been about two months old. At birth, young opossums are the size of bumblebees. They have forepaws capable of grasping the hairs on the mother's body and they crawl to the pouch, enter, and attach themselves to a teat, which is as slender as a thread. The tip of the teat then enlarges, filling the embryo's mouth and forging the firm connection that Catesby noted. Instead of the embryo nursing, the mother exudes milk into it, which accounts for Catesby's inability to make the young reattach to the teat, since they do not suckle.

The Catesby snakes are recognizable. The paintings, as well as the accounts of species, indicate that Catesby was not familiar with the characteristics used by naturalists in separating the species. He painted only dorsal views, as one might see the snake when looking down upon it. Illustrators attempting to convey full information usually draw snakes in a spiral-like display, which shows the dorsal view of the head, a side view of part of the body, and the scaling on the ventral side near the junction of body and tail. Such a view discloses several points of information useful in identifying the specimen.

> I have seen in Carolina eighteen or nineteen sorts of serpents; whereof four are of the Viper kind, the others of the snake kind. It is well known that the most distinguishing characteristicks of the Viper is, that it brings forth its young alive; and of Snakes, that it lays eggs. . . .

The statement contains several inaccuracies, which indicate not only that Catesby did not know much about the snakes of North America but also that he possessed too little information on snakes in general to make any meaningful classification possible. Among other things, one of the commonest snakes in eastern North America, the garter snake, bears its young alive, as do many other nonpoisonous snakes.

Catesby removed many legends from the rattlesnake in his description of the animal. The largest rattler he had seen, he wrote, was about eight feet long and weighed between eight and nine pounds. His reference could have been only to the eastern diamondback rattlesnake, since of all the rattlesnakes it alone approaches such proportions. It is native to the Carolinas. His comments indicate that he was unaware that several species of rattlesnakes exist. He referred to the animal as *Vipera caudisone americana* and called it "the rattle-snake." He said it was

> the most inactive and slow moving Snake of all others. . . . when provoked, they give warning by shaking their rattles. These are commonly believed to be the most deadly venomous serpents of

any in these parts of America; I believe they are so, as being generally the largest, and making a deeper wound, and injecting a greater quantity of poison; though I know not why any of the other three kinds of Vipers may not be as venomous as a Rattle-Snake, if as big; the structure of their deadly fangs being formed alike in all. . . .

Catesby gave a few plant roots that settlers and Indians considered medicine for a rattlesnake bite. He had doubts about the remedies, however.

Having by traveling much with Indians, had frequent opportunities of seeing the direful effects of the bites of these snakes, it always seemed and was apparent to me, that the good effects usually attributed to these their remedies, is owing more to the force of nature, or the bite of a small snake in a muscular part, etc. . . . but where a Rattle-Snake with full force penetrates with his deadly fangs, and pricks a vein or artery, inevitable death ensues; and that, as I have often seen, in less than two minutes. The Indians know their destiny the minute they are bit; and when they perceive it mortal, apply no remedy, concluding all efforts in vain. If the bite happeneth in a fleshy part, they immediately cut it out, to stop the current of the poison.

Catesby described the eastern diamondback rattlesnake (*Crotalus adamanteus*) adequately, including both drawings and a lengthy verbal description of the rattle structure. There were two other species of rattlesnakes in the region he covered, but Catesby possibly thought the other smaller rattlers were young snakes, which would grow to diamond rattler size.

The general soundness of Catesby is illustrated in his final paragraph on the rattlesnake:

The charming, as it is commonly called, or attractive power this Snake is said to have of drawing to it animals, and devouring them, is generally believed in America; as for my own part, I never saw the action; but a great many from whom I have had it related, all agree in the manner of the process; which is, that the animals, particularly birds and squirrels (which principally are their prey) no sooner spy the Snake than they skip from spray to spray, lowering and approaching gradually nearer their enemy, regardless of any other danger; but with distracted gestures and outcries descend, though from the top of the highest trees to the mouth of the Snake, who openeth his jaws, takes them in, and in an instant swallows them.

While Catesby was rather sophisticated for his era regarding most natural history matters, his discussion of bird distribution gives an insight to the prevalent philosophies of early naturalists, most of whom accepted an orthodox religious basis as an explanation of nature's ways. He wrote:

> In America are very few European land birds, but of the water kinds there are many, if not most of those found in Europe, besides the great variety of species peculiar to those parts of the World.
>
> Admitting the World to have been universally replenished with all animals from Noah's ark after the great deluge, and that those European Birds which are in America found their way thither from the old World, the cause of disparity in number of the land and water kinds, will evidently appear by considering their different structure, and manner of feeding, which enables the water fowl to perform a long voyage with more facility than those of the land. . . .

After speculating over the fact that birds from North America often are blown by the north wind to Bermuda, Catesby then suggests that the distance across the Atlantic between Europe and North America may be too great to allow such wind-borne passage between the continents. He then ponders another possibility:

> Though the nearness or joining of the Continents be not known, we may reasonably conclude it to be within or very near the arctic circle, the coasts of the rest of the Earth being well known; so that those few European Land Birds that are in America must have passed thither from a very frigid part of the old World. . . .
>
> Though these reasons occur to me, I am not fully satisfied, nor do I conclude that by this method they passed from one Continent to the other, the climate, and their inability of performing a long flight, may be reasonably objected.
>
> To account therefore for this extraordinary circumstance, there seems to remain but one more reason for their being found on both Continents; which is the nearness of the two parts of the

Earth to each other heretofore, where now flows the vast Atlantic
Ocean. . . .

In this decade during which has emerged a geological theory that
the continents may be adrift on gigantic plates that slowly change
positions, one may place too much emphasis upon Catesby's speculation
that Europe and North America may at some time have been closer
together. Although many scientists now believe that shifting relationships among the continents may explain some of the mysteries of plant
and animal distribution, Catesby probably was speculating wildly. He
had no factual basis for the conjecture. Perhaps he no more believed it
than Jules Verne could accept as attainable his story of a human cir-
cling the earth in only eighty days!

Because Catesby was a botanist, he probably would have been surprised, if he had lived long enough, to find that his bird illustrations
were destined to become more famous than his botanical art. In his
plates, he mingled birds with plants, explaining: "I have adapted the
birds to those plants on which they feed, or have any relation to." The
device enabled him to give his readers far more information, since
more than one object appeared on a single plate. It imparted a sense of
life and reality, since most birds normally are seen in relation to a plant.
It also indicated ecological relationships and allowed a flexibility of
design that a later bird painter named Audubon would bring nearer to
perfection.

Catesby's plates feature 109 birds of the Western Hemisphere and
comprise the first impressive assemblage of these species in full color.
Their value to science was highlighted by the technology of the times.
In that era, present methods of skinning a bird and preserving the skin
with feathers intact as a reference specimen had not been developed. A
rather primitive method of removing the entrails and attempting to
preserve the bird, meat and all, was in vogue. Usually after the bird
was dried by baking and embalmed by various crude spirits, the specimen was arranged in a "natural" position through a process of insert-
ing wires in the body. The result was far less satisfactory than that
achieved by modern taxidermy, for the body of the bird was destined
to rot in a matter of years. One wonders what the museums of the day
must have smelled like.

To some extent it was the ease of preserving natural specimens that
had enabled the botanists to forge ahead of other naturalists of that
period. A botanist could press a complete plant, preserving it indefinitely. He could make several dried specimens and circulate these
with a written description among other botanists. By means of the

process, the botanist presented his contemporaries with the actual plant and his written notes, including the name he had given it. With this material, another botanist could determine readily whether a plant that *he* had found conformed to the dried specimen, which meant it already had been described, or if it varied from all dried specimens available in collections and therefore was a new species.

The existence of type specimens, the actual plants upon which descriptions were based, tended to stabilize the science. A new naturalist in the field could learn rather quickly how a predecessor worked if he could gain access to a herbarium and inspect the complete record, including the type specimens. In a sense, the herbarium was as valuable to the botanist as the alphabet has always been to historians. It makes possible a complete review of what has happened in the past and provides a base for proceeding into the future.

The botanist's problem in Catesby's day was that the discipline had not developed an efficient filing system which would permit a worker in the field instant access to any plant he wished to use for comparison. There are more than 300,000 species of plants on earth, and plant explorers like Catesby were finding too many new species to tuck away in a herbarium that lacked an efficient filing system. The result was chaos.

Catesby and his European supporters were not far removed from the Doctrine of Signatures generally attributed to Paracelsus of Hohenheim, who practiced medicine in the early 1500s. Behind the doctrine was a belief that God had provided all natural objects for man's use and that one need but study the general shape of an object to determine its suggested use, particularly in medicine. Thus the hepatica's liver-shaped leaf suggested that it was a medicine for liver ailments, and the plant became "liverwort" (literally, liver plant). As late as 1664, English botanist Robert Turner wrote: "God hath imprinted upon the Plants, Herbs, and Flowers, as it were in Hieroglyphicks, the very signature of their Vertues." The search for plants of use in medicine, which was accelerated as man emerged from the Middle Ages, had provided a gigantic backlog of specimens.

In Catesby's era, the ornithologist lacked a concrete record of the past. A type specimen that rots and vanishes is not a reliable record. One is left only with a written record, and since he lacks the type specimen, has only a vague idea of the criteria used in compiling the record.

As a result of difficulties in preserving birds, Catesby's paintings served several generations of ornithologists as "type specimens." Although Catesby assured readers that he had depicted all birds of the region, except for oceanic species that might have escaped his notice, we now know that the 109 represent roughly one-fourth of the species that may in some seasons be found in the area he covered. Further, Catesby's knowledge of the birds he painted was incomplete. For instance, he was not familiar with the plumage changes that occur in the "reed-bird," or rice bird, as the bobolink was known in the South. The black-and-white male bobolink of spring goes through a summer molt in northern states and returns south in a duller plumage common to the female. Catesby remarked of the bobolink: "In September when they arrive in infinite swarms to devour the rice, they are all hens not being accompanied by any cock but early in the spring both cocks and hens make a transient visit together."

Catesby also was rather careful that his readers not be misled by common names. For instance, of his *Aquea Capite Albo* he wrote: "This Bird is Called the Bald Eagle, both in Virginia and Carolina, though his head is as much feather'd as the other parts of his body. . . ."

An international system of taxonomy, which would provide naturalists with pigeonholes into which they could tuck new birds, did not exist in Catesby's day. There were ornithologists working in Europe, but they, too, remained below the threshold of a truly organized approach to their subject. Catesby assumed that American birds must have some connection to the birds of Europe, and since he was writing primarily for Europeans anyhow, he often drew comparisons based upon European birds.

A few of Catesby's observations were grossly misleading. He noted that the flicker, which is a common woodpecker in the eastern United States, spent a great deal of time on the ground, and therefore concluded that although it looked much like a woodpecker, it was not a woodpecker. The flicker differs from other woodpeckers in its preference for ground-nesting ants. Catesby's fatal line in the matter: "It differs from Woodpeckers in the hookedness of its bill and manner of feeding which is usually on the ground, out of which it draws worms and other insects."

On the basis of Catesby's description, the Swedish scientist Carolus Linnaeus, who brought order to natural history, classified the flicker as a cuckoo. Linnaeus was to delve into Catesby's work much later, however. At the time Catesby began work, Linnaeus was a student at Uppsala University and had only begun dabbling into the mysteries of plant classification. Catesby had been dead almost a decade before Linnaeus turned his attention to zoology.

The number of copies published of Catesby's *Natural History* may never be known. A second edition, edited by Catesby's friend George Edwards, appeared in 1754. A third edition, which Edwards revised and to which he added a Linnean index, was published in 1771. All involved hand-coloring of plates and were magnificent volumes, intended primarily for the wealthy or institutions.

Among later customers who sought the volumes was Thomas Jefferson, at the time a Virginia delegate to the Continental Congress. In January 1783, Jefferson wrote to Senator Francis Eppes of Virginia:

> Since I came here there has been sold the Westover copy of Catesby's *History of Carolina.* It was held near a twelve month at twelve guineas, and at last sold for ten. This seems to fix what should be given for Mr. Bolling's copy, if you can induce him to let me have it, which I am very anxious for.

Aside from his book, Catesby has one other truly impressive memorial: the largest frog in North America, the bullfrog (*Rana catesbeiana*), was named for him.

Chapter II

Going Native: Bartram, All-American

John Bartram was the king's botanist for George III in North America. The title sounds impressive, but it was a limited honor. George III was not interested in botany.

Although Bartram was the first native-born American naturalist to win international recognition, appointment as king's botanist came late in life. Peter Collinson, London linen draper and gardening enthusiast, who helped finance Catesby and other plant collectors in North America, secured the post for Bartram in 1765. At the time, Bartram was sixty-six years old, an age at which even colonial naturalists found themselves tiring. Bartram was different, however. The fifty British pounds per year which the job paid enabled him to launch immediately a journey into Florida, an area he had longed to visit for many years.

For comparison, one should know that there were two royal botanists in North America and that William Young, who was Queen Anne's botanist, had been appointed two years before Bartram and received a salary of three hundred British pounds. Bartram's contemporaries considered Young a man of minimal accomplishments.

The period of John Bartram's lifetime—1699 to 1777—was an exceptionally productive era for American natural history. The work of Catesby and his contemporaries had suggested that the continent was rich in new forms, particularly botanical species. Wealthy men in Great Britain sought plants for their gardens, which were much in vogue. The grave problem involved in the interaction between British botanists and their American plant hunters, both native European, was the distance separating them and the inefficiencies of transportation. Plants died during the long ordeal at sea in sailing vessels. Shipboard or dock rats ate packets of seeds. Even such hardy and impervious items as acorns dried or mildewed in transit.

Part of Bartram's fame resulted from his ingenious methods of packing seeds and plants so that they could withstand the rigors of oceanic shipment. In his writings one finds frequent references to novel means

WILLIAM BARTRAM (1739–1823) wrote *Travels Through North and South Carolina, Georgia, East and West Florida*, which not only was a great natural history volume but also one of the earliest books by an American author to gain literary acclaim in Europe. Bartram and his father, John Bartram, King George's botanist in North America, founded the natural history tradition that kept Philadelphia the center for such studies for decades.

of protecting seeds in bottles, gourds, and other containers, and of coating individual seeds or placing them in material that kept them viable.

Zoological specimens still were shipped in bottles or casks, preserved in alcohol. The process robbed the material of natural colors, and zoologists usually found themselves working with a soggy, crumpled mass that had been an animal.

In Bartram's period, a Swedish naturalist changed natural history from a philosophy to a science. In 1753 Carolus Linnaeus published his *Species Plantarum*, and the following year, his *Genera Plantarum*. The two volumes established the principle of international recognition of scientific plant names.

Although the system that Linnaeus introduced for classification of plants has been extensively improved, and even today undergoes constant modification, from his ideas grew an enormous catalog that enabled a naturalist for the first time to proceed with the confidence that he or she was working with a plant whose identity had been certified. In effect, the system provided a huge file into which one could tuck any new or known plant and retrieve it for later comparison.

In 1758 Linnaeus established a similar international name bank for the use of zoologists. It appeared in the tenth edition of his *Systemae Naturae*.

Essentially, the Linnean system standardized the terms that a naturalist might use in describing a plant or animal and established a principle, which recognized the name first applied to new material and prevented the application of multiple names to the same species. Coming in a period of intense natural history exploration not only in America but also on other continents, it made manageable the enormous flow of new species and new natural history information into Europe.

The often-changed title to Florida had fallen to the British in 1763. John Bartram had longed to explore that province, which promised a lush flora. When the appointment as king's botanist arrived in the spring of 1765, Bartram immediately saw his fifty-pound salary as the financial backing that would make a Florida trip possible. His lack of procrastination was remarkable, and on July 1, 1765, he sailed from Philadelphia to Charleston, where he would begin his land journey through South Carolina and Georgia into Florida. The trip lasted until April 10, 1766, and was the last, longest, and in some ways most rewarding of a series of journeys he had taken over a thirty-year period. Fortunately, Bartram took his son, William, with him. William was to become the literate Bartram.

On this final journey, Bartram made the discovery for which he is best known today. On October 1, 1765, in the Altamaha River flood plain of Georgia, four miles below Fort Barrington, he found "several very curious shrubs." One he named Franklinia in honor of Benjamin Franklin. Franklinia (*Franklinia altamaha*) proved one of nature's rarities—a plant that existed only in that one stand. Franklinia never again was found in the wild.

John Bartram was a complex person, apparently an intellectual with only a trace of formal schooling. He seems to have mastered a working knowledge of the technical Latin in which educated botanists communicated. He learned to write English well enough to convey his thoughts, but reading his unedited remarks requires considerable skill on the reader's part. He corresponded with all naturalists of note in his era, including Catesby and the great Linnaeus. Bartram's home and garden in Philadelphia was a gathering place for educated men. Yet Bartram was an unschooled farmer whose hobby of making journeys after the annual harvest led him into a familiarity with plants, fossils, geology, and other natural features of America that was unequaled in his period.

When Pehr (Peter) Kalm, a Swedish naturalist, was dispatched to America in 1748 by Linnaeus, one of his instructions was to meet John Bartram and learn as much as possible from him. It is in Kalm's *Travels in North America* that one may read a contemporary's estimate of Bartram:

> Mr. John Bartram is an Englishman, who lives in the country about four miles from Philadelphia. He has acquired a great knowledge of natural philosophy and history, and seems to be born with a peculiar genius for these sciences. In his youth he had no opportunity of going to school, but by his own diligence and indefatigable application he got, without instruction, so far in Latin as to understand all books in that language and even those which were filled with botanical terms. He has in several successive years made frequent excursions into different distant parts of North America with an intention of gathering all sorts of plants which are scarce and little known. Those which he found he has planted in his own botanical garden and likewise sent over their seeds or fresh roots to England. We owe to him the knowledge of many rare plants which he first found and which were never known before. He has shown great judgment and an attention which lets nothing escape unnoticed. Yet with all these qualities he is to be blamed for his negligence, for he did not care to write down his numerous and useful observations. His friends in London once induced him to send them a short account of one of his travels, and they were ready, with a good intention though not with sufficient judgment, to get this account printed. But the book did Mr. Bartram more harm than good, for, as he is rather backward in writing down what he knows, this publication was found to contain but few new observations. It would not however be doing justice to Mr. Bartram's merit if it were to be judged by this performance. He has not filled it with a thousandth part of the great knowledge which he has acquired in natural philosophy and history, especially in regard to North America. I have often been at a loss to think of the sources whence he obtained many things which came to his knowledge. I, also, owe him much, for he possessed that great quality of communicating everything he

knew. I shall therefore in this work frequently mention this gentleman. I should never forgive myself if I were to omit the name of a discoverer and claim that as my contribution which I had learned from another person. . . .

An insight into Kalm's comments upon Bartram's publications and his hints at their general inadequacy may be found in the diary Bartram kept on the Florida journey. Francis Harper, an expert on Bartram, made the following comments concerning his editing of the diary for publication in 1942 by the American Philosophical Society:

> A minimum number of liberties have been taken with the original diary in putting it into print; for I am much in sympathy with Jones's remark (in DeBrahm, 1849, p. 3) on the undesirability of "whitewashing a ruin." It has seemed essential, however, for purposes of readability, to insert some of the punctuation that is missing in John Bartram's manuscript. To a modern it is rather incomprehensible that he should scarcely have learned, during his long life, the need of ending a sentence with some mark of punctuation. In some cases I have been constrained to retain periods in the middle of sentences, although the author must have meant them to have only the force of commas. Commas, however, seemed to form no effective part of his literary equipment. Frequently a colon is used where the construction calls for a period. In numerous places in the manuscript it has seemed impossible to distinguish clearly between comma and period, or between colon and semicolon. I can make no claim to having solved the various problems of punctuation with any particular degree of satisfaction. This task doubtless would have been much simplified if the original had contained no punctuation whatsoever. All inserted punctuation marks are invariably enclosed in square brackets.
>
> Sentences are apparently begun with capitals only by occasional accident, so to speak, but this is a very minor difficulty. Proper nouns appear without capitals as frequently, perhaps, as with them. By some quirk the article 'a' is almost invariably capitalized. I have aimed to make no changes in capitalization. . . .

A sample of Bartram's diary, made more legible by Harper's punctuation, which appears in brackets, concerns the uneasiness of Carolina Low Country people in the hurricane season:

[August] 21[.] thermo[.] 77[.] small rain[.] noon 83[.] then there arose A strong N E wind with rain all night; I find ye towns people is much more terrified & fearfull of A East storm then we are upon ye account of our banks & our store keepers Along water street[;] but our fears & dangers is little in comparison to thairs. I frequently heard ye women talk how fearfull thay was if A thunder gust arose, of ye wind tacking to ye NE & ye danger of A huricane, which I looked upon as A feminin weakness or as ye common Saying[,] more afraid than hurt, as supposeing thes grievous calamities came but once in an age. but upon makeing perticular enquiry of ye ouldest inhabitants I was satisfied that by thair frequent grievous sufferings thay had Sufficient reason for those anctious concerns[.]

ye best account I could obtain of these tremenduous contractions & iregular combinations of water & air, was from one of most substantial in Judgment as well as in honesty & veracity[.] I desired him to give me A perticular account of those within ye reach of his own memory[,] which he did very acurately[.] ye first of which was in ye year 1700[,] which was very severe[,] overthrowing many houses & overflowing ye town: the next of much note was in 1713[;] began ye 5th of september[,] which did conside[r]able damage; if it thunders much ye storm is soon over but if ye wind comes in sudden flaws[,] with intervals calm intervals[,] dangerous[.] ye next was in 1716 September ye 10th[.] ye next I shall transcribe from A note made by an acurate observer of veracity[.]

friday August ye 2^d 1728[.] We had A very violent Huricane[,] ye wind being N.N.E & continuing from N.N.E to ENE for about six hours[,] from 9 of ye clock in ye morning to three in ye afternoon: & as ye tide began to Ebb ye wind shifted to ye SE & ESE[,] still blowing violently untill four of ye clock A Saturday Morning[;] at which time it began to thunder[,] attended with violent showers of rain[,] & then it broke up[.] but ye wind continued at SE. or there about for several days affter; in ye year 1722 in september was ye most violent rain for 3 days & 3 nights without intirmision that ye english inhabitants ever knew[.] it so flowed ye countrey as to cause great destruction of grain & other nessesaries of life[.] it seems as if that collection of vapours that used period[i]cally to operate in currents of wind was discharded in rain[.]

in 1730 they had another storm at NE which did Considerable damage but ye last in 1750[,] september ye 15th[,] which is ye most fresh in ye memory of ye present inhabitants[,] it began as usual in ye north[,] thence to ye east, south & west, upon which this grievous scourge was suddenly removed[,] but ye smart was felt several years affter, by ye great loss most of ye inhabitants sustained. Quere[:] whether these terible currents of air is not some scirts of more southern Huricanes turned upon ye Continent by A northerly wind[,] which setting against ye gulf stream raiseth ye water[,] and ye east wind Joyning ye north heaves ye ye water upon ye shoal wide coast & bay[,] & forcing ye stupendious roleing billows up ye river[,] overwhelmeth ye adjacent land[,] part of which ye town is scituated upon[,] being most of it not above 7 or 8 foot perpendicular above ye surface of ye water at common tides: so that it is but A little way to dig in any garden for water to water ye thir[s]ty plants[,] which[,] by ye help of dung[,] is very fruitefull. about ye year 1686 thay had A very grievous huricane; & ye indians tould the english that thay knew one that raised ye water over ye tops of ye trees where ye town now stands: which perhaps was no other than pavia & chinkapin bushes[,] yapon[,] & dwarf evergreen oaks[.]

There are hints that Bartram's friends may have been sensitive to his lack of formal education. It is possible that such sensitivity may account for the strange contrast that appears in two letters that Dr. Alexander Garden of Charleston, an accomplished botanist, is known to have written. On the other hand, Dr. Garden may have been influenced by some political consideration that time has obscured in his unexplained shift of attitude. Dr. Garden, in beginning his long correspondence with Linnaeus, wrote:

When I came to New York, I immediately inquired for Coldenhamia, the seat of that most eminent botanist, Mr. Colden. Here, by good fortune, I first met with John Bartram, returning from the Blue Mountains, as they are called. How grateful was such a meeting to me! And how unusual in this part of the world! What congratulations and salutations passed between us! How happy should I be to pass my life with men so distinguished by genius, acuteness and liberality, as well as by eminent botanical learning and experience! Men in whom the greatest knowledge and skill are united to the most amiable candour.

Yet six years later, in a letter to John Ellis in London, Dr. Garden wrote:

I have at last met with a man who is to commence nursery man and gardener, and to collect seeds and plants, etc. for the London market. He is a sensible careful man, and has a turn for that business. I must beg your interest in his favour. . . . His name is Young, and any letters to him enclosed to me, will be taken care of.

Bartram had been sending seeds and plants to England for thirty years and Dr. Garden knew it, so it seems strange he should refer to Young, unless Ellis had asked him to recommend someone other than Bartram. Young and Bartram both worked out of Philadelphia, and Bartram's experience certainly overshadowed Young's, who was a relative newcomer to America. The significance of Dr. Garden's remarks may lie in the fact that Young was soon to be named the queen's botanist. Young, it seems, was a young dandy who wore silks and laces. He was almost the reverse of the conservative Quaker Bartram.

Most botanical historians agree that John Bartram introduced no fewer than 200 American plants to cultivation. The exact number never may be certified, for the plants he forwarded to England were usually named by the recipient, rather than by Bartram.

The reason Bartram received so little credit in scientific records for his immense work lies in the method Linnaeus chose for immortalizing plant names. In instances where the discoverer and the describer are not the same person, the describer receives credit for introducing the new material to science. The method worked greatly to Linnaeus's own advantage. He wiped the slate clean of all scientific names that had existed prior to 1753 and proceeded to rename all known plants himself. That is why his name is linked to the scientific name of some 7,700 species of plants, and why one reads at the end of so many scientific names the name Linnaeus or Linn. In 1758, he did the same thing to all animal names and linked his name to 4,400 species in zoology.

As one might guess, such slate wiping held little appeal for his contemporaries, who watched their names disappear and the name Linnaeus appear behind their own discoveries. Only an absolute tyrant could have proposed such seizure of credit. But, on the other hand, only an absolute tyrant could have brought order out of the disarray into which scientific naming had drifted. Linnaeus, who was the sort of man who wrote his own autobiography five times to be certain that he received due credit, was an ideal man for the job.

Linnaeus's success, however, rested less upon his dogged determination that his and no other system of classification should survive, than upon the fact that he indeed had an excellent idea and the guts to carry it out. The man unquestionably was a genius.

There were several competing systems of scientific nomenclature in Linnaeus's time. His won acceptance primarily because of its simplicity. His most valuable contribution, and the one that has endured to the present, was the idea of limiting a scientific name to two words, both Latinized so that they were equally familiar to all naturalists regardless of nationality. Fortunately for him, Linnaeus was skilled in technical Latin. If he had proposed his system in Swedish and suggested Swedish binomials, he probably would have joined a distinguished company of now-forgotten naturalists.

As it was, Linnaeus became known as the dirty old man of botany. He gained the reputation through his artificial system of plant classification, which involved the sexual parts of the flower. The words he chose, although cloaked by Latin or Greek, were sometimes too anatomical for his contemporaries and the system, based upon a count of male and female organs, seemed suggestive. The Rev. Samuel Goodenough wrote: "A literal translation of first principles of Linnaean botany is enough to shock female modesty. It is possible that many virtuous students might not be able to make out the similitude of *Clitoria*." *Clitoria* is a Linnean genus the name of which was suggested by the resemblance of the flower's female organ to the mammalian clitoris. Even Goethe, who was somewhat of a naturalist as well as a poet, suggested that botany was an improper study for women, whose chaste souls might be embarrassed by the textbooks.

Since both John Bartram and his son, William, were alive when the American Revolution began, one may wonder where the sympathies of these naturalists lay. As Quakers, both would have abhorred war. William, at the time, was on his famous journey through Florida; he returned in January 1778 to find his father dead and the colonies at war with King George.

While John Bartram laid a foundation that was to make Philadelphia the intellectual capital of natural history in America, it was William Bartram (1739–1823) who established it firmly. Like his father, William Bartram was acquainted with every naturalist of note in his period. During William's reign at Bartram's Garden, many of the naturalists whose names and works still are known emerged.

Unlike his father, who seemed reluctant even to write letters, William became one of the honored writers of the early United States. He is best known for his *Travels through North and South Carolina, Georgia, East and West Florida*, a chronicle of four years' wandering in the southeastern wilderness. Published in 1791, the volume was translated into Dutch, French, and German. It gained immediate acceptance in Europe, where American productions were suspect. Such eminent English writers as Wordsworth, Coleridge, and Southey found it inspiring. The book can be read at several levels, since it is an account of adventure as well as a report on natural history.

William Bartram differed from his father in several ways. Among other things, he was more of an ornithologist and less of a botanist than his father. John recognized the difference and urged the son to become a merchant, especially since William had shown only minor interest in collecting plants for overseas patrons, the only reliable source of income for botanists of the period. William had little success as a merchant. In 1765 he closed out his store at Cape Fear, North Carolina, and accompanied his father on the first Bartram trip into Florida.

William endured the southeastern mosquitoes in an era when mosquito netting was unknown, became drenched in southern storms because adequate raincoats had not been designed, slept under live oak trees when no pioneer cabins were available, and carried all supplies as well as collection equipment on a single horse, just as his father did. It was excellent training for a naturalist. In addition, he had at least limited formal schooling and grew up not only in Philadelphia but in that focal point where naturalists gathered, Bartram's Garden. The advantages made him one of the better-prepared naturalists of the early Federal period.

Among his other accomplishments, William Bartram was a skillful artist of both flora and fauna. His floral drawings illustrated Dr. Benjamin S. Barton's *Elements of Botany*, one of the pioneer works of scientific botany in the United States, published in 1803. The *Elements* is known to have contained thirty plates by Bartram and to have reached a press run of 500 copies. Barton, who was professor of natural history and botany at the University of Pennsylvania, is best known for his *Fragments of the Natural History of Pennsylvania*, published in 1799. *Fragments* is a highly readable, but not excessively definable, volume. Among Dr. Barton's students was Thomas Nuttall (1786–1859), whose *Manual of Ornithology* was the first handbook on birds of the United States and Canada.

In his field work, William Bartram catalogued 215 species of American birds, the greatest number of species listed by any American worker of that period. Although he named several new species, he often lapsed into using more than two words for the scientific name, thus losing credit for the discovery. Bartram's interest in birds extended beyond descriptive zoology. He collected life history material on various species and investigated migratory habits.

Although William Bartram remains among the more respected observers of nature, he apparently had a fear of alligators that bordered on the psychotic. Either that, or alligators have changed their behavior patterns radically. Alligators today certainly do not display the aggressiveness that Bartram ascribed to those he encountered. It is possible, of course, that under wilderness conditions the reptiles had not developed the wariness of man that the remnant alligator population of our day displays. Indeed, all present alligators may have descended from shy parents, since the brasher ones until recently became shoes or valises. However, modern naturalists tend to question Bartram's account of his battle with alligators as reported in *Travels:*

> But ere I had half-way reached the place, I was attacked on all sides, several endeavouring to overset the canoe. My situation now became precarious to the last degree: two very large ones attacked me closely, at the same instant, rushing up with their heads and part of their bodies above the water, roaring terribly and belching floods of water over me. They struck their jaws together so close to my ears, as almost to stun me, and I expected every moment to be dragged out of the boat and instantly devoured. But I applied my weapons so effectually about me, though at random, that I was so successful as to beat them off a little; when, finding that they designed to renew the battle, I made for the shore, as the only means left me for my preservation; for, by keeping close to it, I should have my enemies on one side of me only, whereas I was before surrounded by them; and there was a probability, if I pushed to the last extremity, of saving myself, by jumping out of the canoe on shore, as it is easy to outwalk them on land, although comparatively as swift as lightning in the water. I found this last expedient alone could fully answer my expectations, for as soon as I gained the shore, they drew off and kept aloof. This was a happy relief, as my confidence was, in some degree, recovered by it.

While in Florida, Bartram observed a spectacular vulture, the king vulture (*Sacoramphus papa*), a bird which never has been reported in the state by any other ornithologist. His restriction of the bird's diet to roasted reptiles may be regarded as an exaggeration, although vultures are notably opportunistic birds and under the circumstances he describes undoubtedly made the most of such fare. The king vulture today seldom occurs north of central Mexico. The reason that Bartram's description can be accepted is that he described the bird quite adequately and obviously did not know its name:

There are two species of vultures in these regions, I think not mentioned in history: the first we shall describe is a beautiful bird, near the size of a turkey buzzard, but his wings are much shorter, and consequently he falls greatly below that admirable bird in sail. I shall call this bird the painted vulture. The bill is long and straight almost to the point, when it is hooked or bent suddenly down and sharp; the head and neck bare of feathers nearly down to the stomach, when the feathers begin to cover the skin, and soon become long and of a soft texture, forming a ruff or tippet, in which the bird by contracting his neck can hide that as well as his head; the bare skin on the neck appears loose and wrinkled, and is of a deep bright yellow colour, intermixed with coral red; the hinder part of the neck is nearly covered with short, stiff hair; and the skin of this part of the neck is of a dun-purple colour, gradually becoming red as it approaches the yellow of the sides and fore part. The crown of the head is red; there are lobed lappets of a reddish orange colour, which lie on the base of the upper mandible. But what is singular, a large portion of the stomach hangs down on the breast of the bird, in the likeness of a sack or half wallet, and seem to be a duplicature of the craw, which is naked and of a reddish flesh colour; this is partly concealed by the feathers of the breast, unless when it is loaded with food (which is commonly, I believe, roasted reptiles), and then it appears prominent. The plumage of the bird is generally white or cream colour, except the quill-feathers of the wings and two or three rows of the coverts, which are of a beautiful dark brown; the tail, which is large and white, is tipped with this dark brown or black; the legs and feet of a clear white; the eye is encircled with a gold coloured iris; the pupil black.

The Creeks or Muscogulges construct their royal standard of the tail feather of this bird, which is called by a name signifying the eagle's tail: this they carry with them when they go to battle, but then it is painted with a zone of red within the brown tips; and in peaceable negotiations it is displayed new, clean, and white: this standard is held most sacred by them on all occasions, and is constructed and ornamented with great ingenuity. These birds seldom appear but when the deserts are set on fire (which happens

almost every day throughout the year, in some part or other, by
the Indians, for the purpose of rousing the game, as also by the
lightning): when they are seen at a distance soaring on the wing,
gathering from every quarter, and gradually approaching the
burnt plains, where they alight upon the ground yet smoking with
hot embers: they gather up the roasted serpents, frogs, and
lizards, filling their sacks with them: at this time a person may
shoot them at pleasure, they not being willing to quit the feast,
and indeed seeming to brave all danger.

If Bartram had been aware of the similarity among cells of all living
tissue, he might have gone even farther in his speculations concerning
the similarities detectable in animal and plant organisms. In his day, of
course, microscopes were primitive. Indeed, only in recent years have
electronic microscopes disclosed in detail a basic similarity in living
organisms. Bartram's comparisons were made at the level where most
naturalists work—the gross organism—a level at which organized tissue
functions with the least similarity. After describing to readers the
actions of several carnivorous plants that trap and ingest insects, Bartram continues:

But admirable are the properties of the extraordinary Dionea
muscipula! A great extent on each side of that serpentine rivulet
is occupied by those sportive vegetables—let us advance to the
spot in which nature has seated them. Astonishing production! see
the incarnate lobes expanding, how gay and sportive they appear!
ready on the spring to intrap incautious deluded insects! what
artifice! there behold one of the leaves just closed upon a struggling fly; another has gotten a worm; its hold is sure, its prey can
never escape—carnivorous vegetable! Can we after viewing this
object, hesitate a moment to confess, that vegetable beings are
endued with some sensible faculties or attributes, familiar to those
that dignify animal nature; they are organical, living, and self-
moving bodies, for we see here, in this plant, motion and volition.
What power or faculty is it, that directs the cirri of the
Cucurbita, Momordica, Vitis, and other climbers, towards the
twigs of shrubs, trees and other friendly support? we see them
invariably leaning, extending, and like the fingers of the human
hand, reaching to catch hold of what is nearest, just as if they
had eyes to see with; and when their hold is fixed, to coil the
tendril in a spiral form, by which artifice it becomes more elastic
and effectual, than if it had remained in a direct line, for every

revolution of the coil adds a portion of strength; and thus collected, they are enabled to dilate and contract as occasion or necessity requires, and thus by yielding to, and humouring the motion of the limbs and twigs, or other support on which they depend, are not so liable to be torn off by sudden blasts of wind or other assaults: is it sense or instinct that influences their actions? it must be some impulse; or does the hand of the Almighty act and perform this work in our sight?

The vital principle or efficient cause of motion and action, in the animal and vegetable system, perhaps may be more familiar than we generally apprehend. Where is the essential difference between the seed of peas, peaches, and other tribes of plants and trees, and the eggs of oviparous animals, as of birds, snakes, or butterflies, spawn of fish, &c.? Let us begin at the source of terrestrial existence. Are not the seeds of vegetables, and the eggs of oviparous animals fecundated, or influenced with the vivific principle of life, through the approximation and intimacy of the sexes? and immediately after the eggs and seeds are hatched, does not the young larva and infant plant, by heat and moisture, rise into existence, increase, and in due time arrive to a state of perfect maturity? The physiologists agree in opinion, that the work of generation in viviparous animals, is exactly similar, only more secret and enveloped. The mode of operation that nature pursues in the production of vegetables, and oviparous animals, is infinitely more uniform and manifest, than that which is or can be discovered to take place in viviparous animals.

The most apparent difference between animals and vegetables is, that animals have the powers of sound, and are locomotive, whereas vegetables are not able to shift themselves from the places where nature has planted them; yet vegetables have the power of moving and exercising their members, and have the means of transplanting and colonising their tribes almost over the surface of the whole earth; some seeds, for instance, grapes, nuts, smilax, peas, and others, whose pulp or kernel is food for animals, will remain several days without being injured in stomachs of pigeons and other birds of passage; by this means such sorts are distributed from place to place, even across seas; indeed some seeds require this preparation by the digestive heat of the stomach of animals, to dissolve and detach the oily, viscid pulp, or to soften the hard shells. Small seeds are sometimes furnished with rays of hair or down; and others with thin light membranes attached to them, which serve the purpose of wings, on which they mount upward, leaving the earth, float in the air, and are carried away by the swift winds to very remote regions before they settle on the earth; some are furnished with hooks, which catch hold of the wool and hair of animals passing by them, and are by that means spread abroad; other seeds ripen in pericarpes, which open with elastic force, and shoot their seed to a very great distance round about; some other seeds, as of the Mosses and Fungi, are so very minute as to be invisible, light as atoms, and these mixing with the air, are wafted all over the world.

As one reads Bartram's *Travels*, one frequently encounters a list of Latin names for plants. The first impression is that the author must be showing off his knowledge. The truth is that many of the plants to which he referred had no common English name in his day, and some still are known only by their scientific names.

Contemporaries reported that as William Bartram aged, he became withdrawn from the world. They considered his mental condition at least slightly aberrant. As evidence, they cited the fact that he frequently wandered in Bartram's Garden barefoot!

Chapter III

Stretching the Limits:
Lewis and Clark

Grizzly bears discovered the Lewis and Clark expedition soon after the American adventurers entered the bears' range in the Upper Missouri River country.

A member of the expedition wounded the first grizzly on the Cannonball River in North Dakota, just below Mandan. Sgt. Patrick Gass, who recorded the event, referred to the animal as "a large white bear." The date was October 20, 1804. After wintering at a Mandan Indian village, the expedition resumed its upstream journey, and from the time the men reached the mouth of the Yellowstone River on April 29, 1805, they were almost constantly in contact with grizzlies along the Missouri River and through the Stony Mountains (now called the Rockies).

There was no naturalist with Lewis and Clark. As one reads the journals, one gets the feeling that the expedition missed the rich rodent complex of the upper Missouri partly because to the leaders a mouse was a mouse and a rat was a rat, and that was that. But grizzly bears made a tremendous impression on everyone with the expedition.

One grizzly chased Capt. Meriwether Lewis into the Missouri River near the great falls of the river. Another grizzly Lewis struck over the head, a blow that shattered his rifle, and when the bear recovered from the stunning, it spent three hours beneath a tree that Lewis had climbed.

The Lewis and Clark journals contain numerous references to the grizzly bears, the authors earnestly advising potential readers that here indeed was a different animal from the black bear, which was docile by comparison. Although they described salmon as different species each time the salmon changed colors in their spawning runs, they made no comparable mistakes about grizzlies. They identified grizzly bears regardless of the rather broad spectrum of colors that characterize the animals' fur. They were so interested in the bears that they even collected information regarding their breeding habits and other behavior.

They reported, for instance, that unlike the black bear of the East, grizzlies could not climb trees. And as for the disposition of this largest of American carnivores, Lewis and Clark endowed it with a ferocity that perhaps only a wounded grizzly deserves. No other mammal except man received such extensive treatment in the journals. A few excerpts from the journals concerning grizzlies follow:

The hunters killed some pheasants, two squirrels, and (Collins) a male and a female bear, the first of which was large, fat, and of a bay color; the second meager, grizzly, and of smaller size. They were of the species (*Ursus horribilis*) common to the upper part of the Missouri, and might well be termed the variegated bear, for they are found occasionally of a black, grizzly, brown, or red color. There is every reason to believe them to be of precisely the same species. Those of different colors are killed together, as in the case of these two, and as we found the white and bay associated together on the Missouri; and some nearly white were seen in this neighborhood by the hunters. Indeed, it is not common to find any two bears of the same color; and if the difference in color were to constitute a distinction of species, the number would increase to almost twenty. Soon afterward the hunters killed a female bear with two cubs. The mother was black, with a considerable intermixture of white hairs and a white spot on the breast. One of the cubs was jet black, and the other of a light reddish-brown or bay color. The foil of these variegated bears [is] much finer, longer, and more abundant than that of the common black bear; but the most striking differences between them are that the former are larger and have longer tusks, and longer as well as blunter talons; that they prey more on other animals; that they lie neither so long nor so closely in winter-quarters; and that they never climb a tree, however closely pressed by the hunters. These variegated bears, though specifically the same with those we met on the Missouri, are by no means so ferocious; probably because the scarcity of game and the habit of living on roots may have weaned them from the practices of attacking and devouring animals. Still, however, they are not so passive as the common black bear, which is also to be found here; for they have already fought with our hunters, though with less fury than those on the other side of the mountains.

A large part of the meat we gave to the Indians, to whom it was a real luxury, as they scarcely taste flesh once in a month. They immediately prepared a large fire of dried wood, on which was thrown a number of smooth stones from the river. As soon as the fire went down and the stones were heated, they were laid next to each other in a level position, and covered with a quantity of branches of pine, on which were placed flitches of the bear; thus placed, the boughs and the flesh alternated for several courses, leaving a thick layer of pine on the top. On this heap was then poured a small quantity of water, and the whole was covered with earth to the depth of four inches. After remaining in this state about three hours the meat was taken off; it was really more tender than that which we had boiled or roasted, though the strong flavor of the pine rendered it disagreeable to our palates. This repast gave them much satisfaction; for though they sometimes kill the black bear, yet they attack very reluctantly the furious variegated bear, and only when they can pursue him on horseback through the plains and shoot him with arrows.

May 31st. Two men visited the Indian village, where they purchased a dressed bear-skin, of a uniform pale reddish-brown color, which the Indians called yackah, in contradistinction to hohhost, or white bear. This remark induced us to inquire more particularly into their opinions as to the several species of bears; we therefore produced all the skins of that animal which we had killed at this place, and also one very nearly white which we had purchased. The natives immediately classed the white, the deep and the pale grizzly red, the grizzly dark brown—in short, all those with the extremities of the hair of a white or frosty color, without regard to the color of the ground of the foil [*sic*], under the name of hohhost. They assured us that they were all of the same species with the white bear; that they associated together, had longer nails than the others, and never climbed trees. On the other hand, the black skins, those which were black with a number of entirely white hairs intermixed, or with a white breast, the uniform bay, the brown, and the light reddish-brown, were ranged under the class yackah, and were said to resemble each other in being smaller, in having shorter nails than the white bear, in climbing trees, and in being so little vicious that they could be pursued with safety. This distinction of the Indians seems to be well founded, and we are inclined to believe: 1st, that the white, grizzly, etc., bear of this neighborhood forms a distinct species (*Ursus horribilis*), which, moreover, is the same with that of the same color on the upper part of the Missouri, where the other species is not found; 2d, that the black, reddish-brown, etc., is a second species (*U. americanus* and its var. *cinnamemeus*), equally distinct from the white bear of this country and (only varietally different) from the black bear of the Atlantic and Pacific oceans, which two last seem to form only one species. The common black bear is indeed unknown in this country; for the bear of which we are speaking, though in most respects similar, differs from it in having much finer, thicker, and longer hair, with a greater proportion of fur mixed with it, and also in having a variety of colors, while the common black bear has no inter-mixture or change of color, but is of a uniform black.

From the extensive entries regarding grizzly bears in the Lewis and Clark journals and from the skin of a grizzly identified as having been shot by a member of the expedition beside the Missouri River, a little above the mouth of the Poplar River in northeastern Montana, George Ord described the grizzly bear in the second American edition of *Guthrie's Geography*, published in 1815. In keeping with the explorers' reports regarding the ferocity of the bear, Ord gave it the scientific name *Ursus horribilis*, the horrible bear. Here is Ord's original description of the grizzly as it appeared in *Guthrie's:*

> *Grizzly Bear.* "This animal," says Mr. Brackenridge, "is the monarch of the country which he inhabits. The African Lion, or the Tiger of Bengal, are not more terrible or fierce. He is the enemy of man, and literally thirsts for human blood. So far from shunning, he seldom fails to attack; and even to hunt him. The Indians make war upon these ferocious monsters, with the same ceremonies as they do upon a tribe of their own species: and in the recital of their victories, the death of one of them gives the warrior greater renown than the scalp of a human enemy.
>
> "He possesses an amazing strength, and attacks without hesita-tion, and tears to pieces, the largest Buffaloe. The colour is usually such as the name indicates, though there are varieties, from black to silvery whiteness. The skins are highly valued for muffs and tippets; and will bring from twenty to fifty dollars each.
>
> "This Bear is not usually seen lower than the Mandan villages. In the vicinity of the Roche Jaune, and of the Little Missouri, they are said to be most numerous. They do not wander much in the prairies, but are usually found in points of wood, in the neighbour-hood of large streams.
>
> "In shape, he differs from the common Bear in being propor-tionally more long and lank. He does not climb trees, a circum-

stance which has enabled hunters, when attacked, to make their escape."

In the history of the expedition under the command of Lewis and Clark, we have much interesting information relating to this dreadfully ferocious animal. These enterprising travellers made many narrow escapes from the attacks of this monster, who in some instances was not brought to the ground until he had received seven or eight balls through his body. As a wonderful proof of the tenacity of life of this animal, one that was killed the nineteenth of May, 1805, ran at his usual pace nearly a quarter of a mile, after having been *shot through the heart*.

The Grizzly Bear has been long known to naturalists; but the above mentioned travellers were the first to give us a particular account of this monarch of the American forests. One killed by them near the Porcupine river measured as follows:

	Feet	Inches
Length from the nose to the extremity of the hind feet	8	7½
Circumference near the fore legs	5	10½
of the neck	3	11
of the middle of the fore leg	1	11
Length of the talons		4⅜

His weight, on conjecture, was between five and six hundred pounds. But this was not the largest Bear that was killed by the party. They give an account of one which measured *nine* feet from the nose to the extremity of the tail; and the talons of another were six and a quarter inches in length. It is said that this animal when full grown and fat will exceed a thousand pounds.

Ord's reference to Mr. Brackenridge concerns comments made by H. M. Brackenridge in his *Views of Louisiana*.

Other mammals collected by Lewis and Clark which Ord described in the 1815 edition of *Guthrie's* included the pronghorn, often called the American antelope, and the black-tailed prairie dog. Ord was a wealthy Philadelphian whose personality made him such a controversial figure in natural history that commentators often overlook the fact that he was a competent zoologist.

Although the Lewis and Clark party was the first group of Americans to ascend the Missouri River beyond the mouth of the Yellowstone River, they certainly were not the first white men to encounter the grizzly bear. The Spanish undoubtedly knew the animal in California. Probably Coronado met grizzlies on his march across the future southwestern states in 1540. Certainly Edward Umfreville of the Hudson's Bay Company, who wintered in Saskatchewan from 1784 to 1787, was familiar with the grizzly. Umfreville was the first to use a form of the word *grizzly* in referring to the beasts. He called them "grizzle" bears and noted that they were savage and ferocious. "The number of maimed Indians to be seen in this country," Umfreville wrote, "exhibit a melancholy proof of their [grizzlies'] power over the human species."

. The obscurity of the grizzly bear obviously was due to the fact that before Lewis and Clark gave their detailed reports on the animal, the grizzly had been lumped with the other bears, as though all bears in North America were members of the same species. Ord made the separation in terms that illuminated the difference.

There are several reasons why the Lewis and Clark collection failed to provide more "firsts" among mammals of the Great Plains and Far West. For one thing, while Americans seldom had ranged so far beyond the Mississippi River, other nationals had. The buffalo, or bison, for instance, was the most numerous large mammal expedition members saw. But the bison had been known to Europe since Cortez in 1521 saw the bull of Mexico with a camel's hump in Montezuma's zoo in Mexico City. Indeed, western creatures as common as the bison and as elusive as the sea otter were so familiar to Europeans that Linnaeus gave both creatures scientific names when he reordered zoology in 1758. At the time of Lewis and Clark's journey, the British and Russians were jostling each other for favored positions in northwestern North America. The Russians had considerable interest in natural history and at various times carried out at least minor biological surveys, particularly along the Alaskan coast, then known as Russian America.

If 1815 seems a bit late for Ord to be describing biological specimens collected by an expedition that ended September 23, 1806, we must remember that the first published report taken directly from the Lewis and Clark journals did not come off the press until February 20, 1814. It is true that there were bastardized editions of the *Nick Carter Nickel Weekly* ilk, all of them mostly fiction, which were published earlier. Sgt. Patrick Gass of the expedition had at least mild financial success and gained some fame from his diary, which appeared in print soon after the expedition ended.

The general disorganization among naturalists of the period explains in part the lateness of scientific descriptions taken from Lewis and

Clark specimens. The federal government had not organized a national museum, and there was no central depository for the specimens.

The first shipment of material collected by Lewis and Clark started down the Missouri River April 4, 1805, from the Mandan village where the explorers wintered. The barge carried the following, presumably all dead although the manifest was not that specific: a male and a female pronghorn (stuffed), a weasel, three squirrels, the skeleton of the prairie wolf (coyote), male and female prairie dog, white weasel, two burrowing squirrels, horns of a mountain ram, a pair of large elk antlers, antlers and tail of a black-tailed deer, some Indian artifacts, one box of plants, and one box of insects. Live animals that started on the barge were listed as one burrowing squirrel, one prairie hen, and four magpies. The material was addressed to Thomas Jefferson, who was the literal, as well as the official, receiver.

It is known that Jefferson took part of the material to Monticello, where it remained as conversation pieces for several months. The larger portion of the Lewis and Clark collection was transferred to Dr. Benjamin S. Barton, whom Jefferson had selected as the scientist to review the material. Some of the specimens went to Peale's Museum in Philadelphia, a private institution that served as a gathering place for naturalists.

Dr. Barton was the famed botany professor at the University of Pennsylvania whose venture in the *Elements of Botany* has been mentioned. When Dr. Barton died in 1815, the records indicate that he had not described a single item collected by the expedition. Frederick Pursh, who was associated with Barton and at one time headed William Hamilton's botanic garden near Philadelphia, undertook the task of sorting Lewis and Clark flora. As a result the scientific names among Rocky Mountain flora are liberally sprinkled with credits to Pursh, or (Pursh) where the genus has been changed. It is among botanical names that Lewis and Clark are best memorialized. This is a bit ironical, because the explorers missed, or rather ignored, the most obvious botanical riches of the Rockies. These remained unappreciated until the intrepid Scot David Douglas went up the Columbia River in April 1825 and returned in March 1827 with specimens of the Douglas fir, the Sitka spruce, and other noble conifers that towered in the Rockies. But Douglas, of course, was not an American naturalist.

Pursh was a German and a graduate of the Royal Botanic Gardens of Dresden. Although he was a forerunner among those who were to establish a great Germanic botanical tradition—so much so that American botanists in the late nineteenth century considered a reading skill in German essential—he was not particularly trusted by many of his contemporaries in America. His *Flora Americae Septentrionalis*, published in 1814, is rated as the first complete record of flora of North America north of Mexico. In view of his accomplishments, it is difficult to conceive of Pursh as being an advanced alcoholic, certainly not to the degree contemporaries reported. It was said that in order for him to work his way through a bale of dried plants, he had to be locked into a room that was free of bottles. Whether he was locked by others or at his own order is not known. Prof. M. L. Fernald of Harvard, in his lectures to graduate students on the early American botanist, always described Pursh as suffering delirium tremens when he died in Montreal on July 11, 1820.

Pursh dedicated to Meriwether Lewis one of the more interesting and beautiful flowers, the bitterroot, which he named *Lewisia rediviva*. The expedition had collected the type specimen in the Bitterroot Valley of western Montana. For Clark, Pursh chose an evening primrose, which still bears no common name other than Clarkia. He named the primrose collected by Clark on the Clearwater River *Clarkia pulchella*. Either plant in its flowering season gives mountainsides a pinkish cast. For himself, Pursh chose *Purshia tridentata*, which may have been in keeping with his personality: *Purshia tridentata* bears the common name of bitterbrush.

Meriwether Lewis did name a bird, but perhaps unintentionally. On September 16, 1804, Lewis noted in his journal: "Killed a bird of the Corvus genus and order of the pica, about the size of a jack-daw with a remarkable long tale." It happened in South Dakota. The bird now is known as *Pica pica*, the black-billed magpie, the scientific name drawn in deference to Lewis's journal entry. Dr. Elliott Coues in his excellent review of the Lewis and Clark natural history material remarked that Lewis's entry was the "solitary instance of our authors venturing a technical Latin name in zoology." Alexander Wilson in his *American Ornithology* says in his account of the magpie: "The drawing was taken from a very beautiful specimen, sent from the Mandan nation, on the Missouri, to Mr. Jefferson, and by that gentleman presented to Mr. Peale of this city, in whose Museum it lived for several months, and where I had an opportunity of examining it."

Other birds from the Lewis and Clark expedition which appeared in Wilson's great work were Lewis's woodpecker, which expedition members collected on July 20, 1805, near Missoula, Montana; Clark's nutcracker, collected by Captain Clark August 22, 1805, near Salmon City, Idaho; and the western tanager, collected by expedition members June 6, 1806, near the Kooskooskee River in Idaho.

The most spectacular bird listed in Captain Clark's report was the

California condor, now reduced to a remnant population confined to a wildlife refuge near Los Angeles, but then an apparently abundant bird along the Columbia River. Following a rather good technical description of the condor, which Clark noted may be the largest bird of North America, he wrote:

> It is not known that this bird preys upon living animals; we have seen him feeding on the remains of the whale and other fishes thrown upon the coast by the violence of the waves. This bird was not seen by any of the party until we had descended the Columbia River below the Great Falls. He is believed to be of the vulture genus. . . .

Clark referred to the bird as a "buzzard," a still common term for a vulture in the South. Clark also included the bat, a mammal, in his bird list, an error that many with limited biological knowledge have made. His attempts at biological descriptions are interesting because they reflect the struggles of an untutored person doing his utmost. As Dr. Coues comments upon the bird list: "It is a personal peculiarity of the writer of this chapter to discover 'sea-green' in the eyes (pupils) of various birds, all of whose pupils are black; and curiously also, he does not notice the green eyes (irides) of the cormorant. . . ."

The failure of Thomas Jefferson to assign at least one naturalist to the Lewis and Clark expedition never has been adequately explained. As early as 1789, Jefferson had suggested to William Bartram that he should make a journey to the upper Missouri River. Although Bartram was only fifty, he refused on the grounds that he was too old. In 1792, Jefferson suggested to the Philosophical Society in Philadelphia that it send a competent person to ascend the Missouri River, cross the Stony (Rocky) Mountains, and descend the nearest river to the Pacific Ocean. Among volunteers for the job was Capt. Meriwether Lewis, an officer in the United States Army and a young fellow Virginian.

Jefferson was personally interested in natural history and was familiar with the coterie of Philadelphia naturalists. He could have tapped the wisdom of the most experienced American naturalists and had them at least recommend a promising young student who might have gained fame on the trip.

Earlier Jefferson had experienced difficulty in assembling reliable natural history information while compiling his then famous *Notes on the State of Virginia*. In it he listed seventy-seven bird species of Virginia with both Linnean and Catesbian references. The list frequently is referred to as the most up-to-date state list of its period, although

Bartram and Dr. Barton's work in Pennsylvania was more sophisticated. Actually, in zoology Jefferson was more of a dabbler than a scientist. Yet it is exactly that level of interest that one might have expected to stimulate him to select a Lewis and Clark naturalist.

Instead, Jefferson ordered Meriwether Lewis, who had become Jefferson's personal secretary when he entered the White House in 1801, to go to Philadelphia and Lancaster, Pennsylvania, and take a quick course in natural history and astronomy from the savants stationed there. During this crash course in 1803, Lewis, always the practical soldier, seems largely to have devoted his efforts to learning how astronomical tools could be used in accurately plotting one's latitude and longitude in mapping. He hardly could have expected to master the natural history field in the few weeks allotted.

It is interesting, and in keeping with the basic purposes of the expedition, that the first mammal listed in Lewis and Clark's mammal account was not a wild animal but the Indian horse. Of it, the explorers said:

> 1. The horse is confined principally to the nations inhabiting the great plains of the Columbia, extending from lat. 40° to 50° N., and occupying the tract of territory lying between the Rocky mountains and a range of mountains which passes the Columbia river about the Great Falls; from long. 116° to 121° W. The Shoshonees, Choppunish, Sokulks, Escheloots, Eneshures, and Chilluckittequaws all enjoy the benefit of that docile, noble, and generous animal, and all of them, except the last three, possess immense numbers.
>
> They appear to be of an excellent race, lofty, elegantly formed, active and durable; many of them appear like fine English coursers; some of them are pied with large spots of white, irregularly scattered, and intermixed with a dark brown bay; the greater part, however, are of an uniform color, marked with stars and white feet, and resemble in fleetness and bottom, as well as in form and color, the best blooded horses of Virginia. The natives suffer them to run at large in the plains, the grass of which affords them their only winter subsistence, their masters taking no trouble to lay in a winter's store for them; notwithstanding, they will, unless much exercised, fatten on the dry grass afforded by the plains during the winter. The plains are rarely, if ever, moistened by rain, and the grass is consequently short and thin. The natives, excepting those of the Rocky mountains, appear to take no pains in selecting their male horses to breed: indeed, those of

that class appear much the most indifferent. Whether the horse was originally a native of this country or not, the soil and climate appear to be perfectly well adapted to the nature of this animal. Horses are said to be found wild in many parts of this extensive country. The several tribes of Shoshonees who reside toward Mexico, on the waters of the Multnomah river, particularly one of them, called Shaboboah, have also a great number of mules, which the Indians prize more highly than horses. An elegant horse may be purchased of the natives for a few beads or other paltry trinkets, which, in the United States, would not cost more than one or two dollars. The abundance and cheapness of horses will be extremely advantageous to those who may hereafter attempt the fur-trade to the East Indies by the way of the Columbia river and the Pacific ocean.

The most specific charge that Lewis and Clark were to carry out was to learn everything they could about the Indians—their numbers and customs, where they summered and wintered, and how they preferred to engage in trade. Jefferson instructed the adventurers in writing to determine whether a fur trade could be established in the upper Missouri River country. In other words, Jefferson was searching for a back-door entrance to a thriving fur trade whose center at that time was the Pacific coast and the Columbia River country. The British were trading in Oregon and northward and were at that time sending traders of the Northwest Company to the edges of the upper Missouri.

The opening paragraph of instructions from Jefferson to Lewis and Clark read: "The object of your mission is to explore the Missouri River, and such principal streams of it, as, by its course and communication with the waters of the Pacific Ocean, whether the Columbia, Oregan [sic], Colorado, or any other river, may offer the most direct and practicable water-communication across the continent, for the purposes of commerce. . . ."

After stressing at length the commercial nature of the journey, Jefferson mentioned toward the end of the mission order "other objects worthy of notice." He suggested that the explorers make notes on the soil, vegetables, animals, minerals, volcanic appearance, and climate. Under climate he included recording the dates when various plants flower, and birds, reptiles, and insects appear.

Under such a priority system, natural history naturally received secondary attention.

Emphasis upon natural history aspects tends to demean the Lewis and Clark expedition's accomplishments. One might mistake it as little more than a buckskin pageant moving across vast voids on a map. Such an impression would be not only unfortunate but also grossly unfair. The Lewis and Clark expedition surely was among the better led in history. Encountering what today would be considered constant hardship, and often forced to make crucial decisions, Lewis and Clark led a party that varied from forty-five to twenty-nine persons for more than two years with the loss of only one life. The single death was that of Sgt. Charles Floyd, who died the second day after being stricken by a "colic," the nature of the affliction not defined. Floyd died in the then wilderness near the present city of Sioux City, Iowa, on October 20, 1804. Among memorials to him was the *Sergeant Floyd,* a snag-boat that the army put to work on the Missouri River to keep open a water supply route to the frontier army post at Fort Leavenworth, Kansas. Coping with the treacherous Missouri snags and sandbars gave the army a priority on the river that eventually was parlayed into one of the most massive river alteration projects in history, resulting in dams that converted the upper Missouri into six massive lakes, plus twenty-four dams and lakes on Missouri tributaries, as well as miles of levees and channel diversions downstream.

A problem that all editors encounter when dealing with the Lewis and Clark narrative is that the adventurers were primarily military men and their journal entries were laconic. For instance, on the return trip a member of the party who was nearsighted in his only eye mistook Lewis for an elk and shot him. The ball passed through Lewis's buttocks, fortunately missing bone and artery, but leaving him in a condition that made both standing and sitting unbearable. The journal records the incident almost with the attitude that such inconveniences should be expected.

The party's harrowing hardships and difficult decisions are recorded with total dispassion. Such trying situations as their final winter in the mountains, when they faced a decision of whether to attempt to move their horses over the hard crust that covered ten feet of snow and take a chance of being trapped by sudden thaws or to remain where they were, must have involved considerable anguish. If they remained where they were, they faced the probability of running out of food and the certainty of having to camp through another winter before reaching St. Louis. They moved across the snow.

The fact that an Indian woman, Sacajawea, guided the party through the rough terrain of the trip and through periods of great trial does not lessen the supposed suffering along the way. Rather it indicates what most biologists know, namely, that the female of a species can withstand any rigors bearable by the male, an adjustment that makes it possible for a species to continue inhabiting the earth. As for Saca-jawea, she gave birth to a son in the Mandan village on February 11, 1805, in a season so bitterly cold that members of the expedition regularly suffered frostbite. The son, Baptiste, became better known as Pompey, a nickname that Clark gave the boy. Sacajawea nursed the child while guiding the expedition to the Pacific, and remained at Fort Clatsop through the winter with him. The child remained in good health until May 16, 1806, when Lewis noted in his journal that "the child is very ill." Baptiste had a high fever and swollen neck, the cause of which remains obscure. Lewis treated the child two weeks with various home remedies while they moved through the Bitterroot Mountains. Baptiste recovered. A few years later the boy was sent to St. Louis and the custody of Clark, who had promised to school him.

One of the things that moderns note in reading Lewis and Clark journal entries is their frequent comments, made in such locations as Iowa or North Dakota, comparing what they have found there with what they were familiar with "in the United States." To them and their contemporaries, what now is the center of the United States was a foreign land.

The task of blending the Lewis and Clark journals into a readable narrative, or history, finally rested upon Nicholas Biddle, a wealthy Philadelphia banker who also was a successful politician and editor. Clark seems to have renewed efforts to bring the journals to publica-tion sometime after Lewis's death from a gunshot wound on October 11, 1809, while he was traveling the infamous Natchez Trace, a road known for its thriving industry of highway robbery. Whether Lewis was killed by the landlord of a tavern where he stopped for the night, as most residents of the area supposed, or committed suicide, as con-temporaries remote from the scene conjectured, never has been estab-lished. At any rate, Clark supplied Biddle with personal comments and extrapolations on the cryptic entries, and Biddle made the rounds in search of a publisher. Finally Bradford and Inskeep, who published natural history books, agreed to undertake Biddle's history of the ex-pedition. The publishers devoted a year to preparation of the history and found themselves in financial troubles which for a time threatened completion of the project.

On August 18, 1813, Paul Allen, a Philadelphia newspaperman who later became the editor of newspapers in Baltimore, wrote Thomas Jefferson a letter asking authority to take over the editing of the jour-nals. Allen said, "I wish very much to enliven the dullness of the [Bid-dle] narrative by something more popular, splendid and attractive." On August 20, 1813, Jefferson wrote Biddle advising him of Allen's offer. Biddle apparently was not satisfied with his own work, and Allen stepped into the role as editor. Although Allen was paid five hundred dollars for his work on the journals, there was little evidence that he made any substantial changes, and the history that was published on February 20, 1814, was referred to then and is still known today as Biddle's version of the Lewis and Clark story.

The story of how Jefferson began quiet negotiations to acquire New Orleans and prevent any future foreign owner from blocking that entry to the Mississippi River and wound up buying a substantial slice of North America highlights the primitiveness of the American political system in that era. None of it illuminates the informality of the times quite so well, however, as the simple fact that when Meriwether Lewis headed for the wilderness, he carried in his pocket a document hand-written by President Jefferson on July 4, 1803, which was an open letter of credit authorizing Lewis to draw unlimited amounts on the U.S. government any time he deemed it necessary.

The grizzly bear serves as a sort of litmus paper by which one may test the still unresolved argument concerning whether or not the Lewis and Clark expedition made significant contributions to American natural history. As the grizzly continued to assert its temperament, the multiple Lewis and Clark diaries became compilations of bear morphology and behavior. Aside from the omission of material on dentition and skull characteristics that one might expect from a competent naturalist, the composite word portrait of the grizzly was the outstanding natural history contribution from the expedition. The expedition members recognized that the grizzly was a quite different bear from the species with which they were familiar. Even more interesting, they recognized the grizzly as a grizzly despite the variable pelage that exists within the species. In a major way, their grizzly records prove that the expedition *could* have been an impressive foray into natural history— if natural history had been a principal concern of the mission.

To appreciate the acumen of the Lewis and Clark troop's recognition of the grizzly bear in all color forms, one might consider the now-classical confusion into which the reputable Dr. C. Hart Merriam descended some decades later when confronted with the puzzling bears of Alaska. Dr. Merriam founded the U.S. Biological Survey, and his credentials were above reproach. In the Alaskan region, south of the polar bear range, there exists an array of bears whose color variations approach the kaleidoscopic. By today's taxonomic standards, the Alaskan region and the western United States are assumed to be populated by one species of large land bear, and what had been until recently the grizzly bear (*Ursus horribilis*) and the Alaskan brown bear

(*Ursus arctos*) have been lumped together as *Ursus arctos,* despite an erratic range of characteristics. The move, of course, canceled Ord's decision that the grizzly was *U. horribilis.* But these modifications occurred long after Merriam's time.

The good Dr. Merriam kept sorting hides and skulls until he had compiled a list of eighty-six bear species and subspecies for the grizzly-brown bear range. He published his results in 1918. Dr. Merriam's count caused considerable discussion in natural history shops and led to the old joke:

"Have you heard about that armchair naturalist in Washington who thinks there are five species of bears on Admiralty Island alone?" a field biologist asked a grizzled old sourdough. "Isn't that ridiculous?"

"It certainly is," replied the old sourdough. "There's at least seven!"

From specimens returned by the expedition, George Ord wrote scientific descriptions not only of the grizzly bear, pronghorn, and black-tailed prairie dog, but also of the bushy-tailed wood rat, eastern wood rat, western gray squirrel, and Columbian ground squirrel. In addition, Ord described three birds: Bonaparte's gull, the whistling swan, and the Columbian sharp-tailed grouse. As stated earlier, Alexander Wilson in his *American Ornithology* published from Lewis and Clark material the first descriptions of Lewis's woodpecker, Clark's nutcracker, and the western tanager. The total is seven mammals and six birds that could be allotted to the expedition despite the fact that their descriptions were published by others.

In botany the expedition did much better. Its score might have been even more impressive except for the fact that misfortune destroyed several bales of plant specimens. As with the fauna, the flora was also described by others. The Lewis and Clark Herbarium, now in custody of the Academy of Natural Sciences of Philadelphia, contains slightly more than 200 dried plants. Of the total of 178 plants described from Lewis and Clark material, 140 were from west of the Continental Divide. A major collection of plants collected east of the Divide was destroyed by spring flood.

One can find more charitable estimates of the scientific worth of the expedition. Perhaps the most charitable is Dr. Paul Russell Cutright's number of species published in *Lewis and Clark: Pioneering Naturalists.* Dr. Cutright credits the expedition with discovery of 12 fish, 15 amphibians and reptiles, 51 birds, and 44 mammals. To achieve such a total requires one to recognize the expedition as having discovered several species that were not differentiated by naturalists until late in the nineteenth century. Dr. Cutright was not alone in the assessment. In fact, most of his credits had been ascribed to the expedition earlier by Dr. Elliott Coues. Dr. Coues, perhaps the most sophisticated zoologist of his era, ferreted out small descriptive passages from the Lewis and Clark journals as a detective might pick up clues at a murder scene and made an educated guess at what the species might have been, basing his estimate upon characteristics of species described by naturalists who worked the region after Lewis and Clark.

The Lewis and Clark expedition was traveling unknown territory between the Yellowstone River at its junction with the Missouri River and the last major falls on the Columbia River toward its mouth. The Pacific coast, at least northward from Fort Clatsop, had been explored in a limited way as early as 1741, when the German naturalist in Russian employ, George Wilhelm Steller, did field studies with the Vitus Bering expedition to Alaska. In addition, Peter Pallas, another German naturalist, had been hired by the St. Petersburg Academy of Sciences in 1768 and had described other eastern Pacific forms collected by Russian traders.

Chapter IV

Listening to Birds: Wilson

On March 29, 1804, Alexander Wilson sent William Bartram a collection of bird drawings with a note in which he said:

> I have now got my collection of Native birds considerably enlarged and shall endeavor if possible to obtain all the smaller ones this summer. Be pleased to mark the Names of each with a pencil as except 3 or 4 I dont know any of them.

The note was not from a youth, but from a man thirty-seven years old. In ten years he would be dead. But in that decade he accomplished one of the landmarks of American natural history—*American Ornithology*, a collection of art and observations on American birds that totaled nine volumes, two of which were published posthumously.

Dr. Elliot Coues, who was among the more astute critics of ornithological literature, commented a half-century later: "Perhaps no other work on ornithology of equal extent is equally free from error; and its truthfulness is illumined by a spark of the 'divine fire.' This means immortality."

As was true of so many early American naturalists, Wilson had no formal preparation for the task of drawing birds or for the collection of scientific data about them. In fact, his schooling in his native town of Paisley, Scotland, appears limited. Wilson's friend and biographer, George Ord, wrote that Wilson was forced to quit school at the age of ten. Records at Paisley, however, indicate that he was thirteen when his mother died and his schooling ended. His stepmother rejected him, forcing him to live with a brother-in-law, William Duncan. Duncan, a weaver, apprenticed Wilson in the trade, and although he spent several years both in Scotland and America as a weaver, he disliked the physical confinement it entailed.

Wilson thought of himself as a poet, but the avocation of rhyming got him into trouble and in part led to his emigration to the United

States. In 1793, during a dispute over labor conditions among Paisley weavers, Wilson wrote a poem entitled "The Shark, or Lang Mills Detected." It was an attack on a leading Paisley manufacturer. Although the piece was anonymous, it was traced to Wilson, and the manufacturer brought libel proceedings against him. It seems that Wilson's only punishment was being forced to burn a copy of the offensive poem in front of the local jail, although some versions speak of a brief imprisonment. Anyhow, Wilson embarked for America and landed at New Castle, Delaware, July 14, 1794. From there he walked to Philadelphia, and on the way shot a red-headed woodpecker, which he thought the most beautiful bird he ever had seen.

At the time Wilson sent his bird drawings and note requesting their identification to William Bartram, he was the unhappy schoolmaster at the Union School at Kingsessing, Pennsylvania, and a near neighbor of Bartram. It was one of several American teaching ventures into which he drifted, and he approached the Pennsylvania school position, as he noted, "with the same sullen resignation that a prisoner re-enters his dungeon or a malefactor mounts the scaffold."

When he asked for Bartram's help, Wilson already had made a major decision which led to his involvement with *American Ornithology,* for in a letter to Alexander Lawson, fellow Scot in Philadelphia who later was to become Wilson's engraver, Wilson wrote on March 12, 1804:

> I am most earnestly bent on pursuing my plan of making a Collection of all the Birds of this part of N. America. Now I dont want you to throw cold water as Shakespeare says on this notion, Quixotic as it may appear. I have been so long accustomed to the building of Airy Castles and brain Windmills that it has become one of my comforts of life a sort of rough Bone that amuses me when sated with the dull drudgery of Life.

Wilson had known both Bartram and Lawson more than a year, and had discussed mutual interests in natural history with Bartram and learned drawing skills from Lawson. They and Charles Willson Peale, Philadelphia painter, amateur scientist, and founder of Peale's Museum, were perhaps the persons most influential in launching Wilson on a new career.

The turning point that made eventual publication of his ornithological work possible came in 1806, when Wilson left schoolteaching to become assistant editor of *Rees New Cyclopedia* in Philadelphia. Samuel E. Bradford was editor of the *Cyclopedia*, and Bradford and

Inskeep were to become the publishers of *American Ornithology*. Wilson's great work began taking form soon after he joined the publishing firm, and early in 1807 the first prospectus was ready for circulation to potential subscribers. In September 1808, the first volume of *American Ornithology* was published.

To fully appreciate the magnitude of the job that Wilson had undertaken, one really needs to be an ornithologist. A review of ornithological literature on American birds that preceded his work discloses that the existing knowledge of bird life was scant, or worse, legendary. His most nearly available scientific source, Bartram, was primarily a botanist, and while Bartram had compiled an impressive list of American bird names, had recorded migration dates at Philadelphia, and had even done some dissecting of birds as well as observing many species in the field, his work was neither as organized nor as penetrating as Wilson would require. The only ornithological work that Wilson owned was Thomas Bewick's *British Birds*, a volume that could serve as a model for the mechanics of assembling an American work but was far from being a well of American information. Thomas Say, another famous Philadelphia naturalist, had loaned Wilson a copy of William Turton's *Linnaeus*, which discussed the binomial system. From the Philadelphia library he borrowed a copy of John Latham's *Synopsis of Birds*. Latham was an English ornithologist of good repute. Latham's special contribution was a standard of bird classification that had international significance, which Wilson rather successfully applied to American birds.

From the text of *American Ornithology* one learns that Wilson acquired access to other volumes on birds, most of which would have been more of a hindrance than a help if he had accepted the authors' assertions.

A rather good assessment of the literature as it applied to American birds, and a clue to Wilson's approach to birds as well as to the literature, appeared in volume 1 of *American Ornithology*, where he wrote of the European authorities and their publications:

> The greatest number of the descriptions, particularly those of the nests, eggs, and plumage, have been written in the woods, with the subjects in view, leaving as little as possible to the lapse of recollection: as to what relates to the manners, habits, &c. of the birds, the particulars on these heads are the result of personal observation, from memorandums taken on the spot; if they differ, as they will in many points, from former accounts, this at least can be said in their behalf, that a single fact has not been advanced

which the writer was not himself witness to, or received from those on whose judgment and veracity he believed reliance could be placed. . . .

As to the state of ornithological science among American naturalists, Wilson wrote with justification:

From the writers of our own country the author has derived but little advantage. The first considerable list of our birds was published in 1787, by Mr. Jefferson, in his celebrated "Notes on Virginia," and contains the names of 109 species, with the designations of Linnaeus and Catesby, and references to Buffon. The next, and by far the most complete that has yet appeared, was published in 1791, by Mr. William Bartram, in his "Travels through North and South Carolina," &c. in which 215 different species are enumerated, and concise descriptions and characteristics of each, added in Latin and English. Dr. Barton, in his "Fragments of the Natural History of Pennsylvania," has favoured us with a number of remarks on this subject: and Dr. Belknap, in his "History of New Hampshire," as well as Dr. Williams, in that of Vermont, have each enumerated a few of our birds. But these, from the nature of the publications in which they have been introduced, can be considered only as catalogues of names, without the detail of specific particulars, or the figured and colored representations of the birds themselves. This task, the hardest of all, has been reserved for one of far inferior abilities, but not of less zeal. With the example of many solitary individuals, in other countries, who have succeeded in such an enterprise, he has cheerfully engaged in the undertaking, trusting for encouragement solely to the fidelity with which it will be conducted.

Wilson had one advantage over previous ornithologists, an advantage from which succeeding generations of ornithologists would benefit: Peale in his museum activities had discovered improved methods of preserving bird skins and had advanced taxidermy to the point where a museum no longer was a repository of rotting bird flesh. This provided a possibility of continuity in type specimens, which would enable others to compare the original bird with the first description by an author. Wilson provided details of the new preserving process on page viii of volume 2 and urged correspondents to clean birds and treat the skins in that manner before forwarding them to

him. Although there has been further technological progress in bird
skinning since 1810, a few practicing ornithologists still follow the
Wilson directions, which begin with an incision beneath a wing. The
more common practice today is to begin the incision at the vent and
proceed along the abdominal line. Despite the value of his advice, it is
obvious that Wilson himself did not always follow it. If he had, the
argument over his "Small-headed Flycatcher" never would have
arisen. Since he did not preserve the specimen, the issue may never
be resolved.

Wilson, of course, made all his ornithological observations by means
of a shotgun. Today incontrovertible proof may be obtained with a
camera equipped with color film and telescopic lens. But in Wilson's
day the optical equipment upon which modern ornithologists place
great reliance was not available. Even had it been, Wilson was too
poor to afford it. His greatest limitation throughout his work was
poverty, although his position as an assistant editor with Bradford
finally resolved it to a degree—he received $900 a year, which he con-
sidered a rather magnificent salary.

Given the known limitations that handicapped Wilson, one would
expect to find the answer to his success in his personality. But even
there he seemed meagerly endowed. Audubon, who seldom had anything complimentary to say of anyone except himself, said of Wilson:

> One fair morning (in Louisville) I was surprised by the sudden
> appearance into our counting room of Mr. Alexander Wilson,
> the celebrated author of *American Ornithology*, of whose exis-
> tence I had never until that moment been apprised. How well do
> I remember him as he then walked up to me. His long hooked
> nose, the keenness of his eyes, and his prominent cheek bones
> stamped his countenance with a peculiar character. His dress,
> too, was of a kind not usually seen in that part of the country,—a
> short coat, trousers, and a waistcoat of grey cloth. . . .

Audubon obviously was not overly impressed with Wilson or his
appearance.

Even more damning of Wilson's personality were the comments
written by his best friend, Ord, in the final volume of *American
Ornithology*:

> But as no one is perfect, Mr. Wilson in a small degree partook
> of the weakness of humanity. He was of the *Genus irritabile*, and
> was obstinate in opinion. It ever gave him pleasure to acknowl-

edge error when the conviction resulted from his own judgment alone, but he could not endure to be told of his mistakes. Hence his associates had to be sparing of their criticisms, through a fear of forfeiting his friendship. With almost all his friends he had occasionally, arising from a collision of opinion, some slight misunderstanding, which was soon passed over, leaving no disagreeable impression. But an act of disrespect, or wilful injury he would seldom forgive.

Interestingly, the picture of Wilson that one may form from the comments of his contemporaries fails to materialize in *American Ornithology*. Within those pages one finds a man who held no bitterness toward the world; an adopted American whose enthusiasm for his country knew few bounds (he even boasts of acquiring in America all ingredients for publication of his book except for a few pigments which he hopes eventually will be American-produced); an astute observer of the American scene as well as of birds; and a man whose cynicism largely is limited to self-evaluation.

Because of the thoroughness, accuracy, and professional quality of *American Ornithology*, Wilson commonly is referred to as "the father of American ornithology." While the title is well deserved, it is to some extent unfortunate, because it implies a stuffiness that cannot be found in a single volume. It was Wilson's good fortune to know as still plentiful some species of birds that either no longer exist, or exist in a population so reduced that the species borders on extinction. One of these, the ivory-billed woodpecker, furnished Wilson with one of his most amusing accounts:

> In looking over the accounts given of the Ivory-billed Woodpecker by the naturalists of Europe, I find it asserted, that it inhabits from New Jersey to Mexico. I believe, however, that few of them are ever seen to the north of Virginia, and very few of them even in that state. The first place I observed this bird at, when on my way to the south, was about twelve miles north of Wilmington in North Carolina. There I found the bird from which the drawing of the figure in the plate was taken. This bird was only wounded slightly in the wing, and on being caught, uttered a loudly reiterated, and most piteous note, exactly resembling the violent crying of a young child; which terrified my horse so, as nearly to have cost me my life. It was distressing to hear it. I carried it with me in the chair, under cover, to Wilmington. In passing through the streets its affecting cries sur-

prised every one within hearing, particularly the females, who hurried to the doors and windows with looks of alarm and anxiety. I drove on, and on arriving at the piazza of the hotel, where I intended to put up, the landlord came forward, and a number of other persons who happened to be there, all equally alarmed at what they heard; this was greatly increased by my asking whether he could furnish me with accommodations for myself and my baby. The man looked blank, and foolish, while the others stared with still greater astonishment. After diverting myself for a minute or two at their expense, I drew my Woodpecker from under the cover and a general laugh took place. I took him up stairs and locked him up in my room, while I went to see my horse taken care of. In less than an hour I returned, and on opening the door he set up the same distressing shout, which now appeared to proceed from grief that he had been discovered in his attempts at escape. He had mounted along the side of the window, nearly as high as the ceiling, a little below which he had begun to break through. The bed was covered with large pieces of plaster; the lath was exposed for at least fifteen inches square, and a hole, large enough to admit the fist, opened to the weather-boards; so that in less than another hour he would certainly have succeeded in making his way through. I now tied a string round his leg, and fastening it to the table, again left him. I wished to preserve his life, and had gone off in search of suitable food for him. As I reascended the stairs, I heard him again hard at work, and on entering had the mortification to perceive that he had almost entirely ruined the mahogany table to which he was fastened, and on which he had wreaked his whole vengeance. While engaged in taking the drawing, he cut me severely in several places, and on the whole, displayed such a noble and unconquerable spirit that I was frequently tempted to restore him to his native woods. He lived with me nearly three days, but refused all sustenance, and I witnessed his death with regret.

American Ornithology contains 76 plates depicting 320 individual birds, all of them hand-colored. Due to financial problems at some stages of producing volumes, Wilson at times was reduced to hand-coloring plates himself when he was unable to employ colorists. All plates except one contain several birds. It is on this single plate, which appeared in volume 9, after Wilson's death, that Wilson's potential as an artist appears. The bird is a peregrine falcon, which Wilson called "Duck Hawk," and here his art and accuracy equal that of any succeeding artist, with the possible exception of Louis Agassiz Fuertes in *his* painting of the peregrine.

In the nine volumes, Wilson—and George Ord, who wrote the ninth volume but pretended only to have edited it—describes 279 species of American birds. While originally the claim was made that the work contained 55 species that had not been described previously, later research into other authors has reduced the list of new discoveries to either 31 or 29, depending in part upon whether two species described by Wilson were valid. It was not a complete list of all the North American birds that had been discovered before Wilson's era, which at the time had reached 384 species, but then the United States occupied a far smaller space on the continent.

The two species whose validity remains under question were the "Small-headed Flycatcher" and the "Blue Mountain Warbler." Although Audubon later was to use both species in his *Birds of America*, no specimen of either species exists today. In fact, a dispute over the "Small-headed Flycatcher" became a pivotal point in what has become known as the Wilson-Audubon controversy. The controversy was misnamed, for it was between George Ord and John James Audubon. Wilson was dead when it arose, and nothing that Wilson wrote in *American Ornithology* in any way casts an aspersion upon Audubon.

Although Ord had injected into his biography of Wilson certain notes that Audubon would recognize as derogatory, even though the average reader would miss the implications, and although Ord was scoffing orally among Philadelphia naturalists, the controversy between Ord and Audubon did not surface publicly until 1840, when Audubon published his comments on the small-headed flycatcher in his *Ornithological Biography*. Despite its odd name, the *Biography* was the text designed to accompany the color plates of *Birds of America*, which were published separately. In his species account of the flycatcher, Audubon wrote:

> The sight of the figure of this species brings to my recollection a curious incident of long-past days, when I drew it at Louisville in Kentucky. It was in the early part of the spring of 1808, thirty-two years ago, that I procured a specimen of it while searching the margins of a pond.
>
> In those happy days, kind reader, I thought not of the minute differences by which one species may be distinguished from another in words, or of the necessity of comparing tarsi, toes, claws, and quills, although I have, as you are aware, troubled you

with tedious details of this sort. When Alexander Wilson visited me at Louisville, he found in my already large collection of drawings, a figure of the present species, which, being at that time unknown to him, he copied and afterwards published in his great work, but without acknowledging the privilege that had thus been granted to him. I have more than once regretted this, not by any means so much on my own account, as for the sake of one to whom we are so deeply indebted for his elucidation of our ornithology.

I consider this Flycatcher as among the scarcest of those that visit our middle districts; for, although it seems that Wilson procured one that "was shot on the 24th of April, in an orchard," and afterwards "several individuals of this species in various quarters of New Jersey, particularly in swamps," all my endeavours to trace it in that section of the country have failed, as have those of my friend Edward Harris, Esq., who is a native of that State, resides there, and is well acquainted with all the birds found in the district. I have never seen it out of Kentucky, and even there it is a very uncommon bird. In Philadelphia, Baltimore, New York, or farther eastward or southward, in our Atlantic districts, I never saw a single individual, not even in museums, private collections, or for sale in bird-stuffers' shops.

In its habits this species is closely allied to the Hooded and Green Blackcapt Flycatchers, being fond of low thick coverts, whether in the interior of swamps, or by the margins of sluggish pools, from which it only removes to higher situations after a continuation of wet weather, when I have found it on rolling grounds, and amid woods comparatively clear of under-growth.

Differing from the true Flycatchers, this species has several rather pleasing notes, which it enunciates at pretty regular intervals, and which may be heard at the distance of forty or fifty yards in calm weather. I have more than once seen it attracted by an imitation of these notes. While chasing insects on wing, although it clicks its bill on catching them, the sound thus emitted is comparatively weak, as is the case with the species above mentioned, it being stronger however in the Green Blackcapt than in this or the Hooded species. Like these birds, it follows its prey to some distance at times, whilst at others, it searches keenly among the leaves for its prey, but, I believe, never alights on the ground, not even for the purpose of drinking, which act it performs by passing lightly over the water and sipping, as it were, the quantity it needs.

All my efforts to discover its nest in the lower parts of Kentucky, where I am confident that it breeds, have proved fruitless; and I have not heard that any other person has been more successful.

In his account, which provided a scientific name and description for the small-headed flycatcher (Wilson hyphenated *small-headed* but Audubon did not), Wilson wrote:

This very rare species is the only one I have met with, and is drawn reduced to half its size, to correspond with the rest of the figures on the same plate. It was shot on the twenty-fourth of April, in an orchard, and was remarkably active, running, climbing and darting about among the opening buds and blossoms with extraordinary agility. From what quarter of the United States or of North America it is a wanderer, I am unable to determine, having never before met with an individual of the species. Its notes and manner of breeding are also alike unknown to me. This was a male: it measured five inches long, and eight and a quarter in extent; the upper parts were dull yellow olive; the wings dusky brown edged with lighter; the greater and lesser coverts tipt with white; the lower parts dirty white, stained with dull yellow, particularly on the upper parts of the breast; the tail dusky brown, the two exterior feathers marked like those of many others with a spot of white on the inner vanes; head remarkably small; bill broad at the base, furnished with bristles, and notched near the tip; legs dark brown; feet yellowish; eye dark hazel.

Since writing the above I have shot several individuals of this species in various quarters of New Jersey, particularly in swamps. They all appear to be nearly alike in plumage. Having found them there in June, there is no doubt of their breeding in that state, and probably in such situations far to the southward; for many of the southern summer birds that rarely visit Pennsylvania, are yet common to the swamps and pine woods of New Jersey. Similarity of soil and situation, of plants and trees, and consequently of fruits, seeds, insects, &c. are doubtless their inducements. The Summer Red-bird, Great Carolina Wren, Pine-creeping Warbler, and many others, are rarely seen in Pennsylvania, or to the northward, tho they are common in many parts of West Jersey.

Audubon clearly had accused Wilson of pirating the details of Audubon's painting of the small-headed flycatcher and—even worse, considering the scientific nature of Wilson's work—faking a description of a bird that he perhaps never had seen.

Ord lost no time in challenging Audubon's charge of plagiarism. The Proceedings of the American Philosophical Society in Philadelphia, which reports on the meeting of September 18, 1840, contains the following:

> The attack upon the reputation of a member of this society, one who, during the long period he dwelt amongst us, was noted for his integrity, ought not to be suffered to pass without examination. Wilson's Small-headed Flycatcher differs in no respect from his ordinary style; that it bears the signet of paternity on its very front. But, as it might be objected that this mode of reasoning is, in conclusion, from the circumstances of several of Mr. Audubon's birds bearing a resemblance to those of Wilson, Mr. Ord obviated this objection, by stating that Mr. Audubon had not scrupled to appropriate the labors of Wilson to his own use; inasmuch as the figures of the female Marsh Blackbird (*Birds of America*, plate 67) and that of the male Mississippi Kite (same work, plate 117) have both been copied from the *American Ornithology*, without the least acknowledgment of the source whence they had been derived. Mr. Ord thought that the charge of plagiarism came with ill grace from one who had been guilty of it himself, as in the instance above named. Wilson states that he shot the bird figured and described in his 6th volume, page 62, in an orchard, on the 24th of April. Mr. Ord confirms this statement, by declaring to this society that he himself was with Wilson on the day in question; that he saw and examined the specimen; and that Wilson assured him it was entirely new to him. Wilson was then residing at the Bartram Botanic Garden near Philadelphia. Mr. Ord further read to the society a letter addressed to him by the artist, Mr. Lawson, who engraved the plate in which the Small-headed Flycatcher is figured. This gentlemen affirms, that all the plates, which he engraved for the American Ornithology, were from Wilson's own drawings, and that in respect to the plate in which the Small-headed Flycatcher appeared, *specimens* of all the birds represented accompanied the drawings; and he, after getting his outlines, worked from them. Mr. Ord laid before the society a proof of the etching of this plate, and re-

marked, that from the minuteness of the details, the point of the engraver had a greater share in producing the desired result, than even the pencil of the ornithologist.

Perhaps the best evidence presented by Ord was Alexander Lawson's letter stating that he had specimens at hand while working on the plate that contained the small-headed flycatcher. Wilson, of course, was not able to testify, as he was dead. But in *American Ornithology* and in letters to friends, Wilson often referred to Lawson as the person who took his sometimes crude drawings and transformed them into art. Not only Lawson but also the Wilson colorists sometimes used actual specimens when completing plates for the book.

It is interesting that the drawings of Audubon and Wilson do not illustrate the same bird, since Wilson's bird wore a conspicuous white eye ring. The illustration rendered by each artist, however, tends to depict a warbler rather than a flycatcher. In his first edition of the *Biography*, Audubon included the line: "The figure in the plate has been copied from the drawing in the possession of my excellent friend and patroness, Miss Eupemia Glifford." While the line was deleted from subsequent editions, it has been interpreted as meaning that Audubon's original drawing of the bird may have been destroyed when rats ruined his collection of art at Henderson, Kentucky, and that he may have redrawn the figure from memory.

The irony not apparent when the controversy gained heat is that the small-headed flycatcher may never have existed. Although in the period during which the dispute continued among ornithologists there were a few instances of fairly reputable men who believed they had *seen* a small-headed flycatcher, no specimen fitting the Wilson-Audubon plates or descriptions ever has been taken to this day.

As the absence of a small-headed flycatcher in nature became prolonged, many Audubon partisans considered the void a proof that Audubon had the only one found and that Wilson quite obviously had copied the bird. Some went so far as to say that the reason Audubon knew that Wilson was guilty of the piracy was because the bird had existed nowhere other than in Audubon's imagination! The accusation, however, is hardly fair to either man, since it implies that Audubon would willingly fake a bird. If one considers the range of Audubon or the thoroughness of Wilson, it seems obvious that neither needed to fake anything. Indeed, their total credibility might be thrown into question and their extensive labors lost over such a valueless object. Both undoubtedly took their work too seriously to contemplate such a frivolous hazard.

In addition, the small-headed flycatcher is not the only nonexistent bird the two authors shared in common. Another species that has not been found in nature since their day is the Blue Mountain Warbler of Wilson, which Audubon obviously accepted as a valid species and credited to Wilson.

In describing the Blue Mountain Warbler, Audubon included his own observations and quoted almost the entire Wilson text regarding the species:

It is somewhat strange, that among the numerous species of birds that visit the United States, a few should have been met with only in rare instances. The present Warbler is in this predicament, as it does not appear that many specimens have been obtained excepting that from which this figure and description were taken. For many years I never met with Bewick's Wren, which is now, however, known to be abundant on the mountains of Virginia, and elsewhere in our Middle and Southern Districts, and still more so along the Columbia river. The same was the case with Henslow's Bunting, which has become a common bird in the State of New Jersey, where it breeds, and in South Carolina and the Floridas, where it spends the winter. Of Townsend's Bunting the only specimen as yet procured is in my possession; and it is only of late years that MacGillivray's Finch has appeared in numbers in the neighbourhood of Charleston. Swainson's Warbler, at one time scarce in South Carolina, where it was discovered by my good friend Dr. Bachman, has since been procured as far eastward as the vicinity of Boston by Thomas M. Brewer, Junr., Esq. The Pipirie Flycatcher was not known to exist eastward of the Floridas until after I had found it there, although now it is not a scarce species, being found breeding in the very heart of the city of Charleston. Traill's Flycatcher, which I first discovered on the Arkansaw river, is now known to abound on the Columbia river. No other person has observed the Rocky Mountain Wren in any part of the country eastward of that great chain besides Dr. Bachman, who shot one within a few miles of Charleston. I might mention several other species, which at one time were extremely rare in the United States, but are now abundant in many of our districts; but prefer returning to the Blue-Mountain Warbler, which it has not been my good fortune to meet with, although it would be in no degree surprising to find it a constant visitor to some portions of our vast country yet untrodden by the ornithologist. My figure was taken from a specimen lent to me by the

Council of the Zoological Society of London, and which had come from California.

Alexander Wilson, to whom we are indebted for our knowledge of this pretty bird, says that it "was first discovered near that celebrated ridge, or range of mountains, with whose name I have honoured it. Several of these solitary Warblers remain yet to be gleaned up from the airy heights of our alpine scenery, as well as from the recesses of our swamps and morasses, whither it is my design to pursue them by every opportunity. Some of these, I believe, rarely or never visit the lower cultivated parts of the country, but seem only at home among the gloom and silence of those dreary solitudes. The present species seems of that family, or subdivision, of the Warblers, that approach the Flycatchers, darting after flies wherever they see them, and also searching with great activity among the leaves. Its song was a feeble screep, three or four times repeated.

"This species is four inches and three-quarters in length; the upper parts a rich yellow-olive; front, cheeks, and chin yellow; also the sides of the neck; breast and belly pale yellow, streaked with black or dusky; vent plain pale yellow; wings black; first and second row of coverts broadly tipped with pale yellowish-white, tertials the same; the rest of the quills edged with whitish; tail black, handsomely rounded, edged with pale olive; the two exterior feathers on each side white on the inner vanes from the middle to the tips, and edged on the outer side with white; bill dark brown, legs and feet purple-brown; soles yellow; eye dark hazel.

"This was a male. The female I have never seen."

At this point, one finds the first great American ornithologist and the foremost American bird artist foolishly recording two birds that so far as anyone else has been able to determine do not now exist and certainly have not existed other than in art and text for a century and a half. But does the absence of specimens or other corroborating evidence mean that they *never* existed? Well, one might turn the proposition around and ask whether the presence of a bona fide bird specimen in a leading museum means that the bird exists. At this time there are two bird skins reposing in the type specimen collection of the United States Museum in Washington which are the only known members of the species they represent that ever were collected or seen by an ornithologist.

As Herbert G. Deignan, associate curator of birds at the museum, comments in his review of type specimens, which supposedly represent typical birds that live, or have lived, in the United States:

Two of our types possess a peculiar interest in being unique of their kind. These are *Tringa cooperi* Baird, a sandpiper taken on the coast of Long Island on May 24, 1833, and *Emberiza Townsendii* Audubon, a bunting collected in Chester County, Pennsylvania, on May 11, 1833. Neither bird (either or each may represent a mutation, a hybrid of uncertain parentage, or the last of a dying race) has ever been seen again and, were the specimens not now extant, each would be considered a chimeral species.

In *American Ornithology*, Wilson made two serious errors of an inexplicable nature: he gave the same scientific name to two different species, and he did it twice. The sharp-shinned hawk, which he called slate-colored hawk, bears the scientific name *Falco pennsylvanicus* on page 13 of volume 2, and the broad-winged hawk described on page 92 of the same volume bears the same scientific name. The sora rail is named *Rallus virginianus* in volume 6, page 27, and in volume 7, page 109, the Virginia rail (he called it "Virginian rail") bears the same scientific name. Wilson knew better, since he obviously recognized and described all four birds as distinct species. One can only consider the errors slips of the mind, which though common to journalism are inexcusable in scientific works. In the Ord-edited reprints of 1824, the broad-winged hawk appears as *Falco latissimus* and the sora rail as *Rallus carolinus*.

The first edition of volume 1, published in September 1808, consisted of 200 copies, a press run that no publisher today could contemplate because of its uneconomic smallness. Wilson toured New England and traveled as far south as Savannah, Georgia, in late 1808 and early 1809, and solicited enough subscribers to justify an additional press run of 300 copies. Unfortunately the pages had been broken and the type had to be reset. Wilson made the most of the opportunity and corrected or restated a few lines that had appeared in the original press run. Thus the additional printing actually constitutes a revised edition, although there is no notation on the title pages to hint at any changes.

One may determine whether the first edition in hand is of the original 200 or of the revised 300 by reading the species account of the wood thrush. Wilson gained a new perspective on the bird in his southern tour for subscriptions. In the original first edition, Wilson wrote: "Tho' it is believed that some of our birds of passage, and among them the present species, winter in the Carolinas, yet they rarely breed there; and when they do, they are certainly vocal." In the revised version, Wilson replaced the sentence with: "I have myself searched the woods of Carolina and Georgia, in winter, for this bird, in vain, nor do I believe that it ever winters in these states."

Wilson's volumes were not only a scientific landmark for the new republic but also a publishing triumph for an infant industry. It was the first combination of art and type on such a major scale to be attempted in the natural history field in North America. How well Bradford and Inskeep succeeded can be attested by the condition of these volumes 168 years after volume 1 left the press. The pages retain fidelity and flexibility because Thomas Amies of the Dover paper mills insisted upon production of the finest rag stock; indeed, he went so far in his patriotism as to insist that only domestic rags be used. Archibald Binney and James Ronaldson designed a superior type and cast the letters. The Philadelphia firm of Robert and William Carr printed the volumes.

George Murry, chief engraver of natural history illustrations for *Rees Cyclopaedia*, engraved plates 3, 7, 9, 15, and 26. Benjamin Tanner did plate 32, and John G. Warnicke, who worked with Tanner, engraved about twenty plates. However, Alexander Lawson was the master engraver who oversaw the work and whose signature appears on fifty of the seventy-six plates. Lawson was not only capable of working from finished drawings, but he could produce a finished plate from mere outlines if he had the specimens in hand.

When Bradford and Inskeep began publication of *American Ornithology*, there was no established house of plate colorists in America such as there were in Europe. Alexander Rider of Philadelphia apparently applied color to more plates than any other colorist who worked on the volumes. Charles Robert Leslie, who later became a well-known artist, applied color to many plates in volume 1. Among the colorists who worked on the volumes were Anna C. Peale (niece of Charles Willson Peale), Eliza Leslie, and Louise Adelersterran. The colorist who later was to become best known in America in his period was John Henry Hopkins, then a youth of eighteen; he was to become the first Episcopal bishop of Vermont.

It is unlikely that Wilson could have been discouraged from at least writing and illustrating *American Ornithology* regardless of the circumstances of the period. In his introduction to the first volume, he says:

In the commencement of a work of such magnitude, and so

novel in this country, some account will necessarily be expected, of the motives of the author, and of the nature and intended execution of the work. As to the former of these, it is respectfully submitted, that, amusement blended with instruction, the correction of numerous errors which have been introduced into this part of the natural history of our country, and a wish to draw the attention of my fellow-citizens, occasionally, from the discordant jarrings of politics, to a contemplation of the grandeur, harmony, and wonderful variety of Nature, exhibited in this beautiful portion of the animal creation, are my principal, and almost only, motives, in the present undertaking. I will not deny that there may also be other incitements. Biassed, almost from infancy, by a fondness for birds, and little less than an enthusiast in my researches after them, I feel happy to communicate my observations to others, probably from the mere principle of self-gratification, that source of so many even of our most virtuous actions; but I candidly declare, that *lucrative* views have nothing to do in the business. In all my wild-wood rambles *these* never were sufficient either to allure me to a single excursion, to discourage me from one, or to engage my pen or pencil in the present publication. My hopes on this head, are humble enough; I ask only support equal to my merits, and to the laudability of my intentions. I expect no more; I am not altogether certain even of this. But leaving the issue of these matters to futurity, I shall, in the meantime, comfort myself with the good old adage, "Happy are they who expect *nothing*, for they shall not be disappointed."

Fortunately for Wilson, a niche into which a costly publication on American birds might fit had been left by Thomas Pennant, prominent British zoologist, who thought of himself as the man most likely to succeed in bringing a full report on American birds to the public. Pennant was at work on the project when the colonials became unruly. Their attitude toward King George disenchanted Pennant, who said:

I thought I had the right to attempt, at a time I had the honour of calling myself a fellow subject with that respectable part of our former great empire; but when the fatal and humiliating hour arrived, which deprived Britain of power, strength, and glory, I felt the mortification which must strike every feeling individual at losing his little share in the boast of ruling over half of the

New World. I could no longer support my clame of entitling myself its humble zoologist; yet unwilling to fling away my labors do now deliver them to the Public under the title of the Arctic Zoology. I added to them a description of the Quadrupeds and Birds of the North of Europe and of Asia from latitude 60 to the farthest known parts of the Arctic World, together with those of Kamtschatka, and the parts of America in the last voyages of the illustrious Cook.

Whatever is wanting in the *American* part I may foresee, will in time be amply supplied. The powers of literature will soon arise, with the other strengths, of the new empire, and some native Naturalist give perfection to that part of the undertaking by observations formed on the spot, in the uses, manners and migrations. Should, at present no one be inclined to take the pen out of my hand, remarks from the other side of the *Atlantic*, from any gentleman of congenial studies, will add peculiar pleasure to a favorite pursuit and be gratefully received.

Although Pennant's two volumes, published in 1784 and 1785, contained birds common in the Carolinas, he avoided mention of North America in his title and called the work *Arctic Zoology*. If Americans had invested in Pennant's work, which contained many color plates, Wilson might have found it more difficult to sell his volumes at the then substantial investment of $120 a set.

With his eighth volume almost ready for the press, Wilson died on August 23, 1813. Ord said that Wilson died from dysentery, although he was known to have suffered from tuberculosis for several years. Audubon, in perhaps the tenderest words he ever had for anyone, later said that Wilson died under a bookseller's lash.

Chapter V

Ahead of Madison Avenue: Audubon

John James Audubon is usually portrayed as a financial incompetent who might have starved except for frequent aid from his wife, Lucy.

Yet Audubon headed a $100,000 enterprise manufacturing and selling a bird book at $1,000 per complete copy. He guided not only the artistic but also the financial phases of the publication. At this he was skillful enough not only to weather the great business depression of 1837 but also to amass a fortune. The final collapse of the Audubon fortune came from the plan of a son to lithograph *Birds of America*.

This observation is not intended to detract from Lucy Bakewell, Audubon's wife, who supported herself and reared their children largely without assistance. It suggests instead that the inability to make good peddling axes and washboards and barrels of flour in a rough frontier village may not be the true measure of a man's worth. At that financial level, Audubon was a complete failure, a fact he proved more than once.

As for Audubon's public figure, he was Madison Avenue personified. He kept himself a mysterious figure but a very prominent one. He paraded in Europe as the great American woodsman. At home in America he was not averse to rumors that he was the lost dauphin of France, the son of Marie Antoinette and King Louis XVI. He would have been a buffoon had not his pure genius elevated him above his own pettiness.

Unquestionably he was the best-known American naturalist of his period and remains the best known today. The very existence of his art, which gained renewed appreciation with each generation, would assure preservation of his memory. The existence of a nationwide conservation group known as the Audubon Society adds to his continuing public recognition. However, in matters of personal life, he is perhaps least known. For while years of scholarship have uncovered many of his adventures, they have been unequal to his own scholarship in obscuring his origins.

When Audubon died at his farm on Manhattan Island on January 27, 1851, newspapers carried obituaries giving his birthplace as Louisiana and his age as seventy-six. Neither statement was correct. While his true birth date may never be known, it is assumed to be 1785. And the place of birth probably was Les Cayes, Santo Domingo (Haiti). Audubon himself always gave his age as greater than it was, although the year of birth varied. Perhaps he had in mind misleading anyone who searched for the truth. When persons lie about their age, they usually suggest a younger age. To suggest an older age might cause researchers to look backward through records, supposing the lie was on the younger side. He often referred to his birthplace as Louisiana. In fact, in the early era of the Audubon Societies, bird journals carried accounts by doting birders who thought they had visited the Audubon birthplace. Later, more serious researchers were to discover that the plantation where he supposedly was born apparently never had existed.

Oddly, Audubon's descendants seemed to have opted for the idea that he was the lost dauphin of France. His own remark that he had roamed the streets of Paris as a common man "when I might have ruled all" was accepted readily by them. It is possible that an alternative explanation, that he was born out of wedlock in Santo Domingo and that the skin color of his mother was unknown, made the dauphin theory more attractive.

Even before the Audubon conservation movement gained momentum, an English biographer, Robert Williams Buchanan, had taken materials supplied by Audubon's widow and produced *The Life and Adventures of John James Audubon*. It was not as adulatory as the family might have hoped. When it became apparent that Audubon as a person was being revived by devotees stimulated by the new Audubon Society, a substitute for Buchanan's biography became imperative. A granddaughter, Maria A. Audubon, undertook the project, producing a two-volume book, *Audubon and His Journals*, published in 1897. As she explained in her introduction: "How much of it was valuable, it is impossible to say; but the fact remains that Mr. Buchanan's book is so mixed up, so interspersed with anecdotes and episodes, and so interlarded with derogatory remarks of his own, as to be practically useless to the world, and very unpleasant to the Audubon family."

Writing an authorized biography was not Maria Audubon's sole service to her grandfather's memory. She also destroyed many of his papers. The extent of Maria's destruction may never be known, since it would be self-defeating to publish a list of what she had destroyed. Neither was her purpose in destroying made clear. She may have been merely prudish. Or she may have worried that her grandfather would become stigmatized because of his racial origins. The destruction of the papers unquestionably has raised more doubts, and perhaps even of a different character, than preservation of the papers would have settled.

Even the name John James Audubon would have lacked validity had not his father, Jean Audubon, a French seaman, adopted the boy and declared himself the natural father. Audubon started life as Jean Rabin, the last name being the name of his mother. As late as July 26, 1817, Audubon identified himself as Jean Rabin in a curious document assigning a brother-in-law, Gabriel Loyen du Puigaudeau, the power of attorney to act in his behalf regarding the settlement of his father's estate in France. The father had referred to Audubon as Jean Rabin in his will. In the document notarized in Henderson, Kentucky, Audubon referred to himself as "Jean Rabin, husband of Lucy Bakewell, of the County of Henderson and State of Kentucky." His foster mother, Anne Moinet Audubon, in her will dated December 4, 1814, referred to her adopted son as "Jean Rabin, créole de Saint-Domingue."

At the adoption proceedings in Nantes, France, March 1, 1794, the naturalist was referred to as "a male child named Fougère." In the same proceedings, a girl named Muguet, later to be known as Rose, also was acknowledged as a natural child by Audubon's father and adopted by Mrs. Audubon. Rose apparently was a half sister of the naturalist. On the roll of passengers on the vessel *Tancrede*, on which Audubon and Rose arrived in France, blacks and mulattos carried the racist designation beside their names. The only passenger whose name bore the notation "white" was Rose. The notation later aroused speculation about her skin color.

The final name, John James Audubon, was of course an Anglicized version of Jean Jacques Audubon, the form into which his name had evolved. At various early periods of his life in America, he had referred to himself as Jean Jacques-Fougère Audubon and Jean Jacques LaForêt Audubon. LaForêt, often Anglicized as LaForest, seems to have been a favorite. His wife, Lucy, called him LaForest, and so did that enchanting but mysterious lady in New Orleans who invited him to her room and posed nude. After a few sessions, the mysterious lady paid $125 for the finest shotgun obtainable in New Orleans and had engraved on its barrel (in French): "Refuse not this gift of a friend who is grateful to thee. May it equal thyself in goodness." On the ramrod was carved: "Property of LaForest Audubon, February 22, 1821."

In a fragmentary autobiography entitled *Myself*, Audubon suggested that his mother was "a lady of Spanish extraction, whom I have been led to understand was as beautiful as she was wealthy." Later biographers decided that his mother was a Mlle Rabin, first name unconfirmed, and that she was part black. Alice Ford in her *John James Audubon*, published in 1964, stated that the naturalist's mother was Jeanne Rabine, 25, a chambermaid, from France's Les Touches parish, who had gone to Santo Domingo. She was the first to bleach Audubon completely.

Dwelling upon Audubon's origin is an exercise in trivia, but one that he stimulated through his furtiveness. Whatever it may have been has little bearing upon that great monument to his genius, *Birds of America*. His trials and tribulations on the American frontier in Kentucky and along the Mississippi River may be regarded as the testing period that most great artists must endure. His interest to naturalists begins in 1824, when, at the age of thirty-nine, he appeared in Philadelphia, an unknown commercial failure making a desperate attempt to break into the most exclusive circle of naturalists in North America.

Audubon carried a portfolio of watercolors of birds to Philadelphia and was in search of two things, both of which he needed desperately. One was membership in the august Academy of Natural Sciences, then the veritable temple in America for certifying naturalists. The other was an engraver and publisher. One man saw to it that Audubon attained neither. That man was George Ord. A wealthy Philadelphian whose hobby was natural history, Ord was a central power in the Academy. Although Ord was a competent zoologist and had made valuable contributions to natural history, much of his fame rested upon his successful editing of the eighth volume of *American Ornithology* and the writing (he always referred to his role as editing) of the ninth and final volume, both done after Alexander Wilson's death. At the time of Audubon's arrival, Ord was contemplating another edition of Wilson's work, He recognized Audubon's plan as a threat.

It was Audubon's misfortune that the most accomplished engraver of natural history subjects in Philadelphia was Alexander Lawson, who did Alexander Wilson's illustrations. Indeed, it seems that some of Wilson's birds were done by Lawson not from Wilson drawings but directly from dead specimens. Lawson was as anxious as Ord to discourage Audubon. He referred to the Audubon paintings as too soft for engraving and criticized them as inaccurate in subject and anatomical detail.

Ord, however, was the principal barrier. He not only attempted to discredit Audubon in America but also enlisted the aid of Europeans in attacking his work, even making a trip to England to further his opposition. According to notes made long after the principals were dead, Miss Malvina Lawson, a daughter of the engravèr and one of his colorists, described Ord thus:

> Mr. Ord was a very singular person, very excitable, almost of pure nervous temperament. Proud, shy and reserved toward strangers; but expansive and brilliant with his friends; an elegant belles-lettres scholar and when he chose, shone in conversation. In his moral character and his business relations he was one of the most upright of men. He had many excellent qualities, was a strong partisan and was charming in conversation when it pleased him to be so. He had much of the nervous grace of a woman when he spoke on literary or sentimental subjects. I remember my father laughing heartily when I was about nine years old; I said I thought Mr. Ord conversed like a woman, and being asked why I thought so, I said: because he could show off all his knowledge to the best advantage. . . .

Unintentionally, although neither man appreciated it at the time, Ord exerted the most profitable influence upon Audubon's life. Because of the Philadelphian, Audubon turned to Europe as the most likely site for publication of *Birds of America*. It was there, first in Scotland and then in England, that he found engravers and colorists capable of meeting the immense challenge that his great work involved. Ord also provided the Lyceum of New York the opportunity of becoming the first scientific group in the world to elect Audubon to its membership, an act accomplished in August 1824, while the naturalist was in New York City pondering the severity of his reception a couple of months earlier in Philadelphia.

Audubon was broke as usual after his calamitous foray on Philadelphia and New York. He returned to Bayou Sara, Louisiana, where Lucy was teaching and keeping the family together. Deciding that Europe was his only hope, he returned to teaching French, drawing, violin, and dancing to raise enough funds for a trip to England. Almost two years later, at the age of forty-one, at New Orleans he boarded a cotton schooner bound for Liverpool. On Friday, July 21,

1826, he arrived at Liverpool, and his life never again was the same. Within a week, he exhibited a collection of paintings at the Royal Institution and was an immediate success. He had offers to purchase his paintings, commissions for portraits, honors—all except an engraver for *Birds of America*. It was, of course, the search for an engraver that had taken him to England. He was to find the man in Edinburgh, Scotland.

To understand the difficulty in finding a proper engraver, one needs to know a little of the dimensions of the project Audubon had in mind. Audubon was determined to publish *Birds* on double-elephant paper, 27 by 40 inches. The size was chosen so that he could portray each bird life-size. The species used for measurement was his famous painting of the turkey cock, an upright representation of the massive bird. Such a gigantic book had never been done before in the field of vertebrate zoology. The 435 colored plates, bound in four volumes, are a portable art museum, and not very portable at that.

Although its total cost to the subscriber was not known, since the number of plates had not been determined, all who participated in the project knew it would be very expensive. The final price turned out to be $1,000 for the four volumes. It is difficult to transcribe the immensity of the price into today's dollars. For instance, if one chose the average income of an American in that period, the sum would be misleading. Most Americans grew some or all of their own food, and economic arrangements on housing and other necessities differed from today's financial arrangements. Audubon's own journal entry indicating that he had bought a "good meal" in Meadville, Pennsylvania, a couple of years earlier for twelve cents may offer some measure. Only the very wealthy could afford the book. Indeed, a few years earlier Alexander Wilson found that his price of $120 for a complete set of *American Ornithology* was an investment only the rich could contemplate. Nevertheless, *The Birds of America* proved over the years to be a most worthwhile investment. Any set sold under $1,000 at any period must have been offered by an uninformed person. The highest price on record was $216,000, paid in 1969 for a complete volume of 435 plates. At the moment, the work of art appears seriously threatened by bids for individual plates, making it more profitable to cut up a set and sell single pages. In 1974, a dealer advertised 116 plates, not including the most famous ones, at a total price of $135,975. The most expensive on that particular list was the canvasback duck, offered at $3,850.

In addition, Audubon demanded of the engraver an almost absolute perfection. He never was satisfied with his own work, the engraver's work, or the colorists' work. Unfortunately for the engraver, Audubon rather regularly visited subscribers, collecting money due for the plates and also inspecting the plates that they had received. He often ordered a subscriber's plate replaced on the basis of his own opinion that it fell short of standards.

On November 19, 1826, Audubon wrote in his journal at Edinburgh, Scotland: "It was settled by Mr. Lizars that he would undertake the publication of the first number of the 'Birds of America'." The engraver was William H. Lizars, an engraver experienced in printing from copper and hand-coloring with watercolors or oil.

The plates were delivered to subscribers in groups of five. On May 1, 1827, Lizars completed the first press run and coloring. Audubon, who had forty-nine subscribers, had ordered fifty groups completed. The plates were the Great American Cock (Wild Turkey), Yellow-billed Cuckoo, Prothonotary Warbler, Purple Finch, and Bonaparte's Fly-catcher. Audubon wrote his wife an enthusiastic letter, pointing out that if he obtained 500 subscribers he could expect a profit of $10,749 per year on *Birds*.

On August 1, 1827, Lizars had completed another group consisting of the Great American Hen and Young (Wild Turkey female and poults), Purple Grackle, White-throated Sparrow, Selby's Fly-catcher, and Brown Titlark. At that time, Lizars advised Audubon to transfer the engraving project to Robert Havell, Jr., of London. Havell not only completed the remaining 425 plates but also retouched the Lizars engravings, which experienced more press runs as subscribers were added.

On June 16, 1838, Havell engraved the last plate, completing *Birds of America*. The news was received with considerable joy by several Audubon subscribers who had complained that the work apparently was designed to drag on forever. They, of course, were buying the plates in groups of five, and the more Audubon and Havell produced, the higher their investment climbed.

Audubon avoided publishing a title page for the book and, indeed, denied that it was a book. He did this in order to circumvent British copyright laws, which decreed that one copy of a copyrighted book must be distributed free to each of nine libraries in Great Britain. The mass of early subscribers was in Europe. When Audubon was ready to export plates to the United States, he was faced with the possibility of paying a fifteen-percent tariff duty. To avoid the tariff, he succeeded in getting a law passed by Congress admitting the art duty-free. As one traces the business angles that he applied to *Birds*, one wonders why he failed as a frontier merchant.

Audubon's goal of 500 subscribers for completed editions of the *Birds* was never attained. His son, Victor Gifford Audubon, once estimated that completed sets consisted of "about 175 copies, of which I should say 80 were in our country [the United States]. The length of time over which the work extended brought many changes to original subscribers, and this accounts for the odd volumes which sometimes are offered for sale." Waldemar H. Fries in his *Double Elephant Folio,* which is the most scholarly survey ever made on the subject, estimates that between 175 and 200 sets were completed. Meanwhile, everything from death to bankruptcy prevented many early subscribers from completing their volumes.

At all times, Audubon exerted strict control over production of the double-elephant plates and forbade the sale of individual prints and refused all but *bona fide* subscribers signed up for the entire work. On a few occasions he debated whether he should bring suit against subscribers who failed to honor the commitment, but he abandoned the idea as nonproductive. His conscientious policing of subscriptions kept production limited and contributed to the final value of each subscriber's investment.

To discuss *Birds of America* becomes a futile exercise in explaining the obvious. Most persons familiar with natural history have at least a passing acquaintance with the work. Unfortunately, the original publication has always been such a scarce item that most persons have seen nothing beyond reproductions. In general, the reproductions are unworthy of the great work itself.

Among other things, Audubon improved upon Catesby's policy of giving the patron his or her money's worth. The 435 plates not only illustrated what Audubon considered to be 497 species of North American birds but also served as an enormous atlas of several branches of natural history. The plates are sprinkled liberally with excellent illustrations of North American plants, fish, insects, reptiles, amphibians, mollusks, and mammals. It was a matter of pride with Audubon that he painted every bird in precisely its natural dimensions, resorting to calipers to assure the exactness. He pointed out that when he bent the necks or turned the bodies of birds that required adjustments in order to fit a double-elephant sheet, he still used perspective in the same careful manner in accounting for the bird's bulk.

Of course, it is not for the exactness alone that Audubon gained fame. It is for masterful design in the plates and the naturalness of his subjects. In this he translated pure illustration into remarkable art. In the use of design, he succeeded on many plates in showing many

sides and attitudes of a species, an accomplishment sadly lacking in
bird guides of today.

Although Audubon seldom permitted others to portray birds, the
backgrounds and botanical art were sometimes done by other artists.
John Woodhouse Audubon, a son, was the only person he credited
with bird paintings that appeared in *Birds*. He acknowledged that the
son painted the American bittern and nine other birds. The first artist
who assisted him was Joseph Mason of Cincinnati, who joined Audubon in 1820 at the age of thirteen. Mason worked two years for
Audubon and journeyed to New Orleans with him. Mason drew backgrounds for fifty-five plates. Audubon said of Mason, "he draws
flowers better than any man probably in America." In 1829, George
Lehman of Lancaster, Pennsylvania, helped Audubon with backgrounds in the Philadelphia area, and then in 1831 accompanied him
to Florida. He was credited with work on thirty plates, including the
background painting of Charleston, South Carolina, in the Long-
billed Curlew plate. On the trip to Florida, Audubon met Miss Maria
Martin, sister-in-law and later wife of the Rev. John Bachman, who
became a botanical artist for Audubon. Miss Martin's work appears on
twenty plates.

The double elephant was published without text. It consisted of
nothing except hand-colored plates. In 1831, after the first volume of
100 plates had been issued, Audubon began publication as a separate
book, *Ornithological Biography*. It was a standard-sized book, not
intended to be bound with the plates. The species accounts, however,
appeared in the same order as the plates.

Ornithological Biography ran to five volumes and was a collabo-
ration of Audubon and William MacGillivray, a young Scottish
ornithologist of Edinburgh. The two worked together from 1830 to
1839, Audubon writing general observations on the behavior of each
species in the wild and MacGillivray scrutinizing and dissecting specimens and writing technical and anatomical details. Audubon made no
pretension to knowledge in the organized science of ornithology, although his paintings reflect his understanding of external anatomy as
well as behavior of the species.

In his introduction to volume 1, Audubon explained the relationship
thus:

I feel pleasure in here acknowledging the assistance which I
have received from a friend, Mr. William MacGillivray, who
being possessed of a liberal education and a strong taste for the

study of the Natural Sciences, has aided me, not in drawing the figures of my illustrations, nor in writing the book now in your hand, although fully competent for both tasks, but in completing the scientific details and smoothing down the asperities of my Ornithological Biographies.

It is in *Ornithological Biography* that one finds evidence of the crosscurrents in the Audubon character. For instance, volume 1 concludes with Audubon's now famous account of Colonel Boon (Daniel Boone), who he said spent a night at Audubon's home in Kentucky. It is such an engaging account that one later is shocked to learn that ever since the publication appeared there has been a debate over whether Audubon ever saw Daniel Boone.

In the same book, however, he often was surprisingly conservative about his observations of birds. As an example, the great auk was known to be scarce in 1833 when Audubon spent the summer cruising to Labrador. He saw the Labrador duck, later to become extinct, but he did not claim to have seen the even more famous great auk. The last great auks, a pair, were killed June 3, 1844. Instead of crediting himself as being among the last observers of the birds, Audubon wrote:

The only authentic account of the occurrence of this bird on our coast that I possess, was obtained from Mr. Henry Havell, brother of my Engraver, who, when on his passage from New York to England, hooked a Great Auk on the banks of Newfoundland, in extremely boisterous weather. On being hauled on board, it was left at liberty on the deck. It walked very awkwardly, often tumbling over, bit every one within reach of its powerful bill, and refused food of all kinds. After continuing several days on board, it was restored to its proper element.

When I was in Labrador, many of the fishermen assured me that the "Penguin," as they name this bird, breeds on a low rocky island to the south-east of Newfoundland, where they destroy great numbers of the young for bait; but as this intelligence came to me when the season was too far advanced, I had no opportunity of ascertaining its accuracy. In Newfoundland, however, I received similar information from several individuals. An old gunner residing on Chelsea Beach, near Boston, told me that he well remembered the time when the Penguins were plentiful about Nahant and some other islands in the bay.

The egg is very large, measuring five inches in length, and

three in its greatest breadth. In form it resembles that of the Common Guillemot; the shell is thick and rather rough to the touch; its colour yellowish-white, with long irregular lines and blotches of brownish-black, more numerous at the larger end.

The *Ornithological Biography* is rich in observations of American scenes and characters, a series of essays unconnected to ornithology which Audubon scattered through the volumes. Although these essays have been reprinted in separate collections, they seldom appear today in reprints of his ornithological reports.

In his introduction to an essay on the Ohio River country, Audubon explained his purpose in including the accounts:

To render more pleasant the task which you have imposed upon yourself, of following an author through the mazes of descriptive ornithology, permit me, kind reader, to relieve the tedium which may be apt now and then to come upon you, by presenting you with occasional descriptions of the scenery and manners of the land which has furnished the objects that engage your attention. The natural features of that land are not less remarkable than the moral character of her inhabitants; and I cannot find a better subject with which to begin, than one of those magnificent rivers that roll the collected waters of her extensive territories to the ocean.

There have been many comments over the years about the seeming contradiction of anointing Audubon as a saint of conservation. In his notes he commented, almost boastfully, that it was a poor day afield in which he shot fewer than 100 birds. On some of his collecting expeditions, particularly in Louisiana and Florida, he related that he and his associates shot so many birds that the pile resembled a haycock. He lived, of course, in an era when portable optical equipment was scarce and unwieldy and the resolution of image was poor. Among other things, spyglasses were of such poor quality that they distorted colors, a deficiency that an artist could not abide. In any event, through his lifetime and for at least seventy-five years after his death, ornithologists commonly shot birds to identify them and were unwilling to rely upon purely visual records. They shot many common birds to determine the amount of variation among even rather standard types. Even in our own era, collection of the specimen by shotgun is considered the most reliable record of the existence of a bird outside its normal range. The bird's skin is then deposited in a museum where later workers can inspect it and determine the validity of the identification. In more recent years, the existence of a good-quality color photograph has been accepted as evidence that a bird was seen and identified outside its normal range. But older ornithologists have been reluctant to accept film records for a number of reasons.

The essay on the Ohio country has considerable relevance to today, because Audubon reported the environmental decline that he had witnessed, a comparison that interests moderns who make like estimates in their own times. He wrote:

When my wife, my eldest son (then an infant), and myself were returning from Pennsylvania to Kentucky, we found it expedient, the waters being unusually low, to provide ourselves with a *skiff*, to enable us to proceed to our abode at Henderson. I purchased a large, commodious, and light boat of that denomination. We procured a mattress, and our friends furnished us with ready prepared viands. We had two stout Negro rowers, and in this trim we left the village of Shippingport, in expectation of reaching the place of our destination in a very few days.

It was in the month of October. The autumnal tints already decorated the shores of that queen of rivers, the Ohio. Every tree was hung with long and flowing festoons of different species of vines, many loaded with clustered fruits of varied brilliancy, their rich bronzed carmine mingling beautifully with the yellow foliage, which now predominated over the yet green leaves, reflecting more lively tints from the clear stream than ever landscape painter portrayed or poet imagined.

The days were yet warm. The sun had assumed the rich and glowing hue which at that season produces the singular phenomenon called there the "Indian Summer." The moon had rather passed the meridian of her grandeur. We glided down the river, meeting no other ripple of the water than that formed by the propulsion of our boat. Leisurely we moved along, gazing all day on the grandeur and beauty of the wild scenery around us.

Now and then, a large cat-fish rose to the surface of the water in pursuit of a shoal of fry, which starting simultaneously from the liquid element, like so many silvery arrows, produced a shower of light, while the pursuer with open jaws seized the stragglers, and, with a splash of his tail, disappeared from our view. Other fishes we heard uttering beneath our bark a rumbling noise, the strange sounds of which we discovered to proceed from the white perch, for on casting our net from the bow we caught several of that species, when the noise ceased for a time.

Nature, in her varied arrangements, seems to have felt a partiality towards this portion of our country. As the traveller ascends or descends the Ohio, he cannot help remarking that alternately, nearly the whole length of the river, the margin, on one side, is bounded by lofty hills and a rolling surface, while on the other, extensive plains of the richest alluvial land are seen as far as the eye can command the view. Islands of varied size and form rise here and there from the bosom of the water, and the winding course of the stream frequently brings you to places where the idea of being on a river of great length changes to that of floating on a lake of moderate extent. Some of these islands are of considerable size and value; while others, small and insignificant, seem as if intended for contrast, and as serving to enhance the general interest of the scenery. These little islands are frequently overflowed during great *freshets* or floods, and receive at their heads prodigious heaps of drifted timber. We foresaw with great concern the alterations that cultivation would soon produce along those delightful banks.

As night came, sinking in darkness the broader portions of the river, our minds became affected by strong emotions, and wandered far beyond the present moments. The tinkling of bells told us that the cattle which bore them were gently roving from valley to valley in search of food, or returning to their distant homes. The hooting of the Great Owl, or the muffled noise of its wings as it sailed smoothly over the stream, were matters of interest to us; so was the sound of the boatman's horn, as it came winding more and more softly from afar. When daylight returned, many songsters burst forth with echoing notes, more and more mellow to the listening ear. Here and there the lonely cabin of a squatter struck the eye, giving note of commencing civilization. The crossing of the stream by a deer foretold how soon the hills would be covered with snow.

Many sluggish flat-boats we overtook and passed: some laden with produce from the different head-waters of the small rivers that pour their tributary streams into the Ohio; others, of less dimensions, crowded with emigrants from distant parts, in search of a new home. Purer pleasures I never felt; nor have you, reader, I ween, unless indeed you have felt the like, and in such company.

The margins of the shores and of the river were at this season amply supplied with game. A Wild Turkey, a Grouse, or a Blue-winged Teal, could be procured in a few moments; and we fared well, for, whenever we pleased, we landed, struck up a fire, and provided as we were with the necessary utensils, procured a good repast.

Several of these happy days passed, and we neared our home, when, one evening, not far from Pigeon Creek (a small stream which runs into the Ohio, from the State of Indiana), a loud and strange noise was heard, so like the yells of Indian warfare, that we pulled at our oars, and made for the opposite side as fast and as quietly as possible. The sounds increased, we imagined we heard cries of "murder"; and as we knew that some depredations had lately been committed in the country by dissatisfied parties of Aborigines, we felt for a while extremely uncomfortable. Ere long, however, our minds became more calmed, and we plainly discovered that the singular uproar was produced by an enthusiastic set of Methodists, who had wandered thus far out of the common way, for the purpose of holding one of their annual camp meetings, under the shade of a beech forest. Without meeting with any other interruption, we reached Henderson, distant from Shippingport by water about two hundred miles.

When I think of these times, and call back to my mind the grandeur and beauty of those almost uninhabited shores; when I picture to myself the dense and lofty summits of the forest, that everywhere spread along the hills, and overhung the margins of the stream, unmolested by the axe of the settler; when I know how dearly purchased the safe navigation of that river has been by the blood of many worthy Virginians; when I see that no longer any Aborigines are to be found there, and that the vast herds of elks, deer and buffaloes which once pastured on these hills and in these valleys, making for themselves great roads to the several salt-springs, have ceased to exist; when I reflect that all this grand portion of our Union, instead of being in a state of nature, is now more or less covered with villages, farms, and towns, where the din of hammers and machinery is constantly heard; that the woods are fast disappearing under the axe by day, and the fire by night; that hundreds of steam-boats are gliding to and fro, over the whole length of the majestic river, forcing commerce to take root and to prosper at every spot; when I see the surplus population of Europe coming to assist in the destruction of the forest, and transplanting civilization into its darkest recesses;—when I remember that these extraordinary changes have all taken place in the short period of twenty years, I pause, wonder, and, although I know all to be fact, can scarcely believe its reality.

Whether these changes are for the better or for the worse, I shall not pretend to say; but in whatever way my conclusions may incline, I feel with regret that there are on record no satisfactory accounts of the state of that portion of the country, from the time when our people first settled in it. This has not been because no one in America is able to accomplish such an undertaking. Our Irvings and our Coopers have proved themselves fully competent for the task. It has more probably been because the changes have succeeded each other with such rapidity, as almost to rival the movements of their pen. However, it is not too late yet; and I sincerely hope that either or both of them will ere long furnish the generations to come with those delightful descriptions which they are so well qualified to give, of the original state of a country that has been so rapidly forced to change her form and attire under the influence of increasing population. Yes; I hope to read, ere I close my earthly career, accounts from those delightful writers of the progress of civilization in our western country. They will speak of the Clarks, the Croghans, the Boons, and many other men of great and daring enterprise. They will analyze, as it were, into each component part, the country as it once existed, and will render the picture, as it ought to be, immortal.

Another glimpse of life in the 1830s is provided in Audubon's essay on the Florida Keys in volume 2 of *Ornithological Biography:*

I left you abruptly, perhaps uncivilly, reader, at the dawn of day, on Sandy Island, which lies just six miles from the extreme point of South Florida. I did so because I was amazed at the appearance of things around me, which in fact looked so different then from what they seemed at night, that it took some minutes' reflection to account for the change. When we laid ourselves down in the sand to sleep, the waters almost bathed our feet; when we opened our eyes in the morning, they were at an immense distance. Our boat lay on her side, looking not unlike a whale reposing on a mud-bank. The birds in myriads were probing their exposed pasture-ground. There great flocks of Ibises fed apart from equally large collections of Godwits, and thousands of Herons gracefully paced along, ever and anon thrusting their javelin bills into the body of some unfortunate fish con-

fined in a small pool of water. Of Fish-Crows I could not estimate the number, but from the havoc they made among the
crabs, I conjecture that these animals must have been scarce by
the time of next ebb. Frigate Pelicans chased the Jaeger, which
himself had just robbed a poor Gull of its prize, and all the
Gallinules ran with spread wings from the mud-banks to the
thickets of the island, so timorous had they become when they
perceived us.

Surrounded as we were by so many objects that allured us,
not one could we yet attain, so dangerous would it have been to
venture on the mud; and our pilot having assured us that nothing
could be lost by waiting, spoke of our eating, and on this hint
told us that he would take us to a part of the island where "our
breakfast would be abundant although uncooked." Off we went,
some of the sailors carrying baskets, others large tin pans and
wooden vessels, such as they use for eating their meals in. Entering a thicket of about an acre in extent, we found on every bush
several nests of the Ibis, each containing three large and beautiful
eggs, and all hands fell to gathering. The birds gave way to us,
and ere long we had a heap of eggs that promised delicious food.
Nor did we stand long in expectation, for, kindling a fire, we
soon prepared, in one way or other, enough to satisfy the crav-
ings of our hungry maws. Breakfast ended, the pilot looking at
the gorgeous sunrise, said, "Gentlemen, prepare yourselves for
fun, the tide is acoming."

Over these enormous mud-flats, a foot or two of water is quite
sufficient to drive all the birds ashore, even the tallest Heron or
Flamingo, and the tide seems to flow at once over the whole ex-
panse. Each of us provided with a gun, posted himself behind a
bush, and no sooner had the water forced the winged creatures
to approach the shore, than the work of destruction commenced.
When it at length ceased, the collected mass of birds of different
kinds looked not unlike a small haycock. Who could not with a
little industry have helped himself to a few of their skins? Why,
reader, surely no one as fond of these things as I am. Every one
assisted in this, and even the sailors themselves tried their hand at
the work.

Our pilot, good man, told us he was no hand at such occupations, and would go after something else. So taking Long Tom
and his fishing-tackle, he marched off quietly along the shores.
About an hour afterwards we saw him returning, when he looked
quite exhausted, and on our inquiring the cause said, "There is a

dewfish yonder and a few balacoudas [Barracudas], but I am not able to bring them, or even to haul them here; please send the sailors after them." The fishes were accordingly brought, and as I had never seen a dewfish, I examined it closely, and took an outline of its form, which some days hence you may perhaps see. It exceeded a hundred pounds in weight, and afforded excellent eating. The balacouda is also a good fish, but at times a dangerous one, for, according to the pilot, on more than one occasion "some of these gentry" had followed him when waist-deep in the water, in pursuit of a more valuable prize, until in self-defence he had to spear them, fearing that "the gentlemen" might at one dart cut off his legs, or some other nice bit, with which he was unwilling to part.

Having filled our cask from a fine well long since dug in the sand of Cape Sable, either by Seminole Indians or pirates, no matter which, we left Sandy Isle about full tide, and proceeded homewards, giving a call here and there at different keys, with the view of procuring rare birds, and also their nests and eggs. We had twenty miles to go "as the birds fly," but the tortuosity of the channels rendered our course fully a third longer. The sun was descending fast, when a black cloud suddenly obscured the majestic orb. Our sails swelled by a breeze, that was scarcely felt by us, and the pilot, requesting us to sit on the weather gunwale, told us that we were "going to get it." One sail was hauled in and secured, and the other was reefed although the wind had not increased. A low murmuring noise was heard, and across the cloud that now rolled along in tumultuous masses, shot vivid flashes of lightning. Our experienced guide steered directly across a flat towards the nearest land. The sailors passed their quids from one cheek to the other, and our pilot having covered himself with his oil-jacket, we followed his example. "Blow, sweet breeze," cried he at the tiller, "and we'll reach land before the blast overtakes us, for, gentlemen, it is a furious cloud yon."

A furious cloud indeed was the one which now, like an eagle on outstretched wings, approached so swiftly, that one might have deemed it in haste to destroy us. We were not more than a cable's length from the shore, when, with imperative voice, the pilot calmly said to us, "Sit quite still, Gentlemen, for I should not like to lose you overboard just now; the boat can't upset, my word for that, if you will but sit still—here we have it!"

Reader, persons who have never witnessed a hurricane, such as not unfrequently desolates the sultry climates of the south, can scarcely form an idea of their terrific grandeur. One would think that, not content with laying waste all on land, it must needs sweep the waters of the shallows quite dry, to quench its thirst. No respite for an instant does it afford to the objects within the reach of its furious current. Like the scythe of the destroying angel, it cuts every thing by the roots, as it were with the careless ease of the experienced mower. Each of its revolving sweeps collects a heap that might be likened to the full sheaf which the husbandman flings by his side. On it goes with a wildness and fury that are indescribable; and when at last its frightful blasts have ceased, Nature, weeping and disconsolate, is left bereaved of her beauteous offspring. In some instances, even a full century is required, before, with all her powerful energies, she can repair her loss. The planter has not only lost his mansion, his crops, and his flocks, but he has to clear his lands anew, covered and entangled as they are with the trunks and branches of trees that are every where strewn. The bark overtaken by the storm, is cast on the lee-shore, and if any are left to witness the fatal results, they are the "wreckers" alone, who, with inward delight, gaze upon the melancholy spectacle.

Our light bark shivered like a leaf the instant the blast reached her sides. We thought she had gone over; but the next instant she was on the shore. And now in contemplation of the sublime and awful storm, I gazed around me. The waters drifted like snow; the tough mangroves hid their tops amid their roots, and the loud roaring of the waves driven among them blended with the howl of the tempest. It was not rain that fell; the masses of water flew in a horizontal direction, and where a part of my body was exposed, I felt as if a smart blow had been given me on it. But enough!—in half an hour it was over. The pure blue sky once more embellished the heavens, and although it was not quite night, we considered our situation a good one.

The crew and some of the party spent the night in the boat. The pilot, myself, and one of my assistants took to the heart of the mangroves, and having found high land, we made a fire as well as we could, spread a tarpaulin, and fixing our insect bars over us, soon forgot in sleep the horrors that had surrounded us.

Next day, the Marion proceeded on her cruize, and in a few more days, having anchored in another safe harbour, we visited other Keys, of which I will, with your leave, give you a short account.

The Deputy-Collector of Indian Isle gave me the use of his

pilot for a few weeks, and I was the more gratified by this, that besides knowing him to be a good man and a perfect sailor, I was now convinced that he possessed a great knowledge of the habits of birds, and could without loss of time lead me to their haunts. We were a hundred miles or so farther to the south. Gay May like a playful babe gambolled on the bosom of his mother nature, and every thing was replete with life and joy. The pilot had spoken to me of some birds, which I was very desirous of obtaining. One morning, therefore, we went in two boats to some distant isle, where they were said to breed. Our difficulties in reaching that Key might to some seem more imaginary than real, were I faithfully to describe them. Suffice it for me to tell you that after hauling our boats and pushing them with our hands, for upwards of nine miles, over the flats, we at last reached the deep channel that usually surrounds each of the mangrove islands. We were much exhausted by the labour and excessive heat, but we were now floating on deep water, and by resting a short while under the shade of some mangroves, we were soon refreshed by the breeze that gently blew from the Gulf. We further repaired our strength by taking some food; and I may as well tell you here, that during all the time I spent in that portion of the Floridas, my party restricted themselves to fish and soaked biscuit, while our only and constant beverage was water and molasses. I found that in these warm latitudes, exposed as we constantly were to alternate heat and moisture, ardent spirits and more substantial food would prove dangerous to us. The officers, and those persons who from time to time kindly accompanied us, adopted the same regimen, and not an individual of us had ever to complain of so much as a headache.

But we were under the mangroves—at a great distance on one of the flats, the Heron which I have named *Ardea occidentalis* was seen moving majestically in great numbers. The tide rose and drove them away, and as they came towards us, to alight and rest for a time on the tallest trees, we shot as many as I wished. I also took under my charge several of their young alive.

At another time we visited the "Mule Keys." There the prospect was in many respects dismal in the extreme. As I followed their shores, I saw bales of cotton floating in all the coves, while spars of every description lay on the beach, and far off on the reefs I could see the last remains of a lost ship, her dismantled hulk. Several schooners were around her; they were wreckers. I turned me from the sight with a heavy heart. Indeed, as I slowly proceeded, I dreaded to meet the floating or cast ashore bodies of some of the unfortunate crew. Our visit to the Mule Keys was in no way profitable, for besides meeting with but a few birds in two or three instances, I was, whilst swimming in the deep channel of a mangrove isle, much nearer a large shark than I wish ever to be again.

"The service" requiring all the attention, prudence and activity of Captain Day and his gallant officers, another cruize took place, of which you will find some account in the sequel; and while I rest a little on the deck of the Lady of the Green Mantle, let me offer my humble thanks to the Being who has allowed me the pleasure of thus relating to you, kind reader, a small part of my adventures.

After the *Birds* and the *Ornithological Biography*, Audubon embarked with his friend the Rev. John Bachman on *The Viviparous Quadrupeds of North America*. Still in his fifties but aging beyond his years, the painter made a trip up the Missouri River in search of specimens. He never again, however, had the vitality that sparkled in the *Birds* paintings. Among other things, his eyesight began to fail. Throughout most of his adult life, Audubon suffered intermittent seizures of "puffiness," which interfered with his painting. From his remarks, one might suspect that he suffered from an allergy that produced a hive condition.

On a trip to Audubon's home on Long Island, Bachman wrote on May 11, 1848: "Alas, my poor friend, Audubon, the outlines of his countenance and his form are there, but his noble mind is all in Ruins."

Audubon was to live on, largely in that condition, until January 27, 1851, when death released him.

LARGEST WHITE BILL'D WOODPECKER, so named
by Mark Catesby, who was the first to describe the now exceedingly rare, if not extinct, ivory-billed woodpecker.
Catesby gave the bird the scientific name *Picus maximus
rostro albo*, following the pre-Linnean style of using several
words. The bird is, or was, the second largest woodpecker
in the world, being exceeded only by the imperial woodpecker of Mexico. The plate is a copy from Catesby's original.

CATESBY'S PLATE 99 in his vegetation series shows what
he called "The Balsam Tree." In his *Natural History of
Carolina, Florida and the Bahama Islands*, Catesby gave the
tree a multiple Latin name of *Cenchramidea arbor saxis
adnascens*. It is now known as *Clusia rosea* and grows as
Catesby said it did "on Bahama Islands, and on many other
islands of America, between the Tropiks." Catesby called it
"balsam" because a balm extracted from the tree was used as
an ointment for man and horse.

CATESBY'S PLATE 22, fishes series, was an accurate and beautiful portrayal of a triggerfish which he called "The Old Wife" and gave the scientific name *Turdus oculo radiato*. A tropical marine fish from the Bahamas, the creature is known now as the Queen triggerfish.

Turdus pilaris, migratorius.
The Fieldfare.

Aristolochia &c.
The Snake-root.

THE FIELDFARE, now known as the American Robin, is a famous although seldom reproduced painting by Mark Catesby.

Ornithogalum luteum &c.

Alauda Magna.
The large Lark.

THE MEADOW LARK resembles a game cock in Catesby's painting which appeared as Plate 33 in his *Natural History of Carolina, Florida and the Bahama Islands*. Catesby called the bird "The Large Lark" and gave it the scientific name *Alauda magna*.

1. *Louisiana Tanager.* 2. *L. Crow.* 3. *L. Woodpecker.*

THREE WESTERN BIRDS, collected by Lewis and Clark in the vast, almost indefinable region then known as "Louisiana" and encompassing most of the present western states, were presented together in this plate by Alexander Wilson in *American Ornithology*. Since the first bird is named "Louisiana tanager," the Ls preceding the other two birds probably meant Louisiana. The text, however, refers to the birds as Louisiana tanager, Clark's crow, and Lewis's woodpecker. On later versions of the plate, Wilson made this change. Clark's crow has since become Clark's nutcracker, and the Louisiana tanager is the western tanager. Only Lewis's woodpecker has survived without name change.

1. Carolina Parrot. 2. Canada Flycatcher. 3. Hooded F. 4. Green black-capt F.

WILSON'S PLATE NO. XXVI in *American Ornithology*
featured the Carolina parrot, a now extinct bird which Wilson himself referred to frequently in the text as a "parakeet." The last known Carolina parakeet died in 1914 in
the Cincinnati Zoo. The grouping together of the other
three birds on the plate typifies Alexander Wilson's acuteness as an observer. He referred to the birds as "flycatchers,"
a name now assigned to a quite different assemblage of
birds. The three species drawn by Wilson comprise the total
membership of the genus *Wilsonia*, a genus of wood warblers.
The bird at the lower left, identified by Wilson as the
green, black-cap't flycatcher, now is known as Wilson's
warbler. The Canada, Hooded, and Wilson's warblers are
exceptionally adroit at catching flying insects.

SOREX CAROLINENSIS, BACH.
CAROLINA SHREW.

THE SHORT-TAILED SHREW depicted on Plate 75 of
The Viviparous Quadrupeds of North America was one of
the illustrations done by John James Audubon, published
between 1849 and 1854. Most of the plates in the volumes
were done by Audubon's son, John Woodhouse Audubon.
The Rev. John Bachman, who wrote the text for the first
great volume on American mammalogy, introduced the
short-tailed shrew to science.

Chapter VI

◆◆◆

Charleston Divine: Bachman

Mustela nigripes (Audubon and Bachman) is the scientific name of the black-footed ferret, possibly North America's rarest mammal.

The Audubon listed beside the scientific name is John James Audubon. The Bachman is the Rev. John Bachman, a Charleston, South Carolina, Lutheran pastor. Now grouped among the lesser-known early naturalists, Bachman was perhaps the leading North American mammalogist of his day.

Born in the second year of George Washington's first term as president, Bachman lived nine years beyond the end of the Civil War. He lived through an era both turbulent and challenging. Not only was the nation growing up, but also basic beliefs that mankind cherished were cast in doubt. It was Bachman's lot to be both a theologian and a scientist when Charles Darwin published *Origin of the Species* in 1859. Darwin's theory that species evolved through natural selection rather than being individually produced by the Creator touched off a major confrontation between theology and science. Bachman accepted the authority of the Bible but attempted to reconcile theology and science. It was a difficult position.

A chance encounter between Audubon and Bachman on a street in Charleston on October 17, 1831, led to the first great book on North American mammals, *The Viviparous Quadrupeds of North America.* Bachman was to write the text for the volume. Indeed, his letters urging Audubon and his sons, John Woodhouse Audubon and Victor Gifford Audubon, to get on with the work and to use care in what they were doing rather confirm Bachman's occasional warning to the Audubons that "you cannot proceed without me."

But in 1831 neither Audubon nor Bachman knew that the *Quadrupeds* lay in their joint futures. At the time, Audubon had begun publication of *Birds of America* and was on the way to Florida to collect more species. With him were two assistants, landscape painter George Lehman and British taxidermist Henry Ward. Audubon's party had

85

spent the first night in a Charleston rooming house that had proved too expensive for Audubon's budget. Among the letters of introduction that Audubon carried on the Florida journey was one to the Rev. John Gilman. Such letters, deeming the bearer worthy of assistance, were common in the colonial and federal eras. The Rev. Gilman helped Audubon find cheaper accommodations.

As Audubon related in a letter to his wife, Lucy:

> He [Mr. Gilman] walked wtih me and had already contrived to procure us cheaper lodgings, when lo, he presented me in the street to the Reverend Mr. Bachman!!—Mr. Bachman!! Why my Lucy, Mr. Bachman would have us all stay at his house. He would not suffer us to proceed farther south for three weeks. He looked as if his heart had been purposely made of the most benevolent materials granted to man by the Creator. . . .

In his collection of essays published as *Delineations of American Scenery and Character,* Audubon gave a different version of the meeting:

> . . . after which we proceeded southward until we arrived at Charleston, in South Carolina. It was there that I formed an acquaintance, now matured into a highly valued friendship, with the Rev. John Bachman, a proficient in general science, and particularly in zoology and botany, and one whose name you will often meet with in the course of my biographies. But I cannot refrain from describing to you my first interview with this generous friend, and mentioning a few of the many pleasures I enjoyed under his hospitable roof, and in the company of his most interesting family and connections.
>
> It was late in the afternoon when we took our lodgings in Charleston. Being fatigued, and having written the substance of my journey to my family, and delivered a letter to the Rev. Mr. Gilman, I retired to rest. At the first glimpse of day the following morning, my assistants and myself were already several miles from the city, commencing our search in the fields and woods, and having procured abundance of subjects, both for the pencil and the scalpel, we returned home, covered with mud, and so accoutred as to draw towards us the attention of every person in the streets. As we approached the boarding-house, I observed a gentleman on horseback close to our door. He looked at me, came up, inquired if my name was Audubon, and on being answered in the affirma-

tive, instantly leaped from his saddle, shook me most cordially by the hand—there is much to be expressed and understood by a shake of the hand—and questioned me in so kind a manner, that I for a while felt doubtful how to reply. At his urgent desire, I removed to his house, as did my assistants. Suitable apartments were assigned to us, and once introduced to the lovely and interesting group that composed his family, I seldom passed a day without enjoying their society. Servants, carriages, horses, and dogs, were all at our command, and friends accompanied us to the woods and plantations, and formed parties for water excursions. Before I left Charleston, I was truly sensible of the noble and generous spirit of the hospitable Carolinians.

Having sailed for the Floridas, we, after some delay, occasioned by adverse winds, put into a harbour near St. Simon's Island, where I was so fortunate as to meet with Thomas Butler King, Esq., who, after replenishing our provision-stores, subscribed to the *Birds of America*. At length we were safely landed at St. Augustine, and commenced our investigation. Of my sojourn in Florida, during the winter of 1831–32, you will find some account in this volume. Returning to Charleston, we passed through Savannah, respecting my short stay in which city you will also find some particulars in the sequel. At Charleston we lived with my friend Bachman, and continued our occupations.

Although Bachman's specialty was mammalogy, the study of animals that at some stage of life wear hair and with a couple of notable exceptions give birth to young alive and nurse them, he was, like most naturalists of the era, a competent commentator on all forms of life. He knew the birds and plants, for instance, more comprehensively than one might expect in a mammalogist today. Thus Bachman and Audubon became comrades in the field of birds.

The contracts between Bachman and Audubon were many. Not only Audubon but also his sons were frequent visitors to Charleston. In 1837 the families merged through John Woodhouse Audubon's marriage to Maria Bachman. Later, Victor Gifford Audubon married Eliza Bachman. Both marriages were brief. Maria died in 1840, leaving two children. Eliza died in 1841 after a few months of marriage.

Audubon spent the winter of 1833–34 with Bachman. In that period, Bachman wrote his then famous "Remarks in Defence of the Author of the 'Birds of America.'" A British journal, *Loudon's Magazine*, had printed a letter questioning Audubon's contention that the turkey vulture lacks the sense of smell and—a far more famous controversial subject—his depiction of mockingbirds repelling a rattlesnake that had climbed into a tree and was menacing the birds' nest.

Bachman sent a rebuttal to *Loudon's* and copies to American natural history societies. The "Defence" was read before the Boston Society of Natural History on February 5, 1834, and published as a major article in the first issue of the Society's *Boston Journal of Natural History*. Below are excerpts regarding the rattlesnake and Bachman's general praise of Audubon's work:

> I have observed in your interesting and valuable Journal a number of remarks calculated to impeach the veracity of Mr. Audubon as a traveller and naturalist, and to injure him in the estimation of the community as an author. Although from my profession and habits I feel no disposition to enter into controversy, yet having had opportunities which few others possess, of becoming acquainted with the occupations and literary acquirements of that gentleman, and being prompted, not by feelings of private friendship alone, but by a desire that full justice should be awarded him for those expenses, sacrifices and privations which he has undergone, I take the liberty of stating what I know on this subject, and I have reason to believe, from the characters of the writers, who have doubted his veracity and the authenticity of his works, that with that generosity of feeling so distinctive of those who are engaged in liberal and kindred pursuits, they will be gratified to assign him the meed of praise which he so undoubtedly merits.
>
> It appears that exception has been taken to two articles by Mr. Audubon—one on the habits of the rattle snake (*Crotalus*) and the other on the habits of the turkey buzzard (*Cathartes aura*, Illig.). The latter publication is now lying before me, the former I have not had an opportunity of seeing; but from what I gather from some communications in your Journal, it appears that he ascribed to the rattle snake some of the habits of the common black snake (*Coluber constrictor*, Linn.) such as ascending trees in search of game, feeding on squirrels, etc. He also mentioned the remarkable fact of its living a considerable length of time in confinement without food, and of its being found in the water, at a considerable distance from the shore.
>
> I do not wish either to defend or perpetuate error, and acknowledge that the rattle snake appears to be a heavy and sluggish reptile; yet it will be recollected that there are now found in this extensive country at least *five* well defined species of rattle snake, and that the habits of some of these are very little known to

naturalists. The fact is now pretty well established, and is generally admitted by naturalists in this country, that one or more of our species of rattle snakes in the South and West have been seen on fences and on trees to a considerable height. . . .

For the last two years and a half I have been intimately acquainted with Mr. Audubon. He has resided in my family for months in succession. From a similarity of disposition and pursuits, he was my companion in my rambles through the woods and fields, and the enlivener of my evening hours. During his absence we were constant correspondents, and his letters, amounting to nearly a hundred, are now lying before me. His journals have been regularly submitted to my inspection. His notes and observations were made in my presence, and a considerable portion of the second volume of his Ornithological Biography was written under my roof. I have carefully compared his first volume with the forthcoming one, and from all these opportunities which I have enjoyed of making a decision, I do not hesitate to state that the second volume will not fall short of the first in purity, vigor, and originality of style, and that it will contain the additional experience and observation of three of the most active years of his life.

The additions already made to American Ornithology by the labors of Audubon are immense; suffice it to say, that he has already added upwards of one hundred species, not figured by Wilson. Some of these have been described in the valuable continuation of Wilson's work by Bonaparte; still, with these deductions, there will be an immense number of new birds published in the Work of Audubon, for a knowledge of which, the public will be solely indebted to his zeal, industry and experience. Amongst the other interesting discoveries made by him, may be noticed a new heron and an eagle (*Falco Washingtonii*, Aud.), the largest in the United States. Two species of pigeon, a humming bird, and a considerable number of the genera of the *Muscicapa, Troglodytes* and *Fringilla*. . . .

Let the literary world but award to Audubon the justice which he merits, let the public continue to be indulgent and liberal, and this work cannot fail to prove a very important acquisition to the Natural History of America. . . .

Ironically, Bachman's defense of Audubon incorporated a blooper. Washington's Eagle (*Falco washingtonii*) proved to be nothing more than an immature bald eagle. Audubon, however, defended *Falco washingtonii* as a valid species for the remainder of his life.

As for the infamous rattlesnake, the presence of that lethargic and almost exclusively ground-dwelling reptile in a tree is less debated by most herpetologists than the snake's anatomy. It is possible, although improbable, that a rattlesnake might climb to a mockingbird's nest, since these birds often build a nest less than a yard above the ground. What herpetologists notice is that Audubon's rattlesnake has a round pupil in the eye, whereas regular rattlesnakes have pupils that are vertical slits. In addition, the Audubon rattler wears a formidable mouthful of teeth in the upper jaw, and normal rattlesnakes have only a pair of fangs. So it was not the position but the rattlesnake itself that was impossible!

Bachman hints in his defense that the blacksnake might have been more appropriate in the mockingbird portrait, and he is correct. Unquestionably Audubon chose the rattlesnake because of its salability in Great Britain. The rattlesnake occurs only in the Western Hemisphere, and Europeans were fascinated by its unusualness, the rattle and all.

For all the furor that the Audubon rattlesnake aroused among naturalists, the improbability of its being in a tree was minor compared to the almost-never-mentioned coral snake shown cavorting on a lichen-covered branch with a pair of chuck-will's-widows. The coral snake is a furtive burrower, seldom seen except by those snake hunters in the deep South who roll logs in search of specimens. But even it remains an improbable, rather than impossible, tree dweller. As one herpetologist remarked: "It could have been lifted into a tree by a flood." Audubon comments on the coral snake: "The beautiful little snake . . . is commonly called the Harlequin Snake, and is, I believe, quite harmless." The coral snake is a relative of the cobra and is among the most deadly in North America!

During his ornithological association with Audubon, Bachman wrote an essay, "On the Migration of North American Birds," which was unusual in its advanced understanding of this still mysterious subject. The essay was published in the *American Journal of Science and Arts* in April 1836. In an era when many believed that birds hibernated, possibly burying themselves in a pond bottom for the winter, Bachman knew that they did not. Further, he understood that the surge of migration begins long before winter and while food remains plentiful. He knew that the young of a species may migrate either before or after the adults and that therefore some "instinct" rather than experience guides them. He sensed that birds migrate to take advantage of more abundant food supplies, rather than to avoid cold. He knew enough of the ecology of birds to suggest: "A large number of the feathered race follow the improvements of civilized man. No sooner does cultivation commence, than many birds which were unknown in the forest around him, are seen in his fields and orchards." He guessed the correct answer to the riddle of why some species that breed in the North are never seen migrating southward through the Carolinas: they either migrate over the sea or select an inland route for the return trip. He felt that birds had an innate sense that predicted favorable weather periods for migration flight, a possibility that students of migration still debate and one that would have obvious survival value to long-distance migrants over open water, such as golden plovers.

Among other interesting facets of "On the Migration of North American Birds," Bachman discussed the attributes of birds as physical functions carried out by the organisms without the constant intervention of God. He wrote from the viewpoint of a scientist rather than a theologian. It is true that at the beginning and end of the essay he brings in the deity as an architect. One might have expected as much from any scientist of the period. Theologians ascribed the minutest behavioral symptoms to God and employed nature as though it existed solely to confirm the Word.

The precise instant in which the Audubons and Bachman decided to collaborate on a mammal book probably has been lost to history. The decision more than likely evolved in conversation among the principals, for their personal contacts were many and prolonged.

Bachman's comments in a letter to Audubon on September 13, 1839, indicate that the volume was still in a formative stage, but at the point where the Audubons had committed themselves publicly to the project.

But are you not a little fast in issuing your prospectus of *The Birds and Quadrupeds*, without having numbers of both works, by which the public can judge of their merits? My idea, in regard to the latter, is that you should carefully get up, in your best style, a volume about the size of "Holbrook's Reptiles." This would enable you to decide on the terms of the book. I think that two thousand subscribers at $1.00 for each number, might be obtained. But it must be no half-way affair.

The animals have never been carefully described, and you will find difficulties at every step. Books cannot aid you much. Long journeys will have to be undertaken. Several species remain to be added, and their habits ascertained. The drawings you can easily make, if you can procure the specimens. I wish I had you here, if for only two days. I think that I have studied the subject more than you have. You will be bothered with the Wolves and the Foxes, to begin with. I have two new species of Bats and Shrews to add. The Western Deer are no joke; and the ever-varying Squirrels seem sent by Satan himself, to puzzle the Naturalists.

A few weeks later, Bachman wrote Audubon:

We will talk when we meet again. We are done with the Birds, but in the Quadrupeds I will show you trap, my boy. Just bring along with you Harlan, Peale, Ord and the other Bipeds and Quadrupeds, and I will row you all up salt river together. I can show the whole concern that they have often been barking with cold noses on the back track. About this partnership in the *Quadrupeds,* we will talk more about it when we meet. I am not ashamed to let my name stand along with yours, and I believe too that it may aid the sale of the work, which, next to its being well got up, is all I can care about. I am also anxious to do something for the benefit of John and Victor, which, alas, in addition to the treasures they have already, is all I can do for them whilst my head is warm. The expenses and the profits will be yours. In due time it will sell as well as the Birds, and if the boys with their good points and industry cannot be independent after all this— they deserve to starve. . . .

Employ yourself in drawing every quadruped you can lay your hands on. If you can possibly get a living ermine—they are common in New York—buy it. . . . Don't flatter yourself that this book is child's play—the birds are a mere trifle compared with this. I have been at it all my life . . . but we all have much to learn in this matter. The skulls and teeth must be studied, and color is as variable as the wind—down, down in the earth they grovel, and in digging and studying we grow giddy and cross. Such works as Godman's and Harlan's could be got up in a month, but I would almost as soon stick my name to a forged bank note as to such a mess of *soup-maigre.*

As work progressed on the *Quadrupeds,* Bachman found himself still having difficulties with his coauthors and illustrators. He wrote to Victor G. Audubon in 1844:

I enclose my plan. I wish always, a month before the time, that you would give me notice of the species you intend to put into the hands of the engraver, and send me, at the same time, the specimen. I cannot describe without it; I will guess at nothing.

I find the labor greater than I expected, and fear that I may break down and, therefore, cry in time, "Help me Cassius or I sink!" Writing descriptions is slow and fatiguing work. I cannot, in the careful manner that I am doing them, write more than three in a week. My son-in-law, Haskell, has copied forty-two closely written pages for me. I cannot shorten the articles, many of them I ought rather to lengthen. With patience and the help of all, I hope, however, to get on—the work may be lighter as we proceed. . . .

The brush of my old friend, Audubon, is a truthteller. I regard his drawings as the best in the world. Let us be very careful to correct any errors of description that have crept in on the plates—I see a few in the lettering—they can be corrected in the letter-press; and let us be so cautious as to have nothing in the future to correct. There is but one principle on which a just man can act; that is, always to seek the truth and to abide by it.

I am pleased with Owen's manner of dissecting, and his anatomical investigations in deciding on closely allied genera. He has, however, given very few of our American quadrupeds. While I do not wish the dissections of others to be copied, we may learn something from them of their manner of dissecting. Our motto must be: *Nature, Truth, and no Humbug!*

A few weeks later, he replied to Victor:

Your letters have been received. About the little mouse—I cannot see a needle in a haystack; or give it a name without knowing what it is. Friend, descriptions cannot be written, as a man works at making Jews-harps—so many dozen in a given time. My credit, as well as your father's, is so deeply concerned, that *I will not publish a day before I am ready*. On the whole, I am rather pleased with the work thus far. If I keep my health, the letter-press [first volume of *Quadrupeds*] will be finished in the Spring, and we shall not be ashamed of it. But if you hurry and worry—why—dyspepsia—temper, and the old fellow I have drawn for you [Satan], I don't know how to figure his horns and his tail! My business and profession is to keep him down—be careful that you don't wake him up!

As a mammalogist, Bachman was interested in the wide variety of small animals, generally overlooked by the public. These include the shrews and mice, many of them only slightly larger than an adult's thumb. An artist working with mammals finds himself indulging in browns, grays, and blacks, perhaps much more than the Audubon temperament desired. In addition, picturing two seemingly identical thumb-sized mammals whose specific differences depend upon a description of tooth and cranial characteristics, rather than outward appearances, did not allow for the flashes of color and spectacular display so typical of Audubon.

When Audubon returned from a trip to the upper Missouri River, he brought back a journal that contains some interesting observations on the American West before settlement. But that was not the purpose of the trip, as Bachman reminds him in a letter expressing disappointment:

> March 6th, 1846
>
> For the last four nights, I have been reading your journal. I am much interested, though I find less about the quadrupeds than I expected. The narrations are particularly spirited, and often instructive, as well as amusing. All that you write on the spot, I can depend on, but I never trust to the memory of others, any more than to my own. I admire a remark of Dr. Wright's on this head. I wished him to give me an account of the glands of the Skunk. He answered, "I must write for my notes, I cannot depend for these particulars on a *fading memory.*" . . .
>
> To return to your Journal. I am afraid that the shadows of the Elk, Buffalo, and Bighorn hid the little Marmots, Squirrels and Jumping Mice. I wish that you had engaged some of the hunters to set traps. I should like to get the Rabbit that led you so weary a chase. Write to S. and find out some way of getting—not his princess brain-eating, horse-straddling squaw, but what is better than such a specimen from the Black-foot country—1st, The Skunk; 2nd, Hares, in Winter colors; and 3rd, the Rabbit that you chased. In your Journal your descriptions of Buffalo hunts are first rate.

A by-product of Audubon's western excursion was the black-footed ferret. The mammal was sent to Audubon after his return east. Alexander Culbertson, chief trader for the American Fur Company at its Fort Union post in eastern Montana, sent the specimen. Culbertson was the husband of the Indian princess who relished the raw, warm brain of a freshly killed buffalo. She was the "brain-eating, horse-straddling squaw" that Bachman referred to in his letter.

In the *Quadrupeds,* Bachman named the black-footed ferret *Putorius nigripes* and discussed its habits thus:

It is with great pleasure that we introduce this handsome new species; it was procured by Mr. Culbertson on the lower waters of the Platte River, and inhabits the wooded parts of the country to the Rocky Mountains, and perhaps is found beyond that range, although not observed by any travellers, from Lewis and Clark to the present day. When we consider the very rapid manner in which every expedition that has crossed the Rocky Mountains, has been pushed forward, we cannot wonder that many species have been entirely overlooked, and should rather be surprised at the number noticed by Lewis and Clark, and by Nuttall, Townsend, and others. There has never yet been a Government expedition properly organized, and sent forth to obtain *all* the details, which such a party, allowed *time* enough for thorough investigation, would undoubtedly bring back, concerning the natural history and natural resources of the regions of the far west. The nearest approach to such an expedition having been that so well conducted by Lewis and Clark. Nor do we think it at all probable that Government will attend to such matters for a long time to come. We must therefore hope that private enterprise will gradually unfold the zoological, botanical, and mineral wealth of the immense territories we own but do not yet occupy.

The habits of this species resemble, as far as we have learned, those of the ferret of Europe. It feeds on birds, small reptiles and animals, eggs, and various insects, and is a bold and cunning foe to the rabbits, hares, grouse, and other game of our western regions.

The specimen from which we made our drawing was received by us from Mr. J. G. Bell to whom it was forwarded from the outskirts or outposts of the fur traders on the Platte River, by Mr. Culbertson. It was stuffed with the wormwood so abundant in parts of that country, and was rather a poor specimen, although in tolerable preservation. We shall have occasion in a future article to thank Mr. Bell for the use of other new specimens, this being only one of several instances of his kind services to us, and the zoology of our country, in this way manifested.

As before stated, the specimen which we have figured and described was obtained on the lower waters of the Platte River. We are not aware that another specimen exists in any cabinet.

From the comments published in 1851, it is obvious that Audubon and Bachman did not appreciate the rarity of the black-footed ferret. Lewis and Clark and other parties in the West hardly could be faulted for failing to collect the mammal. In fact, for more than twenty-five years after publication of the *Quadrupeds* no record of the black-footed ferret appeared in scientific literature or in government surveys. Some mammalogists began to question whether the mammal actually existed. In his review of the black-footed ferret in 1954, Victor H. Cahalane found that fewer than 100 specimens exist in museums. The mammal now is protected as an endangered species, but its numbers remain unknown. Ernest Thompson Seton in his review expressed the opinion that the ferret perhaps always had been rare.

The acuteness of Bachman's mammal knowledge is reflected in his noting the similarity of the American mammal to the ferret of Europe. A less-informed mammalogist might have thought of it as a closer relative of American weasels. It now is regarded as of Asian origin, probably a mammal that crossed the land bridge between Asia and Alaska in the last great glaciation. Neither describer had seen the animal in life, which accounts for Bachman's description of its food. It would appear from more recent observations that the ferret relies mainly upon prairie dogs as prey. By "cabinet" in his report, Bachman meant museum tray.

Putorius nigripes Audubon and Bachman has been changed by later reclassification by mammalogists to *Mustela nigripes* (Audubon and Bachman). Placing the describers' names in brackets signifies that they gave the first accepted description but that the original name and supposed relationship to other mammals have been altered by further scholarship.

One might wonder why John G. Bell, who first owned the specimen, was not credited. A scientific name does not rest with the collector but with the person or persons who wrote the scientific description of the specimen. Priority in such matters can be illustrated in Bachman's letter to Victor G. Audubon which accompanied a mouse to Audubon's London address. Bachman asked Victor to memorize the details of the mouse and then visit the British Museum (Natural History) to learn whether such a specimen was in its collection. He warned Victor not to permit museum mammalogists to see the mouse, suggesting that if he were so careless, someone at the museum would describe it within five minutes and gain credit for the new species.

Another rarity described by Bachman was a shrew, *Sorex longirostris longirostris* Bachman, now known either as the southeastern shrew or Bachman's shrew. This tiny animal is so uncommon that there is some doubt it exists as a valid species, despite a few study skins in museums. Some recent workers have suggested it may be a variant of *Sorex cinereus fontinalis* Hollister, known as the Maryland shrew.

Dr. Roger Tory Peterson has referred to Bachman's warbler, *Vermivora bachmanii*, as "perhaps the rarest North American songbird." The International Union for Conservation of Nature and Natural Resources lists the colorful little warbler as an endangered species and describes it as "A very rare inhabitant of river swamps of southeastern USA with a patchy distribution." Bachman in July 1833 collected a male and female of the then unknown warbler in a swamp near Charleston. He gave them to Audubon, who named them after his friend. The species first was depicted in *Birds of America*.

Bachman's warbler has an erratic and unexplained history of population fluctuation. From 1833 until 1886, when Charles S. Galbraith, a market hunter for the millinery trade, shot a Bachman's warbler near Lake Pontchartrain in Louisiana, no specimen had been available to ornithologists. Serious doubts that the bird even existed were expressed by many ornithologists. Many considered it an Audubon fraud and placed it with the carbonated warbler, *Sylvia carbonate,* as Audubon inventions designed to keep the *Birds* in a class by itself, having birds not illustrated in other ornithologists' works. Another specimen of the carbonated warbler never has been found. Opinions are divided over whether the bird was a fraud, or if Audubon had the good fortune to collect a bird that was on the verge of extinction and since has disappeared from the fauna.

But Bachman's warbler proved more viable than the carbonated. In his notes describing the bird, Audubon wrote: "Shortly after, several were seen in the same neighborhood; and we may still expect an account of its manners, migration, and breeding, although not yet discovered." There was serious doubt about "several" being seen near Charleston until 1888, when the same Galbraith shot thirty-one Bachman's warblers in swampy Louisiana between March 2 and 20. In the next few years, Bachman's warblers were collected in sizable numbers, the largest number being fifty, taken by Arthur T. Wayne in March 1892 along the Suwannee River. Since then the warbler has almost disappeared, with only an occasional report of an authenticated sighting.

Although one seldom sees the *Birds* listed today as a source, mammalogists occasionally cite the *Quadrupeds* in their bibliographies, largely because of the value of the Bachman text. The *Quadrupeds* was published in three volumes, containing 150 plates. The first volume was off the press in 1845, the second in 1846, and the third in 1848. In 1849, five bonus plates by John Woodhouse Audubon were added to the

Quadrupeds and included in an octavo edition. At least seventy-eight of the plates are credited to John James Audubon, with the remainder the work of John Woodhouse Audubon.

In view of Audubon's constant search for new species to illustrate, it is ironic that he failed to recognize that the bighorn, which he recorded near the junction of the Yellowstone and Missouri rivers, was a distinct subspecies. Now extirpated, the Badlands bighorn was named *Ovis canadensis auduboni* in honor of the artist. Mammalogists who have inspected the Audubon plate of the bighorn are not especially surprised at his oversight. The plate depicts the bighorn more as a diagram than a detailed study. It could, as one mammalogist said, be any bighorn.

Indeed, mammalogists are less impressed with Audubon's mammals than ornithologists are with his birds. Some of his squirrels and small mammals appear, as a mammalogist commented, "ferocious and menacing." Even Bachman, who always publicly praised the work as great art, complained privately that one of the skunk plates made the animal appear on two planes. Unquestionably the mammal with the best possible case of defamation of physique is the disheveled bull moose credited to John Woodhouse Audubon.

For scientific publications, Bachman wrote terse descriptions understandable to any modern mammalogist. He gave dental formulas and cranial characteristics and exact measurements in inches. The practice varies today mainly in giving measurements in metric form. An example exists in volume 1, pages 40–41, *Proceedings* of the Boston Society of Natural History, in which he reviewed and named new species in the genus Scalops, now known as Scalopus (moles).

The *Quadrupeds* was aimed at a more general readership, however, and the work was read then and now for Bachman's descriptions of the mammals' behavior. An example is the following excerpt dealing with the striped skunk of the East:

Mephitis Americana, Desm.
Common American Skunk

There is no quadruped on the continent of North America the approach of which is more generally detested than that of the Skunk: from which we may learn that, although from the great and the strong we have to apprehend danger, the feeble and apparently insignificant may have it in their power to annoy us almost beyond endurance. . . .

The Skunk, although armed with claws and teeth strong and sharp enough to capture his prey, is slow on foot, apparently timid, and would be unable to escape from many of his enemies, if he were not possessed of a power by which he often causes the most ferocious to make a rapid retreat, run their noses into the earth, and roll or tumble on the ground as if in convulsions. . . .

This offensive fluid is contained in two small sacs situated on each side of the root of the tail, and is ejected through small ducts near the anus. We have on several occasions witnessed the manner in which this secretion is discharged. When the Skunk is irritated, or finds it necessary to defend himself, he elevates his tail over his back, and by a strong muscular exertion ejects it in two thread-like streams in the direction in which the enemy is observed. He appears to take almost unerring aim, and almost invariably salutes a dog in his face and eyes. . . .

We were once requested by a venerable clergyman, an esteemed friend, who had for many years been a martyr to violent paroxysms of asthma, to procure for him the glands of a Skunk; which, according to the prescription of his medical advisor, were kept tightly corked in a smelling bottle, which was applied to his nose when the symptoms of his disease appeared.

For some time he believed that he had found a specific for his distressing complaint; we were however subsequently informed, that having uncorked the bottle on one occasion while in the pulpit during service, his congregation finding the smell too powerful for their olfactories, made a hasty retreat, leaving him nearly alone in the church. . . .

The Skunk does not support a good character among the farmers. He will sometimes find his way into the poultry-house, and make some havoc with the setting hens; he seems to have a peculiar penchant for eggs, and is not very particular whether they have been newly laid, or contain pretty large rudiments of the young chicken; yet he is so slow and clumsy in his movements, and creates such a commotion in the poultry-house, that he usually sets the watch-dog in motion, and is generally detected in the midst of his depredations; when, retiring to some corner, he is either seized by the dog, or is made to feel the contents of the farmer's fowling piece. . . .

This animal generally retires to his burrow about December, in the Northern States, and his tracks are not again visible until near the tenth of February. He lays up no winter store; and like the bear, raccoon, and Maryland marmot, is very fat on retiring to his winter quarters, and does not seem to be much reduced in flesh at his first appearance toward spring, but is observed to fall off soon afterwards. He is not a sound sleeper on these occasions; on opening his burrow we found him, although dull and inactive, certainly not asleep, as his black eyes were peering at us from the hole, into which we had made an opening, seeming to warn us not to place too much reliance on the hope of finding this striped "weasel asleep."

In the upper districts of Carolina and Georgia, where the Skunk is occasionally found, he, like the raccoon in the Southern States, does not retire to winter quarters, but continues actively prowling about during the night through the winter months. . . .

We have seen the young early in May; there were from five to nine in a litter.

The fur is rather coarse. It is seldom used by the hatters, and never we think by the furriers; and from the disagreeable task of preparing the skin, it is not considered an article of commerce.

Much of the text of the *Quadrupeds* was edited directly from the notes of John James Audubon or John Woodhouse Audubon. This is particularly true of observations on western mammals. It is a credit to Bachman that he appreciated the Audubon flair for writing, a talent that rivaled their work with charcoal or brush. His job was to keep the Audubons within credible limits. In general, observations on mammals in upper New York State or the southeastern states are pure Bachman.

The title, *The Viviparous Quadrupeds of North America*, sounds rather stilted for a book now generally referred to as *Audubon's Animals*. But it had a delimiting value. *Viviparous* means "live-bearing" and is applied to animals that bear their young as viable infants rather than starting them in the world as eggs. It ruled out such quadrupeds as alligators, turtles, and the like. Meanwhile, quadrupeds relieved the authors of dealing with such mammals as whales, dolphins, and seals, all of which are live-bearing but lack four feet.

Bachman always attributed his interest in natural history to tutelage by a slave, George, on his father's farm at Rhinebeck, New York, where he was born. He entered Williams College at Williamstown, Massachusetts, but his health interfered with studies. He left because he suffered "hemorrhaging of the lungs," a condition that bothered him at later periods. Apparently the illness was tuberculosis. He then became an understudy to Lutheran ministers, a pursuit that took him to Philadelphia, where he became acquainted with William Bartram and

Alexander Wilson. Wilson secured Bachman a job teaching in a school where Wilson once had taught.

In 1813, Bachman was licensed as a pastor by the Lutheran church and returned to serve the Gilead Pastorate, a group of Lutheran churches that included his home church. In1815, he received a call to St. John's Lutheran Church in Charleston, which he was to serve until his death in 1874.

The War of 1812 was ending as Bachman left Rhinebeck by stage-coach for Charleston. His notes on the trip read:

> The means of traveling were very different from what they are now in the days of steamers and railroads. The roads were almost impassable; as an evidence of this I would state that, with the exception of a Sunday, on which I preached for Dr. Mayer, of Philadelphia, I came in the regular stage line, which travelled day and night, and arrived at Charleston on the evening of the twenty-ninth day after leaving Dutchess County, which is a hundred miles north of the city of New York. In the meanwhile, our vehicles were either broken or overturned eight times on the journey.
>
> We were in the midst of a three years' war with the most powerful of foreign nations. Fearful battles had occurred on our Northern frontiers, on the ocean, and on the lakes. The traces of devastation and death were visible in the half-covered graves along the highway between Baltimore and Washington. The blackened walls of the Capitol at Washington, and the destruction in every part of the city, presented an awful picture of the horrors of war.

Bachman took with him to Charleston a black woman and her two sons. Later, when New York outlawed slavery, Bachman recognized that had the slaves remained in New York they would have been freed. He offered freedom to the three, and the young men chose it, but the mother remained with Bachman. It was a poor era for liberated females. Even maiden aunts were in effect slaves of the white relatives with whom they lived.

A northern Lutheran minister of abolitionist sentiment attacked Bachman as a disgrace to the denomination because he lived in luxury and indolence at the expense of slaves. Bachman, who had lived with slavery all his life, was evasive in answering the attack. He said that the servants—he always referred to slaves as servants—were his wife's property, thus disposing of the crux of the issue, and devoted the major portion of his defense to denying that he was indolent or indeed lived in luxury.

As the Civil War intensified, Bachman often declared himself as favoring continuation of the Union but refused to preach sermons on any of the issues, declaring them political and unsuited to the pulpit. He did, however, give the invocation, in December 1860, at the South Carolina convention that passed the Ordinance of Secession, and a few months later saw the Charleston batteries fire on Fort Sumter.

Bachman and Audubon were naturalists in a period when naturalists had at least a superficial knowledge of all nature. Rather than having specialities, they had preferences. Audubon's preference was birds; Bachman's, mammals.

So the great Louis Agassiz proved a disappointment to Bachman when he had the Harvard professor as a guest in 1848. Displaying the skin of a European fox, Bachman supposed it would stir nostalgia in the Swiss-born naturalist. "Agassiz, do you know that fellow?" Bachman asked. "No," replied Agassiz. "Why," exclaimed Bachman, "that is the fox of your own native forests." Agassiz answered: "I know little of mammals." From that incident, Bachman felt free to question Agassiz's bolder assertions in natural history.

Agassiz, of course, was a naturalist dealing with fish and mollusks and a great creative thinker in geology and paleontology. Bachman had missed the point in their conversation regarding the fox skin: he had met the new breed, the specialized naturalist.

Chapter VII

Lone Walker and Army Aide: Nuttall and Say

A twenty-five-year-old Englishman who had been in the United States fewer than two years noted in his journal Sunday, June 10, 1810: "To-day I passed thro' a sandy plain covered with the ripe fruit of the *Fragaria* [strawberry], & alive with snakes as the day was warm. I came to a small settlement on *Kiaoga* [River] called *Cleveland*. . . ."

It is obvious from his comments that the Englishman, Thomas Nuttall, had never heard of Cleveland. Neither had Dr. Benjamin Smith Barton of the University of Pennsylvania, who had given Nuttall an exhaustive list of instructions before sending him out for botanical exploration of what then was known as the Northwest Territory. The Kiaoga, to which he referred was, of course, the Cuyahoga River. In 1800, when Connecticut surrendered its claims on the site now occupied by Cleveland, the population of the village was seven persons. It was not until the Erie Canal was begun in 1825 that Cleveland showed any promise of surviving as a place name.

Nuttall, who had been a printer in England, had always had an interest in plants. In the New World he had gravitated to the naturalists' clique in Philadelphia and proven his worth sufficiently that Dr. Barton had chosen him as a field-worker.

On this, the first of several major journeys that Nuttall was to make, Dr. Barton had furnished him with a double-barreled shotgun, a pistol, a dirk, a thermometer, a steel pen, five blank books, and a copy of Hoffman's *Flora Germanica*. Nuttall also carried a list of places he must visit, including Chicago and Detroit, and directions to proceed to Lake Superior and on to Winnipeg, after which he could travel down the Mississippi Valley and return by the Ohio River or whatever course he found proper. He was to conceal plants that he collected from all eyes but his own and Dr. Barton's, in order to avoid piracy by other naturalists, who might rush into print with descriptions and steal credit for the discoveries. For this rather demanding task in a then un-

THOMAS NUTTALL (1786–1859) was a famed botanist
whose versatility in natural history was so great that many
modern naturalists suppose him an ornithologist. Born in
England, he explored the American West, traveling to the
mouth of the Columbia River with the Wyeth Expedition
of 1834–35. He was curator of the Botanical Garden of
Harvard.

certain wilderness, Nuttall was to receive eight dollars a month salary
after his return.

The salary apparently held little interest to Nuttall; he never
bothered to collect it. The binding of secrecy regarding plants that
he collected came to naught. The crafty Frederick Pursh, who had
been Dr. Barton's assistant prior to Nuttall, gained access to Nuttall's
specimens, and for his *Flora Americae Septentrionalis,* published in
London in 1814, hastily arranged an appendix in which he published
many of Nuttall's plants as well as many collected by John Bradbury,
an English botanist who went up the Missouri River with Nuttall.
Thus the scientific names now are attributed to Pursh, rather than to
Nuttall, Bradbury, or Barton.

All of this, however, lay in the future as Nuttall set off happily from Philadelphia to conquer the Old Northwest. In a few weeks he was to learn that the orderliness of Europe had failed to reach that frontier, which consisted in that day of most of the land lying north of the Ohio River and west to the Mississippi River. Indeed, the United States had not conquered these acres, which supposedly were ceded by the treaty ending the Revolution. Nuttall found his identification papers signed by President Madison an almost laughable document to the British fur traders who actually ruled the region. He was to meet surly Indians, unhappy settlers, and semibrigands, and have access to much of the northern and northwestern part of the region closed to him by the fur companies.

Near what appeared to be the end of his trip, Nuttall had the good fortune to join a John Jacob Astor fur trade party at Michilimackinac, a post on Mackinac Island. The fur traders took him to St. Louis. There he met another Astor party, which included the plant collector Bradbury, and traveled up the Missouri River to the Mandan nation in North Dakota with it.

Throughout the journey Nuttall suffered frequent chills and fevers from malaria, then known as ague. He had contracted the disease in 1809, while collecting plants in the Great Cypress Swamp of southern Delaware. While collecting outside the Mandan village, he suffered such a severe attack that he was unable to travel farther and lay down to die. He was convinced that he would have perished had not an Indian found him and returned him to the village. The experience gave Nuttall a new outlook upon Indians. While most naturalists were friendly toward Indians and frequently protested the treatment they received from settlers and the government, Nuttall, more than most, saw them as humans.

Nuttall was at Mackinac Island at the same time as Washington Irving, who was traveling with an Astor party and collecting material for his book *Astoria*. Neither, however, mentions the other in his writings of the period.

Apparently Nuttall traveled from Detroit to Mackinac Island in a birch-bark canoe, a rather hazardous journey along the shore almost the length of Lake Huron. At least he left Detroit on July 29, 1810, in the canoe, apparently with Aaron Greeley, whom he identified only as "surveyor of the territory."

Among the voluminous instructions given by Dr. Barton was the charge to learn all that he could about goiter, an iodine-deficiency ailment that causes the thyroid gland to swell, sometimes doubling the size of a person's neck. Goiter seems to have been prevalent on the frontier and a complete mystery to medical men. Nuttall in several entries in his diary notes that feeding burnt sponge to the victims seemed to offer relief. The burnt sponge theory was on the right track, even though the doctors prescribing it did not know why. The sponge from the sea contained at least small bits of iodine.

In his report on Detroit, written a few days after his arrival there on June 26, 1810, Nuttall said:

Detroit is pleasantly situated on the Western bank of Detroit-river, & contains about 1500 inhabitants mostly French people & Catholicks, & in full possession of all the superstitions peculiar to that religion, Their holidays are so frequent & so strictly observed as to rob the community of much useful labour & to involve themselves in poverty; the Abbe Rishard their priest is a learned & intelligent observer. 3 miles from Detroit at belle fontaine are several high sand hills, which have been raised by the Indians as tumuli or burying-places & are held in veneration by them. Mr. Hervey of Detroit on digging the foundation of a house on one of these sand hills discovered the implements of an Indian chief, viz. a rude axe head of green basalt, cylindric & rounded at one end and wedged at the other, & possessed of a considerable polish. The head of a halbert of rock-crystal about ½ a foot long & 4 inches broad. Several spear-heads well formed, of white hornstone together with several arrow-heads of the same substance. The fragment of a fish-spear of bone barbed on one side, a necklace of human toe or finger joints, & 2 pieces of thin plate copper one in the form of a crescent with 2 small holes in the centre. It is probable the copper is native, & has been beat out & cut by the Indians.

The disease of Bronchocele or Goitre is very prevalent in Detroit & its neighbourhood, both amongst whites & Indians The female sex is much more subject to it than the male, & there are few white women who have not experienced more or less of it. It is sometimes tho' rarely accompanied with fatuity   I saw one instance of this in an Indian man, a poor harmless idiot! It is more distressing to some individuals than others. Many carry about this disease for years without much apparent inconvenience, while others are threatened with suffocation & death.

The situation of Detroit is elevated & airy the soil alluminous, & the surrounding country a stagnant marsh, but the ague is scarcely known.

Different opinions are entertained respecting the origin of this disease; some attributing it to an unknown property in the water of the river; others to drinking snow-water, &c. but this last oppinion is in some measure confuted by the observation of the Abbe Molini. But they never suppose that the abundant & un-healthy miasmata naturally arising from the swamps near the city, have any influence in causing this disease. The water of the lakes is perhaps as pure & generally wholesome as any body of fresh water in the world, & the inhabitants of their banks generally speaking are as healthy or rather more so than in any other part of America, & by no means peculiarly afflicted with Goitre. The opinion of its arrising from exposure to the inclemency of a cold climate; "wading in snow," &c. is not well founded, as women in easy circumstances, are as much if not more liable to it than the poorer ranks, who are necessarily more exposed, & whose constitu-tions here are full as delicate.

Till the nature of this disease becomes better known, little can be done toward a cure, many inert substances, & even charms have had the credit of curing this disease, which baffles reasonable medicine, however, as it comes without any apparent cause so it frequently subsides gradually without the aid of any remedy. amongst the Different substances said to cure this (–) desideratum in medicine (–) are pieces of sponge taken internally—A small woollen bag filled with common salt worn about the neck & fre-quently wet with vinegar; & fomentations of vinegar, or capillary substances wet with vinegar suspended about the neck, which last has been known to dismiss this obstinate tumour in several in-stances.

After spending the winter of 1810–11 in St. Louis, Nuttall accom-panied the Astor party up the Missouri River and spent the summer of 1811 in the Mandan country. After returning to St. Louis, he took a course that never has been explained. Instead of returning to Philadel-phia through Illinois and Indiana, or along the Ohio River, whichever suited him—as Barton had instructed—Nuttall sailed down the Missis-sippi River to New Orleans. There he sorted his collections and notes, packaged Dr. Barton's share, and placed them on a ship for Philadel-phia. Then Nuttall boarded a ship and sailed for England. Perhaps he accounted for his action in a note to Dr. Barton, for the Philadelphia botanist never complained. It generally has been assumed that as a British subject Nuttall may have considered himself unwelcome inas-much as the United States was near the brink of the War of 1812.

How Nuttall spent his time in England remains a mystery. It is known that many of his seeds and plants were propagated in England, for in 1813, Fraser's Nursery at Sloane Square, London, issued a catalog of "New and Interesting Plants Collected in Upper Louisiana, and Principally on the River Missourie, North America." The material corresponds to Nuttall's discoveries. He possibly also did some work on his two-volume *The Genera of North American Plants and a Catalogue of the Species, to the Year 1817*. The work was not completed until 1818, and was published in Philadelphia, Nuttall himself setting at least part of the type. The famed botanist John Torrey, at one time professor at West Point, and later at the College of Physicians and Surgeons and at Princeton, referred to Nuttall's *Genera* as having "contributed more than any other work to the advance of accurate knowledge of the plants of this country."

In 1815 Nuttall had returned to the United States and was traveling through North Carolina, South Carolina, and Georgia. The following year, he traveled down the Ohio River and made a walking trip through Kentucky and Tennessee, returning through the Carolinas.

After completing *Genera*, Nuttall embarked on a personal expedition to explore the Arkansas River for new plants. The 5,000-mile trip by boat, foot, and horseback was made between 1818 and 1820, and provided material for his *Journal of a Journey into the Arkansa Territory*, published in 1821.

In 1822 Nuttall was chosen by Harvard to succeed William Dandridge Peck, who in 1805 had become Harvard's first professor of natural history. Peck died in October of that year. Nuttall, however, did not receive the title of professor, but was named curator of the botanic garden that Peck had founded in Cambridge. He joined the faculty as a lecturer in natural history. In that era, Harvard was a veritable desert for a biologist; its regard for natural history was exemplified by the fact that the subject had but recently arisen above the Aristotelian level. Nuttall found himself without a reference library and with comparatively few persons who had any interest in natural history. He remained at Cambridge eleven years, largely because the salary, though small, was more than he was accustomed to receiving.

Nuttall later was to refer to his years at Cambridge as vegetating with vegetation. He certainly was not entirely unknown in the Boston area, for in 1830, when the Boston Society for Natural History was organized, Nuttall was elected the first president. He was absent from the meeting, being in Philadelphia on that date, and when he returned he declined the office, explaining that he regarded himself as a transient resident of Cambridge.

While at Harvard, Nuttall wrote *An Introduction to Systematic and Physiological Botany*, published in 1827 as a manual for instructing college students. He also wrote the first field guide for birders, *A Manual of the Ornithology of the United States and Canada*, published in two volumes, on land birds (1832) and water birds (1834). Nuttall's journals hint that he was a bird-watcher, perhaps as relaxation from the more strenuous demands of field botany. Although neither as lively in text nor as exact as Wilson or Audubon, the *Manual* has a certain charm, and the two volumes were small enough that one could stuff them into coat pockets. For his ornithological material, Nuttall not only drew upon other authorities but also made two journeys into the South in pursuit of bird information. The *Manual* won him an unusual honor, considering the fact that he attained his fame as a botanist: one of the older American societies of professional and serious amateur ornithologists, the Nuttall Ornithological Club of Cambridge, bears his name.

The *Manual* is a sophisticated discussion that occasionally slumps into folklore not even related to native wild birds, as, for instance, this excerpt from an otherwise excellent introduction:

> The remarkable talent of the Parrot for imitating the tones of human voice has long been familiar. The most extraordinary and well-authenticated account of the actions of one of the common ash-colored species is that of a bird which Colonel O'Kelly bought for a hundred guineas at Bristol. This individual not only repeated a great number of sentences, but *answered* many questions, and was able to whistle a variety of tunes. While thus engaged it beat time with all the appearance of science, and possessed a judgment, or ear so accurate, that if by chance it mistook a note, it would revert to the bar where the mistake was made, correct itself, and still beating regular time, go again through the whole with perfect exactness. So celebrated was this surprising bird that an obituary notice of its death appeared in the "General Evening Post" for the 9th of October, 1802. In this account it is added, that besides her great musical faculties, she could express her wants articulately, and give her orders in a manner approaching to rationality. She was, at the time of her decease, supposed to be more than thirty years of age. The colonel was repeatedly offered five hundred guineas a year for the bird, by persons who wished to make a public exhibition of her; but out of tenderness to his favorite he constantly refused the offer.

The story related by Goldsmith of a parrot belonging to King

Henry the Seventh, is very amusing, and possibly true. It was kept in a room in the Palace of Westminster, overlooking the Thames, and had naturally enough learned a store of boatmen's phrases; one day, sporting somewhat incautiously, Poll fell into the river, but had rationality enough, it appears, to make a profitable use of the words she had learned, and accordingly vociferated, "A boat! twenty pounds for a boat!" This welcome sound reached the ears of a waterman, soon brought assistance to the Parrot, who delivered it to the king, with a request to be paid the round sum so readily promised by the bird; but his Majesty, dissatisfied with the exorbitant demand, agreed, at any rate, to give him what the bird should now award; In answer to which reference, Poll shrewdly cried, "Give the knave a groat!"

The story given by Locke, in his "Essay on the Human Understanding," though approaching closely to rationality, and apparently improbable, may not be a greater effort than could have been accomplished by Colonel O'Kelly's bird. This Parrot had attracted the attention of Prince Maurice, then governor of Brazil, who had a curiosity to witness its powers. The bird was introduced into the room, where sat the prince in company with several Dutchmen. On viewing them, the Parrot exclaimed in Portuguese, "What a company of white men are here!" Pointing to the prince, they asked, "Who is that man?" to which the Parrot replies, "Some general or other." The prince now asked, "From what place do you come?" The answer was, "From Marignan." "To whom do you belong?" It answered, "To a Portuguese." "What do you do there?" To which the Parrot replied, "I look after chickens!" The prince, now laughing, exclaimed, "*You* look after chickens!" To which Poll pertinently answered, "Yes, I,—and I know well enough how to do it;" clucking at the same instant in the manner of a calling brood-hen.

By 1833 Nuttall had had enough of Harvard and resigned the curatorship so that he could join Capt. Nathaniel J. Wyeth's expedition, which left the following spring with a goal of ascending the Missouri River, crossing the Rockies, and descending the Columbia River to the Pacific. With the expedition was a noted field ornithologist, Dr. John Kirk Townsend. The expedition was financed by the Academy of Natural Sciences in Philadelphia.

It was on this expedition that Nuttall and Townsend collected the western birds that Audubon used as models for *Birds of America*. Audubon had finished three volumes of the *Birds* and had returned to the United States in September 1836 in search of subscribers and more birds. Dr. Richard Harlan, naturalist and one of Audubon's few friends in Philadelphia, sent Audubon a letter soon after he landed in New York advising him "that Nuttall & Townsend had forwarded about 100 new species of birds from the Pacific side of the Rocky Mountains" to the Academy of Natural Sciences. The birds were from a region poorly represented in the *Birds*, and Audubon needed the specimens urgently to correct the deficiency. He hurried to Philadelphia, where he quickly learned that absence and success had not made much change in the Philadelphia naturalists' attitude toward him.

As Audubon related in *Ornithological Biography:*

> Having obtained access to the collection sent by Dr. Townsend, I turned over and over the new and rare species, but he was absent at Fort Vancouver, on the shores of the Columbia River; Thomas Nuttall had not yet come from Boston, and loud murmurs were uttered by the *soi-disant* friends of science, who objected to my seeing, much less portraying and describing those valuable relics of birds, many of which had not yet been introduced into our Fauna.

Meanwhile Audubon had begun negotiations through friends to purchase duplicate specimens from the Nuttall-Townsend collection from the Academy. It finally came to fruition with Audubon reporting that it was agreed:

> . . . that I might *purchase duplicates, provided* the specific names agreed upon by Mr. Nuttall and myself were published in Dr. Townsend's name. This latter part of the affair was perfectly agreeable to my feelings, as I have seldom cared much about priority in the naming of species. I therefore paid for the skins which I received, and have now published such as proved to be new, according to my promise. But, let me assure you, Reader, that seldom, if ever in my life, have I felt more disgusted with the conduct of any opponents of mine, than I was with the unfriendly boasters of their zeal for the advancement of ornithological science, who at that time existed in the fair city of Philadelphia.

A more private and jubilant account of the negotiations appeared in a letter Audubon sent to his friend John Bachman:

> Now Good Friend open your Eyes! aye open them tight!! Nay

place specks on your probosis if you chuse! Read aloud!! quite aloud!!! I have purchased *Ninety Three Bird Skins!* Yes 93 Bird Skins!—Well what are they? Why nought less than 93 Bird Skins sent from the Rocky Mountains and the Columbia River by Nuttall and Townsend!—Cheap as Dirt too—only one hundred and Eighty-Four Dollars for the whole of these, and hang me if you do not echo my saying so when *you see them!!* Such beauties! such rarities! Such Novelties! Ah my Worthy Friend how we will laugh and talk over them!

Nuttall had rounded out his tour with the Wyeth expedition by sailing from the West Coast to the Sandwich Islands (now Hawaii), and returning to southern California, where he boarded a ship at Monterey for a trip around Cape Horn to Boston. A crewman on the ship he boarded was Richard Henry Dana, Jr., a Harvard man, who wrote the classic *Two Years Before the Mast.* In the book Dana wrote:

This passenger was no one else than a gentleman whom I had known in my smoother days, and the last person I should have expected to see on the coast of California—Professor Nuttall of Cambridge. I had left him quietly seated in the chair of Botany and Ornithology in Harvard University, and the next I saw of him, he was strolling about San Diego beach in a sailor's pea-jacket, with a wide straw hat, and barefooted, with his trousers rolled up to his knees, picking up stones and shells. . . .

Dana said the second mate informed him that the "old gentleman" spent his time picking flowers and shells and had a dozen boxes and barrels of them on board.

A stroke of good fortune ended Nuttall's career as a naturalist. An uncle died and bequeathed him an estate and fortune in Lancashire, England, with the stipulation that he must live there at least nine months of each year. Nuttall succeeded in completing, however, a project he had begun in Philadelphia, a three-volume supplement to François André Michaux's *North American Sylva.* It dealt largely with trees that Nuttall had discovered on his tours, and included 121 colored plates. The work was finished in 1849. Nuttall managed to combine two three-month periods for his only return trip to the United States, and visited Philadelphia in the winter of 1847–48.

A contemporary of Nuttall, Thomas Say of Philadelphia, appreciated his first big break in natural history because it enabled him to sleep under the skeleton of a horse. Say actually needed the shelter. A few months earlier, he had gone broke in a partnership that operated a drugstore, and so, at the age of twenty-five, when he was elected conservator of the museum of the Academy of Natural Sciences, he needed a place to sleep. His arrangement concerning the horse skeleton never has been fully explained. Presumably he threw a cloak or cloth over the bones to reduce air circulation during the night, somewhat on the order of the canopied four-poster bed of the era.

Although he was a member of a family of some wealth, Say never attempted to recoup his losses. For the remainder of his life, he had no interest in money. When he became manager of the failed Utopian

THOMAS SAY (1787–1834), Philadelphia zoologist whose major interests were insects and shellfish, is considered the founder of American entomology and conchology. Money was the least of Say's interests; he often asked patrons to give him books instead of pay. At one period, his only home was the skeleton of a horse in a Philadelphia museum. He put a raincoat over it each night to make a tent. It was no surprise to his friends that he died penniless at New Harmony, Indiana, where he and his wife were key members of that community dedicated to an ideal life.

community at New Harmony, Indiana, his letters indicate that all he wanted was books, especially books on insects and shells.

That Say should deviate from what one might consider a norm would not surprise anyone acquainted with his family history. His grandfather, also Thomas, was a victim of visions. While hallucinations were not too uncommon in the early 1700s, especially among the religiously motivated, the elder Thomas kept a rather thorough journal of his nocturnal wanderings in the spirit world. Among his more interesting adventures under Morpheus was a death, which permitted his soul to research Heaven. The Says seemed to take these illusions more literally than most persons might, and in 1795 a son, Samuel Say, published a book entitled *A Short Compilation of the Extraordinary Life and Writings of Thomas Say in Which Is Faithfully Copied, from the Original Manuscript, the Uncommon Vision Which He Had When a Young Man.* Samuel was the father of the naturalist.

Say acquired living space at the academy's new museum through the good fortune of being one of eight men who was present on March 17, 1812, to found the academy. It is no reflection on Say's merit to imply that the reason he had such an opportunity related to the fact that he was a member of a leading Philadelphia family, despite his newly acquired poverty. His father was a man of property in the then growing city and an astute manager of money.

As a founder of the academy, Say became a member of that elite group which repulsed Audubon, debunked Rafinesque, and generally disciplined practitioners of natural history. Although Say was quite atypical, the group tended to act as the dons of science in America at that period, which indeed they were. The strict standards they set would elevate the fields of natural history.

The cultural climate toward which Philadelphia already was moving was described by the Englishman Capt. Thomas Hamilton in his *Men and Manners in America*, published in London in 1833. Hamilton had visited the city just as the Philadelphia naturalists were reaching a high-water mark in their leadership of American science. He reported:

> Philadelphia may be called the Bath of the United States, and many individuals who have amassed fortunes in other parts of the Union, select it as the place of their residence. Money-getting is not here the furious and absorbing pursuit of all ranks and conditions of men. On the contrary, every thing goes on quietly. The people seem to dabble in business, rather than follow it with that impetuous energy observable in other cities. The truth is, that a large portion of the capital of the Philadelphians is invested in

New York, where there is ample field for its profitable employment. The extent of their own traffic is limited, and in this respect I should image it to be inferior even to Boston. But, in point of opulence, Philadelphia is undoubtedly first city of the Union. It is the great focus of American capital, the pecuniary reservoir which fills the various channels of profitable enterprise.

In Philadelphia it is the fashion to be scientific, and the young ladies occasionally display the *bas bleu*, in a degree, which in other cities would be considered rather alarming. I remember at a dinner party, being instructed as to the component parts of the atmosphere by a fair spinster, who anticipated the approach of a period when oxygen would supersede champagne, and young gentlemen and ladies would hob or nob in gas. The vulgar term *drunk* would then give place to *inflated*, certainly more euphonious to ears polite, and the coarser stimulants, such as alcohol and tobacco, in all their forms and uses, be regarded with contempt.

There is no American city in which the system of *exclusion* is so rigidly observed as in Philadelphia. The ascent of a *parvenu* into the aristocratic circle is slow and difficult. There is a sort of holy alliance between its members to forbid all unauthorized approach. Claims are canvassed, and pretensions weighed; manners, fortune, tastes, habits, and descent, undergo a rigid examination; and from the temper of the judges, the chances are, that the final oscillation of the scale, is unfavourable to the reception of the candidate. I remember being present at a party, of which the younger members expressed a strong desire to enliven the dulness of the city, by getting up a series of public balls. The practicability of this project became matter of general discussion, and it was at length given up, simply because there were many families confessedly so respectable as to afford no tangible ground for exclusion, and yet so unfashionable as to render their admission a nuisance of the first magnitude.

William Bartram was Say's great-uncle. Bartram encouraged the young Say, who as a youth began collecting butterflies. It was an interest that Say would broaden into a near mania for collecting and naming American insects. The only other interest he allowed to interfere seriously with entomological investigations was the collection and classification of shellfish. His first published work was the first volume of *American Entomology,* in 1817, which consisted of only ten pages including plates and was more or less a prospectus for the larger work that he would accomplish. In the same year, the American edition of

Nicholson's British Cyclopedia published fifteen pages of text and four plates by Say; these comprised the first important paper ever done on American conchology. Say's paper published in 1818 by the Academy of Natural Sciences entitled "An Account of the Crustacea of the United States" is regarded as the first important contribution in that field in North America. For these and his later contributions, Say has been given the title of "father of scientific zoology in the United States." It is not exactly a clear-cut title, for Alexander Wilson preceded him with *American Ornithology*, and not only is ornithology a branch of zoology but also Wilson was as competent as Say. Say did, however, have an aptitude for dealing with the minute and the overlooked creatures, a field that had been largely neglected. As Amos Eaton noted in his *Zoological Text-Book*, published in 1826: "At present but a small proportion of American Animals, excepting those of large size, have been sought out. . . ." Eaton commented that Thomas Say was attempting to correct the situation, but expressed the doubt that he should live so long as to see it accomplished, considering that he had almost no contemporaries in those fields.

Say's greatest accomplishment, at least numerically, was the discovery and description of 1,575 species of American insects new to entomology.

The year 1817 was an exceptionally good one for Say. He not only completed the pioneering publications mentioned, but also had an opportunity to travel to Florida. He made the trip with William Maclure, an outstanding American geologist who later was to become important in Say's life; George Ord; and Titian R. Peale, zoologist and artist. They explored the islands off Georgia; traveled up the St. Johns River in Florida to Picolata, which was favorite Bartram territory; walked overland to St. Augustine; and then on advice of the governor of Florida, who warned them that hostile Indians were a constant threat, returned to Philadelphia.

In 1819 Say was appointed zoologist to Maj. Stephen H. Long's expedition to the Rocky Mountains. Titian R. Peale went along "to prepare the skins of such animals as may be discovered." The party left Pittsburgh by steamer in April 1819, and made such slow progress that by September they had reached only as far as Council Bluffs, Iowa, where they decided to winter. At Council Bluffs Say collected a small wild dog that had been considered a prairie wolf and determined that it was not a wolf but the coyote, *Canis latrans*, as he named it. On this trip Say wrote the first descriptions of the Colorado chipmunk, the golden-mantled ground squirrel, and the swift fox. It was also on this trip that Major Long mistook the wrong mountain for Pike's Peak, a mistake that has been memorialized by naming the mistaken mountain Long's Peak. On the return trip, Long's party explored the Canadian River, under the impression that they were traveling the Red River, an error they discovered when they came to the junction with the Arkansas River. In addition, three soldiers who deserted the expedition robbed the party before leaving, taking all the clothing the men wore. Among the losses were five journals that Say had been keeping. Say had "intermittent fevers" on the trip and suffered from exhaustion. In his official report Major Long noted: "In regard to health we were all highly favored, except Mr. Say, who was more or less indisposed throughout the tour." The expedition crossed part of what now are America's great wheat lands, and Long reported:

> In regard to this extensive section of the country, I do not hesitate in giving the opinion that it is almost wholly unfit for cultivation, and of course uninhabitable by a people depending upon agriculture. . . . This region, however, viewed as a frontier, may prove of infinite importance to the United States, inasmuch as it is calculated to serve as a barrier to prevent too great an extension of our population westward, and secure us against the machinations or incursions of an enemy that might otherwise be disposed to annoy us in that part of our frontier.

On Major Long's second expedition in 1823, Say was among the party that searched for the source of St. Peter's River and explored the region around Lake Winnepeek, now Lake Winnipeg. Present maps indicate that the United States party spent considerable time and effort exploring land that now is in Canada. The border was somewhat unclear in that period. The narrative of the expedition contains what seems a typical Long assessment. He found Chicago to be a miserable village with no current prospects and an uncertain future.

As was Say's custom, his notes on the Lake Winnepeek trip were incorporated into a narrative written by another member of the expedition. In this instance, the compiler was William H. Keating, professor of mineralogy and chemistry at the University of Pennsylvania. Keating had difficulty in describing the frontier in words sanctioned by the grammarians of the day. As he apologized in the volume:

> The compiler found it impossible in the description of the scenery of the Mississippi, etc., to avoid introduction of several words, which, although they are not sanctioned by the dictionaries, seem to be characteristic, and essential to such descriptions;

of this nature are the words bluff, prairie, etc. The term *creek*, being used in different acceptations in England and America, has been avoided in all cases, although with some inconvenience. . . .

In 1826 Say joined the New Harmony, Indiana, communal society, and was to spend the remainder of his life there, dying on October 10, 1834, possibly from typhus. The Dr. Maclure who provided Say his trip to Florida was the final owner of New Harmony, following the collapse of the society in dissension, and Say remained at the colony as Maclure's agent.

While at New Harmony, Say completed his volumes on entomology and conchology. He also eloped with Miss Lucy Way Sistaire, a member of the colony and one of the remarkable women of that period. She was to draw the illustrations for *American Conchology*, signing the work with the unliberated signature of "Mrs. Say."

Although Lucy Sistaire Say often urged her husband to return to New York with her, where she could have lived in modest comfort, he refused. She remained with him to the end, at times sharing rather dire poverty. After his death, Lucy Say returned east, an accomplished conchologist in her own right. In 1841 she was elected the first female member of the Academy of Natural Sciences in Philadelphia.

At the memorial services for Thomas Say in Philadelphia, George Ord in his address commented that Say unfortunately had not written a sentence that would interest laymen. Ord's frankness caused a mild stir among the audience of scientists, many of whom felt he should not have made the remark. It seems, however, a fair assessment.

Chapter VIII

The Weird Spider Man: Hentz

Among Nicholas Marcellus Hentz's idiosyncrasies was his love of spiders.

With the publication in 1821 of his first paper, "A Notice Concerning the Spider Whose Web Is Used in Medicine (*Tegenaria medicinalis*)," Hentz began the first serious pursuit of American spiders. His hobby was culminated almost twenty years after his death by the publication of his collected works under the title *The Spiders of the United States*. This volume, published by the Boston Society of Natural History, largely concerned spiders east of the Mississippi. This, however, was no surprise, for the United States at the time of Hentz's death in 1856 lay largely east of the great river.

What friends noticed most about Hentz was not his fascination with spiders but his unique spirituality. In the midst of a conversation, without warning, Hentz would fall to his knees, clasp his hands across his forehead, direct his eyes to the ceiling, and spend several minutes in silent prayer. He then would resume the conversation. On the door in his room he had painted an "all-seeing-eye" and regularly stopped for prayer before it. The prayer normally was rendered with his forehead pressed against the wall, and it occurred with such frequency that his forehead created an indentation in the wall.

Such reports sound like the undeserved legends that develop concerning naturalists, many of whom were regarded as unusual solely because their fellow citizens considered even a minor interest in natural history erratic. Hentz's aberrance, however, was attested by a son, Charles, who furnished biographical details for the introduction to the *Spiders*.

Hentz was a regular user of morphine, which he injected daily. If he had given one of his spiders a whiff of the drug and then watched the erratic pattern in the web it wove, he might have exercised more care in selecting his medicines. The exact year in which Hentz became addicted is not known. It is probable that he did not consider his

NICHOLAS MARCELLUS HENTZ (1797–1856) was America's first great spider man. Born in France, he came to the United States in 1816 and spent the remainder of his life there. An accomplished painter of miniatures, he earned his living as a teacher, and for a six-year period was professor of modern languages at the University of North Carolina. He changed teaching positions rather frequently, probably because he was an eccentric and a user of narcotics.

slavery to morphine an addiction, since he used it to quiet what he referred to as a nervous condition. Morphine was a relatively new drug in Hentz's day. It first was isolated from opium by a German chemist in 1803. Hentz, who was born in Versailles, France, in 1797, would have been six years old when the alkaloid was discovered. The drug was not illegal in Hentz's day and therefore not as expensive as illicit traffic has made it today. In fact, morphine when properly used is a major medicine of mankind. The more common addictive drugs now in use did not exist in Hentz's day. Cocaine was not extracted from coca until 1855. Heroin, a deadlier opium alkaloid, was not discovered until late in the century. It is interesting that heroin first was used as an ingredient of cough syrups and cocaine as a stimulant that added zip to a "soft" drink. It was easy to become addicted in an era when food and drug restrictions were unknown.

Hentz attributed his nervous condition to certain unscientific folklore that thrived in the period and has not died yet. He thought that his troubled nerves could be traced to his mother's anxiety while she bore him in the womb. In the period of her pregnancy, Hentz's father, a Paris lawyer, had found himself in a losing political clique and the family had fled from Paris to Versailles, where they lived under an assumed name.

With the fall of Napoleon, the Hentz family found it advisable to flee Europe. They arrived in New York on March 19, 1816. The flight interfered with the young Hentz's study of medicine at the Hospital Val-de-Grace. In the winter of 1820–21, Hentz enrolled as a medical student at Harvard but soon abandoned the discipline. The remainder of his life he spent as a teacher or tutor, his specialties being French and miniature painting. While teaching at the Round Hill School for Boys at Northampton, Massachusetts, Hentz married Caroline Lee Whiting, who became modestly famous as a poet and novelist.

Soon after the marriage, Hentz moved to the State University at Chapel Hill, North Carolina, where he held the chair in modern languages. In 1830 the Hentzes moved to Covington, Kentucky, where he became headmaster at a female seminary. He later taught school at Florence, Tuscaloosa, and Tuskegee, all in Alabama, and in Columbus, Georgia. His health finally failed and he died at the home of a son, Charles, in Marianna, Florida.

In his studies of spiders, Hentz was aware of the deficiencies that a general disregard of spiders, even among naturalists, placed upon his work. He had almost no correspondents, although he received some help and specimens from Dr. Thaddeus W. Harris of Massachusetts, after whom he named a son, T. W. Hentz, and from the work of John Abbot, the Georgia entomologist famed for his unpublished bird paintings. Hentz himself had been an entomologist before he became specialized in the allied but separate field of spiders.

As a painter of miniatures, Hentz found spiders little beauties, worthy of meticulous work. The knowledge of spiders, of course, has increased since Hentz's day, and better classification has entered the field. He has been charged with almost consistently painting the creatures' legs too short. It is possible that the optical equipment he used may have distorted them. Throughout his career, his preoccupation with spiders remained a hobby, pursued at odd hours away from his profession. He did, however, do considerable field work, observing the creatures in their natural habitats as well as in laboratory jars.

One of his favorites was the group known as wolf spiders, members of the genus *Lycosa*. The group includes the housekeeper spider of the South, an agile hunter of insects that was appreciated highly in the days before persistent pesticides. The group also includes several agile spiders that run down or pounce upon prey, rather than entrapping it in webs.

The following is a composite taken from *Spiders*. It involves what Hentz considered three species of the genus *Lycosa*. In it is reflected much of his feeling for these creatures which most persons malign.

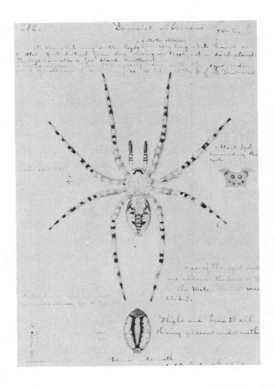

MYGALE TRUNCATA, as drawn by Nicholas Marcellus Hentz, occupied one section of seventeen plates which the naturalist published in the *Boston Journal of Natural History*. The species is now known as *Cyclocosmia truncata*.

Lycosa, (Latr.)—Eyes 8, unequal in size; legs 4. 1. 2. 3. wandering about in quest of prey found under stones, in holes, etc., bearing their cocoons attached to their anus, and carrying their young on their back. Eleven species known to me. Dr. Charles Pickering, of Salem, Mass., presented me with a collection of Araneides, in which were six or perhaps seven new species from New England, but which are too much dried up to be well delineated or described. That single fact shows how far this is from being a complete list of North American Spiders. The famous Tarantula of the south of Europe, the bite of which for many years was supposed to produce a disease that music alone could cure, belongs to this genus; and I found on Round Hill, Mass., a species (*Lycosa fatifera*, my catalogue) which is probably very closely related to the European species, and which dwells in holes nearly a foot deep. These holes seem to be dug by the spider, and to be increased gradually, as its size may require; the opening has a ring of filaments woven by the spider to prevent the filling up of the cavity by rain. It is in this genus also that we may witness astonishing instances of maternal tenderness and courage; and that, too, in the most cruel race of animals, a race in which ferocity renders even the approach of the sexes a perilous act, and condemns every individual to perpetual solitude, and apprehensions of its own kind. When a mother is found with the cocoon containing its progeny, if this be forcibly torn from her, she turns round and grasps it with her mandibulae. All her limbs, one by one, may then be torn from her body without forcing her to abandon her hold. But if, without mangling the mother, the cocoon be skillfully removed from her, and suddenly thrown out of sight, she instantaneously loses all her activity, seems paralyzed, and coils her tremulous limbs as if mortally wounded; if the bag be returned, her ferocity and strength are restored the moment she has any perception of its presence, and she rushes to her treasure to defend it to the last.

Habits. Araneides making no web, wandering for prey, hiding under stones and frequently making holes in the ground in which they dwell, making at the orifice a ring of silk, forming a consolidated entrance; cocoon usually orbicular, often carried about by the mother, the young borne on the back of her abdomen.

Observations. The subgenus Lycosa is not variable in its characters like Dolomedes. The lower row of eyes is straight in some species and more or less curved in others, but I could not avail myself of this to make any satisfactory subdivision. The upper

mammulae, it is true, are longer in *Lycosa lenta,* but I found them
to vary in length in others so imperceptibly that I could not adopt
any of the three families of Walckenaer, which appear to me quite
artificial. These spiders are the eagles and lions of the family. They
are found swarming on the ground, running with great agility, a
property belonging to those spiders in which the fourth pair of
legs is longest. Most are usually found wandering for prey, except
when engaged in maternal duties; others dwell in holes several
inches deep, well rounded and supplied with a ring of silk and
little straws, consolidated so as to prevent the crumbling of the
earth. I have found one of these in the winter which was supplied
with a lid, and probably they all close the orifice for hibernation.
The mother carries its cocoon attached to the posterior part of the
abdomen. Small species ramble about with these; but the larger
ones watch them in their habitation or under stones. The moment
the young ones are hatched they climb on the abdomen of the
mother and remain there for a considerable time. They give a
monstrous and horrible appearance to the mother, which seems
hairy, and twice as large as usual. If the parent be touched, or
forcibly arrested, the young spiders instantly disperse and disappear. . . . It is extremely difficult to distinguish the different
species of Lycosa, owing to the infinite varieties in colors, mark-
ing and size. Future writers will probably clear the confusion
which I boast not of having removed during twenty years of
studious attention to this subgenus.

Lycosa fatifera—Description. Bluish black; cephalothorax deeper
in color at the sides; cheliceres covered with rufous hairs and with
a red elevation on their external side near the base; one of the
largest species.

Observations. This formidable species dwells in holes ten or
twelve inches in depth, in light soil, which it digs itself; for the
cavity is always proportionate to the size of the spider. The orifice
of the hole has a ring, made chiefly of silk, which prevents the
soil from falling in when it rains. This Lycosa, probably as large
as the *Tarantula* of the South of Europe, is common in Massachusetts; but we have not heard of serious accidents produced by
its bite. Its poison, however, must be of the same nature and as
virulent. The reason perhaps why nothing is said of its venom, is,
that so very few instances can have occurred of its biting any
body. All persons shun spiders, and these shun mankind still
more. Moreover, their cheliceres cannot open at an angle which
can enable them to grasp a large object. Without denying its

powers to poison, which it certainly has, it is well to expose popular errors, such as that of the Romans in regard to the bite of the shrew, which it is now proved cannot open its mouth wide enough to bite at all. This spider, when captured, shows some combativeness, and has uncommon tenacity of life. It is a laborious task to dig down its deep hole with the care necessary not to injure it. I have at times introduced a long slender straw downward, till I could feel a resistance, and also the struggle of the tenant; and I could perceive that it bit the straw. In one or two instances, by lifting the straw gradually, I brought up the enraged spider still biting the inert instrument of its wrath. It probably lives many years. A piceous variety is found in Alabama, with the two first joints of the legs, pectus and abdomen yellowish underneath, or lighter in color.

Habitat. Massachusetts, North Alabama.

Chapter IX

◆◆◆

Madness or Genius?
Rafinesque

Constantine Samuel Rafinesque was one of the most universal as well as erratic thinkers of the early American naturalists. Among his many proposals not bearing on natural history is the currently used system of printing bonds coupons, which investors clip and cash.

The best-known personality sketch of Rafinesque was written by John James Audubon and published in his *Ornithological Biography*. The sketch records Rafinesque's visit to Audubon's home in Henderson, Kentucky, in 1818, the year before Rafinesque became professor of natural history at Transylvania University in Lexington, Kentucky, an aspiring institution on the then American frontier. Rafinesque was "M. de T." in Audubon's account:

> "What an odd-looking fellow!" said I to myself, as, while walking by the river, I observed a man landing from a boat, with what I thought a bundle of dried clover on his back; "how the boatmen stare at him! sure he must be an original!" He ascended with a rapid step, and approaching me asked if I could point out the house in which Mr. Audubon resided. "Why, I am the man," said I, "and will gladly lead you to my dwelling."
>
> The traveller rubbed his hands together with delight, and drawing a letter from his pocket handed it to me without any remark. I broke the seal and read as follows: "My dear Audubon. I send you an odd fish, which you may prove to be undescribed, and hope you will do so in your next letter. Believe me always your friend B." With all the simplicity of a woodsman I asked the bearer where the odd fish was, when M. de T. (for, kind reader, the individual in my presence was none else than that renowned naturalist) smiled, rubbed his hands, and with the greatest good-humor said, "I am that odd fish I presume, Mr. Audubon." I felt confounded and blushed, but contrived to stammer an apology.
>
> We soon reached the house, when I presented my learned guest

CONSTANTINE SAMUEL RAFINESQUE (1783–1840) was born in Constantinople. He pioneered in the study of American fishes, particularly those of the Ohio River. He was one of the first professors of natural history in North America, being named to the post at Transylvania University in Lexington, Kentucky, in 1818. He was eccentric to a degree that many contemporaries considered insane. One of the most prolific writers of natural history, he was usually impoverished and died in debt in a Philadelphia garret.

to my family, and was ordering a servant to go to the boat for M. de T.'s luggage, when he told me he had none but what he brought on his back. He then loosened the pack of weeds which had first drawn my attention. The ladies were a little surprised, but I checked their critical glances for the moment. The naturalist pulled off his shoes, and while engaged in drawing his stockings, not up, but down, in order to cover the holes about the heels, told us in the gayest mood imaginable that he had walked a great distance, and had only taken a passage on board the *ark*, to be put on this shore, and that he was sorry his apparel had suffered so much from his late journey. Clean clothes were offered, but he would

not accept them, and it was with evident reluctance that he per-
formed the lavations usual on such occasions before he sat down
to dinner.

At table, however, his agreeable conversation made us all
forget his singular appearance; and, indeed, it was only as we
strolled together in the garden that his attire struck me as exceedingly remarkable. A long loose coat of yellow nankeen, much the
worse for the many rubs it had got in its time, and stained all
over with the juice of plants, hung loosely about him like a sac.
A waistcoat of the same, with enormous pockets, and buttoned up
to his chin, reached below over a pair of tight pantaloons, the
lower parts of which were buttoned down to the ankles. His beard
was as long as I have known my own to be during some of my
peregrinations, and his lank black hair hung loosely over his
shoulders. His forehead was so broad and prominent that any
tyro in phrenology would instantly have pronounced it the
residence of a mind of strong powers. His words impressed an
assurance of rigid truth, and as he directed the conversation to
the study of the natural sciences, I listened to him with as much
delight as Telemachus could have listened to Mentor. He had
come to visit me, he said, expressly for the purpose of seeing my
drawings, having been told that my representations of birds were
accompanied with those of shrubs and plants, and he was desirous
of knowing whether I might chance to have in my collection any
with which he was unacquainted. I observed some degree of im-
patience in his request to be allowed at once to see what I had.
We returned to the house, where I opened my portfolios and laid
them before him.

He chanced to turn over the drawing of a plant quite new to
him. After inspecting it closely, he shook his head, and told me no
such plant existed in nature; for, kind reader, M. de T., although
a highly scientific man, was suspicious to a fault, and believed
such plants only to exist as he had himself seen, or such as, having
been discovered of old, had, according to Father Malebranche's
expression, acquired a "venerable beard." I told my guest that the
plant was common in the immediate neighborhood, and that I
should show it to him on the morrow. "And why tomorrow, Mr.
Audubon? Let us go now." We did so, and on reaching the bank
of the river I pointed to the plant. M. de T., I thought, had gone
mad. He plucked the plants one after another, danced, hugged me
in his arms, and exultingly told me that he had got not merely a new

species, but a new genus. When we returned home, the naturalist opened the bundle which he had brought on his back, and took out a journal rendered water-proof by means of a leather case, together with a small parcel of linen, examined the new plant, and wrote its description. The examination of my drawings then went on. You would be pleased, kind reader, to hear his criticisms, which were of the greatest advantage to me, for, being well acquainted with books as well as with nature, he was well fitted to give me advice.

It was summer, and the heat was so great that the windows were all open. The light of the candles attracted many insects, among which was observed a large species of Scarabaeus. I caught one, and, aware of his inclination to believe only what he should himself see, I showed him the insect, and assured him it was so strong that it would crawl on the table with the candlestick on its back. "I should like to see the experiment made, Mr. Audubon," he replied. It was accordingly made, and the insect moved about, dragging its burden so as to make the candlestick change its position as if by magic, until coming upon the edge of the table, it dropped on the floor, took to wing, and made its escape.

When it waxed late, I showed him to the apartment intended for him during his stay, and endeavored to render him comfortable, leaving him writing materials in abundance. I was indeed heartily glad to have a naturalist under my roof. We had all retired to rest. Every person I imagined was in deep slumber save myself, when of a sudden I heard a great uproar in the naturalist's room. I got up, reached the place in a few moments, and opened the door, when to my astonishment, I saw my guest running about the room naked, holding the handle of my favorite violin, the body of which he had battered to pieces against the walls in attempting to kill the bats which had entered by the open window, probably attracted by the insects flying around his candle. I stood amazed, but he continued jumping and running round and round, until he was fairly exhausted, when he begged me to procure one of the animals for him, as he felt convinced they belonged to "a new species." Although I was convinced of the contrary, I took up the bow of my demolished Cremona, and administering a smart tap to each of the bats as it came up, soon got specimens enough. The war ended, I again bade him good-night, but could not help observing the state of the room. It was strewed with plants, which it would seem he had arranged into groups, but which were now scattered about in confusion. "Never mind, Mr. Audubon," quoth the eccentric naturalist, "never mind, I'll soon arrange them again. I have the bats, and that's enough."

Some days passed, during which we followed our several occupations. M. de T. searched the woods for plants, and I for birds. He also followed the margins of the Ohio, and picked up many shells, which he greatly extolled. With us, I told him, they were gathered into heaps to be converted into lime. "Lime! Mr. Audubon; why, they are worth a guinea apiece in any part of Europe." One day, as I was returning from a hunt in a cane-brake, he observed that I was wet and spattered with mud, and he desired me to show him the interior of one of these places, which he said he had never visited.

The cane, kind reader, formerly grew spontaneously over the greater portions of the State of Kentucky and other western districts of our Union, as well as in many farther south. Now, however, cultivation, and introduction of cattle and horses, and other circumstances connected with the progress of civilization, have greatly altered the face of the country, and reduced the cane within comparatively small limits. It attains a height of from twelve to thirty feet, and a diameter of from one to two inches, and grows in great patches resembling osierholts, in which occur plants of all sizes. The plants frequently grow so close together, and in course of time become so tangled, as to present an almost impenetrable thicket. A portion of ground thus covered with canes is called a *cane-brake*.

If you picture to yourself one of these cane-brakes growing beneath the gigantic trees that form our western forests, interspersed with vines of many species, and numberless plants of every description, you may conceive how difficult it is for one to make his way through it, especially after a heavy shower of rain or a fall of sleet, when the traveller, in forcing his way through, shakes down upon himself such quantities of water as soon reduce him to a state of the utmost discomfort. The hunters often cut little paths through the thickets with their knives, but the usual mode of passing through them is by pushing one's self backward, and wedging a way between the stems. To follow a Bear or a Cougar pursued by dogs through these brakes is a task the accomplishment of which may be imagined, but of the difficulties and dangers accompanying which I cannot easily give an adequate representation.

The canes generally grow on the richest soil, and are particularly plentiful along the margins of the great western rivers. Many of our new settlers are fond of forming farms in their vicinity, as the plant is much relished by all kinds of cattle and horses, which feed upon it at all seasons, and again because these brakes are plentifully stocked with game of various kinds. It sometimes happens that the farmer clears a portion of the brake. This is done by cutting the stems—which are fistular and knotted, like those of other grasses—with a large knife or cutlass. They are afterwards placed in heaps, and when partially dried set fire to. The moisture contained between the joints is converted into steam, which causes the cane to burst with a smart report, and when a whole mass is crackling, the sounds resemble discharges of musketry. Indeed, I have been told that travellers floating down the rivers, and unacquainted with these circumstances, have been induced to pull their oars with redoubled vigor, apprehending the attack of a host of savages, ready to scalp every one of the party.

A day being fixed, we left home after an early breakfast, crossed the Ohio, and entered the woods. I had determined that my companion should view a cane-brake in all its perfection, and after leading him several miles in a direct course, came upon as fine a sample as existed in that part of the country. We entered, and for some time proceeded without much difficulty, as I led the way, and cut down the canes which were most likely to incommode him. The difficulties gradually increased, so that we were presently obliged to turn our backs to the foe, and push ourselves on the best way we could. My companion stopped here and there to pick up a plant and examine it. After a while we chanced to come upon the top of a fallen tree, which so obstructed our passage that we were on the eve of going round instead of thrusting ourselves through amongst the branches, when, from its bed in the centre of the tangled mass, forth rushed a Bear, with such force, and snuffing the air in so frightful a manner, that M. de T. became suddenly terror-struck, and, in his haste to escape, made a desperate attempt to run, but fell amongst the canes in such a way that he looked as if pinioned. Perceiving him jammed in between the stalks, and thoroughly frightened, I could not refrain from laughing at the ridiculous exhibition which he made. My gayety, however, was not very pleasing to the savant, who called out for aid, which was at once administered. Gladly would he have retraced his steps, but I was desirous that he should be able to describe a cane-brake, and enticed him to follow me by

telling him that our worst difficulties were nearly over. We proceeded, for by this time the Bear was out of hearing.

The way became more and more tangled. I saw with delight
that a heavy cloud, portentous of a thunder gust, was approaching. In the mean time, I kept my companion in such constant
difficulties that he now panted, perspired, and seemed almost overcome by fatigue. The thunder began to rumble, and soon after a
dash of heavy rain drenched us in a few minutes. The withered
particles of leaves and bark attached to the canes stuck to our
clothes. We received many scratches from briers, and now and
then a switch from a nettle. M. de T. seriously inquired if we
should ever get alive out of the horrible situation in which we
were. I spoke of courage and patience, and told him I hoped we
should soon get to the margin of the brake, which, however, I
knew to be two miles distant. I made him rest, and gave him a
mouthful of brandy from my flask; after which, we proceeded on
our slow and painful march. He threw away all his plants, emptied
his pockets of the fungi, lichens, and mosses which he had thrust
into them, and finding himself much lightened, went on for
thirty or forty yards with a better grace. But, kind reader, enough
—I led the naturalist first one way, then another, until I had nearly
lost myself in the brake, although I was well acquainted with it,
kept him tumbling and crawling on his hands and knees until
long after mid-day, when we at length reached the edge of the
river. I blew my horn, and soon showed my companion a boat
coming to our rescue. We were ferried over, and on reaching the
house, found more agreeable occupation in replenishing our
empty coffers.

M. de T. remained with us for three weeks, and collected multitudes of plants, shells, bats, and fishes, but never again expressed
a desire of visiting a cane-brake. We were perfectly reconciled
to his oddities, and, finding him a most agreeable and intelligent
companion, hoped that his sojourn might be of long duration. But,
one evening when tea was prepared, and we expected him to join
the family, he was nowhere to be found. His glasses and other
valuables were all removed from his room. The night was spent
in searching for him in the neighborhood. No eccentric naturalist
could be discovered. Whether he had perished in a swamp, or had
been devoured by a Bear or a Garfish, or had taken to his heels
were matters of conjecture, nor was it until some weeks after that
a letter from him, thanking us for our attention, assured me of
his safety.

As one may gather, Rafinesque was not an ordinary citizen. Oddly, although Rafinesque and other naturalists knew the identity of M. de T., the professor never objected to the profile.

Most contemporaries considered Rafinesque mad and apparently assumed that he always had been mad. His biographers, however, have often speculated about the event or point in time which either drove him to madness or permitted him to slip into a mental state toward which his whole life seemed to have been headed.

As early as 1804, Dr. Benjamin Smith Barton, physician and University of Pennsylvania professor, detected erratic strains in Rafinesque's writing, and in the following year, when he became editor of *Philadelphia Medical and Physical Journal,* refused to publish Rafinesque manuscripts. Barton's attitude developed during Rafinesque's first visit to America, which lasted from 1802 to 1805 and was spent largely in Philadelphia. After his return to America in 1815, Rafinesque aroused the ire of Benjamin Silliman, Sr., Yale's first professor of chemistry and natural history, who was destined to become the most influential scientific editor of the period. Silliman founded the *American Journal of Science* in 1818 and later boasted that he had banned all Rafinesque manuscripts after 1819. Perhaps the Silliman decision more than any other effectively barred Rafinesque from access to the few reputable channels for scientific publication. After rejection by his peers, Rafinesque turned to both the popular press and privately financed publication, and his prolific production resulted in what must be the most scattered distribution of papers in American natural history.

From 1805 to 1815, Rafinesque lived in Palermo, Sicily, serving part of the period as an employee of the U.S. consulate there. He wrote extensively on the flora of Sicily and devoted much attention to the fishes of the Mediterranean. He corresponded with Baron Cuvier of France, among others, and Cuvier, who had asked for some fish specimens, soon complained that Rafinesque was inundating him with hundreds of them. The baron was unable to reconcile the colorless specimens preserved in alcohol with Rafinesque's descriptions of fresh specimens, and at last decided that Rafinesque was touched.

It is interesting, however, that when Cuvier's most distinguished student, Dr. Louis Agassiz, a renowned ichthyologist, decided to visit America some thirty years later, one of his announced goals was to visit the Ohio River and see in life the marvelous fishes that Professor Rafinesque had described.

Several biographers have concluded that the events of 1815 brought a mental decline upon Rafinesque. In that year, his common-law wife, Josephine Vaccaro, with whom he had been living in Sicily since 1809, ran off with an actor, Giovanni Pizzalous (whom Rafinesque always referred to as "the comedian"), and took their daughter, Emily, with her. On the night of November 2, 1815, Rafinesque, who was returning to America in hopes of bettering his dismal fortune, was shipwrecked on Race Rocks in Long Island Sound and somehow reached safety at New London, Connecticut. In the wreck he lost all his scientific writings, journals, natural history specimens, indeed, all that he owned except the clothing in which he arrived ashore.

Others regard Rafinesque as retaining mental lucidness after the shipwreck and through the period from 1819 to 1826 when he served as a professor at Transylvania University. The consensus seems to be that after 1830, while he had periods of lucidity, he lived generally in a mental fog.

Whatever else he accomplished, Rafinesque disproved an old maxim which says that academics, and more especially those in biological sciences, either must publish research papers or perish from the profession. Rafinesque both published and perished on the grand scale. He is known to have published at least 939 papers, ranging from single paragraphs to complete books. Yet the more he published, the less attention his contemporaries gave him. When the impoverished Rafinesque died in a garret on Race Street in Philadelphia in 1840, the landlord attempted to sell the body to a medical school to recover unpaid rent.

At the time of his death, Rafinesque had a herbarium of 50,000 plants which he valued at $6,000 and a library which he valued at $1,250. An auction of his goods brought $131.42, which fell $13.43 short of satisfying creditors' claims against the estate. One item listed by the auctioneer as "waste paper" brought $20.25. It is assumed that the entry covered unsold books that Rafinesque had produced. If so, that auction imparted a then unappreciated value to Rafinesque originals, because such items now are among the rarest natural history relics in America.

However quaint or unbalanced Rafinesque may have seemed to his contemporaries, there were periods in which he not only was quite lucid but also showed considerable genius. As one reads his autobiography, *A Life of Travels*, published in 1836, and scans his myriad of scientific or semiscientific papers and books, one discovers a personality that explains to some extent the rejection he suffered among contemporaries. He was a vain egocentric who was quite convinced that he was smarter than his fellows. As he wrote in the autobiography:

Versatility of talents and of professions, is not uncommon in

America; but those which I have exhibited in these few pages, may appear to exceed belief: and yet it is a positive fact that in knowledge I have been a Botanist, Naturalist, Geologist, Geographer, Historian, Poet, Philosopher, Philologist, Economist, Philanthropist. . . . By profession a Traveller, Merchant, Manufacturer, Collector, Improver, Professor, Teacher, Surveyor, Draftsman, Architect, Engineer, Pulmist, Author, Editor, Bookseller, Librarian, Secretary. . . . and I hardly know myself what I may not become as yet: since whenever I apply myself to any thing, *which I like,* I never fail to succeed if depending on me alone, unless impeded and prevented by lack of means, or the hostility of the foes of mankind.

Rafinesque was not exaggerating. He indeed had published in all the fields he listed. That was his trouble. He viewed himself as an expert in all fields. The value of his work varied, but he was a pioneer in several areas. For instance, his papers on Indian mounds and Indian languages were among the first on then neglected subjects.

The universality of Rafinesque appears as one glances through the scientific names of North American organisms. He named the mule deer, the white-footed mouse, the mountain beaver, and a few bats. Among fishes, thirty-five species including the channel catfish, from the Ohio River valley, bear his name as their first describer. The names of thirty genera of flowering plants were supplied by Rafinesque, and at least seventy other genera, which he named first, and apparently validly, exist under the names of later botanists. He also described many shelled invertebrates of American fresh waters and the Mediterranean.

In the naming of birds, Rafinesque had less luck at acceptance. He had one triumph of the spirit in that field, however. On his famous visit to Audubon, the artist sketched him an imaginary swallow, which Rafinesque named as a new genus and species: the red-headed swallow. Although Audubon considered this hilarious, he probably did not appreciate the fact that on the same trip Rafinesque discovered and named the cliff swallow, a species that had long been flitting right before Audubon's unseeing eyes!

The red-headed swallow was only one of the fictitious creatures that Audubon painted for the unsuspecting Rafinesque. He also gave Rafinesque ten paintings of fishes that did not exist. Audubon, however, was not prepared for the consequences of his jokes. Rafinesque not only published the nonexistent fishes in his *Ichthyologia Ohiensis* (Fishes of the Ohio River), but also commented upon the unusualness

of the creatures and gave Audubon credit for their discovery! Here is
a typical description which he gave to an Audubon "species":

> 3d Species. BLACK DOTTED PERCH. *Perca nigropunctata.* Perche
> a-points-noirs.
> Upper jaw longer; body brown, covered all over with black
> dots, breadth one sixth of the length, lateral line nearly straight,
> the anal fins very long, tail truncate. I have not seen this species,
> I describe it from a drawing made by Mr. Audubon. I am there-
> fore doubtful, whether it is a real perch, particularly since the
> drawing does not show the serratures and spines of the gill cover.
> It might be a *Sciena*, or a *Dipterodon*, yet the shape of the body
> and the distant dorsal fins, induce me to rank it with the G. *Perca*
> until better known; when it may even turn out to be a peculiar
> genus, which the flexuose opercule, long anal fin and vent in the
> middle of the body, seem to indicate, and should it be a real perch,
> it must form a peculiar subgenus, which may be called *Poma-
> campsis* in either case.

While it may seem unusual today that a naturalist would describe
and name a species on the basis of a painting, it was not unique in the
early 1800s. Linnaeus in his tenth editions of *Systema*, published in
1758, named fifty-nine species of North American birds solely on the
basis of Mark Catesby's paintings, and in the twelfth edition he added
ten more Catesbian species.

It is a wonder that the red-headed swallow and artificial fish esca-
pades failed to damage seriously Audubon's reputation as a naturalist.
Since the artist's brush was Audubon's principal tool in the profession,
one hardly would expect him to lie with it. Audubon's ability to
escape serious censure undoubtedly lay in the attitude that most naturalists held toward Rafinesque.

Perhaps Rafinesque's soundest work was in ichthyology. Even in
that field, however, he encountered severe criticism from the few contemporaries who pursued the discipline. He was, of course, a generalist. The orderly influence of Louis Agassiz was to enter the field later.
And the genius that David Starr Jordan contributed to ichthyology
lay decades ahead. Rafinesque suffers more by comparison with knowledgeable experts of a later era than he does by comparison with contemporaries. Most of them were still pioneering, and North American
standards remained primitive, especially in comparison with European
standards.

Born near Constantinople, Turkey, in 1783, Rafinesque was the son of a French merchant. He boasted in his *Life of Travels* that although he did not attend college, he was tutored. He had read 1,000 books by the age of twelve, he said.

Rafinesque's education in the classics probably exceeded that of most of his contemporaries, a few of whom were almost illiterate. He published papers and books in French, Italian, and Latin, as well as in English. He spoke of a proficiency in Greek and several other languages.

Because of what he described as a prejudice against the French in Sicily, he added his mother's maiden name of Schmaltz to his own, explaining that it helped him "to pass for an American."

One seldom hears Rafinesque spoken of with affection by modern botanists. The reason: he was the most disruptive practitioner of the science in America. He considered himself especially skillful in botany, and it was in that field that he sowed the greatest chaos.

Rafinesque was critical of the Linnean system in botany. He recognized the system as "artificial." Rafinesque pointed out that the basis of Linnaeus's botanical system consisted of a comparative device that often did not reflect reality. Linnaeus had chosen the flower structure as the indicator of relationships among plants. His system was artificial in that classifications were based upon the numbers of stamens (male organs) and stigmata (female organs). As critics later were to point out, the system was equivalent to dividing the furniture in a room into groups based upon the number of legs, and in the process designating a four-legged chair as more closely related to a four-legged bed than to a three-legged stool. A more "natural" system would group furniture in accordance with its use rather than its design. The fact that botanists long since have abandoned Linnaeus's classification system—without losing, however, his great contribution to botanical stability, the two-word Latinized scientific name—justifies Rafinesque's contention. It was not he, however, who effected the change.

In the matter of Linnean genera (described by the first word in a scientific name and designating a group of closely-related organisms), Rafinesque also was correct in stating that Linnaeus had suggested far too few. It was in this field, however, that Rafinesque created havoc. Linnaeus had suggested about 1,440 generic names. Rafinesque added to the literature 2,700 additional generic names, the all-time record for an individual. In addition, Rafinesque proposed 6,700 binomials as scientific names of plants which he claimed to have discovered and which he said were new to botany. Only 30 of Rafinesque's generic names are now recognized by botanists, one of the lowest scores by any botanist in relation to proposals.

In his *Flora Telluriana*, published in 1837, Rafinesque wrote: "I am never at a loss for names, as Linnaeus was when he framed *Quisqualis;* I could readily supply 20,000, all good." That possibly was the most conservative statement he ever published.

His own estimate of his qualifications appeared in his *New Flora of North America* (1838):

> As I think that I am gifted with a peculiar sharp sagacity in discriminating Genera and Species of Plants and Animals, it behoves me to use it in order to rectify these objects and the sciences relating thereto. It is what I have often done, am now doing, and will continue to do as long as I live, not being prevented by the sneer or neglect of any one whom I consider less sagacious than myself, who cannot discriminate between the most conspicuous characters blended by the Linneists or modern Blenders and Shufflers.

To understand how Rafinesque was disruptive, one must know what he was disrupting. Among other things, he attempted to displace the prevailing Linnean system with a new system of his own devising. Since the system was not accepted, his publications associated with it became a mass of meaningless scientific terms. He also objected to many Linnean scientific names as being either too long or too short. He published new names which he felt corrected those imperfections. Such actions flooded more meaningless scientific names into the field. In addition, he frequently published as new a description of a previously described plant. He also tended to split existing genera into a multitude of species, often without justification. As an example, he split the genus *Trillium* into 34 species and 67 varieties. The miniscular differences that he magnified have not appealed to other botanists, who rejected all but four of his trillium suggestions. At times he announced that he had broken a genus into six or seven genera, but refused to explain the basis of his action. Such a spate of words which cannot be connected to physical entities would ruin the stability of botany if taken seriously.

Also disruptive was his method of continuing publication after scientific journals had denied him access. Rafinesque succeeded in placing articles containing new generic and specific names in such popular publications as *Cincinnati Literary Gazette, American Monthly Magazine, Saturday Evening Post, Kentucky Gazette,* and *The Casket.*

The priority of scientific names depends upon the date of publication, and not upon the journal in which it appears. Some scientific names have appeared first in garden catalogs. The botanical code assigns the same respect to them as though they had been published in the leading scientific journal of the day. The scatter effect of Rafinesque's unusual outlets, plus the fact that his contemporaries ignored his papers, has made the collection of his priorities in publication particularly tedious.

Further complicating the record, Rafinesque finally resorted to financing publication of his papers. One of his early attempts at self-publication occurred while he was at Transylvania University. He launched a new magazine, *The Western Minerva*. He had a printer in Lexington, Kentucky, in 1821 print 300 copies of *Minerva*. When the printer discovered that Rafinesque had no money to pay for the job, he destroyed all but three copies, which Rafinesque managed to get out of the shop. Three copies, however, constitute publication, and all items within the journal become validly published. *Minerva* is among the rarest Rafinesque publications; only one original copy is known to exist. It is in the library of the Academy of Natural Sciences in Philadelphia.

The Rafinesque experience indicated that the scientific press in America was maturing. It is possible that some of his early work was rejected because editors lacked the training that would enable them to evaluate it. Nevertheless, they recognized in his spate of words a lack of discipline dangerous to scientific progress. With more self-discipline and greater concentration, Rafinesque might have made impressive contributions, especially in botany, ichthyology, or malacology. He was an anachronism; a universal generalist in an era in which naturalists were progressing through greater attention to details.

For generations after Rafinesque, scientific papers were subjected to more scrutiny and scientists were more reluctant to rush unprepared into print. The pursuit of perfection in scientific papers continued intensifying until after World War II. The postwar system of grants placed greater emphasis upon publication than upon findings, and thus weakened the rigid criteria. In addition, the employment of scientists by industry has colored reports in many fields.

At the same time, however, the influence of fads, which may have entered to some degree in the evaluation of Rafinesque's work, has not disappeared. Scientific disciplines, as well as other human endeavors, have cycles in which acceptability is determined by the fashionable approach that prevailing scientists approve. A recent editorial in *Ecology* (1974, vol. 55, no. 5) accents the indestructibility of cyclical fads that involve acceptability more than validity. Two ecological scientists complain in the editorial that mathematical ecologists, whose speciality is computer science, have attempted to ban from publication the more traditional ecologists who work with living organisms. They write :

> When a new scientific approach becomes respectable, it often happens that its adherents try to suppress other views. This is now occurring to some extent in ecology. . . .
> Item: An eminent population biologist recently advocated criteria for doctoral theses that would actually have made *The Origin of Species* unacceptable for a Ph.D. . . .
> New ideas are unorthodox by definition and therefore are automatically hard to publish. This, together with the monopoly on theory appropriated for itself by the new Establishment, is partly why the journal *Evolutionary Theory* was founded. But the new orthodoxy goes further; it is not much of a caricature to say that gathering facts (if more than data points) is thought a waste of time. The study of real organisms is a second-class occupation. . . .

After leaving Transylvania University in 1825, Rafinesque moved to Philadelphia. He tried to earn a living as a lecturer in physical geography and natural history in the Franklin Institute. Eventually he drifted into the practice of medicine. In fact, he became a specialist in lung ailments. Considering that he had no training in medical science, his limited success in the field gives an idea of medical practice at the time. He explained in his *Life:*

> Having cured myself completely in 1828 of my chronic complaint, which was the fatal Phthisis, caused by my disappointments, fatigues, and the unsteady climate; which my knowledge in medical botany enabled me to subdue and effect a radical cure: I entered into arrangements for establishing a Chemical manufacture of vegetable remedies against the different kinds of Consumption. This succeeded well. I introduced also a new branch of medical knowledge and art. I became a Pulmist, who attended only to diseases of the lungs, as a Dentist attends only to the teeth. Being thus the first Pulmist, and perhaps the only one here or elsewhere. This new Profession changed my business for awhile; yet enabling me to travel again in search of plants or to spread my practice, and to put my collections in better order, publishing many pamphlets, &c.
> In 1829 I gave a public proof of my art, in printing a small book

called the Pulmist or the art to cure the Consumption, and many hundreds of individuals, whom I have cured or relieved are another striking proof of the beneficial results of my new practice.

Although later writers referred to Rafinesque as a "quack doctor," modern biographers point out that he apparently was sincere and believed that he had found a cure for consumption, which was a prevalent American malady in the cities of that day.

Among the many fields in which he was more modern than his contemporaries was evolution. Rafinesque accepted mutations among species as a fact. Almost without exception, American naturalists of that era considered the idea heretical. As he often did, Rafinesque credited another naturalist with implanting the evolution idea. He ascribed it to Adanson, who wrote *Familles des Plantes* in 1763. In *Herbarium Rafinesquianum*, published in 1833, Rafinesque wrote:

I shall soon come out with my avowed principles about G[enera] and Sp[ecies] partly announced 1814 in my principles of Somiology, and which my experience and researches ever since have confirmed. The truth is that *Species and perhaps Genera also, are forming in organized beings* by gradual deviations of shapes, forms and organs, taking place in the lapse of time. There is a tendency to deviations and mutations through plants and animals by gradual steps at remote irregular periods. This is a part of the great universal law of PERPETUAL MUTABILITY in every thing.

Thus it is needless to dispute and differ about new G[enera] Sp[ecies] and varieties. Every variety is a deviation which becomes a Sp[ecies] as soon as it is permanent by reproduction. Deviations in essential organs may thus gradually become N[ew] G[enera]. Yet every deviation in form ought to have a peculiar name; it is better to have only a generic and specific name for it than 4 when deemed a variety. It is not impossible to ascertain the primitive Sp[ecies] that have produced all the actual; many means exist to ascertain it: history, locality, abundance, &c. This view of the subject will settle botany and zoology in a new way and greatly simplify those sciences. The races, breeds or varieties of men, monkeys, dogs, roses, apple, wheat . . . and almost every other genus, may be reduced to one or a few primitive Sp[ecies] yet admit of several actual Sp[ecific] names [which] may and will multiply as they do in geography and history by time and changes, but they will be reducible to a better classification by a kind of genealogical order or tables.

My last work on Botany if I live and after publishing all my
N[ew] Sp[ecies] will be on this, and the reduction of our Flora
from 8000 to 1200 or 1500 primitive Sp[ecies] with genealogical
tables of the gradual deviations having formed our actual
Sp[ecies]. If I cannot perform this give me credit for it, and do it
yourself upon the plan that I trace.

The idea of evolution, of course, was not original with Rafinesque;
Adanson and others had suggested it much earlier. And he did not advance the idea to higher plateaus. The mechanism that might make
evolutionary conjectures more plausible had not been discovered yet.
However, in the same year that Rafinesque published his opinions, a
young scientist named Charles Darwin was on the east coast of South
America in a vessel named H.M.S. *Beagle.* In two years the *Beagle*
would make her way to the Galápagos Islands, where Darwin would
notice some strange finches.

Chapter X

Searching for Antarctica: Wilkes

On December 26, 1839, Lieutenant Charles Wilkes sailed from Sydney, New South Wales, traveling southward, and in the next two months bumped along through shroudlike fogs, snowstorms, and unbelievable gales. The lieutenant claimed intermittent glimpses of what he interpreted as land. Indeed, Lieutenant Wilkes was certain that he not only had laid eyes on the unexplored continent of Antarctica but also had skirted at least 1,500 miles of its coastline.

For the next century there was a debate over whether Wilkes and his companions had really seen Antarctica. Critics contended that even if the lieutenant had seen land, the land might have been islands. It is, however, to Wilkes's credit that he made no claim to have seen Antarctica on his first attempt to reach the then mythical land. On the first try, Wilkes had sailed from Tierra del Fuego in the *Flying Fish*. He claimed for that trip, in the Antarctic summer of 1839–40, to have reached latitude 74 degrees and 14 minutes south, with no sight of land. On the second attempt, Wilkes had many witnesses, since he was accompanied by the vessels *Vincennes, Peacock, Porpoise*, and *Flying Fish*.

Whatever Wilkes saw on that foggy voyage may have been controversial, but it was nothing compared to the controversy he later was to encounter as he strove with congressmen and scientists to establish a published record of the great venture he headed: the U.S. Exploring Party sent out to explore the world. The side trip to Antarctica was only a minor feature of this most ambitious undertaking for an infant nation that then remained uncertain of even its own geographical boundaries.

Later explorations have tended to confirm the possibility, if not probability, that Wilkes did see Antarctica. In any event, the area that he would have skirted according to his navigational calculations now is known as Wilkes Land.

As for the expedition, it continued until June 1842, when two of the original vessels, *Vincennes* and *Porpoise*, plus other vessels that had replaced those lost or traded, sailed into New York Harbor after three years and ten months at sea. Wilkes, who had expected praise for an outstanding accomplishment, returned to discover that the Democrats who sent him on the journey had lost an election and that the Whigs in power were indifferent to his exploits.

For the next thirty-two years, Wilkes fought for appropriations from Congress to complete what certainly is a jewel among natural history publications: *An Account of the Discoveries Made by the Exploring Expedition, Under Command of Lieutenant Wilkes of the United States Navy.* It could have been an even greater contribution. Unfortunately, when Congress halted appropriations for the publishing project in 1874, several volumes, including a few potentially great ones, had not been published and were condemned to languish either as manuscripts or thoughts in someone's head.

Publication of the *Account* covered such a span of years that Charles Wilkes had advanced from lieutenant to rear admiral and had been retired from naval service eight years by the time Congress refused further funding of the project. A headstrong, often impulsive character, Wilkes pressed Congress for more and more money, demanded quality work from the scientists—even rejecting some volumes and assigning the work to specialists who had not made the voyage—and insisted upon quality printing jobs.

Always a controversial figure, Wilkes was the naval officer who early in the Civil War seized the British mail ship *Trent* in Bahamian waters and removed the Confederate commissioners John M. Mason and James Slidell. The incident almost plunged the embattled Union into war with Great Britain. He was such a hard driver and strict disciplinarian that within days after the exploring expedition returned, several officers filed charges against him and he faced a naval court, which cleared him.

Regardless of how shoddily Congress at times treated the results of the expedition, the total effect was to elevate natural history in the United States. The collection and publication of natural history reports became a recognized function of the federal government. Naturalists like Asa Gray, who had been paying collectors for specimens taken from the American West, could now rely upon government-paid collectors.

The volume of material collected by the exploring expedition was so vast that establishment of the U.S. National Museum could be justified to house it. The exploring expedition specimens became the core collection of the new institution in Washington.

The expedition's material was recognized as public property from the beginning. The attitude marked a radical departure from the procedure used in disposing of the Lewis and Clark specimens, an assembly of natural history and Indian artifacts whose ownership seemed in doubt. The Lewis and Clark material was treated as the personal property of the President. Jefferson displayed the most interesting specimens at Monticello before deciding to ship them to Philadelphia. At Philadelphia the material entered a private collection, Peale's Museum, there being no governmental repository.

The first institution to receive the exploring expedition's specimens was the National Institute, an agency formed for the express purpose. The specimens were housed in the halls of the U.S. Patent Office, and current accounts indicate that the collection inundated the edifice. From there it was moved to the new National Museum.

When the expedition sailed from Norfolk, Virginia, on August 18, 1838, the civilian scientific personnel consisted of Horatio Hale, philologist; Charles Pickering and Titian R. Peale, naturalists; J. P. Couthouy, conchologist; James D. Dana, mineralogist; William Rich, botanist; William D. Brackenridge, horticulturist and assistant botanist; and Alfred T. Agate and Joseph Drayton, draftsmen. The scientists were on the payroll at $2,500 a year plus rations; the draftsmen, or artists, at $2,000.

While the expedition was afield, the navy served primarily as a water transport to the scientists. Wilkes personally made most of the oceanographic observations and wrote the marine reports. The scientists were put ashore for such chores as crossing the Andes to the sources of the River Amazon; to range Brazil, the Polynesian Islands, New Zealand, and New Holland; to walk overland from Fort Vancouver to San Francisco; to travel up the Columbia River to the Blue Mountains—in short, to sample many of the lesser-known areas of the world.

Publication of the expedition's volumes proved quite an experience for Congress as well as the scientists. When Congress authorized the expedition in 1836, it appropriated $150,000, which it seemed to assume was sufficient to cover all costs. By the time the expedition returned to the United States, the bill had run up to $928,183.62. This caused some astonishment in Washington. At that point, there was neither money available for publication of the expedition's results nor much support for such a project. The first move toward publication was an attempt by President Tyler to assign Robert Greenhow, a State Department translator, to write a report and publish the journal of the expedition. This was the critical test, and Wilkes turned the tide against what seemed an obvious attempt to dismiss the whole matter in little more than a pamphlet. In August 1842, Congress appropriated $20,000 for publication of the expedition's reports, with Wilkes in charge. The law limited printing to 100 copies, although printers in that era charged a flat rate for 250 copies or less. In other words, Congress more or less rejected 150 free copies, probably to the printers' delight. Printing of the volumes was done by private printing firms, because most were issued before 1860, when the Government Printing Office was organized. Most of the volumes were done by the Sherman plant in Philadelphia.

The history of piecemeal appropriations by Congress is a rather dull recitation of underfunding. Money was appropriated almost annually up to 1861, when the Civil War began. By 1859, the total had reached $279,131, and the end was far from in sight. The final sums were $11,036.26 in 1861, $2,000 in 1862, and $9,000 in 1872.

That the volumes were published at all came as a surprise to many citizens, among them John James Audubon, who on July 30, 1842, wrote to his young friend Spencer Fullerton Baird:

> I have some very strong doubts whether the results of the Antarctic Expedition will be published for some time yet; for, alas, our Government has not the means, at present, of paying some *half a Million of Dollars*, to produce publications such as they should publish, and connected with the vast stores of Information, collected by so many Scientific Men in no less than Four Years of Constant Toil and privation, and which ought to come to the World of Science at least as brightly as the brightest rays of the Orb of Day during the Mid-summer Solstice. Oh, my dear young friend, that I did possess the wealth of the Emperor of Russia, or of the King of the French; then indeed I would address the Congress of our Country, ask of them to throw open these stores of Natural Curiosities, and Comply with mine every wish to publish, and to *Give Away* Copies of the invaluable Works thus produced to every Scientific Institution throughout our Country, and throughout the World.

Baird was nineteen when he received the note. Although Audubon did not live to witness the chain of events, Baird was destined to head the National Museum, which would house the "Antarctic Expedition" collection. Indeed, Baird eventually was to superintend compilation of the herpetology volume of the expedition, published in 1858.

The taxpayer always has had alleged champions ready to condemn government publication of what commonly has been referred to as "the love life of the bullfrog." The most erudite opponent of the exploring expedition reports was U.S. Senator John P. Hale of New Hampshire. Perhaps the most famous of his many attacks was the one in 1859 in which, during debate on the Senate floor, Hale said:

> When I first read Dickens's *Bleak House,* and his description of that everlasting chancery suit, Jarndyce *vs.* Jarndyce, I thought it was an exaggeration; but I think really, that the Wilkes exploring expedition has performed a thing of romance that will tax credulity vastly more than Jarndyce *vs.* Jarndyce.

Never noted for leaving well enough alone, Congress set its own ground rules on how the reports should proceed: chauvinistically, they were to be an all-American production, shunning foreign advice or participation, and they were to contain only new material. Fortunately, the scientists managed to subvert both restrictions—and almost any other restriction except underfinancing. The value of the volumes as reference works stemmed largely from that subterfuge.

James D. Dana, who wrote the volume on zoophytes, explained that his discoveries, particularly in the field of corals, had so revolutionized classifications that it would require less space to completely redo the field than to publish his new material and attempt to relate it to vast changes in existing literature. So Dana proceeded to write a complete report covering the entire field of zoophytes. Asa Gray, the great Harvard botanist, said of Dana's zoophyte volume: "If the other volumes of the scientific part of the Exploring Expedition equal this both in its fine generalizations, and in accurate detail, our country may be truly proud of the results of the Expedition."

Asa Gray, who eventually inherited the task of describing the seed plants collected in foreign areas, broke the injunction against an all-American production by farming out segments of the collection to foreign botanists who were specialists. Gray completed one volume and worked on a second dealing with seed plants. The second never was published. The manuscript reverted to the Gray Herbarium at Harvard. Gray still was at work on the project when Congress halted further appropriations in 1874. John Torrey, Gray's first mentor and himself a famed American botanist, earlier had described new seed plants collected on the North American West Coast.

The involvement of such experts as Gray, Torrey, John Cassin, Augustus A. Gould, Charles Girard and Louis Agassiz, none of whom had made the voyage with the expedition, resulted from Wilkes's disappointment in the scientific staff and his demand for excellence in the volumes.

Titian R. Peale, for instance, completed in 1848 the volume on mammals and birds. Wilkes was so unsatisfied with Peale's work that in letters to various persons associated with the publication project, he suggested that they urge Peale to submit his manuscript to the scrutiny of friends in Philadelphia "and by this means we may preserve both the Country and Expedition from being disgraced." The press run of Peale's volume, with the exception of a few volumes that had been distributed, was destroyed by a fire in the Library of Congress storage space in December 1851. Wilkes capitalized on the misfortune by not reprinting Peale's volume. Instead, he assigned the zoologist John Cassin to study the mammal and bird collection, and Cassin's new volume on the subject was published in 1858.

On reading William Rich's manuscript on the botany of the expedition, Wilkes wrote in 1847: "I am sorry to say that Mr. Rich's manuscript is not in any way worthy of the Expedition. If published as it is, it would bring disgrace upon the Expedition and himself." Rich's manuscript never was published, and the botanical volumes were assigned to others.

A major volume of the expedition which failed to attain publication, despite the fame of its author, was the ichthyology volume assigned to Louis Agassiz, then at Harvard and acclaimed as a world authority on fishes. Wilkes called in Agassiz in 1849, when it became apparent that the artist Joseph Drayton, who had begun the fishes phase, was unable to complete it, and that the naturalist Charles Pickering, despite his skills in other zoological fields, might never make his way through the fish collection. By March 1855, Congress was becoming edgy about the Agassiz volume. Senator James A. Pearce of Maryland, chairman of the Joint Library Committee, wrote Wilkes: "Mr. Agassiz after six years service and receiving $3965.50 has not yet finished a page for the press and his numerous other engagements render it highly improbable that he ever will complete the work. . . ." Wilkes defended Agassiz, contending that he already had named forty-seven new genera of fishes from the expedition collection and that in view of Agassiz's standing as a scientist, "he best not be thrown overboard." After a lapse of three more years, Wilkes was becoming concerned about the slow progress of the ichthyology volume and wrote Agassiz a letter to prod him along. Agassiz replied:

I am as much surprised as grieved by your letter. You know very well that I am not an employee of the government. . . . I will remain what I have been all my life, an independent man of science. Could I have suspected that my connection with the Exploring Expedition would lead me into such difficulties nothing in the world could have induced me to touch any of its specimens. . . .

Agassiz's delay seems related to a new classification system for zoologists, which he had introduced in his *Contributions to the Natural History of the United States*, published in 1857. In a letter to Wilkes in 1857, Agassiz reported that he was having difficulty with his eyes but that an assistant was continuing with the fish studies. At the same time, he wrote to a friend:

I have not finished the fishes of the Expl. Exp., but I have about a thousand pages of Mss descriptive of those which I have thoroughly examined. I have besides compared again & again the whole series, related what should be drawn, caused many hundred figures to be drawn besides the general views of the most interesting species, the whole of the drawings filling a portfolio, of about four inches bulk, all of which are ready for the engraver. If you wish more details they are at your service. Should your question relate to the time of publication, I would add that I can give over a large parcel of it at very short notice, but I am now extremely reluctant to have any thing printed, before I can submit it to an entire revision. When you see my first volume Amer. Contrib. you will understand why. The fact is that I have remodelled the principles of Zoology in a most radical way, & that every thing I write now is likely to be scrutinized & compared with the principles I advocate in my new book, either to test them, or to find me at fault in the application of my own principles. You cannot conceive what kind & what amount of work I am now doing, in order to bring myself up to the practice of my own principles. . . .

And now to return to the fishes, I wish to apply to this class all the improvements I look forward as flowing from what I have been doing these last two years, as I intend with your leave to take time enough with the Corals to do it fully for my Report to you upon the Coral Reef & the Reef builders. If the publication of the fishes, is urged, then of course I must give up what I have, as it is; but if time is granted, in a sensible way the volume on fishes, may be made the first work in which the new principles are applied upon a large scale. In order to be prepared for this task, I have now an assistant entirely employed in making skeletons of fishes, upon which he has now been engaged for about one year & I intend, if I am allowed to have my own way in the matter to incorporate the results of this investigation in the volume on fishes without enlarging it, in the least, on the contrary, reducing its bulk by the possibility I am acquiring by these studies of condensing the characteristics of families into more definite formula, instead of verbous descriptions. This preliminary enquiry bearing upon a radical revision of the whole class of fishes I have made entirely at my own expense. But I am desirous of giving it up for the benefit of the U.S. Expl. Exp. volume, because the large number of new species to be described there, would afford the best opportunity of illustrating my principles upon an extended scale. In order to carry on all these investigations simultaneously I have now five assistants, besides three artists. With my appointments of $1500 it requires no little industry on my part to do all this without any assistance. For more than three or four years I have not claimed a cent from Capt Wilkes, though I have in the mean time done much that relates to his work.

With the outbreak of the Civil War, funding of Agassiz's project ceased and he suspended work on the volume. Although Wilkes noted in 1859 that the manuscript in preparation by Agassiz promised to fill 2,000 printed pages, no trace of the writing has been found. Several plates by J. H. Richard and Joseph Drayton drawn for the volume are in possession of the U.S. National Museum.

Still unexplained more than a century later is the mystery of why the zoologist Charles Frederic Girard was not credited with authorship of the herpetology volume, which was published in 1858 as compiled "under the superintendence of Spencer Fullerton Baird." Girard came to America with Agassiz in 1847 and lived three years in Cambridge before moving to Washington to become Baird's assistant at the Smithsonian Institution in 1850. He was an expert on fish and reptiles and classified much of the material in those fields that was collected in the Far West. Girard's biographer, G. Brown Goode, said of the volume:

> This book was not written by Professor Baird, who assures me that he did not touch pen to it. The book was done entirely by Dr. Charles Girard, but through some technicality his name was not allowed to appear on the title page by the naval authorities

having the matter in charge, who insisted in publishing the book under the name of Professor Baird, to whom the original contract was given out.

Girard returned to France in 1860, and when the Civil War began the following year, he joined the Confederate cause and traveled Virginia and the Carolinas as the Confederate agent for surgical and medical supplies.

While Wilkes wrested from Congress what seemed financial crumbs in relation to what he was trying to accomplish, another publisher who used government channels to produce great volumes of natural history was rising to his prime.

The successful publisher was Spencer Fullerton Baird, the same Baird whose name appeared on the Exploring Expedition's herpetology volume, a work with which he often denied having any close association. In 1850, Baird was named an agent for the then four-year-old Smithsonian Institution by its first secretary, Joseph Henry. He was authorized to prepare instructions for collecting of natural history specimens, take charge of such collections, and work out cooperative agreements with army, navy, and private collectors that would promote the flow of specimens to the Smithsonian. A few months later he was named assistant secretary of the Smithsonian, at the age of twenty-seven, and devoted the remainder of his life to promoting natural history projects through the Smithsonian. He supervised construction of the U.S. National Museum and organized its first displays, became the first U.S. commissioner of fisheries in 1871, and established the Marine Biological Laboratory at Woods Hole, Massachusetts.

Baird published more than 1,000 papers on mammals, birds, fishes, and reptiles; attached naturalists to every type of government expedition from the surveys for railroad routes to surveys of national boundaries; encouraged naturalists who were serving with the U.S. Army in Indian territory; and edited the most influential natural history volumes of his period.

Baird revolutionized systematics and classifications by setting new standards in the fields of mammalogy and ornithology. In fact, his imprint was such that the period from 1858 to his death in 1887 is commonly referred to as the Bairdian epoch in ornithology.

In spite of his renown and research, Baird was elected to the National Academy of Sciences in 1864 only over the opposition of Louis Agassiz, who had contended that Baird was no more than a descriptive zoologist who had contributed nothing to science. It is true that he gained considerable fame from describing 70 new species of mammals and 216 new species of birds in comprehensive monographs based on American collections by fifteen government surveys in the West. But more importantly, in the process he completely recast the nomenclature and classifications in the two classes. He was the first American ornithologist to use more than one specimen in describing a species, thus taking into account the individual variations that occur within a species rather than assuming that one specimen is the standard to which all other members of the species must conform.

Baird's "Distribution and Migrations of North American Birds," published in the *American Journal of Science* in 1866, was among early papers that suggested evolutionary links among American birds.

Like most naturalists, Baird got his start in natural history by roaming the countryside near his home, in his case Reading, Pennsylvania, where he was born in 1823. He first attracted attention from a senior naturalist when, as a boy of fifteen, then living in Carlisle, Pennsylvania, he sent an interesting squirrel skin he had obtained from a dealer to John James Audubon. A few years later Audubon and Bachman described the skin in the *Viviparous Quadrupeds* as "the Annulated Marmot Squirrel." Audubon and Bachman referred to the animal as a ground squirrel "obtained on the Western Prairies, we believe on the east of the Mississippi River; the locality was not particularly stated. . . . It was politely presented to us by Professor Spencer F. Baird of Carlisle, Pennsylvania, a young Naturalist of eminent attainments." Between the time he sent Audubon the skin as a gift of admiration and the date of publication, young Baird had become professor of natural history at Dickinson College. Baird had no information concerning the squirrel's geographical origin. In later years, during his service at the Smithsonian, he concluded that the mysterious squirrel specimen must have been collected in Africa. In 1877, however, he discovered that his new-found friends had been partly correct although geographically askew. A second specimen of the squirrel appeared at the Smithsonian, and it was a ground squirrel collected in the tropics of western Mexico. Its common name today is the ringtailed ground squirrel, and though it has been assigned to the genus *Citellus*, its species name remains the same as Audubon and Bachman gave it: *annulatus*.

If one opens a copy of volume 9 of *Explorations and Surveys for a Railroad Route from the Mississippi River to the Pacific Ocean*, one quickly discovers that it is not about railroads or railroad construction, but about the birds of North America. Not the birds between the Mississippi and Pacific, mind you, but about birds from the Arctic to Mexico, including those that venture no nearer the Mississippi than northern Maine. In fact, Ross's gull, which never had been seen in North America south of Point Barrow, Alaska, until 1975, when one appeared on the Merrimack River estuary at Salisbury, Massachusetts, is described on page 857 of the volume. It is evident that the Congressional injunction limiting publication to only new material that resulted directly from the survey, which applied to the exploring expedition's volumes, did not apply to Baird, who wrote volume 9 of the *Railroad Survey*. It was published by the government in 1858.

Should one find the text of it familiar, it may be because one has already read *The Birds of North America* by Spencer Fullerton Baird, assistant secretary of the Smithsonian Institution, in cooperation with John Cassin of the Academy of Natural Sciences in Philadelphia and George N. Lawrence of the Lyceum of Natural History in New York. For the *Railroad Survey* volume was reprinted commercially the next year by J. B. Lippincott and Company of Philadelphia as *The Birds of North America*.

Elliott Coues later was to say of volume 9, or the *Birds:*

> The appearance of so great a work, from the hands of a most methodical, learned, and sagacious naturalist, aided by two of the leading ornithologists of America, exerted an influence perhaps stronger and more widely felt than that of any of its predecessors, Audubon's and Wilson's not excepted, and marked an epoch in the history of American ornithology. . . . Such a monument of original research is likely to remain for an indefinite period a source of inspiration to lesser writers, while its authority as a work of reference will always endure.

While refinement in classification of birds has continued to the present, Baird rather adequately rounded out the descriptive phase of American ornithology and moved forward. In the future, ornithologists would devote more effort to determining how each species fits and functions within nature's framework. It was an investigation well begun by Wilson and carried forward by others into what today is known as systematics and ecology.

The interjection of Baird's happier publishing experiences at this point seems illustrative of a negative bias that dogged Wilkes and his scientific crew throughout the post expedition phase. A comparison of publishing dates discloses that many of Baird's successful pressruns occurred at the same time that Congress was unresponsive to Wilkes.

Aside from the often abrasive personality of Wilkes, there were other considerations that may have tilted congressional approval toward the more diplomatic Baird. Perhaps as much as anything was the fact that while Baird was dealing with the natural history of the United States, Wilkes was promoting the broader field of the natural history of the world. Indeed, if it were not for the U.S. Exploring Expedition's foray on the West Coast, in Hawaii and in Samoa, all of which later were to become part of the United States or U.S. territory, one hardly could justify including its work in a volume limited to natural history exploration within America.

Congress was interested in the oceanographic survey work done by Wilkes. His navigation charts and similar technical work valuable to the marine trades were welcomed and praised. As one inspects the background that led to authorization of the exploring expedition, congressional coldness to pure science becomes more understandable. The first proposal that the United States undertake a major exploring expedition seems to have originated among sealers who worked largely out of Stonington, Connecticut. Having used up the supply of seals that could be found on readily available islands in the Southern Hemisphere, the sealers urged Congress to equip an expedition that might open unknown sealing grounds in the Antarctic.

In addition, the whaling fleets of New Bedford and Nantucket were finding that the slow whales which wind- and oar-powered vessels could overtake and which floated after death were becoming scarce. And the sandalwood trade in the Sandwich Islands (now Hawaii), which had produced fortunes, had reached a point where its base resource faced exhaustion.

Agitation for an exploring expedition began early in the 1820s. Many congressmen, however, viewed a search for new natural resources as a matter better left to commercial enterprise than to the government. Indeed, the U.S. Senate proved so adamant regarding public financing of Southern Hemisphere exploration that in October 1829, three vessels under the command of Stonington sealers set out to undertake the exploration under combined backing of commercial and scientific groups. In the fleet were the *Seraph*, commanded by Benjamin Pendleton; the *Annawan*, commanded by Nathaniel B. Palmer; and the *Penguin*, commanded by Nathaniel's brother, Alexander Palmer. All three Stonington skippers were experienced Antarctic hands. Nathaniel Palmer in 1820 had discovered what now is known as the Palmer Peninsula, the tongue of Antarctica that juts toward South America and the most northward land in that polar continent. As with most polar explorations—although Palmer was a sealer whose interest in exploration was limited to quarry—Palmer's discovery long was regarded as a possible island rather than a projection of the continent. The Stonington expedition swept around Cape Horn and up the coast of Chile. Unfortunately, all hands, except the scientists Jeremiah N. Reynolds and James Eights and the scientific artist John Frampton Watson, had signed on for the traditional shares of sealers. Having failed to find anything worthwhile in pelts, the crews were at a point of rebellion, and the leaders turned back at Chile. The expedition's chief contribution to science was negative: it proved that no islands existed in the areas it visited. Reynolds, who went ashore with Watson, spent two years exploring Chile. The expedition did return with fifteen chests of scientific material, which were distributed to learned societies. In addition, Reynolds collected plants, shells, minerals, and four hundred bird skins, which he gave to the Boston Society of Natural History.

When one considers that the U.S. Exploring Expedition originated from such a background, one begins to understand why congressmen were not enthusiastic about publishing new discoveries regarding minute coral animals that lived around islands that had no obvious commercial worth.

There seems to be no adequate record of how extensive the U.S. Exploring Expedition's collections were. Among other things, massive shipments either were lost at sea or, equally as bad, put ashore at Philadelphia or Boston, where the local savants quite often helped themselves to specimens. Friends of congressmen immediately began demanding seeds and plants, and many of the demanders were commercial nurserymen. Many of the chests landed at Philadelphia were discovered to have a label on the underside declaring them the personal property of Titian Peale, an overstatement that was corrected, but perhaps not before the disappearance of some chests. In a few instances, cartons that were transshipped from Philadelphia to Washington were found, when opened at the capital, to contain nothing except wood shavings or shredded recent issues of Philadelphia newspapers.

In spite of diversions, however, chests of specimens had flooded the National Institute and the Patent Office long before the vessels of the expedition returned with shiploads. The natural history establishment, which was accustomed to dealing with a few small packets from overland expeditions, was wholly unprepared to cope with the largess.

Meanwhile, the scientists who had accompanied the expedition and their onshore successors did not permit the reluctance of Congress to finance publication to rob them of credit for new discoveries. In order to establish the priority of publication necessary in natural history, they began mailing manuscripts to any possible publisher. *The American Journal of Science* at Philadelphia and the *Proceedings* of the old Boston Society of Natural History, as well as other journals, were benefactors of the necessity to publish.

As a measure of the expedition's contribution to science, among 400 species of coral, 200 either were entirely new or the animals that formed the coral had not been described; of 1,000 species of crustacea, some 600 were new to science; the expedition's botanical collection became the United States National Herbarium and the mounted specimens filled 1,300 shelves; the 200-plus navigation charts not only were more accurate than earlier charts but also freed American seamen from dependence upon foreign publications; the total contributions in all fields gave the United States a preeminence in scientific exploration that was not to be equaled until the British *Challenger* expedition of 1873–76.

Chapter XI

Harpoons and Pens: Melville and Scammon

To accommodate the whale, Linnaeus changed man and his hairy cousins into mammals.

To earlier workers in zoology, most animals now known as mammals had been referred to as viviparous quadrupeds. The term meant that they were four-legged animals who bore their young alive, rather than from external eggs. Those who dared the speculation, since it was a sacrilegious thought, considered man a viviparous quadruped, his two arms counting as legs.

Actually Linnaeus had several tries at sorting out the animals and dropping them into convenient slots. In the first edition of his *Systema Naturae* (1735), he went along with prevailing opinion and dropped the hairy ones into the class *Quadrupedia*. It was not until the tenth edition of *Systema* (1758) that he made a clean break with the past and established *Mammalia*. This was the result of his pondering the problem of what to do about the whale.

Man gave Linnaeus little trouble. He assigned man the scientific name *Homo sapiens*, meaning the wise man. Those who considered Linnaeus vain always reported that the Swedish master had no difficulty in finding the type specimen for *sapiens*, the individual animal that best characterized the attribute of wisdom—and that for this honor, he chose himself. But he went a step farther. He placed man in the order *Primates*. To accompany man in that order, Linnaeus placed also the apes and monkeys, lemurs, and, for some odd reason, the bats. Thus man officially became recognized as similar to monkeys and apes and the monkeylike lemurs. The transition was achieved without a murmur from theologians. Perhaps the uproar was delayed almost a century to Darwin's era because Linnaeus did not enter into speculation on the origin of species. He accepted man as a special creation and supposed that all existing species proceeded from the hand of God and had remained unaltered.

The whale was more of a problem. Because they swam like fish and had evolved into the streamlined form common to fish, whales generally had been considered fish. Yet 2000 years before Linnaeus, Aristotle had described the whales rather accurately. As men had known for centuries before him, Aristotle knew that whales breathed air, had reproductive organs similar to other mammals, gave birth to young alive and nursed them, and were warm-blooded creatures. In other words, whales were four-footed creatures that did not have four feet. They were viviparous but not quadrupeds.

A cartoon hangs on a wall in Linnaeus's study in his home at Uppsala. It shows a baby whale connected to its mother by an umbilical cord. Historians say it was this cartoon that led Linnaeus to suppress *Quadrupedia* and establish the class *Mammalia*. In his sorting of mammals, Linnaeus relied heavily upon the creatures' tooth structure. But the determining factor, the one that elevated the whale above the fishes, was the mammary glands, the milk-producing organs of female mammals. They became the credentials for inclusion in class *Mammalia*. Female whales had them.

Linnaeus placed the whales, with dolphins and porpoises, in the order *Cetae* (from the Greek word for "whale"). Over the years the name has been enlarged to *Cetacea*, a sort of code word for what probably is the least-known group of mammals.

Why the life histories of whales are little understood can be explained by economics. A scientist may erect a blind consisting of sticks and burlap and acquire an enormous file of observations and facts concerning a bird species. But to follow the life of the whale requires a ship and crew, sophisticated underwater equipment, and months at sea. In short, one must assemble a costly expedition to pursue leviathan and for his effort acquire but fleeting glimpses of his quarry.

Of those who actively pursued the whale with pen or quill, as well as harpoon, the outstanding memoirs came from William Scoresby, Jr., Herman Melville, and Charles M. Scammon. Perhaps the least sensitive of the three was Scammon. It is interesting, however, that all three retired the harpoon and turned to other careers. For all the glamour of sailing days, whaling was a bloody business that turned the sea red while men held fast in fear of their own lives and stabbed with lances a struggling monster whose refusal to die sometimes carried the work through hours.

The chauvinistic bent of this volume excludes Scoresby, for although he frequented the Arctic whaling grounds familiar to Americans of the era, he was an Englishman. His interest was more in exploration and science than in whale oil. Two years after publication of his *Account of the Arctic Region with a History and Description of the Northern Whale Fishery* in 1820, Scoresby entered the Anglican ministry.

Herman Melville was born in New York City in 1819, and after an unrewarding career as a bank clerk, decided to go to sea. He was a crew member of the whaler *Acushnet* through 1841 and 1842, until he jumped ship at Marquesas Island in July 1842, preferring to live among cannibals.

There are those who consider his *Moby Dick*, written in 1851, as the great American novel. His contemporaries did not agree with that verdict, and the book was a financial failure. One may want to accept the assumption that Ahab's struggles with the great white whale represent Calvinistic man struggling with an angry God. Nevertheless, *Moby Dick* remains the most readable book on whaling. Many who have read *Moby Dick* in modern editions, however, may not know that Melville inserted between chapters of the novel a complete, if not at all times scientific, report on cetology as he saw it. Many abridged editions appear without the chapters devoted to the zoology of the whale.

Melville introduces the subject of whales as living, rather than fictional, characters, as Moby Dick was, in chapter 32:

Already we are boldly launched upon the deep; but soon we shall be lost in its unshored, harborless immensities. Ere that come to pass; ere the Pequod's weedy hull rolls side by side with the barnacled hulls of the Leviathan; at the outset it is but well to attend to a matter almost indispensable to a thorough appreciative understanding of the more special leviathanic revelations and allusions of all sorts which are to follow.

It is some systematized exhibition of the whale in his broad genera, that I would now fain put before you. Yet it is no easy task. The classification of the constituents of a chaos, nothing less is here essayed. Listen to what the best and latest authorities have laid down.

"No branch of Zoology is so much involved as that which is entitled Cetology," says Captain Scoresby, A.D. 1820.

"It is not my intention, were it in my power, to enter into the inquiry as to the true method of dividing the cetacea into groups and families. * * * Utter confusion exists among the historians of this animal" (Sperm Whale), says Surgeon Beale, A.D. 1839.

"Unfitness to pursue our research in the unfathomable waters." "Impenetrable veil covering our knowledge of the cetacea." "A field strewn with thorns." "All these incomplete indications but serve to torture us naturalists."

Thus speak of the whale, the great Cuvier, and John Hunter, and Lesson, those lights of zoology and anatomy. Nevertheless, though of real knowledge there be little, yet of books there are a plenty; and so in some small degree, with Cetology, or the science of whales.

Melville, who had witnessed the chopping of whales on the *Acushnet* deck, was attending the same classroom that most whale experts attended. True, he lacked the training in anatomy that most professional whale students had. Yet up to the present, most of the data that men have compiled in regard to whales have come from this same source: watching whalers cut up the catch. As a watcher, one becomes a supercargo and somewhat of a nuisance. Whales are flensed for oil and profit, and a guest with pencil and clipboard is more tolerated than humored. Nevertheless, much valuable information on the whale as an organism, although a dead one, has come from such observations.

In various chapters, Melville details the innards of whales; indeed, both sperm and right whales. His living whale, the type of whale that interests naturalists, emerges most clearly in his chapter entitled "The Tail."

Other poets have warbled the praises of the soft eye of the antelope, and the lovely plumage of the bird that never alights; less celestial, I celebrate a tail.

Reckoning the largest sized Sperm Whale's tail to begin at that point of the trunk where it tapers to about the girth of a man, it comprises upon its upper surface alone, an area of at least fifty square feet. The compact round body of its root expands into two broad, firm, flat palms or flukes, gradually shoaling away to less than an inch in thickness. At the crotch or junction, these flukes slightly overlap, then sideways recede from each other like wings, leaving a wide vacancy between. In no living thing are the lines of beauty more exquisitely defined than in the crescentic borders of these flukes. At its utmost expansion in the full grown whale, the tail will considerably exceed twenty feet across.

The entire member seems a dense webbed bed of welded sinews; but cut into it, and you find that three distinct strata compose it:—upper, middle, and lower. The fibres in the upper and lower layers, are long and horizontal; those of the middle one, very short, and running crosswise between the outside layers. This triune structure, as much as anything else, imparts power to the tail. To the student of old Roman walls, the middle layer will furnish a curious parallel to the thin course of tiles always alternating with the stone in those wonderful relics of the antique, and which undoubtedly contribute so much to the great strength of the masonry.

But as if this vast local power in the tendinous tail were not enough, the whole bulk of the Leviathan is knit over with a warp and woof of muscular fibres and filaments, which passing on either side the loins and running down into the flukes, insensibly blend with them, and largely contribute to their might; so that in the tail the confluent measureless force of the whole whale seems concentrated to a point. Could annihilation occur to matter, this were the thing to do it.

Nor does this—its amazing strength, at all tend to cripple the graceful flexion of its motions; where infantileness of ease undulates through a Titanism of power. On the contrary, those motions derive their most appalling beauty from it. Real strength never impairs beauty or harmony, but it often bestows it; and in everything imposingly beautiful, strength has much to do with the magic. Take away the tied tendons that all over seem bursting from the marble in the carved Hercules, and its charm would be gone. As devout Eckermann lifted the linen sheet from the naked corpse of Goethe, he was overwhelmed with the massive chest of the man, that seemed as a Roman triumphal arch. When Angelo paints even God the Father in human form, mark what robustness is there. And whatever they may reveal of the divine love in the Son, the soft, curled, hermaphroditical Italian pictures, in which his idea has been most successfully embodied; these pictures, so destitute as they are of all brawniness, hint nothing of any power, but the mere negative, feminine one of submission and endurance, which on all hands it is conceded, form the peculiar practical virtues of his teachings.

Such is the subtle elasticity of the organ I treat of, that whether wielded in sport, or in earnest, or in anger, whatever be the mood it be in, its flexions are invariably marked by exceeding grace. Therein no fairy's arm can transcend it.

Five great motions are peculiar to it. First, when used as a fin for progression; Second, when used as a mace in battle; Third, in sweeping; Fourth, in lobtailing; Fifth, in peaking flukes.

First: Being horizontal in its position, the Leviathan's tail acts in a different manner from the tails of all other sea creatures. It never wriggles. In man or fish, wriggling is a sign of inferiority. To the whale, his tail is the sole means of propulsion. Scroll-wise coiled forwards beneath the body, and then rapidly sprung backwards, it is this which gives that singular darting, leaping motion to the monster when furiously swimming. His side-fins only serve to steer by.

Second: It is a little significant, that while one Sperm Whale fights another Sperm Whale only with his head and jaw, nevertheless, in his conflicts with man, he chiefly and contemptuously uses his tail. In striking at a boat, he swiftly curves away his flukes from it, and the blow is inflicted only by the recoil. If it be made in the unobstructed air, especially if it descend to its mark, the stroke is then simply irresistible. No ribs of man or boat can withstand it. Your only salvation lies in eluding it; but if it comes sideways through the opposing water, then partly owing to the light buoyancy of the whale-boat, and the elasticity of its materials, a cracked rib or a dashed plank or two, a sort of stitch in the side, is generally the most serious result. These submerged side blows are so often received in the fishery, that they are accounted mere child's play. Some one strips off a frock, and the hole is stopped.

Third: I cannot demonstrate it, but it seems to me, that in the whale the sense of touch is concentrated in the tail; for in this respect there is a delicacy in it equalled only by the daintiness of the elephant's trunk. This delicacy is chiefly evinced in the action of sweeping, when in maidenly gentleness the whale with a certain soft slowness moves his immense flukes from side to side upon the surface of the sea; and if he feel but a sailor's whisker, woe to that sailor, whiskers and all. What tenderness there is in that preliminary touch! Had this tail any prehensile power, I should straightway bethink me of Darmonodes' elephant that so frequented the flower-market, and with low salutations presented nosegays to damsels, and then caressed their zones. On more accounts than one, a pity it is that the whale does not possess this prehensile virtue in his tail; for I have heard of yet another elephant, that when wounded in the fight, curved round his trunk and extracted the dart.

Fourth: Stealing unawares upon the whale in the fancied security of the middle of solitary seas, you find him unbent from the vast corpulence of his dignity, and kitten-like, he plays on the ocean as if it were a hearth. But still you see his power in his play. The broad palms of his tail are flirted high into the air; then smiting the surface, the thunderous concussion resounds for miles. You would almost think a great gun had been discharged; and if you noticed the light wreath of vapor from the spiracle at his other extremity, you would think that that was the smoke from the touch-hole.

Fifth: As in the ordinary floating posture of the Leviathan the flukes lie considerably below the level of his back, they are then completely out of sight beneath the surface; but when he is about to plunge into the deeps, his entire flukes with at least thirty feet of his body are tossed erect in the air, and so remain vibrating a moment, till they downwards shoot out of view. Excepting the sublime *breach*—somewhere else to be described—this peaking of the whale's flukes is perhaps the grandest sight to be seen in all animated nature. Out of the bottomless profundities the gigantic tail seems spasmodically snatching at the highest heaven. So in dreams, have I seen majestic Satan thrusting forth his tormented colossal claw from the flame Baltic of Hell. But in gazing at such scenes, it is all in all what mood you are in; if in the Dantean, the devils will occur to you; if in that of Isaiah, the archangels. Standing at the mast-head of my ship during a sunrise that crimsoned sky and sea, I once saw a large herd of whales in the east, all heading towards the sun, and for a moment vibrating in concert with peaked flukes. As it seemed to me at the time, such a grand embodiment of adoration of the gods was never beheld, even in Persia, the home of the fire worshippers. As Ptolemy Philopater testified of the African elephant, I then testified of the whale, pronouncing him the most devout of all beings. For according to King Juba, the military elephants of antiquity often hailed the morning with their trunks uplifted in the profoundest silence.

The chance comparison in this chapter, between the whale and the elephant, so far as some aspects of the tail of the one and the trunk of the other are concerned, should not tend to place those two opposite organs on an equality, much less the creatures to which they respectively belong. For as the mightiest elephant is but a terrier to Leviathan, so, compared with Leviathan's tail, his trunk is but the stalk of a lily. The most direful blow from the elephant's trunk were as the playful tap of a fan, compared with the measureless crush and crash of the Sperm Whale's ponderous flukes, which in repeated instances have one after the other hurled entire boats with all their oars and crews into the air, very much as an Indian juggler tosses his balls.*

The more I consider this mighty tail, the more do I deplore my inability to express it. At times there are gestures in it, which, though they would well grace the hand of man, remain wholly inexplicable. In an extensive herd, so remarkable, occasionally, are these mystic gestures, that I have heard hunters who have declared them akin to Free-Mason signs and symbols; that the whale, indeed, by these methods intelligently conversed with the world. Nor are there wanting other motions of the whale in his general body, full of strangeness, and unaccountable to his most experienced assailant. Dissect him how I may, then, I but go skin deep; I know him not, and never will. But if I know not even the tail of this whale, how understand his head? much more, how comprehend his face, when face he has none? Thou shalt see my back parts, my tail, he seems to say, but my face shall not be seen. But I cannot completely make out his back parts; and hint what he will about his face, I say again he has no face.

Scammon retired from eleven years of whaling at the outbreak of the Civil War and joined the U.S. Revenue Marine (now the Coast Guard), a service in which he devoted the remainder of his active years, retiring on disability in 1895. Born in Pittston, Maine, in 1825, Scammon was among New Englanders who headed for California in the great gold rush of 1849.

In his *Marine Mammals of the Northwest Coast of North America*, Scammon tells us that he found gold prospecting not to his liking. Explaining that he was a "seafaring man," he took command in 1852 "of a brig bound on a sealing, sea-elephant, and whaling voyage." In 1856, Scammon made a discovery that was a contribution to zoological science. He found that the female gray whales of the eastern Pacific congregated each year in the shallow and hidden Laguna Ojo de Liebre of Baja California to give birth to young. Unfortunately, Scammon and others exploited the discovery to an extent that almost

---

* Though all comparison in the way of general bulk between the whale and the elephant is preposterous, inasmuch as in that particular the elephant stands in much the same respect to the whale that a dog does to the elephant; nevertheless, there are not wanting some points of curious similitude; among these is the spout. It is well known that the elephant will often draw up water or dust in his trunk, and then elevating it, jet it forth in a stream.

extirpated the gray whale. The lagoon now is known throughout the whaling world as Scammon's Lagoon.

In his section of the *Marine Mammals* devoted to the history of the American whale fishery, Scammon tells of the lagoon discovery and the difficulties of whaling in the shallows:

> On the third day the gale abated, when the brig and her con-
> sort made the best of their way up to the head of the hitherto
> unexplored waters. Here the whales were found in great num-
> bers. On the next day the boats were sent in pursuit, and two
> large cows were captured without difficulty, which gave all
> hands confidence in our ultimate success. Early the next morning,
> the boats were again in eager pursuit; but before the animal was
> struck, it gave a dash with its flukes, staving the boat into frag-
> ments, and sending the crew in all directions. One man had his
> leg broken, another had an arm fractured, and three others were
> more or less injured—the officer of the boat being the only one
> who escaped unharmed. The relief boat, while rescuing the
> wounded men, was also staved by a passing whale, leaving only

THE BOWHEAD WHALE, drawn by Charles S. Scammon for his *Marine Mammals of the Northwestern Coast of
North America*, now is one of the rarest living whales. The
bowhead was a slow moving whale which floated when
killed and as a result was almost extirpated in the days when
whalers operated under sail and harpooned by hand from
hand-rowed boats.

one boat afloat. The tender being near at hand, however, a boat from that vessel rendered assistance, and all returned to the brig. When the first boat arrived with her freight of crippled passengers, it could only be compared to a floating ambulance crowded with men—the uninjured supporting the helpless. As soon as they reached the vessel, those who were maimed were placed on mattresses upon the quarter-deck, while others hobbled to their quarters in the forecastle. The next boat brought with it the remains of the two others, which were complete wrecks. Every attention was given to the wounded men, their broken limbs were set, cuts and bruises were carefully dressed, and all the injured were made as comfortable as our situation would permit; but the vessel, for several days, was a contracted and crowded hospital. During this time no whaling was attempted, as nearly half of the crew were unfit for duty, and a large portion of the rest were demoralized by fright. After several days of rest, however, two boat's crews were selected, and the pursuit was renewed. The men, on leaving the vessel, took to the oars apparently with as much spirit as ever; but on nearing a whale to be harpooned, they all jumped overboard, leaving no one in the boat, except the boat-header and the boat-steerer. On one occasion, a bulky deserter from the U.S. Army, who had boasted of his daring exploits in the Florida War, made a headlong plunge, as he supposed, into the water; but he landed on the flukes of the whale, fortunately receiving no injury, as the animal settled gently under water, thereby ridding itself of the human parasite.

It was useless to attempt whaling with men who were so completely panic-stricken; and the officers and boat-steerers combined could not muster the complement to man two boats. Our situation was both singular and trying. The vessel lay in perfect security in smooth water; and the objects of pursuit, which had been so anxiously sought, were now in countless numbers about us. It was readily to be seen that it was impossible to capture the whales in the usual manner with our present company, and no others could be obtained before the season would be over. Among the officers there were two who had been considered good shots with the bomb-lance gun, one of whom we personally knew to be unequaled as a marksman. There seemed to be but one way to successfully capture these sprightly animals, and that was by using the bomb-lance. The officers were called together, and the matter plainly set before them; the best marksmen were selected, and informed that if they could kill a whale without expending more than three bomb-lances, our supply was ample to insure a "full ship." They were then directed to place their boats on the side of the narrowest channel in the lagoon, near where the whales passed, but in shallow water, so that they could not possibly reach the boat, and there wait until one would come within gunshot. The idea was a novel one, and to old whalemen it seemed impracticable. Three boats were at once dispatched—two prepared for shooting, and the third as a relief boat in case of emergency. They took their positions as ordered, and it was not long before three whales had been "bombed"—the third one was killed instantly and secured. On returning to the vessel, the officers reported their good luck; and on the following day they were again dispatched, but with instructions to first board the tender, and take a look from her mast-head for the whales that had been bombed the day previous, as we confidently expected that either one, or both, would be found dead not far from where they were shot. It was a pleasant surprise to the chief officer, when, on going half-way up the tender's rigging, both whales were seen floating dead near the head of the lagoon; and no time was lost in securing them.

From that time, whaling was prosecuted without serious interruption.

Scammon was known as "the gentleman whaler," partly because he gave his crew Sunday off, but expected them to work twice as hard on Monday to make up the lost time. One should remember that the slaughter in Scammon's Lagoon was among the most wasteful forms of whaling. For each usable whale killed, two died, and one of the two dead, the calf, represented the future of the species. Scammon seems rather laconic in giving such details as the whale mother's desperate efforts to protect her calf. But whaling is not a vocation for the faint of heart.

From Scammon's species account of the gray whale, called in his day "California gray whale":

The California Gray Whale is only found in north latitudes, and its migrations have never been known to extend lower than 20 degrees north. It frequents the coast of California from November to May. During these months the cows enter the lagoons on the lower coast to bring forth their young, while the males remain outside along the sea-shore. The time of gestation is about one year. Occasionally a male is seen in the lagoons with the

cows at the last of the season, and soon after both male and female, with their young, will be seen working their way northward, following the shore so near that they often pass through
the kelp near the beach. It is seldom they are seen far out at sea.
This habit of resorting to shoal bays is one in which they differ
strikingly from other whales. In summer they congregate in the
Arctic Ocean and Okhotsk Sea. It has been said that this species
of whale has been found on the coast of China and about the
shores of the island of Formosa, but the report needs confirmation.

In October and November the California Grays appear off the
coast of Oregon and Upper California, on their way back to their
tropical haunts, making a quick, low spout at long intervals;
showing themselves but very little until they reach the smooth
lagoons of the lower coast, where, if not disturbed, they gather
in large numbers, passing and repassing into and out of the
estuaries, or slowly raising their colossal forms midway above
the surface, falling over on their sides as if by accident, and dashing the water into foam and spray about them. At times, in calm
weather, they are seen lying on the water quite motionless, keeping one position for an hour or more. At such times the sea-gulls
and cormorants frequently alight upon the huge beasts. The first
season in Scammon's Lagoon, coast of Lower California, the
boats were lowered several times for them, we thinking that the
animals when in that position were dead or sleeping, but before
the boats arrived within even shooting distance they were on the
move again.

About the shoals at the mouth of one of the lagoons, in 1860,
we saw large numbers of the monsters. It was at the low stage of
the tide, and the shoal places were plainly marked by the constantly foaming breakers. To our surprise we saw many of the
whales going through the surf where the depth of water was
barely sufficient to float them. We could discern in many places,
by the white sand that came to the surface, that they must be
near or touching the bottom. One in particular, lay for a half-
hour in the breakers, playing, as seals often do in a heavy surf;
turning from side to side with half-extended fins, and moved
apparently by the heavy ground-swell which was breaking; at
times making a playful spring with its bending flukes, throwing
its body clear of the water, coming down with a heavy splash,
then making two or three spouts, and again settling under water;
perhaps the next moment its head would appear, and with the

heavy swell the animal would roll over in a listless manner, to all appearance enjoying the sport intensely. We passed close to this sportive animal, and had only thirteen feet of water.

The habits of the Gray have brought upon it many significant names, among which the most prominent are, "Hard-head," "Mussel-digger," "Devil-fish," "Gray-back," and "Rip-sack." The first-mentioned misnomer arose from the fact of the animals having a great propensity to root the boats when coming in contact with them, in the same manner that hogs upset their empty troughs. Moreover, they are known to descend to soft bottoms in search of food, or for other purposes; and, when returning to the surface, they have been seen with head and lips besmeared with the dark ooze from the depths below; hence the name of "Mussel-digger." "Devil-fish" is significant of the danger incurred in the pursuit of the animal. "Gray-back" is indicative of its color, and "Rip-sack" originated with the manner of flensing.

As the season approaches for the whales to bring forth their young, which is from December to March, they formerly collected at the most remote extremities of the lagoons, and huddled together so thickly that it was difficult for a boat to cross the waters without coming in contact with them. Repeated instances have been known of their getting aground and lying for several hours in but two or three feet of water, without apparent injury from resting heavily on the sandy bottom, until the rising tide floated them. In the Bay of Monterey they have been seen rolling, with apparent delight, in the breakers along the beach.

In February, 1856, we found two whales aground in Magdalena Bay. Each had a calf playing about, there being sufficient depth for the young ones, while the mothers were lying hard on the bottom. When attacked, the smaller of the two old whales lay motionless, and the boat approached near enough to "set" the hand-lance into her "life," dispatching the animal at a single dart. The other, when approached, would raise her head and flukes above the water, supporting herself on a small portion of the belly, turning easily, and heading toward the boat, which made it very difficult to capture her. It appears to be their habit to get into the shallowest inland waters when their cubs are young. For this reason the whaling-ships anchor at a considerable distance from where the crews go to hunt the animals, and several vessels are often in the same lagoon.

The first streak of dawn is the signal for lowering the boats, all pulling for the head-waters, where the whales are expected to be found. As soon as one is seen, the officer who first discovers it sets a "waif" (a small flag) in his boat, and gives chase. Boats belonging to other vessels do not interfere, but go in search of other whales. When pursuing, great care is taken to keep behind, and a short distance from the animal, until it is driven to the extremity of the lagoon, or into shoal water; then the men in the nearest boats spring to their oars in the exciting race, and the animal, swimming so near the bottom, has its progress impeded, thereby giving its pursuers a decided advantage: although occasionally it will suddenly change its course, or "dodge," which frequently prolongs the chase for hours, the boats cutting through the water at their utmost speed. At other times, when the cub is young and weak, the movements of the mother are sympathetically suited to the necessities of her dependent offspring. It is rare that the dam will forsake her young one, when molested. When within "darting distance" (sixteen or eighteen feet), the boat-steerer darts the harpoons, and if the whale is struck it dashes about, lashing the water into foam, oftentimes staving the boats. As soon as the boat is fast, the officer goes into the head, and watches a favorable opportunity to shoot a bomb-lance. Should this enter a vital part and explode, it kills instantly, but it is not often this good luck occurs; more frequently two or three bombs are shot, which paralyze the animal to some extent, when the boat is hauled near enough to use the hand-lance. After repeated thrusts, the whale becomes sluggish in its motions; then, going "close to," the hand-lance is set into its "life," which completes the capture. The animal rolls over on its side, with fins extended, and dies without a struggle. Sometimes it will circle around within a small compass, or take a zigzag course, heaving its head and flukes above the water, and will either roll over, "fin out," or die under water and sink to the bottom.

Thus far we have spoken principally of the females, as they are found in the lagoons. Mention has been made, however, of that general habit, common to both male and female, of keeping near the shore in making the passage between their northern and southern feeding-grounds. This fact becoming known, and the bomb-gun coming into use, the mode of capture along the outer coast was changed. The whaling parties first stationed themselves in their boats at the most favorable points, where the thickest beds of kelp were found, and there lay in wait watching for a good chance to shoot the whales as they passed. This was called "kelp whaling."

The first year or two that this pursuit was practiced, many of the animals passed through or along the edge of the kelp, where the gunners chose their own distance for a shot. This method, however, soon excited the suspicions of these sagacious creatures. At first, the ordinary whale-boat was used, but the keen-eyed "Devil-fish" soon found what would be the consequence of getting too near the long, dark-looking object, as it lay nearly motionless, only rising and falling with the rolling swell. A very small boat—with one man to scull and another to shoot—was then used, instead of the whale-boat. This proved successful for a time, but, after a few successive seasons, the animals passed farther seaward, and at the present time the boats usually anchor outside the kelp. The mottled fish being seen approaching far enough off for the experienced gunner to judge nearly where the animal will "break water," the boat is sculled to that place, to await the "rising." If the whale "shows a good chance," it is frequently killed instantly, and sinks to the bottom, or receives its death-wound by the bursting of the bomb-lance. Consequently, the stationary position or slow movement of the animal enables the whaler to get a harpoon into it before sinking. To the harpoon a line is attached, with a buoy, which indicates the place where the dead creature lies, should it go to the bottom. Then, in the course of twenty-four hours, or in less time, it rises to the surface, and is towed to the shore, the blubber taken off and tried out in pots set for that purpose upon the beach.

Another mode of capture is by ships cruising off the land and sending their boats inshore toward the line of kelp; and, as the whales work to the southward, the boats, being provided with extra large sails, the whalemen take advantage of the strong northerly winds, and, running before the breeze, sail near enough to be able to dart the hand-harpoon into the fish. "Getting fast" in this way, it is killed in deep water, and, if inclined to sink, it can be held up by the boats till the ship comes up, when a large "fluke-rope" is made fast, or the "fin-chain" is secured to one fin, the "cutting-tackle" hooked, and the whale "cut in" immediately. This mode is calling "sailing them down." Still another way of catching them is with "Greener's Harpoon Gun," which is similar to a small swivel-gun. It is of one and a half inch bore, three feet long in the barrel, and, when stocked, weighs seventy-five pounds. The harpoon, four feet and a half long, is projected with considerable accuracy to any distance under eighty-four yards. The gun is mounted on the bow of the boat. A variety of manoeuvres are practiced when using the weapon: at times the boat lying at anchor, and, again, drifting about for a chance-shot. When the animal is judged to be ten fathoms off, the gun is pointed eighteen inches below the back; if fifteen fathoms, eight or ten inches below; if eighteen or twenty fathoms distant, the gun is sighted at the top of its back.

Still another strategic plan has been practiced with successful results, called "whaling along the breakers." Mention has been already made of the habit which these whales have of playing about the breakers at the mouths of the lagoons. This, the watchful eye of the whaler was quick to see, could be turned to his advantage.

After years of pursuit by waylaying them around the beds of kelp, the wary animals learned to shun these fatal regions, making a wide deviation in their course to enjoy their sports among the rollers at the lagoons' mouths, as they passed them either way. But the civilized whaler anchors his boats as near the roaring surf as safety will permit, and the unwary "Mussel-digger" that comes in reach of the deadly harpoon, or bomb-lance, is sure to pay the penalty with its life. If it come within darting distance, it is harpooned; and, as the stricken animal makes for the open sea, it is soon in deep water, where the pursuer makes his capture with comparative ease; or if passing within range of the bomb-gun, one of the explosive missiles is planted in its side, which so paralyzes the whale that the fresh boat's-crew, who have been resting at anchor, taking to their oars, soon overtake and dispatch it.

The casualties from coast and kelp whaling are nothing to be compared with the accidents that have been experienced by those engaged in taking the females in the lagoons. Hardly a day passes but there is upsetting or staving of boats, the crews receiving bruises, cuts, and, in many instances, having limbs broken; and repeated accidents have happened in which men have been instantly killed, or received mortal injury. The reasons of the increased dangers are these: the quick and deviating movements of the animal, its unusual sagacity, and the fact of the sandy bottom being continually stirred by the strong currents, making it difficult to see an object at any considerable depth. When a whale is "struck" at sea, there is generally but little difficulty in keeping clear. When first irritated by the harpoon, it attempts to escape by "running," or descending to the depths below, taking out more or less line, the direction of which, and the movements of the boat, indicate the animal's whereabouts. But in a lagoon, the object of pursuit is in narrow passages, where frequently there is a swift tide, and the turbid water prevents the whaler from seeing far beneath the boat. Should the chase be made with the current, the fugitive sometimes stops suddenly, and the speed of the boat, together with the influence of the running water, shoots it upon the worried animal when it is dashing its flukes in every direction. The whales that are chased have with them their young cubs, and the mother, in her efforts to avoid the pursuit of herself and offspring, may momentarily lose sight of her little one. Instantly she will stop and "sweep" around in search, and if the boat comes in contact with her, it is quite sure to be staved. Another danger is, that in darting the lance at the mother, the young one, in its gambols, will get in the way of the weapon, and receive the wound, instead of the intended victim. In such instances, the parent animal, in her frenzy, will chase the boats, and, overtaking them, will overturn them with her head, or dash them in pieces with a stroke of her ponderous flukes.

Sometimes the calf is fastened to instead of the cow. In such instances the mother may have been an old frequenter of the ground, and been before chased, and perhaps have suffered from a previous attack, so that she is far more difficult to capture, staving the boats and escaping after receiving repeated wounds. One instance occurred in Magdalena Lagoon, in 1857, where, after several boats had been staved, they being near the beach, the men in those remaining afloat managed to pick up their swimming comrades, and, in the meantime, to run the line to the shore, hauling the calf into as shallow water as would float the dam, she keeping near her troubled young one, giving the gunner a good chance for a shot with his bomb-gun from the beach. A similar instance occurred in Scammon's Lagoon, in 1859.

The testimony of many whaling-masters furnishes abundant proof that these whales are possessed of unusual sagacity. Numerous contests with them have proved that, after the loss of their cherished offspring, the enraged animals have given chase to the boats, which only found security by escaping to shoal water or to shore.

After evading the civilized whaler and his instruments of destruction, and perhaps while they are suffering from wounds received in their southern haunts, these migratory animals begin their northern journey. The mother, with her young grown to half the size of maturity, but wanting in strength, makes the best of her way along the shores, avoiding the rough sea by passing between or near the rocks and islets that stud the points and capes. But scarcely have the poor creatures quitted their southern homes before they are surprised by the Indians about the Strait of Juan de Fuca, Vancouver and Queen Charlotte's Islands. Like enemies in ambush, these glide in canoes from island, bluff, or bay, rushing upon their prey with whoop and yell, launching their instruments of torture, and like hounds worrying the last life-blood from their vitals. The capture having been effected, trains of canoes tow the prize to shore in triumph. The whale-men among the Indians of the North-west Coast are those who delight in the height of adventure, and who are ambitious of acquiring the greatest reputation among their fellows. Those among them who could boast of killing a whale, formerly had the most exalted mark of honor conferred upon them by a cut across the nose; but this custom is no longer observed.

Many of the marked habits of the California Gray are widely different from those of any other species of *balaena*. It makes regular migrations from the hot southern latitudes to beyond the Arctic Circle; and in its passages between the extremes of climate it follows the general trend of an irregular coast so near that it is exposed to attack from the savage tribes inhabiting the sea-shores, who pass much of their time in the canoe, and consider the capture of this singular wanderer a feat worthy of the highest distinction. As it approaches the waters of the torrid zone, it presents an opportunity to the civilized whalemen—at sea, along the shore, and in the lagoons—to practice their different modes of strategy, thus hastening the time of its entire annihilation. This species of whale manifests the greatest affection for its young, and seeks the sheltered estuaries lying under a tropical sun, as if to warm its offspring into activity and promote comfort, until grown to the size Nature demands for its first northern visit. When the parent animals are attacked, they show a power of resistance and tenacity of life that distinguish them from all other Cetaceans. Many an expert whaleman has suffered in his encounters with them, and many a one has paid the penalty with his life. Once captured, however, this whale yields the coveted reward to its enemies, furnishing sustenance for the Esquimaux whaler, from such parts as are of little value to others. The oil extracted from its fatty covering is exchanged with remote tribes for their fur-clad animals, of which the flesh affords the venders a feast of the choicest food, and the skins form an indispensable article of clothing. The North-west Indians realize the same comparative benefit from the captured animals as do the Esquimaux, and look forward to its periodical passage through their circumscribed fishing grounds as a season of exploits and profit.

The civilized whaler seeks the hunted animal farther sea-ward, as from year to year it learns to shun the fatal shore. None of the species are so constantly and variously pursued as the one we have endeavored to describe; and the large bays and lagoons, where these animals once congregated, brought forth and nurtured their young, are already nearly deserted. The mammoth bones of the California Gray lie bleaching on the shores of those silvery waters, and are scattered along the broken coasts, from Siberia to the Gulf of California; and ere long it may be questioned whether this mammal will not be numbered among the extinct species of the Pacific.

Scammon was quite right about the decline of the gray whale. No one knows in detail how low its numbers became before the animal received complete protection in 1947. Since then it has bounced back rather impressively. The current (1975) estimate of gray whale numbers in the eastern Pacific ranges from a pessimistic 6,000 to an optimistic 11,000 animals.

The recovery of the gray is rather unusual. Three other species, two right whales and the bowhead whale, were hunted almost to extirpation. Despite the fact that they now have complete protection, except from northern native hunters, and have not been a commercially important factor in a century, they still remain at depressed levels. Man knows so little about whales that a satisfactory explanation for the right and bowhead whales' failures does not exist.

Chapter XII

Nature's Great Thinker: Thoreau

On Tuesday of his *Week on the Concord and Merrimack Rivers*, Henry David Thoreau relates how he and his brother, John, shot a passenger pigeon "that had lingered too long upon its perch."

"It is true," Thoreau continued, "it did not seem to be putting this bird to its right use to pluck off its feathers, and extract its entrails, and broil its carcass on the coals; but we heroically persevered, nevertheless, waiting for further information."

The incident the Concord, Massachusetts, philosopher recorded happened in 1839. At the time, Thoreau was twenty-two years old and two years out of Harvard College. He was to die twenty-two years later at the age of forty-four. All those intervening years were spent, not "waiting for," but actively pursuing "further information."

The hot pursuit of information brought Thoreau to a view largely rejected not only in his own day but also by succeeding generations of Americans. It was a view that rubbed adversely against both theology and human vanity. It was best expressed in the opening paragraph of his essay entitled "Walking," his final work, which he completed with the aid of his sister, Sophia, and which appeared in the *Atlantic Monthly* in June 1862, one month after his death. He wrote:

> I wish to speak a word for Nature, for absolute freedom and wildness, as contrasted with a freedom and culture merely civil— to regard man as an inhabitant, or a part and parcel of Nature, rather than a member of society. I wish to make an extreme statement, an emphatic one, for there are enough champions of civilization: the minister, and the school committee, and every one of you will take care of that.

It is in Thoreau that one senses most clearly what has become known as "reverence for life." In looking through the winter ice, Thoreau sees not just a pickerel but a finny cousin. Exalted man has become just another living creature. Thoreau had no need of a Darwin. He stripped the veneer of civilization and returned the beast to its nakedness by instinct born of introspection. When the so-called postindustrial cult arrived sixteen decades later, the participants found in Thoreau a ready-made saint. He had covered the ground before them. He did it in a largely agricultural society that was suffering its first disruptions by the expansion of railroads in America.

It may surprise residents of the last quarter of the twentieth century to learn that for decades the question of whether Thoreau should be classified as a naturalist was in dispute. There were those who denied him membership in the cult. Others said that although he was a naturalist, he was a very poor one. Today the argument has been resolved largely in his favor. Both ornithologists and botanists working in the Concord area now view his contributions, made in his journal, as among the early observations of substance.

Except for occasional contributions to magazines, Thoreau published little during his lifetime. Most of what now are accepted as books written by him actually are compilations of notes from his journal, edited by others and published after the author's death. His serious natural history observations are strewn at random in the journal. Although most of the observations have validity, they are of uneven literary quality when amassed and published as a volume, a fate for which they were not intended.

The Thoreau classic is *Walden*. That he never exceeded it is not surprising. Too few writers have even approached it. The only other Thoreau volume that bears the author's final imprint, since it was the only other one that he followed to completion, is the report on the Concord and Merrimack rivers excursion.

The following sample of Thoreau's work, "A Winter Walk," was chosen because it is less readily available and because it is among the pieces attributed to him which he wrote, rather than a work compiled by another from a Thoreau journal. It also illustrates elements of Thoreau's insight into nature and the nature of man. The piece originally appeared in *Dial*, a literary magazine of Thoreau's era.

The wind has gently murmured through the blinds, or puffed with feathery softness against the windows, and occasionally sighed like a summer zephyr lifting the leaves along, the livelong night. The meadow mouse has slept in his snug gallery in the sod, the owl has sat in a hollow tree in the depth of the swamp, the rabbit, the squirrel, and the fox have all been housed. The watch-dog has lain quiet on the hearth, and the cattle have stood silent in their stalls. The earth itself has slept, as it were its first, not its last sleep, save when some street sign or woodhouse door has faintly creaked upon its hinge, cheering forlorn nature at her midnight work—the only sound awake 'twixt Venus and Mars—advertising us of a remote inward warmth, a divine cheer and fellowship, where gods are met together, but where it is very bleak for men to stand. But while the earth has slumbered, all the air has been alive with feathery flakes descending, as if some northern Ceres reigned, showering her silvery grain over all the fields.

We sleep, and at length awake to the still reality of a winter morning. The snow lies warm as cotton or down upon the window sill; the broadened sash and frosted panes admit a dim and private light, which enhances the snug cheer within. The stillness of the morning is impressive. The floor creaks under our feet as we move toward the window to look abroad through some clear space over the fields. We see the roofs stand under their snow burden. From the eaves and fences hang stalactites of snow, and in the yard stand stalagmites covering some concealed core. The trees and shrubs rear white arms to the sky on every side; and where were walls and fences, we see fantastic forms stretching in frolic gambols across the dusky landscape, as if Nature had strewn her fresh designs over the fields by night as models for man's art.

Silently we unlatch the door, letting the drift fall in, and step abroad to face the cutting air. Already the stars have lost some of their sparkle, and a dull, leaden mist skirts the horizon. A lurid brazen light in the east proclaims the approach of day, while the western landscape is dim and spectral still, and clothed in a somber Tartarean light, like the shadowy realms. They are Infernal sounds only that you hear—the crowing of cocks, the barking of dogs, the chopping of wood, the lowing of kine, all seem to come from Pluto's barnyard and beyond the Styx—not for any melancholy they suggest, but their twilight bustle is too solemn and mysterious for earth. The recent tracks of the fox or otter, in the yard, remind us that each hour of the night is crowded with events, and the primeval nature is still working and making tracks in the snow. Opening the gate, we tread briskly along the lone country road, crunching the dry and crisped snow under our feet, or aroused by the sharp, clear creak of the wood sled, just starting for the distant market, from the early farmer's door, where it has lain the summer long, dreaming amid the chips and stubble; while far through the drifts and powdered windows we see the farmer's early candle, like a paled star, emitting a lonely beam, as if some severe virtue were at its matins there. And one by one the smokes begin to ascend from the chimneys amid the trees and snows.

> The sluggish smoke curls up from some deep dell,
> The stiffened air exploring in the dawn,
> And making slow acquaintance with the day
> Delaying now upon its heavenward course,
> In wreathèd loiterings dallying with itself,
> With as uncertain purpose and slow deed
> As its half-awakened master by the hearth,
> Whose mind still slumbering and sluggish thoughts
> Have not yet swept into the onward current
> Of the new day—and now it streams afar,
> The while the chopper goes with step direct,
> And mind intent to swing the early axe.
> First in the dusky dawn he sends abroad
> His early scout, his emissary, smoke,
> The earliest, latest pilgrim from the roof,
> To feel the frosty air, inform the day;
> And while he crouches still beside the hearth,
> Nor musters courage to unbar the door,
> It has gone down the glen with the light wind,
> And o'er the plain unfurled its venturous wreath,
> Draped the treetops, loitered upon the hill,
> And warmed the pinions of the early bird;
> And now, perchance, high in the crispy air,
> Has caught sight of the day o'er the earth's edge,
> And greets its master's eye at his low door,
> As some refulgent cloud in the upper sky.

We hear the sound of woodchopping at the farmers' doors, far over the frozen earth, the baying of the housedog, and the distant clarion of the cock—though the thin and frosty air conveys only the finer particles of sound to our ears, with short and sweet vibrations, as the waves subside soonest on the purest and lightest liquids, in which gross substances sink to the bottom. They come clear and bell-like, and from a greater distance in the horizon, as if there were fewer impediments than in summer to make them faint and ragged. The ground is sonorous, like seasoned wood, and even the ordinary rural sounds are melodious, and the jingling of the ice on the trees is sweet and liquid. There is the least possible moisture in the atmosphere, all being dried up or congealed, and it is of such extreme tenuity and elasticity that it becomes a source of delight. The withdrawn and tense sky seems groined like the aisles of a cathedral, and the polished air sparkles as if there were crystals of ice floating in it. As they who have resided in Greenland tell us that when it freezes "the sea smokes like burning turf-land, and a fog or mist arises, called frost-smoke," which "cutting smoke frequently raises blisters on the face and hands, and is very pernicious to the health." But this pure, stinging cold is an elixir to the lungs, and not so much a frozen mist as a crystallized midsummer haze, refined and purified by cold.

The sun at length rises through the distant woods, as if with the faint clashing, swinging sound of cymbals, melting the air with his beams, and with such rapid steps the morning travels, that already his rays are gilding the distant western mountains. Meanwhile we step hastily along through the powdery snow, warmed by an inward heat, enjoying an Indian summer still, in the increased glow of thought and feeling. Probably if our lives were more conformed to nature, we should not need to defend ourselves against her heats and colds, but find her our constant nurse and friend, as do plants and quadrupeds. If our bodies were fed with pure and simple elements, and not with a stimulating and heating diet, they would afford no more pasture for cold than a leafless twig, but thrive like the trees, which find even winter genial to their expansion.

The wonderful purity of nature at this season is a most pleasing fact. Every decayed stump and moss-grown stone and rail, and the dead leaves of autumn, are concealed by a clean napkin of snow. In the bare fields and tinkling woods, see what virtue survives. In the coldest and bleakest places, the warmest charities still maintain a foothold. A cold and searching wind drives away all contagion, and nothing can withstand it but what has a virtue in it, and accordingly, whatever we meet with in cold and bleak places, as the tops of mountains, we respect for a sort of sturdy innocence, a Puritan toughness. All things beside seem to be called in for shelter, and what stays out must be part of the original frame of the universe, and of such valor as God himself. It is invigorating to breathe the cleansed air. Its greater fineness and purity are visible to the eye, and we would fain stay out long and late, that the gales may sigh through us, too, as through the leafless trees, and fit us for the winter—as if we hoped so to bor-

PLATE LXVII

CANIS LUPUS, LINN. (VAR. ATER.)
BLACK AMERICAN WOLF.

THE BLACK AMERICAN WOLF was painted by John James Audubon for *The Viviparous Quadrupeds of North America*. Time and more taxonomic experience have merged this animal with the gray wolf.

PUTORIUS FRENATA, LINN.
BRIDLED WEASEL

THE BRIDLED WEASEL of Audubon and Bachman, as
shown on Plate 60 of *The Viviparous Quadrupeds of North
America,* now has been "lumped," along with Bachman's
white weasel, little nimble weasel, and little American brown
weasel, into the single species known as the long-tailed
weasel. Called *Putorius frenata* on the plate, the animal now
is known as *Mustela frenata.* It is a member of the same
species that, among northern members, each winter turns
into a white weasel that furnishes the fur for ermine coats.

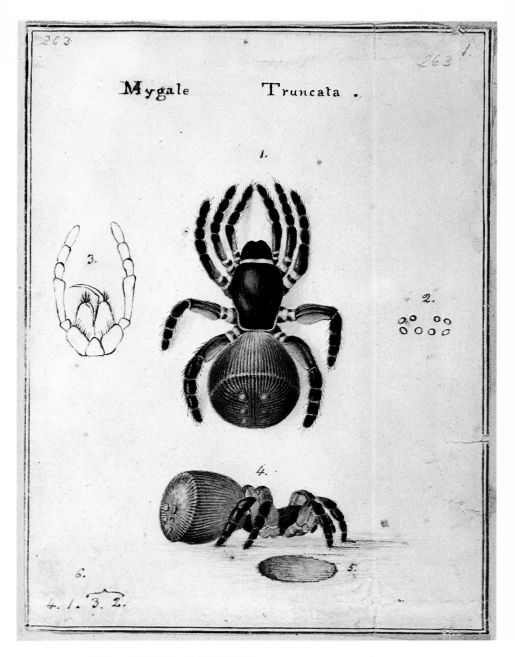

DOLOMEDES ALBINEUS is an ashy-gray southern water spider painted by Nicholas Marcellus Hentz, the first American arachnidologist of note. *Albineus* spends much time perched head-downward on a tree trunk, prepared to dive into the water.

THE BLANDING'S TURTLE was introduced to science
on Plate 3, Volume I, of John Edwards Holbrook's *North
American Herpetology*, published in 1842. Holbrook named
the turtle *Cistuda Blandingii* and in his text commented that
it "was first observed by Dr. William Blanding of Philadelphia, an accurate naturalist, whose name I have given to
the species." Later taxonomists changed the turtle's name to
Emys blandingii.

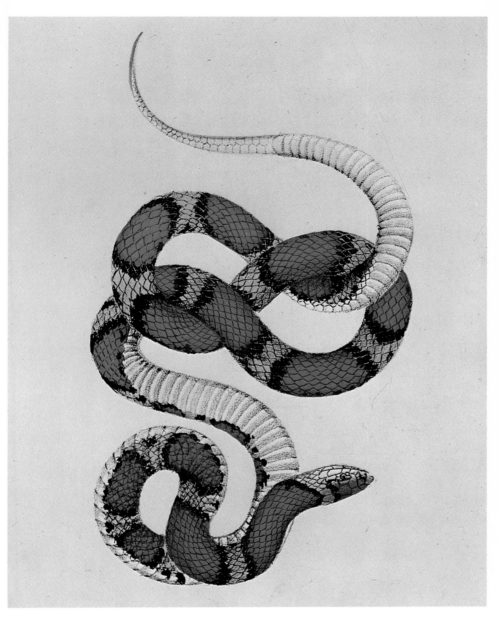

THE SCARLET SNAKE, which slightly resembles the
scarlet kingsnake, was named *Rhinostoma coccinea* in Holbrook's *North American Herpetology* where it appears on
Plate XXX of Volume III. The reptile now bears the scientific name *Cemophora coccinea*. Holbrook pointed out, as
do modern authorities, that an identifying characteristic is
that "the whole abdomen is silver white." The mark distinguishes it from snakes of similar pattern whose rings extend around the body.

THE HORNED TOAD which posed for Plate XI, Volume
II, of Holbrook's *North American Herpetology* was brought
to Holbrook "by Mr. Gregg from the neighborhood of
Santa Fe, near the confines of the United States . . ." which
was a fair geographical description before the Mexican
War.

THE RUFFED GROUSE in a coniferous forest is an example of bird art by Louis Agassiz Fuertes. It differs from his more familiar work in that it was executed for a New England patron and was never intended for reproduction. Among other things, it has a detailed background and gives hints of the protective coloration which fits birds and other animals to their environment.

THE PEREGRINE FALCON, identified under the older name of duck hawk, appears on Plate 43, Volume II of *Birds of Massachusetts and the Other New England States* by Edward Howe Forbush. Considered by many the finest bird portrait ever done, it is an excellent example of an illustration by Louis Agassiz Fuertes.

row some pure and steadfast virtue, which will stead us in all seasons.

There is a slumbering subterranean fire in nature which never goes out, and which no cold can chill. It finally melts the great snow, and in January or July is only buried under a thicker or thinner covering. In the coldest day it flows somewhere, and the snow melts around every tree. This field of winter rye, which sprouted late in the fall, and now speedily dissolves the snow, is where the fire is very thinly covered. We feel warmed by it. In the winter, warmth stands for all virtue, and we resort in thought to a trickling rill, with its bare stones shining in the sun, and to warm springs in the woods, with as much eagerness as rabbits and robins. The steam which rises from swamps and pools is as dear and domestic as that of our own kettle. What fire could ever equal the sunshine of a winter's day, when the meadow mice come out by the wall-sides, and the chickadee lisps in the defiles of the wood? The warmth comes directly from the sun, and is not radiated from the earth, as in summer; and when we feel his beams on our backs as we are treading some snowy dell, we are grateful as for a special kindness, and bless the sun which has followed us into that by-place.

This subterranean fire has its altar in each man's breast; for in the coldest day, and on the bleakest hill, the traveler cherishes a warmer fire within the folds of his cloak than is kindled on any hearth. A healthy man, indeed, is the complement of the seasons, and in winter, summer is in his heart. There is the south. Thither have all birds and insects migrated, and around the warm springs in his breast are gathered the robin and the lark.

At length, having reached the edge of the woods, and shut out the gadding town, we enter within their covert as we go under the roof of a cottage, and cross its threshold, all ceiled and banked up with snow. They are glad and warm still, and as genial and cheery in winter as in summer. As we stand in the midst of the pines in the flickering and checkered light which straggles but little way into their maze, we wonder if the towns have ever heard their simple story. It seems to us that no traveler has ever explored them, and notwithstanding the wonders which science is elsewhere revealing every day, who would not like to hear their annals? Our humble villages in the plain are their contribution. We borrow from the forest the boards which shelter and the sticks which warm us. How important is their evergreen to the winter, that portion of the summer which does not fade, the permanent year, the unwithered grass! Thus simply, and with little expense of altitude, is the surface of the earth diversified. What would human life be without forests, those natural cities? From the tops of mountains they appear like smooth-shaven lawns, yet whither shall we walk but in this taller grass?

In this glade covered with bushes of a year's growth, see how the silvery dust lies on every seared leaf and twig, deposited in such infinite and luxurious forms as by their very variety atone for the absence of color. Observe the tiny tracks of mice around every stem, and the triangular tracks of the rabbit. A pure elastic heaven hangs over all, as if the impurities of the summer sky, refined and shrunk by the chaste winter's cold, had been winnowed from the heavens upon the earth.

Nature confounds her summer distinctions at this season. The heavens seem to be nearer the earth. The elements are less reserved and distinct. Water turns to ice, rain to snow. The day is but a Scandinavian night. The winter is an arctic summer.

How much more living is the life that is in nature, the furred life which still survives the stinging nights, and, from amidst fields and woods covered with frost and snow, sees the sun rise!

> The foodless wilds
> Pour forth their brown inhabitants.

The gray squirrel and rabbit are brisk and playful in the remote glens, even on the morning of the cold Friday. Here is our Lapland and Labrador, and for our Esquimaux and Knistenaux, Dog-ribbed Indians, Novazemblaites, and Spitzbergeners, are there not the ice-cutter and woodchopper, the fox, muskrat, and mink?

Still, in the midst of the arctic day, we may trace the summer to its retreats, and sympathize with some contemporary life. Stretched over the brooks, in the midst of the frost-bound meadows, we may observe the submarine cottages of the caddisworms, the larvae of the Plicipennes; their small cylindrical cases built around themselves, composed of flags, sticks, grass, and withered leaves, shells, and pebbles, in form and color like the wrecks which strew the bottom,—now drifting along over the pebbly bottom, now whirling in tiny eddies and dashing down steep falls, or sweeping rapidly along with the current, or else swaying to and fro at the end of some grass-blade or root. Anon they will leave their sunken habitations, and, crawling up the stems of plants, or to the surface, like gnats, as perfect insects henceforth, flutter over the surface of the water, or sacrifice their short lives in the flame of our candles at evening. Down yonder little glen the shrubs are drooping under their burden, and the red alderberries contrast with the white ground. Here are the marks of a myriad feet which have already been abroad. The sun rises as proudly over such a glen as over the valley of the Seine or the Tiber, and it seems the residence of a pure and self-subsistent valor, such as they never witnessed—which never knew defeat nor fear. Here reign the simplicity and purity of a primitive age, and a health and hope far remote from towns and cities. Standing quite alone, far in the forest, while the wind is shaking down snow from the trees, and leaving the only human tracks behind us, we find our reflections of a richer variety than the life of cities. The chickadee and nuthatch are more inspiring society than statesmen and philosophers, and we shall return to these last as to more vulgar companions. In this lonely glen, with its brook draining the slopes, its creased ice and crystals of all hues, where the spruces and hemlocks stand up on either side, and the rush and sere wild oats in the rivulet itself, our lives are more serene and worthy to contemplate.

As the day advances, the heat of the sun is reflected by the hillsides, and we hear a faint but sweet music, where flows the rill released from its fetters, and the icicles are melting on the trees; and the nuthatch and partridge are heard and seen. The south wind melts the snow at noon, and the bare ground appears with its withered grass and leaves, and we are invigorated by the perfume which exhales from it, as by the scent of strong meats.

Let us go into this deserted woodman's hut, and see how he has passed the long winter nights and the short and stormy days. For here man has lived under this south hillside, and it seems a civilized and public spot. We have such associations as when the traveler stands by the ruins of Palmyra or Hecatompolis. Singing birds and flowers perchance have begun to appear here, for flowers as well as weeds follow in the footsteps of man. These hemlocks whispered over his head, these hickory logs were his fuel, and these pitch pine roots kindled his fire; yonder fuming rill in the hollow, whose thin and airy vapor still ascends as busily as ever, though he is far off now, was his well. These hemlock boughs, and the straw upon this raised platform, were his bed, and this broken dish held his drink. But he has not been here this season, for the phoebes built their nest upon this shelf last summer. I find some embers left as if he had but just gone out, where he baked his pot of beans; and while at evening he smoked his pipe, whose stemless bowl lies in the ashes, chatted with his only companion, if perchance he had any, about the depth of the snow on the morrow, already falling fast and thick without, or disputed whether the last sound was the screech of an owl, or the creak of a bough, or imagination only; and through his broad chimney-throat, in the late winter evening, ere he stretched himself upon the straw, he looked up to learn the progress of the storm, and, seeing the bright stars of Cassiopeia's Chair shining brightly down upon him, fell contentedly asleep.

See how many traces from which we may learn the chopper's history! From this stump we may guess the sharpness of his axe, and from the slope of the stroke, on which side he stood, and whether he cut down the tree without going round it or changing hands; and, from the flexure of the splinters, we may know which way it fell. This one chip contains inscribed on it the whole history of the woodchopper and of the world. On this scrap of paper, which held his sugar or salt, perchance, or was the wadding of his gun, sitting on a log in the forest, with what interest we read the tattle of cities, of those larger huts, empty and to let, like this, in High Streets and Broadways. The eaves are dripping on the south side of this simple roof, while the titmouse lisps in the pine and the genial warmth of the sun around the door is somewhat kind and human.

After two seasons, this rude dwelling does not deform the scene. Already the birds resort to it, to build their nests, and you may track to its door the feet of many quadrupeds. Thus, for a long time, nature overlooks the encroachment and profanity of man. The wood still cheerfully and unsuspiciously echoes the strokes of the axe that fells it, and while they are few and seldom, they enchance its wildness, and all the elements strive to naturalize the sound.

Now our path begins to ascend gradually to the top of this high hill, from whose precipitous south side we can look over the broad country of forest and field and river, to the distant snowy mountains. See yonder thin column of smoke curling up through the woods from some invisible farmhouse, the standard raised over some rural homestead. There must be a warmer and more genial spot there below, as where we detect the vapor from a spring forming a cloud above the trees. What fine relations are established between the traveler who discovers this airy column from some eminence in the forest and him who sits below! Up goes the smoke as silently and naturally as the vapor exhales from the leaves, and as busy disposing itself in wreaths as the housewife on the hearth below. It is a hieroglyphic of man's life, and suggests more intimate and important things than the boiling of a pot. Where its fine column rises above the forest, like an ensign, some human life has planted itself—and such is the beginning of Rome, the establishment of the arts, and the foundation of empires, whether on the prairies of America or the steppes of Asia.

And now we descend again, to the brink of this woodland lake, which lies in a hollow of the hills, as if it were their expressed juice, and that of the leaves which are annually steeped in it. Without outlet or inlet to the eye, it has still its history, in the lapse of its waves, in the rounded pebbles on its shore, and in the pines which grow down to its brink. It has not been idle, though sedentary, but, like Abu Musa, teaches that "sitting still at home is the heavenly way; the going out is the way of the world." Yet in its evaporation it travels as far as any. In summer it is the earth's liquid eye, a mirror in the breast of nature. The sins of the wood are washed out in it. See how the woods form an amphitheater about it, and it is an arena for all the genialness of nature. All trees direct the traveler to its brink, all paths seek it out, birds fly to it, quadrupeds flee to it, and the very ground inclines toward it. It is nature's saloon, where she has sat down to her toilet. Consider her silent economy and tidiness; how the sun comes with his evaporation to sweep the dust from its surface each morning, and a fresh surface is constantly welling up; and annually, after whatever impurities have accumulated herein, its liquid transparency appears again in the spring. In summer a hushed music seems to sweep across its surface. But now a plain sheet of snow conceals it from our eyes, except where the wind has swept the ice bare, and the sere leaves are gliding from side to side, tacking and veering on their tiny voyages. Here is one just keeled up against a pebble on shore, a dry beech leaf, rocking still; as if it would start again. A skillful engineer, methinks, might project its course since it fell from the parent stem. Here are all the elements for such a calculation. Its present position, the direction of the wind, the level of the pond, and how much more is given. In its scarred edges and veins is its log rolled up.

We fancy ourselves in the interior of a larger house. The surface of the pond is our deal table or sanded floor, and the woods rise abruptly from its edge, like the walls of a cottage. The lines set to catch pickerel through the ice look like a larger culinary preparation, and the men stand about on the white ground like pieces of forest furniture. The actions of these men, at the distance of half a mile over the ice and snow, impress us as when we read the exploits of Alexander in history. They seem not unworthy of the scenery, and as momentous as the conquest of kingdoms.

Again we have wandered through the arches of the wood, until from its skirts we hear the distant booming of ice from yonder bay of the river, as if it were moved by some other and subtler tide than oceans know. To me it has a strange sound of home, thrilling as the voice of one's distant and noble kindred. A mild summer sun shines over forest and lake, and though there is but one green leaf for many rods, yet nature enjoys a serene health. Every sound is fraught with the same mysterious assurance of health, as well now the creaking of the boughs in January, as the soft sough of the wind in July.

> When Winter fringes every bough
>   With his fantastic wreath,
> And puts the seal of silence now
>   Upon the leaves beneath;
>
> When every stream in its penthouse
>   Goes gurgling on its way,
> And in his gallery the mouse
>   Nibbleth the meadow hay;
>
> Methinks the summer still is nigh,
>   And lurketh underneath,
> And that same meadow mouse doth lie
>   Snug in that last year's heath.
>
> And if perchance the chickadee
>   Lisp a faint note anon,
> The snow is summer's canopy,
>   Which she herself put on.
>
> Fair blossoms deck the cheerful trees,
>   And dazzling fruits depend;
> The north wind sighs a summer breeze,
>   The nipping frosts to fend,

Bringing glad tidings unto me,
  The while I stand all ear,
Of a serene eternity,
  Which need not winter fear.

Out on the silent pond straightway
  The restless ice doth crack,
And pond sprites merry gambols play
  Amid the deafening rack.

Eager I hasten to the vale,
  As if I heard brave news,
How nature held high festival,
  Which it were hard to lose.

I gambol with my neighbor ice,
  And sympathizing quake,
As each new crack darts in a trice
  Across the gladsome lake.

One with the cricket in the ground,
  And fagot on the hearth,
Resounds the rare domestic sound
  Along the forest path.

Before night we will take a journey on skates along the course of this meandering river, as full of novelty to one who sits by the cottage fire all the winter's day as if it were over the polar ice, with Captain Parry or Franklin; following the winding of the stream, now flowing amid hills, now spreading out into fair meadows, and forming a myriad coves and bays where the pine and hemlock overarch. The river flows in the rear of the towns, and we see all things from a new and wilder side. The fields and gardens come down to it with a frankness, and freedom from pretension, which they do not wear on the highway. It is the outside and edge of the earth. Our eyes are not offended by violent contrasts. The last rail of the farmer's fence is some swaying willow bough, which still preserves its freshness, and here at length all fences stop, and we no longer cross any road. We may go far up within the country now by the most retired and level road, never climbing a hill, but by broad levels ascending to the upland meadows. It is a beautiful illustration of the law of obedience, the flow of a river; the path for a sick man, a highway down which an acorn cup may float secure with its freight. Its slight occasional falls, whose precipices would not diversify the landscape, are celebrated by mist and spray, and attract the traveler from far and near. From the remote interior, its current conducts him by broad and easy steps, or by one gentler inclined plane, to the sea. Thus by an early and constant yielding to the inequalities of the ground it secures itself the easiest passage.

No domain of nature is quite closed to man at all times, and now we draw near to the empire of the fishes. Our feet glide swiftly over unfathomed depths, where in summer our line tempted the pout and perch, and where the stately pickerel lurked in the long corridors formed by the bulrushes. The deep, impenetrable marsh, where the heron waded and bittern squatted, is made pervious to our swift shoes, as if a thousand railroads had been made into it. With one impulse we are carried to the cabin of the muskrat, that earliest settler, and see him dart away under the transparent ice, like a furred fish, to his hole in the bank; and we glide rapidly over meadows where lately "the mower whet his scythe," through beds of frozen cranberries mixed with meadowgrass. We skate near to where the blackbird, the pewee, and the kingbird hung their nests over the water, and the hornets builded from the maple in the swamp. How many gay warblers, following the sun, have radiated from this nest of silver birch and thistledown! On the swamp's outer edge was hung the supermarine village, where no foot penetrated. In this hollow tree the wood duck reared her brood, and slid away each day to forage in yonder fen.

In winter, nature is a cabinet of curiosities, full of dried specimens, in their natural order and position. The meadows and forest are a *hortus siccus*. The leaves and grasses stand perfectly pressed by the air without screw or gum, and the birds' nests are not hung on an artificial twig, but where they builded them. We go about dryshod to inspect the summer's work in the rank swamp, and see what a growth have got the alders, the willows, and the maples; testifying to how many warm suns, and fertilizing dews and showers. See what strides their boughs took in the luxuriant summer—and anon these dormant buds will carry them onward and upward another span into the heavens.

Occasionally we wade through fields of snow, under whose depths the river is lost for many rods, to appear again to the right or left, where we least expected; still holding on its way underneath, with a faint, stertorous, rumbling sound, as if, like the bear and marmot, it too had hibernated, and we had followed its faint summer trail to where it earthed itself in snow and ice.

At first we should have thought that rivers would be empty and dry in midwinter, or else frozen solid till the spring thawed them; but their volume is not diminished even, for only a superficial cold bridges their surfaces. The thousand springs which feed the lakes and streams are flowing still. The issues of a few surface springs only are closed, and they go to swell the deep reservoirs. Nature's wells are below the frost. The summer brooks are not filled with snow-water, nor does the mower quench his thirst with that alone. The streams are swollen when the snow melts in the spring, because nature's work has been delayed, the water being turned into ice and snow, whose particles are less smooth and round, and do not find their level so soon.

Far over the ice, between the hemlock woods and snow-clad hills, stands the pickerel-fisher, his lines set in some retired cove, like a Finlander, with his arms thrust into the pouches of his dreadnaught; with dull, snowy, fishy thoughts, himself a finless fish, separated a few inches from his race; dumb, erect, and made to be enveloped in clouds and snows, like the pines on shore. In these wild scenes, men stand about in the scenery, or move deliberately and heavily, having sacrificed the sprightliness and vivacity of towns to the dumb sobriety of nature. He does not make the scenery less wild, more than the jays and muskrats, but stands there as a part of it, as the natives are represented in the voyages of early navigators, at Nootka Sound, and on the Northwest coast, with their furs about them, before they were tempted to loquacity by a scrap of iron. He belongs to the natural family of man, and is planted deeper in nature and has more root than the inhabitants of towns. Go to him, ask what luck, and you will learn that he too is a worshiper of the unseen. Hear with what sincere deference and waving gesture in his tone he speaks of the lake pickerel, which he has never seen, his primitive and ideal race of pickerel. He is connected with the shore still, as by a fish-line, and yet remembers the season when he took fish through the ice on the pond, while the peas were up in his garden at home.

But now, while we have loitered, the clouds have gathered again, and a few straggling snowflakes are beginning to descend. Faster and faster they fall, shutting out the distant objects from sight. The snow falls on every wood and field, and no crevice is forgotten; by the river and the pond, on the hill and in the valley. Quadrupeds are confined to their coverts and the birds sit upon their perches this peaceful hour. There is not so much sound as in fair weather, but silently and gradually every slope, and the gray walls and fences, and the polished ice, and the sere leaves, which were not buried before, are concealed, and the tracks of men and beasts are lost. With so little effort does nature reassert her rule and blot out the traces of men. Hear how Homer has described the same: "The snowflakes fall thick and fast on a winter's day. The winds are lulled, and the snow falls incessant, covering the tops of the mountains, and the hills, and the plains where the lotus tree grows, and the cultivated fields, and they are falling by the inlets and shores of the foaming sea, but are silently dissolved by the waves." The snow levels all things, and infolds them deeper in the bosom of nature, as, in the slow summer, vegetation creeps up to the entablature of the temple, and the turrets of the castle, and helps her to prevail over art.

The surly night wind rustles through the wood, and warns us to retrace our steps, while the sun goes down behind the thickening storm, and birds seek their roosts, and cattle their stalls.

> Drooping the lab'rer ox
> Stands covered o'er with snow, and *now* demands
> The fruit of all his toil.

Though winter is represented in the almanac as an old man, facing the wind and sleet, and drawing his cloak about him, we rather think of him as a merry woodchopper, and warm-blooded youth, as blithe as summer. The unexplored grandeur of the storm keeps up the spirits of the traveler. It does not trifle with us, but has a sweet earnestness. In winter we lead a more inward life. Our hearts are warm and cheery, like cottages under drifts, whose windows and doors are half concealed, but from whose chimneys the smoke cheerfully ascends. The imprisoning drifts increase the sense of comfort which the house affords, and in the coldest days we are content to sit over the hearth and see the sky through the chimney-top, enjoying the quiet and serene life that may be had in a warm corner by the chimney-side, or feeling our pulse by listening to the low of cattle in the street, or the sound of the flail in distant barns all the long afternoon. No doubt a skillful physician could determine our health by observing how these simple and natural sounds affected us. We enjoy now, not an Oriental, but a Boreal leisure, around warm stoves and fireplaces, and watch the shadow of motes in the sunbeams.

Sometimes our fate grows too homely and familiarly serious ever to be cruel. Consider how for three months the human destiny is wrapped in furs. The good Hebrew Revelation takes no cognizance of all this cheerful snow. Is there no religion for the temperate and frigid zones? We know of no scripture which records the pure benignity of the gods on a New England winter night. Their praises have never been sung, only their wrath deprecated. The best scripture, after all, records but a meager faith. Its saints live reserved and austere. Let a brave, devout man spend the year in the woods of Maine or Labrador, and see if the Hebrew Scriptures speak adequately to his condition and experience, from the setting in of winter to the breaking up of the ice.

Now commences the long winter evening around the farmer's hearth, when the thoughts of the indwellers travel far abroad, and men are by nature and necessity charitable and liberal to all creatures. Now is the happy resistance to cold, when the farmer reaps his reward, and thinks of his preparedness for winter, and, through the glittering panes, sees with equanimity "the mansion of the northern bear," for now the storm is over,

> The full ethereal round,
> 　Infinite worlds disclosing to the view,
> Shines out intensely keen; and all one cope
> 　Of starry glitter glows from pole to pole.

Chapter XIII

Darwin's Debate in America: Agassiz and Gray

When Darwin's theory of evolution emerged in 1859, it was opposed by the most eloquent spokesman for science in America and championed by a Harvard professor who dreaded speaking to such an extent that he even had difficulty lecturing to students.

The opponent was Swiss-born, German-educated Dr. Jean Louis Rodolphe Agassiz, the living symbol of science in the United States. When New England industrialists captured Agassiz for Harvard University while the Swiss professor was visiting the United States in 1846, the news was greeted with an excitement now reserved for the signing of a multifigured contract by a sports figure. Educated at Lausanne, Zurich, Heidelberg, and Munich, an associate of the famed Humboldt and a research student under Baron Cuvier, Dr. Agassiz was considered an outstanding scientist throughout Europe. Americans seldom had seen his academic equal even as a visitor. He was famed as a zoologist, the author of several remarkable books on living and fossil fishes, and was the man who developed fully the idea that glaciers had covered parts of the earth.

In the United States, Dr. Agassiz became the leading administrator of science. He founded the famed Museum of Comparative Zoology at Harvard, raising the then unbelievably large sum of money in a matter of months. He moved in social circles that included not only the wealthy of Boston but also such intellectual leaders as Oliver Wendell Holmes, Henry Wadsworth Longfellow, James Russell Lowell, and Ralph Waldo Emerson. The corpulent professor, who was an incessant cigar smoker, had all the right connections. When he needed a vessel for biological exploration, the U.S. Coastal Survey or the U.S. Navy always was ready to provide it. Even the common people revered him. When he delivered his lecture on "The Plan of Creation in the Animal Kingdom" at the Tremont Temple in Boston, 5,000 persons vied for seats. He was not a man to be trifled with. He had organized in the United States a so-called Scientific Lazzaroni

LOUIS AGASSIZ (1807–1883), Swiss-born, German-educated naturalist, was the social lion of American natural history from the day of his arrival in the United States in 1846. He became professor of zoology and geology at Harvard and founded there the famed Museum of Comparative Zoology. Although his work with fossils furnished impressive evidence of evolution, Agassiz was the most outspoken opponent of Darwin's theory in North America.

dedicated to waging war on old fogyism, charlatanism, and quackery. It functioned, however, to exclude from scientific consideration anyone who did not agree with Agassiz.

At the first meeting of the American Association for Advancement of Science in Philadelphia, in September 1848, Agassiz not only dominated all sessions but also delivered twelve lectures in the fields of geology, ichthyology, and botany.

In the same period, quiet Dr. Asa Gray, Harvard botanist, was having difficulty raising enough money to replace the broken pickets in the fence around Harvard's botanical garden. That he prevailed over Agassiz was a tribute both to the soundness of Darwin's work and to his own standing among American scientists.

Agassiz and Gray were among a rather small group in America who understood fully the implications of Darwin's *Origin of Species.*

The tempest that quickly embroiled Darwin in England, where he developed and announced the theory, occurred much later in the United States. The theory was debated on a rather high plane in Cambridge, where it was of interest principally to scientists. The initial exchanges between Agassiz and Gray were in terms not readily understood by the few intellectuals and literary persons privileged to attend. Diary entries by several auditors indicated that they either completely misunderstood what the scientists discussed or thought that the discussion "had something to do with Lamarck." The firebrands who could have brought the debate to a boiling point were busy leading their fellow citizens into a civil war. It was the year in which John Brown led a raid that seized the federal arsenal and armory at Harpers Ferry, Virginia, an act that Brown hoped would spark an insurrection of slaves in the South. The issues of slavery and federal allegiance, which were tearing the nation apart, took precedence over the esoteric

ASA GRAY (1810–1888) elevated American botany into a science. Trained as a physician, he became affiliated with the great John Torrey, the preeminent field botanist of the era. Darwin personally chose Gray to champion his theory of natural selection in the United States. In the Agassiz-Gray debates on evolution, Gray, working at great odds against the public figure of Agassiz as the greatest American naturalist, convinced American scientists of the worth of Darwin's theory.

idea that many animals and plants had changed since Noah's Ark grounded.

The theory that Darwin announced July 1, 1858, through the reading of a brief paper before the Linnaean Society of London stirred rabid reactions in England largely because it struck at a basic tenet of Western religion: that man was a special creation made in the image of God. It was debated so fiercely along this line that even today many persons suppose that Darwin's major hypothesis rested upon the idea that man descended from monkeys.

The title of the paper, however, if not more illuminating, is clearly more descriptive of Darwin's theory. He called it "On the tendency of species to form varieties; and on the perpetuation of varieties and species by natural means of selection." The treatise was published under that title in the Linnaean Society's *Journal of Proceedings,* August 20, 1858. In this initial effort to explain thoughts he had harbored more than twenty years, Darwin appeared as joint author with Alfred Russel Wallace, a young naturalist working in the Malay Archipelago, who had in that year sent Darwin a letter in which he outlined an evolutionary theory that surprisingly corresponded to Darwin's own conclusions. The actual publication of Darwin's complete explanation of his theory, *Origin of Species,* occurred on November 24, 1859. The first printing of this book which was to shake the scientific world consisted of only 1,250 copies. One of the copies was mailed by Darwin to Asa Gray. That copy, with Gray's meticulous handwritten notes on the margins and end papers, is now in the Gray Herbarium at Harvard.

Darwin was not the first naturalist to suggest that evolution had occurred among plants and animals. The French naturalist known as Lamarck some sixty years earlier had proclaimed that existing life forms had evolved through the geologic ages through modification. But Lamarck had failed to develop a logical cause that might explain the modifications. He assumed that species arose to take advantage of environmental opportunities; for instance, that the giraffe's neck had grown long because generations of giraffes had stretched their necks browsing treetops and that this acquired characteristic had been inherited by their offspring. While Lamarck attracted considerable attention, many naturalists before him had noted similarities between existing species which suggested a common ancestry.

The new element that Darwin injected was "natural selection." The mechanism through which speciation occurred, he said, was the selective pressures that nature exerts. In accordance with Darwin's theory, the giraffe has a long neck because in past ages an occasional giraffe had a longer-than-normal neck. The long neck gave the animal the advantage of browsing higher into trees than its fellow giraffes. As a result, it thrived, bred with other giraffes, and passed on through breeding the advantages it had enjoyed. As a result of their success in obtaining food, giraffes with long necks became the successful models and established a long-neck trend among the animals.

The Darwin theory supposes that there are mutations or changes that occur in any animal or plant population. Since the species is already successful in nature, most of these modifications are handicaps and nature eliminates them. When a modification occurs that has survival and breeding value to the individual, this inheritance is passed on to descendants.

Thus, instead of there being a constant type form among plants and animals, there is a fluidity that tends to modify existing species even in those cases where a species does not break into two species. In the modern understanding of the theory, when an advantageous modification arises in a population, the animals or plants that inherit the advantage tend to displace their less successful relatives until the whole species drifts toward the more successful form. Separation into two species occurs when some physical barrier splits the range of a species and the successful modification occurs on only one side of the barrier. Ancient forms which have existed through geological ages are creatures so excellently adapted to a way of life that no modification has proved advantageous to the species.

The best-known illustration of Darwin's theory involves the so-called Darwin's finches, a group of birds that Darwin noted on the Galápagos Islands, a 200-square-mile archipelago lying 600 miles west of the coast of Ecuador in the Pacific Ocean. In 1825, as a twenty-six-year-old naturalist on H.M.S. *Beagle*, Darwin spent five weeks on the Galápagos. Many people consider that period the most productive five weeks in the history of biology.

While on the Galápagos, Darwin noticed that there were thirteen species of dingy little sparrows, or finches, which were quite similar in most details but lived different life-styles. In addition, the Galápagos finches, while being different, were similar to a finch species that he had seen on the South American mainland. The question of why God might have gone to the trouble to create thirteen different species for an area as small as the Galápagos, and never again used the same model anywhere else in the world, troubled Darwin for three years. He finally concluded that a flock of mainland finches must have reached the Galápagos and through the ages undergone modification into thirteen new species. The finches are a classic example of evolution, because they not only illustrate the physical separation brought about by mainland birds invading an island that is far enough from the mainland to discourage further chance invasions but also provide an illustration of a second evolution mechanism: ecological separation within a species inhabiting the same territory. Apparently when the finches arrived, there were no other land birds to compete with them. Thus, there were many available food sources that finches do not exploit. Over the years, mutations occurred among the finches which made it possible for modified birds to exploit additional food sources. These modified birds, since they were not competing with the original finch type for traditional finch foods, were able to thrive and did not displace the type form. Darwin found among the thirteen finches an array of birds that existed in diverse food niches. They ranged from traditional seed-eating finches to birds that were using thorns to pry insects from bark as woodpeckers do with their bills, and even finches that had modified toward hummingbird tendencies, with the frayed tongues of nectar-eaters, which enabled them to gain a living from flowers.

To understand the departure that Darwin's theory made from traditional concepts of species, one needs to know the prevailing attitude up to the acceptance of his theory. Linnaeus had organized his system of species as a series of mental pigeonholes into which one might catalog the new types of plants and animals then being discovered by a worldwide surge of exploration. He had established order so that one might retrieve a specimen and determine the obvious extent to which something new might differ from something already known. While the system involved the grouping together of creatures that were similar in outward appearance, the arrangement did not suppose that there was a relationship between similar but different species. The general concept was that God had created each species independently and that their descendants carried on the original characteristics as though they had been cast from the original mold. When a variation, which is a slightly different individual but still recognizable as a member of a species, occurred, it was assumed that a slight accident had happened in the molding and that the deviation was not transmittable. The legend of God's creative week as outlined in Genesis was accepted without question, although some preferred an emphasis upon Noah's rescue of prevailing species.

The one problem that Darwin could not overcome was the general lack of knowledge by all biologists of the era regarding genetic inheritance and genetic variability. Although Darwin was certain that what he had observed proved his theory, he could not supply any evidence that there was any physiological attribute within a creature which could cause it to vary from the norm. Indeed, he knew none of the rules of inheritance, and the empiric rules that existed among biologists were against his theory. Direct observation tended to confirm the old proverb that like begets like.

The cautious Professor Gray, who preferred scientific proof to philosophical speculation, was acutely aware of Darwin's deficiency in the matter of internal mechanisms that might cause modifications. It troubled him greatly. But, as he often pointed out in Darwin's defense, neither did scientists have any idea of the mechanism that produced succeeding generations that looked alike.

Unknown to both Darwin and his supporters, an Austrian monk named Gregor Johann Mendel, who kept a garden at an Augustinian monastery in Brno, had learned at least part of the secret of inheritance. Mendel had crossed varieties of garden peas. He carried out thousands of experiments. What he learned is a basic law of heredity. He discovered that in cross-breeding there is a contribution of genes by the two parents, and among genes there are dominant and recessive genes. He demonstrated that a cross between a pea that has red blossoms and a pea that has white blossoms does not result in pink blossoms. Instead, all peas resulting from the cross will have red blossoms. The reason is that red is the dominant gene in such crosses. However, each pea from the combination inherits one dominant red gene and one recessive white gene. If one interbreeds the all-red hybrids, the next generation consists of three plants with red blossoms to one plant with white blossoms. Mendel tested seven characteristics of peas and found that the formula works in every case. The first generation looks like one parent. In the second generation, three-quarters of the peas resemble their parents but the other quarter revert to the grandparent whose contribution was not evident in the intervening generation. The formula usually is expressed in capital letters for dominant genes and lower case for recessives. For instance, the two genes that control color in red peas become AA, since they are dominant. The two genes controlling color in white peas are aa, since they are recessive. In a cross, each pea contributes one letter to make up the two-letter genetic component of their progeny. Thus, each pea in the first generation has the genetic composition of Aa. Under such circumstances, the A, which is red, prevails over a, which is white. However, if one makes random crosses of Aa peas, probability dictates the following distributions: AA, Aa, and aA, all of which will be red since A predominates. However, there should be one chance in four of the combination aa occurring, and that pea will be white.

Mendel published his experimental results in an obscure journal in 1866 and achieved instant oblivion. No one saw the significance of the discovery. Mendel had been dead sixteen years when biologists rediscovered his work in 1900.

Although the basic components of Darwin's hypothesis are accepted today by most workers in biology, the theory itself remains as unprovable as Professor Agassiz recognized it to be. Although there are many indications that Darwin was correct, and although his hypothesis seems more valid than the many creation legends, the time element, involving geological eras, defies human longevity, and so the missing link still is missing.

A major contribution to biology that arose from the questions that Darwin posed has been a clearer definition of what constitutes a species. Darwin's arguments had thrown the whole species concept into disarray. No longer could one answer that a species was a type created by God and should not be questioned. Time has shown that the old concept was not viable under any circumstances. Although it required almost a century to reach the agreement, the general consensus today is that a species is a breeding population of plants or animals. The line of demarcation falls upon any barrier that prevents a reasonable genetic exchange. As a result, the concept of species has ceased being a theory and become an actuality. And, as reality often does, it has produced unusual consequences. For instance, under the older rule of separating birds that do not have nearly identical appearances, the blue goose and the snow goose were classified as different species. Ornithologists now know that blue and snow geese interbreed and that indeed the blue goose is no more than a color form of the snow goose. So the two quite different appearing geese now are recognized as a single species. Meanwhile, among the flycatchers once known as Traill's flycatcher, there occur two identical populations, inseparable by any rules of visual inspection. However, the two populations sing quite different songs and breed in very different environments. They do not interbreed. So, although they cannot be told apart by appearance, the two populations have been divided into alder flycatchers and willow flycatchers.

In this age in which academic degrees account for so much, Asa Gray's preparation for the burden of establishing Darwin's theory among American scientists seems slender. Gray was a poor boy from upstate New York. His family's circumstances were such that it was unable to finance a college education and instead sent him to medical school. In the autumn of 1826, Gray enrolled in the College of Physicians and Surgeons of the Western District of New York, an institution more familiarly known as Fairfield Medical School, because it was in Fairfield, New York. The course consisted of sixteen weeks of lectures. The student then was expected to apprentice himself to a practicing physician and serve three years. The student then, or at a later date, returned for the same sixteen weeks of lectures and received a diploma. Gray received his on January 25, 1831.

If Fairfield Medical School sounds like a diploma mill, it is only because one may be unfamiliar with early American medical practice. Many American physicians in that era practiced without having attended any formal course of instruction. Stricter qualifications for medical men have largely arisen within the last century. When Charles W. Eliot became president of Harvard in 1869, the first professional school that attracted his attention was Harvard Medical School, which turned out physicians in one year and operated largely independently of Harvard College. In fact, it has often been said that until the 1890s the best health care in America was enjoyed by those too poor to visit a physician.

The insubstantial nature of Gray's academic credentials was not as great a handicap as one might suppose. Although Gray did not realize it, he had been chosen by Darwin himself as North American spokesman for evolution by natural selection. Gray was perhaps the first American botanist whom European scientists considered a peer. He had developed the field of plant geography and was among the first scientists to appreciate the relationship of North American plants with the plants of the world. The famous English botanist Joseph Hooker had called Darwin's attention to Gray. Darwin and his friends had recognized Agassiz as a potential threat to the Darwinian theory and were searching for a competent scientist to defend the theory in America. Darwin began his testing of Gray in April 1855. He wrote him a letter seeking information on plant distribution. The exchange of correspondence continued on that plane into 1857. At that time, Darwin wrote Gray a capsule of his views on evolution. Darwin urged that the matter remain confidential.

Gray had become a professor at Harvard in 1842 and organized the college's botany department. He had achieved eminence in botany through an apprenticeship with Dr. John Torrey, who preceded Gray in the role of physician-turned-botanist. At the time Gray began collaborating with him on a flora of North America, Torrey unquestionably was the outstanding botanist of the United States. Torrey was a student of the famed teacher Amos Eaton, but he soon surpassed Eaton, who remained faithful until death to the botanical rules of Linnaeus. Torrey became the first American botanist to adopt what was then known as the "natural system" in botany. In many ways, the natural system prepared the way for Darwin's theory, for it recognized the prevailing natural relationships among plants. In 1826, Torrey published an account of Dr. Edwin James's plant collection, made on Major Long's expedition to the Rocky Mountains in 1820. The account is a landmark in American botany, for it was the first paper done by an American in which all plants were classified in accordance with natural order. Although Torrey served as a professor at West Point, the College of Physicians and Surgeons in New York (now Columbia), and the College of New Jersey (now Princeton), he taught only chemistry. His experience indicates the general disregard of botany in America, even by leading institutions. Torrey did the classifications for most of the great expeditions into the American West, including the Pacific Railroad and the Mexican Boundary reports. Torrey was so highly regarded by fellow botanists that genus *Torreya*, a rare relative of the yews, was named in his honor. Even Rafinesque attempted to name a genus in Torrey's honor. But, unfortunately, that erratic naturalist had goofed again, this time by an incorrect dismemberment of genus *Cypreus*.

Gray surpassed Torrey through progression beyond the excellent base that their association produced, the usual course by which a truly brilliant student improves upon the fund of knowledge he has received. It was this growth, this continued mental acuity in the search for knowledge, that set Gray apart from Agassiz and enabled him to triumph at least among their scientific colleagues.

Despite his sterling credentials, Agassiz had paid a grim price for his great social and financial success in America. He was too busy erecting buildings, administering science, and maintaining social contacts to devote more than superficial attention to research. This became evident in 1857, when the first volume of Agassiz's *Contributions to the Natural History of the United States* rolled off the press. The promotion that had preceded publication of *Contributions* had been unparalleled in natural history. Agassiz maintained a nationwide network of correspondents whom he kept busy running errands and collecting specimens. It was one of those operations in which the ordinary citizen found himself a companion in research to the world's greatest scientist. It was enormously effective in making a tough word like Agassiz a common household term. Although it undoubtedly did some good, especially for the correspondents, it had a strong flavor of public relations, a contrivance of which Madison Avenue might be proud. The word went out over the network that Agassiz soon would favor his adopted land with *Contributions*, which was to be a compendium of knowledge the likes of which a scientifically deprived nation never had seen.

When Gray read the first volume of *Contributions*, he ceased worrying about the coming and inevitable confrontation over Darwin's theory. He knew that he had Agassiz at bay, at least among scientific colleagues whose opinions both could respect. For *Contributions* disclosed that Agassiz had remained fundamentally unchanged since leaving Munich. At Munich, Agassiz had been drilled in a Germanic philosophy usually identified as *Naturphilosophie*. He embraced it fully, and his mental processes through the remainder of life were tainted by it. As with all complex philosophical systems, it embodied more, but simplification characterizes it as a statement that the Creator placed a firm pattern upon the world and the role of an investigator examining evidence is to determine what God had in mind. Agassiz's now famous essay on classification, which appeared in volume 1, was riddled with *Naturphilosophie* and proved him an incurable captive of the system.

That modern apostle of evolution, Dr. Ernst Mayr, director emeritus of the very institution that Agassiz founded, the Museum of Comparative Zoology, has said of Agassiz, "He was a victim of the thoroughness of his education."

A now famous line of Agassiz's which appeared in volume 1 illustrates his basic attitude toward creation, evolution, and natural history. He wrote: "Natural history must, in good time, become the analysis of the thoughts of the Creator of the Universe, as manifested in the animal and vegetable kingdoms."

Actually in his work in glaciation and with fossils, Agassiz had amassed an enormous fund of information that supported Darwin's theory. Many of Agassiz's views coincided with evolutionary theory, or at least were not divergent from it. He wrote in volume 1:

Is there an investigator, who having recognized such a similarity between certain faculties of Man and those of the higher animals, can feel prepared in the present stage of our knowledge to trace the limit where this natural community ceases? And yet to ascertain the characters of all these faculties there is but one road, the study of the habits of animals and a comparison between them and the earlier stages of development of Man. I confess I could not say in what the mental faculties of a child differ from those of a young Chimpanzee.

It is interesting that in the American debate, Gray was the orthodox Christian and Agassiz, while godly, was the iconoclast. Agassiz believed firmly in Baron Cuvier's theory of cataclysms. He maintained that the biological slate had been wiped clean by cataclysms many times and that each time the Creator had created a new population of animals. He supposed that these re-creations had been accomplished on different time scales in each zoological region and that the races of man furnished an excellent example of these independent creations. This was readily seized upon by slavery enthusiasts in the South as proof that white and black races bore no direct relationships. He limited the creation story in Genesis as having no application beyond the Jewish nation. Other peoples, he said, had a different origin and history.

Gray was adroit at pointing out that Darwin's theory of direct descent from a single creation fit the Biblical record more neatly than Agassiz's beliefs.

Since evolution was understood in the era as the process through which an egg was transformed into a creature, the term was not used by Darwin nor employed in the Gray-Agassiz debates. The common term used for what we now call "evolution" was "transmutation." Since Darwin's theory has so infiltrated our thinking, it may be difficult for the modern reader to appreciate the finer points that the debaters stressed. Much of it perhaps makes sense only to those who can recapture the major themes of biology as they existed in 1859.

One must remember that neither Gray nor Agassiz had been exposed to the modern idea that each parent provides one-half of the genetic information that goes into an embryo. Or that these two pieces of information must fuse correctly to reproduce a typical organism. It is a lottery in which the chances of mutation are high. But neither man knew the secret of how like produces like, nor why at times an imprecise copy resulted.

The written word provides the best record of the two scientists' attitudes. Their auditors at oral debates often incorrectly interpreted their remarks. Gray fired the first written volley. It was the lead article in the *American Journal of Science and Arts* for March 1860; it ran to thirty-three pages of rather small type and was entitled "Review of Darwin's Theory on the Origin of Species by Means of Natural Selection." The following are excerpts.

Who, upon a single perusal, shall pass judgment upon a work like this, to which twenty of the best years of the life of a most able naturalist have been devoted? And who among those naturalists who hold a position that entitles them to pronounce summarily upon the subject, can be expected to divest himself for the nonce of the influence of received and favorite systems? In fact, the controversy now opened is not likely to be settled in an off-hand way, nor is it desirable that it should be. A spirited conflict among opinions of every grade must ensue, which,—to borrow an illustration from the doctrine of the book before us— may be likened to the conflict in nature among races in the struggle for life, which Mr. Darwin describes; through which the views most favored by facts will be developed and tested by "Natural Selection," the weaker ones be destroyed in the process, and the strongest in the long run alone survive. . . .

The ordinary and generally received view assumes the independent, specific creation of each kind of plant and animal in a primitive stock, which reproduces its like from generation to generation, and so continues the species. Taking the idea of species from this perennial succession of essentially similar individuals, the chain is logically traceable back to a local origin in a single stock, a single pair, or a single individual, from which all the individuals composing the species have proceeded by natural generation. Although the similarity of progeny to parent is fundamental in the conception of species, yet the likeness is by no means absolute: all species vary more or less, and some vary remarkably—partly from the influence of altered circumstances, and partly (and more really) from unknown constitutional causes which altered conditions favor rather than originate. But these variations are supposed to be mere oscillations from a normal state, and in Nature to be limited if not transitory; so that the primordial differences between species and species at their beginning have not been effaced, nor largely obscured, by blending through variation. Consequently, whenever two reputed species are found to blend in nature through a series of intermediate forms, community of origin is inferred, and all the forms, however diverse, are held to belong to one species. Moreover, since bisexuality is the rule in nature (which is practically carried out, in the long run, far more generally than has been suspected), and the heritable qualities of two distinct individuals are mingled in the offspring, it is supposed that the general sterility of hybrid progeny, interposes an effectual barrier against the blending of the original species by crossing.

From this generally accepted view the well-known theory of Agassiz and the recent one of Darwin diverge in exactly opposite directions.

That of Agassiz differs fundamentally from the ordinary view only in this, that it discards the idea of a common descent as the real bond of union among the individuals of a species, and also the idea of a local origin,—supposing, instead, that each species originated simultaneously, generally speaking over the whole geographical area it now occupies or has occupied, and in perhaps as many individuals as it numbered at any subsequent period.

Mr. Darwin, on the other hand, holds the orthodox view of the descent of all the individuals of a species not only from a local birth-place, but from a single ancestor or pair; and that each species has extended and established itself, through natural agencies, wherever it could; so that the actual geographical distribution of any species is by no means a primordial arrangement, but a natural result. He goes farther, and this volume is a protracted argument intended to prove that the species we recognize have not been independently created, as such, but have descended, like varieties, from other species. Varieties, on this view, are incipient or possible species: species are varieties of a larger growth and a wider and earlier divergence from the parent stock: the difference is one of degree, not of kind.

The ordinary view—rendering unto Caesar the things that are Caesar's—looks to natural agencies for the actual distribution and perpetuation of species, to a supernatural for their origin.

The theory of Agassiz regards the origin of species and their present general distribution over the world as equally primordial, equally supernatural; that of Darwin, as equally derivative, equally natural.

The theory of Agassiz, referring as it does the phenomena both of origin and distribution directly to the Divine will,—thus removing the latter with the former out of the domain of inductive science (in which efficient cause is not the first, but the last word),—may be said to be theistic to excess. The contrasted theory is not open to this objection. Studying the facts and phenomena in reference to proximate causes, and endeavoring to trace back the series of cause and effect as far as possible, Darwin's aim and processes are strictly scientific, and his endeavor, whether successful or futile, must be regarded as a legitimate attempt to extend the domain of natural or physical science. For though it well may be that "organic forms have no physical or secondary cause," yet this can be proved only indirectly, by the failure of every attempt to refer the phenomena in question to causal laws. But, however originated, and whatever be thought of Mr. Darwin's arduous undertaking in this respect, it is certain that plants and animals are subject from their birth to physical influences, to which they have to accommodate themselves as they can. How literally they are "born to trouble," and how incessant and severe the struggle for life generally is, the present volume graphically describes. Few will deny that such influences must have gravely affected the range and the association of individuals and species on the earth's surface. Mr. Darwin thinks that, acting upon an inherent predisposition to vary, they have sufficed even to modify the species themselves and produce the present diversity. Mr. Agassiz believes that they have not even affected the geographical range and the actual association of species, still less their forms; but that every adaptation of species to climate and of species to species is as aboriginal, and therefore as inexplicable, as are the organic forms themselves. . . .

The actual causes of variation are unknown. Mr. Darwin favors the opinion of the late Mr. Knight, the great philosopher of horticulture, that variability under domestication is somehow connected with excess of food. He also regards the unknown cause as acting chiefly upon the reproductive system of the parents, which system, judging from the effect of confinement or cultivation upon its functions, he concludes to be more susceptible than any other to the action of changed conditions of life. The tendency to vary certainly appears to be much stronger under domestication than in free nature. But we are not sure that the greater variableness of cultivated races is not mainly owing to the far greater opportunities for manifestation and accumulation —a view seemingly all the more favorable to Mr. Darwin's theory. The actual amount of certain changes, such as size or abundance of fruit, size of udder, stands of course in obvious relation to supply of food.

Really, we no more know the reason why the progeny occasionally deviates from the parent than we do why it usually resembles it. Though the laws and conditions governing variation are known to a certain extent, those governing inheritance are apparently inscrutable. "Perhaps," Darwin remarks, "the correct way of viewing the whole subject would be, to look at the inheritance of every character whatever as the rule, and noninheritance as the anomaly." This, from general and obvious considerations, we have long been accustomed to do. Now, as exceptional instances are expected to be capable of explanation, while ultimate laws are not, it is quite possible that variation may be accounted for, while the great primary law of inheritance remains a mysterious fact. . . .

It is not surprising that the doctrine of the book should be denounced as atheistical. What does surprise and concern us is, that it should be so denounced by a scientific man, on the broad assumption that a material connection between the members of a series of organized beings is inconsistent with the idea of their being intellectually connected with one another through the Deity, i.e., as products of one mind, as indicating and realizing a preconceived plan. An assumption the rebound of which is somewhat fearful to contemplate, but fortunately one which every natural birth protests against. . . .

We wished under the light of such views, to examine more critically the doctrine of this book, especially of some questionable parts;—for instance, its explanation of the natural development of organs, and its implication of a "necessary acquirement of mental power" in the ascending scale of gradation. But there is room only for the general declaration that we cannot think the Cosmos a series which began with chaos and ends with mind, or of which mind is a result: that if by the successive origination of species and organs through natural agencies, the author means a series of events which succeed each other irrespective of a continued directing intelligence,—events which mind does not order and shape to destined ends,—then he has not established that doctrine, nor advanced towards its establishment, but has accumulated improbabilities beyond all belief. Take the formation and the origination of the successive degrees of complexity of eyes as a specimen. The treatment of this subject, upon one interpretation is open to all the objections referred to; but if, on the other hand, we may rightly compare the eye "to a telescope, perfected by the long continued efforts of the highest human intellects," we could carry out the analogy, and draw satisfactory illustrations and inferences from it. The essential, the directly intellectual thing is the making of the improvements in the telescope or the steam-engine. Whether the successive improvements, being small at each step, and consistent with the general type of the instrument, are applied to some of the individual machines, or entire new machines are constructed for each, is a minor matter. Though if machines could engender, the adaptive method would be most economical; and economy is said to be a paramount law in nature. The origination of the improvements, and the successive adaptations to meet new conditions or subserve other ends, are what answer to the supernatural, and therefore remain inexplicable. As to bringing them into use, though wisdom foresees the result, the circumstances and the natural competition will take care of that, in the long run. The old ones will go out of use fast enough, except where an old and simple machine remains still best adapted to a particular purpose or condition,—as, for instance, the old Newcomen engine for pumping out coal-pits. If there's a Divinity that shapes these ends, the whole is intelligible and reasonable; otherwise, not.

We regret that the necessity of discussing philosophical questions has prevented a fuller examination of the theory itself, and of the interesting scientific points which are brought to bear in its favor. One of its neatest points, certainly a very strong one for the local origination of species, and their gradual diffusion under natural agencies, we must reserve for some other convenient opportunity.

The work is a scientific one, rigidly restricted to its direct object; and by its science it must stand or fall. Its aim is, probably not to deny creative intervention in nature,—for the admission of the independent origination of certain types does away with all antecedent improbability of as much intervention as may be required,—but to maintain that Natural Selection in explaining the facts, explains also many classes of facts which thousand-fold repeated independent acts of creation do not explain, but leave more mysterious than ever. How far the author has succeeded, the scientific world will in due time be able to pronounce. . . .

Agassiz's reply was a halfhearted rehash of his speciation theories that appeared in volume 1 of *Contributions*. It was later to be included in the introduction of volume 3, but it first appeared in the *American Journal of Science and Arts* dated July 1860. It required thirteen pages of small type. These are excerpts:

Darwin in his recent work on the "Origin of a Species," has also done much to shake the belief in the real existence of species, but the views he advocates are entirely at variance with those I have attempted to establish. For many years past I have lost no opportunity of urging the idea that while species have no material existence, they yet exist as categories of thought, in the same ways as genera, families, orders, classes, and branches of the animal kingdom. Darwin's fundamental idea, on the contrary, is that species, genera, families, orders, classes, and any other kind of more or less comprehensive divisions among animals do not exist at all, and are altogether artificial, differing from one another only in degree, all having originated from a successive differentiation of a primordial organic form, undergoing successively such changes as would at first produce a variety of species; then genera, as the difference became more extensive and deeper; then families, as the gap widened still farther between the groups, until in the end all that diversity was produced which has existed or exists now. Far from agreeing with these views, I have, on the contrary, taken the ground that all the natural divisions in the animal kingdom are primarily distinct, founded upon different categories of characters, and that all exist in the same way, that is, as categories of thought, embodied in individual living forms. I have attempted to show that branches in the animal kingdom are founded upon different plans of structure, and for that very reason have embraced from the beginning representatives between which there could be no community of origin. . . .

Had Mr. Darwin or his followers furnished a single fact to show that individuals change, in the course of time, in such a manner as to produce at last species different from those known before, the state of the case might be different. But it stands recorded now as before, that the animals known to the ancients are still in existence, exhibiting to this day the characters they exhibited of old. The geological record, even with all its imperfections, exaggerated to distortion, tells now, what it has told from the beginning, that the supposed intermediate forms between the species of different geological periods are imaginary beings, called up merely in support of a fanciful theory. The origin of all the diversity among living beings remains a mystery as totally unexplained as if the book of Mr. Darwin had never been written, for no theory unsupported by fact, however plausible it may appear, can be admitted in science.

It seems generally admitted that the work of Darwin is particularly remarkable for the fairness with which he presents the facts adverse to his views. It may be so; but I confess that it has made a very different impression upon me. I have been more forcibly struck by his inability to perceive when the facts are fatal to his argument, than by anything else in the whole work. His chapter on the Geological Record, in particular, appears to me, from beginning to end, as a series of illogical deductions and misrepresentations of the modern results of Geology and Palaeontology. I do not intend to argue here, one by one, the questions

he has discussed. Such arguments end too often in special plead-
ing, and any one familiar with the subject may readily perceive
where the truth lies by confronting his assertions with the geological record itself. But since the question at issue is chiefly to
be settled by palaeontological evidence, and I have devoted the
greater part of my life to the special study of the fossils, I wish
to record my protest against his mode of treating this part of the
subject. Not only does Darwin never perceive when the facts are
fatal to his views, but when he has succeeded by an ingenious
circumlocution in overleaping the facts, he would have us believe
that he has lessened their importance or changed their meaning.
He would thus have us believe that there have been periods during which all that had taken place during other periods was destroyed, and this solely to explain the absence of intermediate
forms between the fossils found in successive deposits, for the
origin of which he looks to those missing links; whilst every
recent progress in Geology shows more and more fully how
gradual and successive all the deposits have been which form the
crust of our earth.—He would have us believe that entire faunae
have disappeared before those were preserved, the remains of
which are found in the lowest fossiliferous strata; when we find
everywhere non-fossiliferous strata below those that contain the
oldest fossils now known. It is true, he explains their absence by
the supposition that they were too delicate to be preserved; but
any animals from which Crinoids, Brachiopods, Cephalopods,
and Trilobites could arise, must have been sufficiently similar to
them to have left, at least, traces of their presence in the lowest
non-fossiliferous rocks, had they ever existed at all.—He would
have us believe that the oldest organisms that existed were simple
cells, or something like the lowest living beings now in existence;
when such highly organized animals as Trilobites and Ortho-
ceratites are among the oldest known.—He would have us believe that these lowest first-born became extinct in consequence
of the gradual advantage some of their more favored descendants
gained over the majority of their predecessors; when there exist
now, and have existed at all periods in past history, as large a
proportion of more simply organized beings, as of more favored
types, and when such types as Lingula were among the lowest
Silurian fossils, and are alive at the present day.—He would have
us believe that each new species originated in consequence of
some slight change in those that preceded; when every geological
formation teems with types that did not exist before.—He would

have us believe that animals and plants became gradually more and more numerous; when most species appear in myriads of individuals, in the first bed in which they are found. He would have us believe that animals disappear gradually; when they are as common in the uppermost bed in which they occur as in the lowest, or any intermediate bed. Species appear suddenly and disappear suddenly in successive strata. That is the fact proclaimed by Palaeontology; they neither increase successively in number, nor do they gradually dwindle down; none of the fossil remains thus far observed show signs of a gradual improvement or of a slow decay.—He would have us believe that geological deposits took place during the periods of subsidence; when it can be proved that the whole continent of North America is formed of beds which were deposited during a series of successive upheavals. I quote North America in preference to any other part of the world, because the evidence is so complete here that it can only be overlooked by those who may mistake subsidence for the general shrinkage of the earth's surface in consequence of the cooling of its mass. In this part of the globe, fossils are as common along the successive shores of the rising deposits of the Silurian system, as anywhere along our beaches; and each of these successive shores extends from the Atlantic States to the foot of the Rocky Mountains. The evidence goes even further; each of these successive sets of beds of the Silurian system contains peculiar fossils, neither found in the beds above nor in the beds below, and between them there are no intermediate forms. And yet Darwin affirms that "the littoral and sub-littoral deposits are continually worn away, as soon as they are brought up by the slow and gradual rising of the land within the grinding action of the coast waves." Origin of Species, p. 290.—He would also have us believe that the most perfect organs of the body of animals are the product of gradual improvement, when eyes as perfect as those of the Trilobites are preserved with the remains of these oldest animals.—He would have us believe that it required millions of years to effect any one of these changes; when far more extraordinary transformations are daily going on, under our eyes, in the shortest periods of time, during the growth of animals.—He would have us believe that animals acquire their instincts gradually; when even those that never see their parents, perform at birth the same acts, in the same way, as their progenitors.—He would have us believe that the geographical distribution of animals is the result of accidental transfers; when most species are so narrowly confined within the limits of their natural range, that even slight changes in their external relations may cause their death. And all these, and many other calls upon our credulity, are coolly made in the face of an amount of precise information, readily accessible, which would overwhelm any one who does not place his opinions above the records of an age eminently characterized for its industry, and during which, that information was laboriously accumulated by crowds of faithful laborers.

It would be superfluous to discuss in detail the arguments by which Mr. Darwin attempts to explain the diversity among animals. Suffice it to say, that he has lost sight of the most striking of the features, and the one which pervades the whole, namely, that there runs throughout Nature unmistakable evidence of thought, corresponding to the mental operations of our own mind, and therefore intelligible to us as thinking beings, and unaccountable on any other basis than that they owe their existence to the working of intelligence; and no theory that overlooks this element can be true to nature. . . .

The fallacy of Mr. Darwin's theory of the origin of species by means of natural selection, may be traced in the first few pages of his book, where he overlooks the difference between the voluntary and deliberate acts of selection applied methodically by man to the breeding of domesticated animals and the growing of cultivated plants, and the chance influences which may effect animals and plants in the state of nature. To call these influences "natural selection," is a misnomer which will not alter the conditions under which they may produce the desired results. Selection implies design; the powers to which Darwin refers the order of species, can design nothing. . . .

Were the transmutation theory true, the geological record should exhibit an uninterrupted succession of types blending gradually into one another. The fact is that throughout all geological times each period is characterized by definite specific types, belonging to definite genera, and these to definite families, referable to definite orders, constituting definite classes and definite branches, built upon definite plans. Until the facts of Nature are shown to have been mistaken by those who have collected them, and that they have a different meaning from that now generally assigned to them, I shall therefore consider the transmutation theory as a scientific mistake, untrue in its facts, unscientific in its method, and mischievous in its tendency.

To the day of his death fourteen years later, Agassiz maintained that Darwin's theory was ridiculous. By that time, however, the issue had been resolved within the scientific community in Darwin's favor, and even Agassiz's students had deserted to Darwinism. Ironically, Agassiz lost face primarily among his scientific colleagues. With the public, and especially with the wealthy of Boston, Agassiz was an idol to the end.

Chapter XIV

Meticulous Reptile Sorter: Holbrook

Dr. John Edwards Holbrook specialized in that segment of natural history which even many naturalists refer to as "the creepy crawlies," that poorly defined collection that Linnaeus referred to as Class Amphibia, which served as a catchall for the creatures that fell between birds and fishes.

Linnaeus, a botanist, consigned to Amphibia what naturalists now call reptiles and amphibians, and went a step farther in throwing in a few troublesome fishes such as the sturgeon.

Actually, Holbrook was not the first naturalist to cope with the reptiles and amphibians of North America. Thomas Say and Richard Harlan had tried the field, if not with a genuinely encyclopedic approach. And Catesby had delineated a few of the more interesting and obvious snakes and frogs in his pioneering natural history.

Holbrook, however, was to bring new vision into the field—and for the first time was to attempt a description of all reptiles and amphibians of the United States east of the Rocky Mountains. How well he succeeded may be determined by Louis Agassiz's estimate of Holbrook's great work, *North American Herpetology:*

Holbrook's elaborate history of American herpetology was far above any previous work on the same subject. In that branch of investigation Europe had at that time nothing which could compare with it.

For proper appreciation, one should know that Agassiz, himself a product of European science and natural history disciplines, had prefaced his remarks with the comment that European studies in natural history in general were superior to American productions.

Holbrook not only was meticulous but also demanded of himself a degree of quality that exceeded the current standards. He published *North American Herpetology* in four volumes between 1836 and

214

JOHN EDWARDS HOLBROOK (1794–1871), a founder of the Medical College of South Carolina, was the first great American naturalist specializing in snakes and amphibians. He was such a stickler for accuracy that he became dissatisfied with the first edition of his *American Herpetology,* bought up all the copies which he could find of those that had been sold, and burned the lot in a backyard bonfire.

1840. The illustrations and, perhaps, sections of text displeased him, however. So he recovered as many sets from the public as he could and burned them in a bonfire that contained his entire stock of the work. The conflagration took place in his backyard in Charleston, South Carolina. He then in 1842 reissued a better-quality *Herpetology* in five volumes. The bonfire made the previous edition of *Herpetology* one of the rarer books of natural history. Many excellent collections of natural history volumes contain fewer than the four volumes from the early edition.

Born in Beaufort, South Carolina, in 1796, Holbrook was taken to Wrentham, Massachusetts, as a baby by his parents. He was educated in New England and graduated from Brown University before studying medicine in Philadelphia. He practiced briefly in Boston, then attended medical school in Edinburgh, Scotland, and while in Europe studied at the famed Jardin des Plantes in Paris.

On returning to the United States, he became professor of anatomy at the medical school in Charleston, South Carolina, where he spent the remainder of his life. Although he returned each summer to Wrentham, and indeed died in 1871 in North Wrentham, by then Norfolk, Massachusetts, he remained rather cosmopolitan in his attitude.

When the Civil War erupted, Holbrook, then a man of seventy, joined the Confederate Army as a medical man and spent considerable time in field hospitals. At the end of the war, he returned to his Massachusetts summer home and immediately resumed relationships with a large circle of friends.

As an anatomist, Holbrook sharpened the details of descriptive zoology as it pertains to reptiles and amphibians. He extended synonymy in the field back to Catesby, reconciling six to ten names that had been applied to reptiles by various less careful workers who had been either unable or unwilling to recognize that predecessors had worked on various species. In addition, he extended the field observations of the creatures, drawing together rather accurate life histories of each species. In other words, he went beyond description and gave sensible accounts of how and why each reptile species existed.

The state of herpetology when he began his work is adequately described in his introduction to *Herpetology* and gives one an idea of what he was about and how he proceeded:

> Reptiles form the third great class of vertebrated animals. They are beings provided with lungs, a simple heart, low temperature, slow digestion, and oviparous generation; having neither hair, feathers, nor mammae.
>
> Naturalists have experienced much difficulty in giving an appropriate name to this great class of animals. Linnaeus, observing some of the most remarkable phenomena in the economy of Reptiles—as their being able to live on land or in water—called them amphibia. The term is inappropriate; for it can be applied but to a very small number; as many never approach the water, and few, like the Sirens, can respire in this element;—breathing with lungs, others must approach its surface for atmospheric air. The respiration of young Batrachia is indeed only in water; but they have gills, and when the animal arrives at its perfect state of development, these disappear, and are succeeded by lungs. An ani-

mal, to respire equally well on land or in water, must have both
gills and lungs; gills to breathe in the water, as Fishes, and lungs
to respire atmospheric air, as Birds and Mammalia. The Sirens of
our rice-fields, and the Menobranchi of the great northern lakes,
are the only North American Reptiles that have this structure;
and are consequently our only really amphibious animals. However inapplicable the term amphibia may be to these animals,
many writers have followed the example of the great Swedish
naturalist. Brisson was the first who arranged them under the
name Reptiles; which term will be adopted in this work as more
indicative of their habits than the word amphibia.

The science which treats of the forms, organization, habits,
and history of Reptiles, is named Herpetology; and has been
more neglected than all other branches of Zoology; for the study
of Reptiles offers difficulties more numerous and insurmountable
than those presented by any other class of vertebrated animals.
Inhabiting, for the most part, deep and extensive swamps, in-
fected with malaria, and abounding with diseases during the summer months, when Reptiles are most numerous, time is wanting to
observe their modes of life with any prospect of success. Regarded, moreover, by most persons as objects of detestation,
represented as venomous, and possessed of the most noxious
properties, few have been hardy enough to study their character
and habits.

Though wanting the gracefulness of form of some Mammalia,
—though without the beauty of plumage of some Birds, or the
intelligence of others,—though they lack the brilliancy of colour
and wonderful instinct of the insect tribe,—still the Reptiles offer
many striking points of interest to the student of nature. To one
who would trace the chain of organized bodies, their connexion,
their relation with each other, and with the great whole, the
study of Herpetology is highly interesting and important. The
Reptiles occupy a prominent place in the scale of creation.
Neither the highest, nor yet the lowest of vertebrated animals,
they fill a space between the Birds and Fishes, and without them
a vast link in the chain of animated beings would be wanting.
Elevated above the Fish by the presence of lungs and articulated
members, yet inferior to Birds from having cold blood, a simple
heart, and a less degree of sensibility, these animals, by their
multiplied and extremely diversified forms, make the medium of
connexion between beings of the most opposite character. The
Testudo connects them with the inferior Mammalia, as with the

Armadillo, on the one hand, while the Siren approximates them
to the cartilaginous Fishes on the other. Serpents form a link of
another series, connecting this class with osseous Fishes, as with
the Eel; and the Flying Lizard connects them with the Birds. In
order to estimate properly the rank these animals hold in the
scale of creation, it is necessary to examine the general and principal points of their organization—to study the number of their
senses, and their degree of perfection. Without this, we cannot
understand the diversified forms and the shades of life that present themselves in such infinite variety among them. Their
conformation and modes of life are so different—some being organized for creeping, others for walking, for swimming, and even
for flying, that it would be impossible to generalize their anatomical forms or structure. We cannot give the structure of one as
the type of organization in all the others; for their variation in
shape and figure is attended with modifications of their internal
organs. These differences of structure will be fully described in
the anatomical part of this work; at this time, according to the
plan proposed above, it can only be said that the difference of
organization observed in different species, led Brogniart to arrange them all in four great orders—I. Chelonia. II. Sauria. III.
Ophidia. IV. Batrachia.

John K. Townsend, the ornithologist whose western birds were
used by Audubon in *Birds of America*, had returned from the Pacific
Coast with several reptiles before Holbrook completed his work.
Holbrook, however, refused to include the material, because accurate
information on the creatures did not exist and because he declined to
use models pickled in alcohol for illustrations. Pickling destroys the
animal's colors. Although he tried to picture, classify, and give a life
history of all species east of the Rockies, Holbrook missed a rather
large reptile of the United States, confined largely to extreme southern Florida: the American crocodile. His only crocodillian was the
alligator. The following is an excerpt from his *Alligator mississippiensis:*

Colour. The whole superior surface of the Alligator is dusky
in the old animal, but in the young it is banded with dirty yellowish-white, most remarkable on the tail. The throat is yellowish-
white; the plates of the abdomen are straw colour on their
posterior half and dusky on their anterior, lightest in the young

animal. The tail is coloured below like the belly, but still more dusky.

Dimensions. Length of head, 14 inches; length of body, 3 feet 1 inch; length of tail, 5 feet; total length, 9 feet 5 inches. The Alligator, however, frequently reaches dimensions much greater; I have seen one in Carolina 13½ feet long. Bartram says in Florida they exceed the length of 23 feet, a size almost incredible.

Habits. Alligators abound in the low, stagnant ponds and deep morasses of the southern states, where hundreds of them can be seen at a time, either on the flat marshy banks of creeks and rivers, or on sandy or muddy shores left dry by the ebb of the tide. Here they remain motionless for hours, apparently asleep, and are often mistaken for logs of dead and decaying wood, as well from their colour as from their perfect immobility; but when disturbed by the approach of enemies, they suddenly retreat to the water. At other times they may be observed floating on the surface of the water and only directed by its current; suddenly they skim along with the greatest velocity, either in search of food or of their mate.

Such Alligators as dwell in ponds and streams out of the influence of tidewater, wander much further from the banks, and are not unfrequently seen a mile or more from water; this happens, however, most commonly when they migrate for some reason or other from one pool to another.

The Alligator in his native state is exceedingly voracious, and feeds on any animal substance that may fall in his way; though he seems mostly attracted by fish, and by other animals in motion, as minks, musk-rats, dogs, &c., so as to render it almost impossible for them to cross even small streams without danger, at certain seasons of the year. These the Alligator seizes, drags under water, suffocates, and conveys to his lair, to be devoured at leisure.

Having no prehensile organs but the mouth and strong teeth with which they seize their prey, drag and retain it under water, and breathing as they do, only atmospheric air, and with lungs, it follows that they might as soon be suffocated, when thus submerged, as their struggling prey. A curious arrangement of the soft palate prevents this; it hangs down to meet a broad cartilaginous plate that projects upwards from the lingual bone, so as to close completely the fauces, (in which the trachea is placed,) when the mouth is widely opened, and effectually prevents the introduction of water to the lungs, which would cause the death of the animal.

Alligators are said to lie in wait for their prey on the banks of creeks and rivers, and when it approaches, they sweep it into the water with their tail; and it is certain that the animal uses the tail in defence, striking with it the enemy, and turning the head to the same side, at the same instant, so as to represent nearly a circle; further than this it cannot be carried, in consequence of the extreme length of the transverse process of the cervical vertebrae.

The Alligator takes the hook readily enough, when baited with flesh, but it requires strong tackle, such as is used in shark-fishing, to secure them, so great is the strength of an adult animal. When taken, they emit a disagreeable odour of musk, which proceeds from glands placed under the lower jaw. These glands are sometimes preserved and used as a substitute for musk in perfumery.

Besides the natural food of the animal, there is at all times found in the stomach of the Alligator, various extraneous substances, as stones, pieces of wood, fragments of glass, broken bottles, &c., and these latter have their angles rounded, probably by trituration with other hard substances. Many persons suppose these foreign matters are destined to keep the stomach distended, during the long fast the animal undergoes in winter: others think they aid digestion, as particles of gravel operate in the gizzards of birds. It is not easy to say what may be the precise use of these foreign substances found in the stomach of the Alligator, but there can be little doubt of their subserviency to the function of digestion, when it is remembered that they are universally present in the adult, and most commonly also in the young animal.

The Alligator is much more timid than is commonly supposed, at least when on land; even Catesby says "it seldom attacks men and cattle, yet it is a great devourer of hogs." There is, I believe, no well authenticated instance with us in Carolina, of their having preyed on man; yet Lacoudrenière (Journal de Physique) says it often happens in Louisiana, and that they greatly prefer the flesh of the black to the white!! Alligators will, however, defend themselves boldly when on land and at certain seasons of the year; nor can they be made to retreat from their position, as I have more than once observed, yet on these occasions I have never known them the aggressors. Bartram gives a different account; he says, they are very ferocious, and that he "was nearly devoured" by one; his description should however be received with some caution; and yet, perhaps, the encroachments of man upon their dwelling-places, since Bartram wrote, may have rendered them more timid and distrustful.

The Alligator moves but slowly and with difficulty on land, in consequence of the shortness of the extremities compared with the great length of the body. He raises himself on his legs, advances for a short distance, dragging along the thick, heavy tail; now he falls upon the belly, apparently to rest for a time, before he proceeds on his journey. In water, however, he moves from place to place with great velocity, being propelled by his broad, strong, fin-like tail: besides, the peculiar structure of the heart—the large lungs—the nostrils closed with valves, make him eminently aquatic, and enables him to remain for a long time beneath the surface without injury. "Some of the organs of sense even are constructed to receive impressions under water as well as on land: thus the ear is covered with two movable lips, which are closed in one instance and separated in the other, as the impression is to be made by elastic or liquid fluids."

The female Alligator mounts small sandy hillocks, or she constructs small mounds, with mud and vegetable substances, in which she deposits her eggs; these are hatched by the heat of the sun in about thirty days. As soon as the young are disengaged from the shell, they seek the water "and shift for themselves," the parents taking no further care of them, though they may remain for some weeks in the same locality. Bosc says he once captured several young Alligators and preserved them for a time, and that their only food was insects, and to them they were not attracted unless they were in motion: I have never seen Alligators take any food whatever in confinement.

In the spring of the year and early summer months, and during the time of incubation, and especially on cloudy days or in the evening, Alligators make a great noise; their croak is not unlike that of the bull-frog, but louder and less prolonged; Bartram compares it to distant thunder!

On the approach of winter, these animals seek out holes in the earth, where they remain torpid until spring, or until the warmth of the weather excites them again to life and activity. In this state of hibernation, many are dug out of their retreats by the slaves, who esteem the tail as an article of food, and which, indeed, is tolerable.

Geographical Distribution. The Alligator is first observed on the Atlantic border of the United States at the mouth of the

Neus river, in North Carolina; those that are occasionally seen farther north, must be considered as stragglers rather than permanent residents. From this point they abound near the mouths of all the creeks and rivers that empty into the Atlantic ocean, or into the Gulf of Mexico, as far as New Orleans, ascending up the Mississippi as high as the entrance of Red river, six hundred miles. Cuvier, in his *Mémoire* on the Crocodiles, says, "Cette espèce (Lucius) va assez loin au Nord; elle remonte le Mississippi jusque à la rivière rouge."

Dumeril and Bibron give the Alligator a still wider range; they say it apparently inhabits all parts of North America—"Qu'elle semble habiter dans toute son étendue,"—a striking proof of the inaccuracy of foreign herpetologists in arranging the geographical limits of our reptiles. In fact, the Alligator is never found north of lat. 35° on the Atlantic shore, and does not even reach the same parallel on the Mississippi, but stops at 33° 50″, the entrance of Red river—and what is this to the whole extent of North America? It may safely be affirmed, that nine-tenths of the territory of the United States east of the Rocky mountains, is uninhabited by this reptile.

General Remarks. Catesby first described this animal, and gave a tolerable figure of it, under the name Alligator, in his *History of Carolina*, &c. Linnaeus next reviewed it in the twelfth edition of the *Systema Naturae*, but he seems to have regarded it but as a variety of the Nilotic crocodile, in which opinion he was followed by many naturalists of that time. In fact, the elder herpetologists "are in some degree excusable for their ignorance of the different species of Crocodiles, for the specific characters applied to them were variable, and often little accordant with nature."

It is to Cuvier that we owe nearly all that is worth knowing on this subject; it was he who first observed the differences of the Crocodiles of the old and new world. In a *Mémoire* read before the Institute of France, and afterwards published in Weidmann (Archiv. Zoot., b. ii. p. 161, Brunswick, 1801), he recognised the peculiarly shaped head of the Alligator—"flat, and resembling that of the pike"—and seems to have regarded it as distinct from the South American animal; yet he observes that further observations of several individuals will be necessary to determine if it be really a distinct species.

Daudin next published an account of our animal in his Natural History of Reptiles, (1802) under the name Crocodilus Mississippiensis, the description being taken from a "specimen killed on the borders of the Mississippi," and furnished him by Michaux the botanist. Cuvier having completed (1807) his most interesting observations on this family of animals, now described the Alligator as a new species, in the *Annales du Museum,* under the name "Alligator lucius," from the shape of the head resembling that of the common pike of Europe, (Esox lucius.)

This specific name, although perfectly appropriate, so far as regards the form of the head, cannot be retained, as that of Mississippiensis, imposed by Daudin, has the undoubted right of priority. Dr. Leach, an excellent English naturalist, afterwards reproduced this animal in his Zoological Miscellany as a new species, and dedicated it to Cuvier (Crocodilus Cuvieri), which specific name is liable to the same objection as that imposed by Cuvier himself; it is subsequent to that given by Daudin.

There exists some doubt as to the etymology of the term Alligator, by which the animal is now universally known; some have supposed it derived from the word "Legateer" or "Allegater," a name by which the young Crocodile is distinguished in some parts of India. Cuvier says it is much more probable that it is a corruption of the Portuguese "Lagarto," derived from the Latin "Lacerta," as Hawkins writes it "Alagartos;" and Sloan, in his History of Jamaica, spells it "Allagator."

Chapter XV

The Incompatibles: Muir and Burroughs

Publication in the New York *Tribune* of December 5, 1871, of a story headlined "Yosemite Glaciers" marked the beginning of a new era in American natural history, the emergence of the preservationist.

John Muir wrote the report, which he had titled "The Death of a Glacier." Fortunately the editor changed the title, because a month after he wrote the story, and more than a month before its publication, Muir found a live glacier in the Merced Range of the Sierras. In two years, Muir was to find a total of sixty-five living glaciers in the California mountains.

John Daniel Runkle, president of the Massachusetts Institute of Technology, earlier in 1871 had urged Muir to write a glacier report. Runkle had visited Muir in the Yosemite Valley and became among the first scientific men impressed by Muir's evidence that glaciation had formed the valley. The prevailing theory, endorsed by leading geologists of the period, ascribed formation of Yosemite Valley to a cataclysm. Muir's newspaper report was printed in the leading science periodical, *Silliman's Journal*, in January 1872, elevating Muir's opinion to a hypothesis worthy of scientific discussion.

It was not the content of the glacier story but the fact that it was published that launched a campaign to save great Western landscapes that kept Muir intermittently busy until his death in 1914. Muir learned for the first time that he was a readable writer. He soon turned his pen from science writing to the even more controversial field of demanding that the federal government take title for the public to lands from which others hoped to make great profits. The battle turned the Yosemite Valley into a national park, and Muir's pleas and the work of his associates led to the founding of the National Park Service. Behind the service was an idea wholly new to Americans, that some vast landscapes were worthy of saving solely for their intrinsic value as beautiful land areas.

It is true that before Muir the nation had indulged in what one might call "after-the-fact" protective laws. These laws largely were enacted by state legislatures, the role of the federal government remaining questionable in such internal matters. Massachusetts had declared a closed season on deer as early as 1696, and by 1718 the Legislature had declared a three-year moratorium on killing deer. Enforcement, however, was lax in all states, and in general closed seasons were declared only after the animal to be protected had already been extirpated, or the season was closed during the time of year in which the creature normally was not hunted, and therefore no one was offended by the law.

An occasional naturalist had raised questions concerning man's rapacious dealings with nature. Thoreau had expressed reservations, but many of his best thoughts were buried in his personal journal. Whether they ever were intended for publication became moot only after his death, and editors began making generous use of his work. Audubon in his old age, his mind tottering, wondered whether he and his generation had been overactive in the killing of wildlife. His pondering came late, almost as a mother of eight who after the menopause becomes concerned about the burgeoning population.

Muir's concern was active and current. His interest was in the irreplaceable, gigantic sequoias of the Sierra and the 2500-year-old redwoods of the California coast. The state forest practices that came after his campaigns, such as buying forest acreage which had been logged to stumps and holding the land for natural reforestation, would not serve his purpose. One either saves a 2000-year-old tree as it stands or ends the option of humans seeing a similar tree for at least 100 generations—assuming of course that a logged redwood grove would regenerate giants.

Muir usually referred to the redwood as "the greatest of living things," qualifying the statement with "as far as I know." He undoubtedly was honest in his estimate, but wrong. Apparently the largest tree that ever lived was the monkey-thorn tree, *Acacia galpinii*, of the Transvaal region of South Africa. One giant monkey-thorn may have had a basal girth of 146 feet and a height of at least 400 feet, according to measurements made of remains. There are monkey-thorn trees today, but no giants. The monkey-thorn did not have a John Muir.

The following report from Muir on his search for redwoods was published by *Atlantic* in September 1901, and later was included in his book *Our National Parks*, which consisted of ten stories that *Atlantic* had published. The series rounded out a seventeen-year campaign by Muir to transfer the Yosemite Valley, then held as a state park by California, to federal control. Muir contended that California politicians had abused the valley since 1864, when President Lincoln signed a bill ceding Yosemite and the Mariposa Big Tree Grove to California. The battle ended on June 11, 1906, when President Theodore Roosevelt signed legislation making the area a national park. The following by Muir is entitled "Hunting Big Redwoods":

The Big Tree (*Sequoia gigantea*) is nature's forest masterpiece, and, as far as I know, the greatest of living things. It belongs to an ancient stock, as its remains in old rocks show, and has a strange air of other days about it, a thoroughbred look inherited from the long ago, the auld lang syne of trees. Once the genus was common, and with many species flourished in the now desolate Arctic regions, the interior of North America, and in Europe; but in long eventful wanderings from climate to climate only two species have survived the hardships they had to encounter, the *gigantea* and *sempervirens:* the former now restricted to the western slopes of the Sierra, the other to the Coast Mountains, and both to California, excepting a few groves of redwood which extend into Oregon.

The Pacific coast in general is the paradise of conifers. Here nearly all of them are giants, and display a beauty and magnificence unknown elsewhere. The climate is mild, the ground never freezes, and moisture and sunshine abound all the year. Nevertheless, it is not easy to account for the colossal size of the sequoias. The largest are about three hundred feet high and thirty feet in diameter. Who of all the dwellers of the plains and prairies and fertile home forests of round-headed oak and maple, hickory and elm, ever dreamed that earth could bear such growths? Sequoias are trees that the familiar pines and firs seem to know nothing about, lonely, silent, serene, with a physiognomy almost godlike, and so old that thousands of them still living had already counted their years by tens of centuries when Columbus set sail from Spain, and were in the vigor of youth or middle age when the star led the Chaldean sages to the infant Saviour's cradle. As far as man is concerned, they were the same yesterday, today, and forever, emblems of permanence.

Excepting the sugar pine, most of its neighbors with pointed tops seem to be forever shouting "Excelsior!" while the Big Tree, though soaring above them all, seems satisfied, its rounded head poised lightly as a cloud, giving no impression of trying to go higher. Only in youth does it show, like other conifers, a heavenward yearning, keenly aspiring with a long quick-growing top.

Indeed, the whole tree, for the first century or two, or until a hundred to a hundred and fifty feet high, is arrowhead in form, and compared with the solemn rigidity of age, is as sensitive to the wind as a squirrel tail. The lower branches are gradually dropped as it grows older, and the upper ones thinned out, until comparatively few are left. These, however, are developed to great size, divide again and again, and terminate in bossy rounded masses of leafy branchlets, while the head becomes dome-shaped. Then, poised in fullness of strength and beauty, stern and solemn in mien, it glows with eager, enthusiastic life, quivering to the tip of every leaf and branch and far-reaching root, calm as a granite dome— the first to feel the touch of the rosy beams of the morning, the last to bid the sun good night.

Perfect specimens, unhurt by running fires or lightning, are singularly regular and symmetrical in general form, though not at all conventional, showing infinite variety in sure unity and harmony of plan. The immensely strong, stately shafts, with rich purplish-brown bark, are free of limbs for a hundred and fifty feet or so, though dense tufts of sprays occur here and there producing an ornamental effect, while long parallel furrows give a fluted, columnar appearance. The limbs shoot forth with equal boldness in every direction, showing no weather side. On the old trees the main branches are crooked and rugged, and strike rigidly outward, mostly at right angles from the trunk, but there is always a certain measured restraint in their reach which keeps them within bounds. No other Sierra tree has foliage so densely massed or outlines so finely, firmly drawn and so obediently subordinate to an ideal type. A particularly knotty, angular, ungovernable-looking branch, five to eight feet in diameter and perhaps a thousand years old, may occasionally be seen pushing out from the trunk, as if determined to break across the bounds of the regular curve; but, like all the others, as soon as the general outline is approached, the huge limb dissolves into massy bosses of branchlets and sprays, as if the tree were growing beneath an invisible bell glass against the sides of which the branches were molded, while many small varied departures from the ideal form give the impression of freedom to grow as they like.

Except in picturesque old age, after being struck by lightning and broken by a thousand snowstorms, this regularity of form is one of the Big Tree's most distinguishing characteristics. Another is the simple sculptural beauty of the trunk and its great thickness as compared with its height and the width of the branches; many of them being from eight to ten feet in diameter at a height of two hundred feet from the ground and seeming more like finely modeled and sculptured architectural columns than the stems of trees, while the great strong limbs are like rafters supporting the magnificent dome head.

The root system corresponds in magnitude with the other dimensions of the tree, forming a flat, far-reaching, spongy network, two hundred feet or more in width, without any taproot; and the instep is so grand and fine, so suggestive of endless strength, it is long ere the eye is released to look above it. The natural swell of the roots, though at first sight excessive, gives rise to buttresses no greater than are required for beauty as well as strength, as at once appears when you stand back far enough to see the whole tree in its true proportions.

The bark of full-grown trees is from one to two feet thick, rich cinnamon brown, purplish on young trees and shady parts of the old, forming magnificent masses of color with the underbrush and beds of flowers. Toward the end of winter the trees themselves bloom, while the snow is still eight or ten feet deep. The pistillate flowers are about three eighths of an inch long, pale green, and grow in countless thousands on the ends of the sprays. The staminate are still more abundant, pale yellow, a fourth of an inch long, and when the golden pollen is ripe they color the whole tree and dust the air and the ground far and near.

The cones are bright grass green in color, about two and a half inches long, one and a half wide, and are made up of thirty or forty strong closely packed rhomboidal scales, with four to eight seeds at the base of each. The seeds are extremely small and light, being only from an eighth to a fourth of an inch long and wide, including a filmy surrounding wing, which causes them to glint and waver in falling and enables the wind to carry them considerable distances from the tree.

The faint lisp of snowflakes, as they alight, is one of the smallest sounds mortal can hear. The sound of falling sequoia seeds, even when they happen to strike on flat leaves or flakes of bark, is about as faint. Very different are the bumping and thudding of the falling cones. Most of them are cut off by the Douglas squirrel and stored for the sake of the seeds, small as they are. In the calm Indian summer these busy harvesters with ivory sickles go to work early in the morning, as soon as breakfast is over, and nearly all day the ripe cones fall in a steady pattering, bumping shower. Unless harvested in this way, they discharge their seeds and remain on the tree for many years. In fruitful seasons the trees are fairly laden. On two small specimen branches, one and a half and two inches in diameter, I counted four hundred and eighty cones. No other California conifer produces nearly so many seeds, excepting perhaps its relative, the redwood of the Coast Mountains. Millions are ripened annually by a single tree, and the product of one of the main groves in a fruitful year would suffice to plant all the mountain ranges of the world.

The dense tufted sprays make snug nesting places for birds, and in some of the loftiest, leafiest towers of verdure thousands of generations have been reared, the great solemn trees shedding off flocks of merry singers every year from nests like the flocks of winged seeds from the cones.

The Big Tree keeps its youth far longer than any of its neighbors. Most silver firs are old in their second or third century, pines in their fourth or fifth, while the Big Tree, growing beside them, is still in the bloom of its youth, juvenile in every feature, at the age of old pines, and cannot be said to attain anything like prime size and beauty before its fifteen hundredth year, or, under favorable circumstances, become old before its three thousandth. Many, no doubt, are much older than this. On one of the Kings River giants, thirty-five feet and eight inches in diameter, exclusive of bark, I counted upwards of four thousand annual wood rings, in which there was no trace of decay after all these centuries of mountain weather.

There is no absolute limit to the existence of any tree. Their death is due to accidents, not, as of animals, to the wearing out of organs. Only the leaves die of old age—their fall is foretold in their structure—but the leaves are renewed every year, and so also are the other essential organs, wood, roots, bark, buds. Most of the Sierra trees die of disease. Thus the magnificent silver firs are devoured by fungi, and comparatively few of them live to see their three hundredth birth year. But nothing hurts the Big Tree. I never saw one that was sick or showed the slightest sign of decay. It lives on through indefinite thousands of years, until burned, blown down, undermined, or shattered by some tremendous lightning stroke. No ordinary bolt ever seriously hurts sequoia. In all my walks I have seen only one that was thus killed outright.

I have seen silver firs, two hundred feet high, split into long peeled rails and slivers down to the roots, leaving not ·even a stump; the rails radiating like the spokes of a wheel from a hole in the ground where the tree stood. But the sequoia, instead of being split and slivered, usually has forty or fifty feet of its brash knotty top smashed off in short chunks about the size of cordwood, the beautiful rosy-red ruins covering the ground in a circle a hundred feet wide or more. I never saw any that had been cut down to the ground, or even to below the branches, except one in the Stanislaus Grove, about twelve feet in diameter, the greater part of which was smashed to fragments, leaving only a leafless stump about seventy-five feet high. It is a curious fact that all the very old sequoias have lost their heads by lightning.

The great age of these noble trees is even more wonderful than their huge size, standing bravely up, millennium in, millennium out, to all that fortune may bring them; triumphant over tempest and fire and time, fruitful and beautiful, giving food and shelter to multitudes of small fleeting creatures dependent upon their bounty.

One of my own best excursions among the sequoias was made in the autumn of 1875, when I explored the then unknown or little-known sequoia region south of the Mariposa Grove for comprehensive views of the belt and to learn what I could of the peculiar distribution of the species and its history in general. In particular, I was anxious to try to find out whether it had ever been more widely distributed since the glacial period; what conditions, favorable or otherwise, were affecting it; what were its relations to climate, topography, soil, and the other trees growing with it, and so forth; and whether, as was generally supposed, the species was nearing extinction.

I have done nearly all my mountaineering on foot, carrying as little as possible, depending on campfires for warmth, so that I might be light and free to go wherever my studies might lead. But on this sequoia trip, which promised to be long, I was persuaded to take a small wild mule with me to carry provisions and a pair of blankets. The friendly owner of the animal, having noticed that I sometimes looked tired when I came down from the peaks to replenish my bread sack, assured me that his "little Brownie mule" was just what I wanted—tough as a knot, perfectly untirable, low and narrow, just right for squeezing through brush, able to climb like a chipmunk, jump from boulder to boulder to boulder like a wild sheep, and go anywhere a man could go. But tough as he was, and accomplished as a climber, many a time in the course of our journey, when he was jaded and hungry, wedged fast in rocks or struggling in chaparral like a fly in a spider web, his troubles were sad to see, and I wished he would leave me and find his way home alone.

We set out from Yosemite about the end of August, and our first camp was made in the well-known Mariposa Grove. Here and in the adjacent pine woods I spent nearly a week, carefully examining the boundaries of the grove for traces of its greater extension without finding any. Then I struck out into the majestic trackless forest to the southeastward, hoping to find new groves or traces of old ones in the dense silver fir and pine woods about the head of Big Creek, where soil and climate seemed most favorable to their growth; but not a single tree or old monument of any sort came to light until I climbed the high rock called Wamellow by the Indians. Here I obtained telling views of the fertile forest-filled basin of the upper Fresno. Innumerable spires of the noble yellow pine were displayed rising one above another on the braided slopes, and yet nobler sugar pines with superb arms outstretched in the rich autumn light, while away toward the southwest, on the verge of the glowing horizon, I discovered the majestic domelike crowns of Big Trees towering high over all, singly and in close grove congregations. There is something wonderfully attractive in this king tree, even when beheld from afar, that draws us to it with indescribable enthusiasm, its superior height and massive smoothly rounded outlines proclaiming its character in any company; and when one of the oldest of them attains full stature on some commanding ridge, it seems the very god of the woods.

I ran back to camp, packed Brownie, and steered over the divide and down into the heart of the Fresno Grove. Then, choosing a camp on the side of a brook where the grass was good, I made a cup of tea and set off free among the brown giants, glorying in the abundance of new work about me. One of the first special things that caught my attention was an extensive landslip. The ground on the side of a stream had given way to a depth of fifty feet, and with all its trees had been launched into the bottom of the stream ravine. Most of the trees—pines, firs, incense cedar, and sequoia—were still standing erect and uninjured, as if unconscious that anything out of the common had happened. Tracing the ravine alongside the avalanche, I saw many trees whose roots had been laid bare, and in one instance discovered a sequoia, about fifteen feet in diameter, growing above an old prostrate trunk that seemed to belong to a former generation. This slip had occurred seven or eight years ago, and I was glad to find not only that most of the Big Trees were uninjured, but that many companies of hopeful seedlings and saplings were growing confidently on the fresh soil along the broken front of the avalanche. These young trees were already eight or ten feet high, and were shooting up vigorously, as if sure of eternal life, though young pines, firs, and libocedrus were running a race with them for the sunshine, with an even start. Farther down the ravine I counted five hundred and thirty-six young sequoias on a bed of rough bouldery soil not exceeding two acres in extent.

Although there were many busy naturalists in the last quarter of the nineteenth century, the persons whom the press kept prominent were "the two Johns." Often referred to as John o' the Mountains and John o' the Woods, in deference to their Scottish ancestry—although only Muir was born in Scotland—John Muir of California fame and John Burroughs, the Hudson River naturalist, were linked together in the public mind. It was a strange linkage, largely uncomfortable to both principals. The only thing they truly had in common, besides the first name, was that both wrote in the natural history field.

Burroughs often commented in his journals about his reluctance to enter a controversy over the environment, or any other subject. Muir, when he was in action, was all fight. Comments by friends of the men, and occasional paragraphs in journals or letters, indicate that they at least were uncomfortable in each other's presence. It was not an unusual state of affairs for two writers mining similar veins. Muir felt that Burroughs was hiding on the banks of the Hudson refusing to contribute his talent to great issues. Burroughs, in visits to Muir country, found the mountaineer loquacious, perhaps a show-off, and occasionally quite probably wrong. Burroughs even questioned Muir's glacier theory regarding Yosemite long after experts had accepted it.

Muir differed from his contemporaries, and indeed from those who came after him, in having a vision far ahead of his time. Although the words to describe the philosophy did not exist in his day and therefore he never used the term, he was trying to save ecosystems. He knew that giant redwoods cannot survive alone. Winds or floods would overthrow them. He seemed to sense at least that the big trees existed as part of a community of living things. In any event, he was interested in saving whole wild landscapes, whole mountain ranges, vast acreages in which man could experience the wildness he had experienced.

In his lectures and writings, Muir referred to the interconnected structure of nature. "As soon as we take one thing by itself," he wrote, "we find it hitched to everything in the universe." Although Muir's use of the idea in relation to a living landscape may have been new, the idea was not original. It had been expressed many times in ancient religions and philosophies, usually illustrated by the example of grasping a loose thread only to discover that pulling it unraveled a fabric. Muir's vision of the oneness of nature foresaw the interlocking ramifications that can result in an unexpected disaster to some species that seems at best remotely connected. The concept that an alteration in the environment can have repercussions extending an unexpected distance became largely accepted only in the mid-twentieth century.

Muir acquired the feeling that all nature was connected not only from his own experiences in the Sierras but also from the writing of an exceptional Vermonter, George Perkins Marsh. A Burlington lawyer, Marsh in 1864 published *Man and Nature*, which often in recent years has been referred to as the first substantial work on American ecology.

The exact period in which Muir fell under Marsh's influence is indefinite. At the time *Man and Nature* was published, Muir was twenty-six years old and recently separated from the University of Wisconsin, where he studied two and a half years. The fact that he was a Marsh disciple, however, has been attested by Muir's copy of the book, which bears voluminous marginal notes. Marsh, who had served Vermont as a congressman, became a member of the U.S. diplomatic corps and served as minister to Turkey and later to Italy. Posts in the Mediterranean and Middle East gave him opportunities to rove over man-abused landscapes and helped shape the outlook expressed in his book. The substance of what he learned was well expressed in Marsh's statement: "The ravages committed by man subvert the relations and destroy the balance which nature had established . . . and she avenges herself upon the intruder by letting loose her destructive energies." A revival of *Man and Nature* a century later by modern environmentalists disclosed a close parallel between what environmentalists see now and what Marsh saw then, particularly in his warning that continued abuse of the land by man threatened "the depravation, barbarism, and perhaps even extinction of the species."

The other great influence upon Muir was Alexander von Humboldt's thirty-volume account of the naturalist's explorations in South America. Muir was so impressed by Humboldt that he resolved as a young man to visit the River Amazon. The Amazon was to elude him until 1911, when at the age of 73 he made the journey. He not only sailed up the Amazon, but also ventured on the Rio Negro and Rio Iguassu, crossed South America to Chile, where he found a forest of monkey-puzzle trees on a high slope of the Andes, and capped off the expedition by sailing to Africa and crossing that continent from South Africa to the Nile Valley.

In contrast, Burroughs was a disciple of more sedentary masters. His penultimate hero, perhaps, was Walt Whitman. Burroughs's critical acclaim of the message the Brooklyn poet expounded in *Leaves of Grass* came at a time when other critics were suffering cultural shock from its free spirit. Burroughs's alternate hero was the Concord philosopher Ralph Waldo Emerson. A former schoolmaster, journalist, and clerk, Burroughs always retained a broad streak of educator, which appears constantly in his writing. He was essentially a teacher, and his books were classrooms in which natural history was taught.

As is true of most persons, and perhaps even truer of writers, their personal lives are at times in conflict with the message they give others. Burroughs, who counseled patience, often was impatient. From his journals it would appear that he could be cantankerous despite the lovable image he always projected to visitors. Despite his message of kindliness to all beasts, he hated groundhogs. He shot them regularly, and on at least one occasion tore down a stone wall so that his dogs could kill a groundhog that had outwitted them. A guest who witnessed the procedure was shocked by the unequalness of the contest and Burroughs's obvious glee. He also trapped chipmunks. These acts were in defense of his garden, as though he were a farmer who made a living from growing peas, rather than a writer who profited from the wildlife that surrounded him.

Like Muir, Burroughs was appalled by war. He visited an army field hospital late in the Civil War and was sickened by the wounds and the grisly amputations. He saw an army column moving toward the front line and admitted that had he been a member of it he might have fainted from the shock.

Muir expressed his sentiments about the Civil War in a letter to a friend: "if we must cut the throats of the Secessionists, let it be done solemnly, as when a judge sheds tears on pronouncing the doom of an atrocious murderer." Late in the war, when it became evident that there were few remaining men of draftable age in his home Wisconsin county, Muir went to Canada, where he found employment and remained until the war's end. Muir always hated guns and never could understand hunters. He was disturbed by the hunting enthusiasm of his friend President Theodore Roosevelt, and in comments to Roosevelt implied that it hinted of immaturity. Roosevelt assured him that his interest in hunting had become limited to procuring specimens for museums, and from then on Roosevelt accented specimen collecting as his public image while continuing the sport he dearly loved.

In his battles to save the Sierras, Muir often was accused by his opponents of being a despoiler himself. They accused him of operating a sawmill, grazing sheep, and working for the hotel industry in the Yosemite. The naturalist indeed had done those things, but not in the scope that the accusers implied or on the scale of exploitation they had in mind. In fact, his experiences in those fields convinced him of the rightness of his position in demanding that the Yosemite be saved from abuse. They gave him an insight that an uninvolved person might have missed.

Burroughs cultivated a different approach to nature than Muir. While both are readable, Burroughs was more relaxed, and perhaps is more comfortable for the reader. Traits of both writers may be exemplified by comparing Muir's comments on the majestic and unique redwoods to Burroughs's handling of the commonplace and ubiquitous strawberry in these passages from a chapter of *Locusts and Wild Honey*:

Was it old Dr. Parr who said or sighed in his last illness, "Oh, if I can only live till strawberries come!" The old scholar imagined that, if he could weather it till then, the berries would carry him through. No doubt he had turned from the drugs and the nostrums, or from the hateful food, to the memory of the pungent, penetrating, and unspeakably fresh quality of the strawberry with the deepest longing. The very thought of these crimson lobes, embodying as it were the first glow and ardor of the young summer, and with their power to unsheathe the taste and spur the flagging appetite, made life seem possible and desirable to him.

The strawberry is always the hope of the invalid, and sometimes, no doubt, his salvation. It is the first and finest relish among fruits, and well merits Dr. Boteler's memorable saying, that "doubtless God could have made a better berry, but doubtless God never did."

On the threshold of summer, Nature proffers us this her virgin fruit; more rich and sumptuous are to follow, but the wild delicacy and fillip of the strawberry are never repeated,—that keen feathered edge greets the tongue in nothing else.

Let me not be afraid of overpraising it, but probe and probe for words to hint its surprising virtues. We may well celebrate it with festivals and music. It has that indescribable quality of all first things,—that shy, uncloying, provoking barbed sweetness. It is eager and sanguine as youth. It is born of the copious dews, the fragrant nights, the tender skies, the plentiful rains of the early season. The singing of birds is in it, and the health and frolic of lusty Nature. It is the product of liquid May touched by the June sun. It has the tartness, the briskness, the unruliness of spring, and the aroma and intensity of summer.

Oh, the strawberry days! how vividly they come back to one! The smell of clover in the fields, of blooming rye on the hills, of the wild grape beside the woods, and of the sweet honeysuckle and the spiraea about the house. The first hot, moist days. The daisies and the buttercups; the songs of the birds, their first reckless jollity and love-making over; the full tender foliage of the trees; the bees swarming, and the air strung with resonant musical chords. The time of the sweetest and most succulent grass, when the cows come home with aching udders. Indeed, the strawberry belongs to the juiciest time of the year.

What a challenge it is to the taste! how it bites back again! and is there any other sound like the snap and crackle with which it salutes the ear on being plucked from the stems? It is a threat to one sense that the other is soon to verify. It snaps to the ear as it smacks to the tongue. All other berries are tame beside it.

The plant is almost an evergreen; it loves the coverlid of the snow, and will keep fresh through the severest winters with a slight protection. The frost leaves its virtues in it. The berry is a kind of vegetable snow. How cool, how tonic, how melting, and how perishable! It is almost as easy to keep frost. Heat kills it, and sugar quickly breaks up its cells.

Is there anything like the odor of strawberries? The next best thing to tasting them is to smell them; one may put his nose to the dish while the fruit is yet too rare and choice for his fingers. Touch not and taste not, but take a good smell and go mad! . . .

Ovid mentions the wood strawberry, which would lead one to infer that they were more abundant in his time and country than in ours.

This is, perhaps, the same as the alpine strawberry, which is said to grow in the mountains of Greece, and thence northward. This was probably the first variety cultivated, though our native species would seem as unpromising a subject for the garden as club-moss or wintergreens.

Of the field strawberry there are a great many varieties,—some growing in meadows, some in pastures, and some upon mountain-tops. Some are round, and stick close to the calyx or hull; some are long and pointed, with long, tapering necks. These usually grow upon tall stems. They are, indeed, of the slim, linear kind. Your corpulent berry keeps close to the ground; its stem and foot-stalk are short, and neck it has none. Its color is deeper than that of its tall brother, and of course it has more juice. You are more apt to find the tall varieties upon knolls in low, wet meadows, and again upon mountain-tops, growing in tussocks of wild grass about the open summits. These latter ripen in July, and give one his last taste of strawberries for the season.

But the favorite haunt of the wild strawberry is an uplying meadow that has been exempt from the plow for five or six years, and that has little timothy and much daisy. When you go a-berrying, turn your steps toward the milk-white meadows. The slightly bitter odor of the daisies is very agreeable to the smell, and affords a good background for the perfume of the fruit. The strawberry cannot cope with the rank and deep-rooted clover, and seldom appears in a field till the clover has had its day. But the daisy with its slender stalk does not crowd or obstruct the plant, while its broad white flower is like a light parasol that tempers and softens the too strong sunlight. Indeed, daisies and strawberries are generally associated. Nature fills her dish with the berries, then covers them with the white and yellow of milk and cream, thus suggesting a combination we are quick to follow. Milk alone, after it loses its animal heat, is a clod, and begets torpidity of the brain; the berries lighten it, give wings to it, and one is fed as by the air he breathes or the water he drinks.

Then the delight of "picking" the wild berries! It is one of the fragrant memories of boyhood. Indeed, for a boy or man to go a-berrying in a certain pastoral country I know of, where a passer-by along the highway is often regaled by a breeze loaded with a perfume of the o'er-ripe fruit, is to get nearer to June than by almost any course I know of. Your errand is so private and confidential! You stoop low. You part away the grass and the daisies, and would lay bare the inmost secrets of the meadow. Everything is yet tender and succulent; the very air is bright and new; the warm breath of the meadow comes up in your face; to your knees you are in a sea of daisies and clover; from your knees up, you are in a sea of solar light and warmth. Now you are prostrate like a swimmer, or like a surfbather reaching for pebbles or shells, the white and green spray breaks above you; then, like a devotee before a shrine or naming his beads, your rosary strung with luscious berries; anon you are a grazing Nebuchadnezzar, or an artist taking an inverted view of the landscape. . . .

Chapter XVI

⚬⚬⚬

Rattling Bones: Marsh versus Cope

A major fact in the battle over bones between Othniel Charles Marsh and Edward Drinker Cope was that, despite the bitterness of the contest, neither man sacrificed his scientific integrity while striving to win.

Otherwise, in reviewing the dirty tricks and defamations that elevated paleontology to the unlikely position of front-page news in the New York *Herald,* one might lose sight of the fact that both contestants were honored men, respected in the profession. At times they seemed more like spoiled adolescents.

On January 12, 1890, the feud over fossils, which had raged for years in academic circles, broke in the *Herald.* Cope was forty-nine years old and recently appointed a professor at the University of Pennsylvania. Marsh was fifty-eight and had been a professor at Yale for twenty-three years. While libeling each other, they attempted to embroil every professional in paleontology on both sides of the Atlantic in the fray.

Rivalry between or among naturalists and scientists who are contemporaries in the same field is commonplace. Indeed, it almost is a way of life and particularly was so in the post–Civil War era that Cope and Marsh shared. Seldom, however, does rivalry reach the level achieved by these two paleontologists, and perhaps neither before nor since has it approached such a self-destructive pitch. That both survivéd it with their reputations intact remains one of the more implausible achievements in natural history.

For credibility, it is a story best related through beginning at the end. From the summation in the two contestants' obituaries, one may gain a perspective that easily could be lost in considering only what generally has been related as the sole focal point of their lives: the clash of temperaments in the *Herald.*

Among other accomplishments, both Cope and Marsh were respected ornithologists and as such were entitled to obituaries in the

EDWARD DRINKER COPE (1840–1897) was deemed by contemporaries the greatest naturalist that America had produced. The opinion was not unanimous, however. Othneil Charles Marsh, Yale professor of paleontology, held the minority view. The battle between Cope and Marsh over priority in fossil discoveries in the American West became the bitterest public dispute in the history of American science. Cope almost bankrupted himself in the contest, since his limited fortune was far from equal to Marsh's great wealth. The irony of the situation was that both were honest, competent men, who had the misfortune of striving for the same goal.

American Ornithologists' Union journal, *The Auk*. Fortunately, both obituaries were written by the same author, Dr. Joel Asaph Allen, editor of *The Auk* for twenty-eight years. As a contemporary and a respected scientist himself (he was dean of the scientific staff of the American Museum of Natural History), Dr. Allen was in a unique position to render judgment on the two men in a spirit that seems to reflect the opinion of their peers.

Of Cope, Dr. Allen wrote:

Cope, Professor Edward Drinker, died at his home in Philadelphia, April 12, 1897, at the age of nearly 57 years, he having been born July 28, 1840. In his death science has lost one of the greatest naturalists America has yet produced. As a vertebrate zoologist and palaeontologist, the world has seen few that can be ranked as his equal. Although not especially recognized as an ornithologist, as he published little on recent birds, he is known to have possessed, and on occasions displayed, a profound general knowledge of the class, and to have had a good field knowledge of the birds of eastern North America. In other departments of vertebrate zoology he has long been recognized as one of the highest authorities, especially in reptiles, both recent and extinct, while his contributions to mammalian palaeontology have been almost unrivalled. He is also the author of several epoch-making schemes of classification, including especially one of fishes, and is properly recognized as one of the chief founders of the Neo-Lamarckian school of evolutionists, of which he was one of the most able exponents. He was gifted with a powerful intellect, remarkable keenness of observation, and, in the main, admirable judgment. As one writer has tersely and wisely said of him, "One hesitates which to admire the most, the tenacity of his memory, the brilliancy of his wit, or the ease with which he used his enormous erudition. To any community, and at any time, the loss of such a man is a calamity." It is therefore more than fitting that a few lines should be here devoted to his memory. As editor for many years of the "American Naturalist," he is doubtless well known to the readers of "The Auk," who will find elsewhere the record of his achievements and honors.

Of Marsh, he wrote:

Marsh, Professor Othniel Charles, of Yale University, died at New Haven, March 18, in the 68th year of his age. He was born at Lockport, N.Y. in 1831, and was graduated at Yale in 1860. He subsequently studied several years under leading specialists in Europe, returning to New Haven in 1866, where he has since occupied the chair of Palaeontology. He has long been recognized throughout the world as one of the leading authorities in vertebrate palaeontology. His explorations in various parts of the West for fossil vertebrates began in 1868, and in subsequent years he amassed the immense collections which have been so long famous. The results of his investigations have been published in a long series of papers and memoirs, numbering nearly three hundred titles, covering a period of more than twenty-five years. His unrivalled collections of fossils, as yet only partly worked up, he presented to Yale University, with a considerable endowment for carrying on and publishing the results of further investigation of this great mass of material. Professor Marsh is well known to ornithologists for his numerous publications on fossil North American birds, including his great quarto memoir "Odontornithes: a Monograph of the Extinct Toothed Birds of North America," published in 1880. Probably five-sixths of the known extinct North American birds have been described by Professor Marsh. His scientific work brought him many honors both at home and abroad. In 1878 he was chosen President of the American Association for the Advancement of Science, and from 1883 to 1896 he was President of the National Academy of Sciences.

One may note that while Marsh was the expert on fossil birds and therefore a more deserving member of the American Ornithologists' Union, Allen pays the ultimate tribute to Cope in his remark that Cope was "one of the greatest naturalists America yet has produced." Dr. Allen wisely avoided the newspaper dispute and the long history of power plays between the two. Among his peers, Cope had been forgiven for dashing into print and publicly airing the animosity between him and Marsh. The general consensus was that Cope had been fighting for his professional life. Marsh had placed Cope in an untenable position, denying him publication outlets, and perhaps was involved in the final insult that brought Cope out fighting: a demand from the federal government that Cope surrender all the fossil material that he had collected. For Cope, going public through the columns of the *Herald* was a desperate gamble. He had spent his moderate fortune fighting Marsh and he knew that Marsh forces would bring pressure to have him ousted from the job he so recently had acquired at the University of Pennsylvania.

Marsh had nothing to lose. Marsh was paleontologist of the U.S. Geological Survey, and two of his close allies, Clarence King and Maj. John W. Powell, were successive directors of the survey. They blocked Cope's publication of his fossil discoveries made on an early government survey. Marsh also had an influential friend in Dr. Silliman, editor of the *American Journal of Science*, and succeeded in cutting off Cope from possible publication there. In the meantime, Cope had gone broke publishing the *American Naturalist*, a journal that he had purchased to provide an avenue of publication.

The situation could be summed up thus: an impoverished Cope faced almost certain defeat and ruin at the hands of his old adversary Marsh. And Marsh had behind him the vast wealth he had inherited from his uncle, George Peabody, one of America's wealthy men. Most of their peers saw the situation that way. And it was most fortunate for Cope that they did. The only thing that they resented was Cope's attempt to drag several of them into the controversy through naming them publicly as persons not completely enamored of Marsh.

Since most persons today have never heard of King or Powell, or of Lucius Q. C. Lamar, William F. Vilas, or John W. Noble, the last three of whom served as U.S. secretary of interior, the political figures mentioned in the Cope-Marsh newspaper exchange now have little meaning to readers. It also is probable that many of the finer points of paleontology, particularly as practiced in that era, will have no relevance to today's readers, as they undoubtedly had no relevance to the newspaper readers of 1890. The complete record as published in the *Herald* filled pages set in the pinhead-sized type of the era. Reset in modern type, it becomes a complete book whose total message is abstruse at best. So, perhaps, the tenor of the exchange may be illustrated best by a few outrageous statements the contestants made.

Cope was the instigator of the six newspaper stories, which began appearing in the *Herald* January 12, 1890. The author of the series, however, was William Hosea Ballou, a free-lance writer specializing in science. He sold the stories to the *Herald*. The series was not especially well written. Ballou often has been charged with spicing the material, and even Cope referred to Ballou as "a rough customer." The truth seems to be, however, that Ballou did not need to contribute his ideas to the feud. Cope had saved material on Marsh for years, and Marsh was quite adequate in returning insults.

In the opening salvo, Ballou wrote:

It is asserted vigorously, and evidence in abundance is offered by many men high in power, that Major John W. Powell, director of the [U.S. Geological] survey, and Professor Marsh, its principal salaried officer, are partners in incompetency, ignorance and plagiarism. . . .

As a result, it is alleged that Marsh has sent out large field collecting parties into the Territories [now the Western states], which were instructed to gather everything of use to the survey and break all specimens which it was unnecessary to bring East, in order that other scientists should not have them, or, rather, should not be able to anticipate the work of the survey. Beside breaking specimens and destroying the possibility of any competition in the acquirement of knowledge, Professor Marsh is now charged with retaining the salaries of members of his field parties.

But the most astounding charge against Professor Marsh is that all of the work purporting to be his, as published by the government, is not his own, but in part that of his employees, the remainder being a collection of plagiarisms. . . .

Ballou then reports the following interview with Cope:

"What is the origin, Professor, of this war against the Geological Survey?" I asked.

"It may be found in the outrageous order I have received from the Secretary of the Interior to turn over my collections to the National Museum at Washington. I have no more than a bushel of specimens belonging to the government, and to these it is welcome. The fact is, I sent out my own exploring parties and secured my collections at an expense of about $80,000 of my own money, to say nothing of the value of the time I have expended upon them."

"Who is the author of the order?"

"Why to be sure, who but Major Powell. The object of this absurd order to place my collections in the National Museum is to gain control of them, so that my work may be postponed until it has been done by Professor Marsh, of Yale College, and this in spite of the fact that the preliminary work has been already published by me, and that the truth is sure to come out at some future time."

"What is this charge of plagiarism against Professor Marsh?"

"First, his alleged discovery of the evolution of the horse. It will be remembered that this paper attracted great public attention some years ago as showing the divided hoofs of the ancestors of the horse. This work was mostly plagiarized from Professor Kowalevsky, of Moscow, who complained bitterly when here of Professor Marsh's theft of his important life work.

"Second, his alleged work on toothed birds (*Odontornithes*) was written by his assistants, one of whom was Professor Williston. Third, his work on the *Dinocerata*, or horned mammals, was done chiefly by his assistants. The generalizations were dictated by George Baur, who repeated what he knew from my own work on the subject, Marsh changing the names of divisions of classification. This attempted theft from my work is making a laugh all over Europe.

"Fourth, Professor Marsh's work on the saurians of the West was written by Williston, and fifth, his paper on the mammals of the Laramie formation was really written by himself, and is the most remarkable collection of errors and ignorance of anatomy and the literature on the subject ever displayed. Sixth, his papers on the horned saurians of the Laramie is a pretended discovery which I fully described thirteen years since.

"Notwithstanding the fact that I described these animals so long ago—from my work he might, in accordance with his usual freedom, have taken correct data—he has described one of these horned saurians as a species of bison. Ought a man who does not know the difference between a saurian and a bison, and who supposes because the saurian had a horn that it must be a bison, be intrusted with scientific work for this great government?"

Cope was quite willing to drag in his friends and used correspondence that seemed of confidential nature to wage his attack. Published as a part of the *Herald* story was a letter from a young professor of anatomy at Yale College, S. W. Williston:

I wait with patience the light that will surely be shed over Professor Marsh and his work. Is it possible for a man whom all his colleagues call a liar to retain a general reputation for veracity! . . . I do not worry about his ultimate position in science. He will find his level, possibly fall below it. There is one thing I have always felt was a burning disgrace—that such a man should be chosen to the highest position in science as the president of the National Academy of Sciences, while men of the deepest erudition and unspotted reputation are passed by unnoticed. Professor Marsh did once indirectly request me to destroy Kansas fossils rather than let them fall into your hands. It is necessary for me to say that I only despised him for it.

Another young professor, W. B. Scott, who held the chair of geology and paleontology at Princeton, was quoted in part by Ballou thus:

I could corroborate all that are made against Professor Marsh if I were in a position to do so. Marsh distinguished himself by an open theft some years ago. He listened to an address by Professor Cope before the National Academy of Sciences on the Permean [Permian] reptiles. He took notes, and as soon as the address was completed hurried to New Haven and held back the *Journal of Science* until he could print and bring out the discoveries announced by Cope as his own. In science priority of discovery is secured by first publication. It is in this manner that Professor Marsh has won his laurels as a scientist.

Major John W. Powell made a dignified reply to Cope's allegations in the original report. Powell had been given the opportunity of reading the report before publication, a move that Ballou had made to avert libel action. In one paragraph summing his opinion of Cope, Powell wrote:

> I am not willing to be betrayed into any statement which will do injustice to Professor Cope. He is the only one of the coterie who has scientific standing. The others are simply his tools and act on his inspiration. The Professor himself has done much valuable work for science. He has made great collections in the field and has described these collections with skill. Altogether he is a fair systematist. If his infirmities of character could be corrected by advancing age, if he could be made to realize that the enemy which he sees forever haunting him as a ghost is himself, and if he could be made to see that it is of importance that he should promptly fulfil his engagements with other men, he could yet do great work for science.

Marsh, who had been quoted in the *Herald* as prepared to make a reply to Cope at the proper opportunity, found that opportunity in the January 19 edition. He opened his reply with:

> The author of the recent attack upon me and my work is Professor E. D. Cope, and he has at last placed publicly on record the slanders he has secretly been repeating for years. Whether he makes the statements directly or conceals them in the form of an interview with himself or others they are his own. He has devoted some of his best years to its preparation and to the preparation of the public for it, and it may thus be regarded as the crowning work of his life. . . .
>
> Little men with big heads, unscrupulous in warfare, are not confined to Africa, and Stanley will recognize them here when he returns to America. Of such dwarfs we have unfortunately a few in science, and some of them have fallen ready victims to the wiles of Professor Cope's flattery and promises of friendship. How reliable his friendship is many, both dwarfs and larger men, have learned to their cost.

The lawyers have a saying, "Set a man to write three letters and we will hang him." If Professor Cope and his partners have heard this proverb they surely have not heeded it. I leave the verdict to the public, with a faint suspicion that they will find it a case of suicide. . . .

In what purports to be an interview with Professor Cope, he repeats some of the previous charges and adds others that he now puts in print under his own name. His first charge in this series is that my publications on the evolution of the horse were mostly taken from Kowalevsky, of Moscow, without due credit.

This is a most unfortunate charge for Professor Cope to make. In the first place it is not true, and in the second he compels me to state things that, for the credit of science at least, might well be omitted.

My work on the genealogy of the horse was entirely my own and my conclusions were based on specimens I collected myself. I never saw Kowalevsky's work until my own was completed and partly published. I first laid my full conclusions, as shown by my own specimens, before Professor Huxley, when he visited me in New Haven, in 1876. I was already familiar with his works on the genealogy of the horse in Europe, and as my conclusions differed essentially from his, and my specimens seemed to show clearly that the horse originated in the New World and not in the Old, I laid the whole matter before him, and he spent nearly two days going over my specimens with me and testing each point I made.

He informed me that this was all new to him, and that my facts demonstrated the evolution of the horse beyond question and for the first time indicated the direct line of descent of an existing animal. With the generosity of true greatness he gave up his own opinions in the face of new truth and took my conclusions as the basis of his famous New York lecture on the horse. I think I need say no more on this point.

Professor Cope compels me to add something more about Kowalevsky and himself, in many respects the counterparts of each other, twin brothers in work and methods. I have already alluded to Professor Cope's depredations on the museums of the scientific world. Kowalevsky's were of similar character, although less known, but the cunning of his hand has been felt even in America.

During the recent International Geological Congress in London

I attended a conference of museum authorities who met to consider the depredations they had suffered from visiting scientists. The cases of Cope and Kowalevsky were fully discussed and the extent and skill of their respective work were topics of lively interest.

The general opinion was that it was a close race between them and no competitors in sight. Like the famous race between the dog and the wolf it was a case of nip and tuck, and the general conclusion seemed to be that, as in many more honorable international contests, the American was a little ahead.

Kowalevsky was at last stricken with remorse and ended his unfortunate career by blowing out his own brains. Cope still lives, unrepentant.

[Editor's note: Professor Kowalevsky, whose name was misspelled quite commonly among American paleontologists, was Vladimir O. Kovalevsky, an associate professor at Moscow University. He did blow his brains out, but not in remorse over the horse, as Marsh well knew. The professor was involved in financial speculations that backfired, and killed himself in 1883. He was an expert on fossil horses.]

Professor Cope charges once more that I have endeavored to pre-empt the land where he was exploring in the West.

What he means by this I know not, but I have often been obliged to protect not only localities I have myself discovered, but my personal property, from Professor Cope or the unscrupulous adventurers in his confidence and service. I can give specific instances, if necessary, and full evidence to substantiate what I say. . . .

It is stated in this attack, apparently to Professor Cope's credit, that he is now the editor of the *American Naturalist*.

To many readers this would be regarded as his crowning disgrace. The *American Naturalist* was long a scientific journal of repute and standing. Its editors and contributors were men of ability and respected in science. Among its contributors were some of the most distinguished men in America.

At the end of 1877 Professor Cope bought this journal, removed it to Philadelphia and became its proprietor and editor. How this act was regarded by the scientific men of the country who had hitherto sustained it is shown by the following circular, which was promptly issued when it was known that Professor Cope would in future absolutely control this journal: —

CIRCULAR

The undersigned, who have in past years contributed articles and by other means helped to support the *American Naturalist,* protest against the continued use of their names in the same connection under the new conditions advertised in the December number of 1877.

December 10, 1877.

Alexander Agassiz, Asa Gray, J. D. Whitney, H. A. Hagen, N. S. Shaler, J. A. Allen, W. G. Farlow, James D. Dana, O. C. Marsh, A. E. Verrill, J. S. Newberry, A. R. Grote, Samuel Lockwood.

The result anticipated has been more than realized. Professor Cope at once made the *Naturalist* his personal organ and used it for the abuse of honored names. He announced his own discoveries and discredited those of others, who were seldom allowed to reply, and even then their replies were sometimes garbled. He in every way prostituted this periodical to his own purposes. . . .

My acquaintance with Professor Cope dates back twenty-five years, when I was a student in Germany at the University of Berlin. Professor Cope called upon me and with great frankness confided to me some of the many troubles that even then beset him. My sympathy was aroused, and, although I had some doubts as to his sanity, I gave him good advice and was willing to be his friend.

As in any bitter struggle, there were casualties among bystanders as Cope and Marsh flailed each other. The major casualties occurred early, long before the principals were press figures. Among the first was Dr. Joseph Leidy, professor of anatomy at the University of Pennsylvania. Leidy usually is referred to as perhaps the last naturalist familiar with the entire spectrum of life, from amoeba to man. Leidy had been active in paleontology, and in his first publications in 1847 proved that there had been fossil horses in America. Ironically, Leidy taught the only college course that Cope ever formally attended, a three-month course of lectures on comparative anatomy at the University of Pennsylvania given in 1860.

The pioneer in scientific paleontology in North America, Leidy withdrew from the field around 1877, explaining publicly that although earlier almost all fossil specimens collected in North America had been forwarded to him, the Cope-Marsh rivalry and the money they were paying for specimens had dried up his sources. Privately, he told friends that he withdrew to avoid becoming embroiled between Cope and Marsh. Leidy had an experience early in the Cope-Marsh feud that justified his caution. Cope had found an extinct giant reptile in Kansas which he named *Elasmosaurus*. He wrote numerous papers on the fossil in 1869 and reconstructed the skeleton in the museum of the Philadelphia Academy of Sciences. Marsh visited the skeleton in 1870 and "noticed that the articulations of the vertebrae were reversed and suggested to him gently that he had the whole thing wrong and foremost." Marsh recalled Cope's indignation as "great." Marsh then took Professor Leidy to see the skeleton. Leidy quietly declared that the creature seemed to have an exceedingly long neck because Cope had assembled it backward and placed the skull on the end of the tail. As Marsh recalled in the newspaper battle, "when I informed Professor Cope of it, his wounded vanity received a shock from which it has never recovered, and he has since been my bitter enemy."

While Marsh was correct about Leidy's observations on the skeleton that Cope had assembled backward, he was concealing the truth about the length of the Cope-Marsh dispute and the incident that initiated it.

The truth was that in March 1868, Cope had taken his then friend Othniel C. Marsh to Haddonfield, New Jersey, to visit a marl pit where Cope and, earlier, Leidy had unearthed several good fossil animals. During the week the two friends spent in the marl pits area, Marsh made arrangements with local men to send him specimens of fossils for pay. Cope later was to charge that when he returned to the pit area, which was close to his home, "I found everything closed to me and pledged to Marsh for money."

Marsh's propensity for scattering money as a barrier to competitors has been detailed by so many naturalists of the period that it must be true. Professor William B. Scott in his autobiographical notes wrote:

> Othniel Charles Marsh, a nephew of the wealthy philanthropist, George Peabody, was from 1866 to his death in 1899 a professor at Yale and, like Cope, a man of wealth, as riches were measured in those days. I did not meet him until considerably later, and I always heartily disliked him; indeed, his hostility had a really detrimental effect upon my career. Like Charles Lamb, in the story which Woodrow Wilson was fond of repeating, I could

not really "hate a fellow I knew," but Marsh's egoism, his intense selfishness, and his unscrupulous duplicity aroused in me very strong feelings of resentment. Our dear professor of geology, Doctor Arnold Guyot, one of the gentlest and most kindly of men, never forgave Marsh for the way in which Marsh had euchred him out of a very fine Mastodon skeleton. Doctor Guyot had bought the skeleton from a man who found it on his farm, somewhere in New York State, and the bones were boxed and addressed to Princeton and lying ready for shipment in the railroad station. Marsh heard of the discovery, chartered a special engine and reached the station in time to induce the discoverer to accept a higher price and send the bones to New Haven. Not-

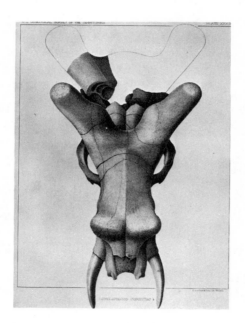

THE BATTLE OVER BONES between E. D. Cope and O. C. Marsh, one of the bitterest public disputes in the history of science, began over credit for discovery of the ancient beast whose fossil remains were depicted in Plate XXXIX in Volume III of the *Report of the U.S. Geological Survey of the Territories.* The book was titled *The Vertebrata of the Tertiary Formations of the West* but became known in the paleontology trades as "Cope's Bible," since it ran 1009 pages with 134 lithographic plates.

withstanding all this, Marsh was a very able man and rendered immense services to American palaeontology, really deserving his great reputation here and in Europe.

At one point in the heated contest to gain priority in publication of scientific names, Cope sent a telegram in hopes of beating Marsh, whom he suspected of having found a similar specimen. It occurred in the Bridge Basin of Wyoming. On August 17, 1872, Cope wired his printer in Philadelphia reporting the discovery of a skull of a gigantic creature which he named *Loxolophodon.* Some place along the line between Black Buttes, Wyoming, and Philadelphia, the word melted into *Lefalophodon,* and Cope's separate issued two days later bore the misspelling. Cope had resorted to "separates," the publication of a printed page and its circulation before regular publication of a journal, in order to beat Marsh in priority. For in paleontology as well as in all other fields of natural history, the first person who reaches print and circulation receives credit for the discovery.

The Cope-Marsh battle generated scores of double and triple names for the same species of fossils, since each was certain that the other had not described the extinct beast properly, or at least, hoped so. In addition, both contestants also were describing and renaming creatures that Leidy had already described correctly. As a result, some creatures' fossils bore a Marsh name, a Cope name, and a Leidy name. Later paleontologists devoted about thirty years to sorting specimens and determining priorities that would establish an acceptable name.

Government efficiency finally brought Marsh and Cope into their final conflict. In 1871, when Cope made his first trip into the American West with the F. V. Hayden Expedition, there were four government agencies engaged in Western surveys. In 1879, Congress decided to consolidate the efforts into one unit and organized the U.S. Geological Survey. In the scuffle for positions that ensued, Cope backed Hayden for director of the new agency. The position was won by Clarence King, who had headed one of the four replaced units. King was a friend of Marsh and acutely aware that Cope had opposed him. King soon was replaced by Major John W. Powell, who had headed another of the quadruple surveys. He was a Marsh admirer. Marsh meanwhile had been named paleontologist of the combined surveys.

The trend of events was a disaster for Cope. He had been working with the Hayden Survey not only to gain access to fossils in the West but also to secure government financing of the publication of his discoveries. Cope worked for the survey without pay. Cope's greatest triumph from association with the Hayden Survey was the publication, dated 1884 but circulated in 1885, of *The Vertebrata of the Tertiary Formations of the West,* a tome of 1,009 pages and 134 lithographic plates that became known as "Cope's Bible." The then new U.S. Geological Survey printed the volume on the grounds that it had been authorized through the original commission of the Hayden Survey. Cope, however, had another volume in manuscript, which he had entitled *Tertiary and Permian Vertebrata* and which he expected the government to publish. Major Powell ruled that there were no funds for Cope's second work. Indeed, Powell, in inspecting the bulk of the manuscript, suspected that Cope had produced two or three additional volumes. Cope immediately began pestering congressmen, successive secretaries of the interior, and any other reachable government official in an attempt to override Powell's decision and get the volume published.

The capping climax to Cope's despair came in mid-December 1889, when Secretary of Interior John Noble sent Cope a letter ordering him to turn over all his fossil specimens on the grounds that the material had been collected on a government expedition and therefore was government property. It was then that Cope called in Ballou and gave him his file of purported misdeeds by Marsh and Powell.

The postscript: Marsh was ousted as paleontologist for the U.S. Geological Survey in 1892 through abolition of the position by congressmen who could see no value in searching for birds with teeth; he continued, however, in his main position, professor at Yale. Powell resigned as director of the Geological Survey in 1894, a move he had been contemplating even before the newspaper skirmish. Cope kept his fossils and continued in his position at the University of Pennsylvania. Cope never succeeded in his campaign for publication of volume 2—except in a belated and truncated way. In 1915, some eighteen years after Cope's death, Dr. W. D. Matthew of the American Museum of Natural History, in cooperation with the U.S. Geological Survey, had the lithograph plates that had been printed for Cope's volume bound and distributed. The text never was printed.

Chapter XVII

────── ••• ──────

Superb but Mystic:
Coues

Dr. Elliott Coues was among the most respected American ornithologists when in 1880, at the age of thirty-eight, he followed a female guru known as Madame Blavatsky into the Theosophical Society of India. The transformation of a scientist into a mystic left his friends embarrassed as well as mystified. The reputation of a lesser man might not have survived such peregrination, but there was nothing lesser about Coues.

The curious event caused widespread speculation and spawned gossip. It perhaps may best be dealt with by a passage from the eulogy that Coues's lifelong friend Daniel Girard Elliot delivered before the eighteenth congress of the American Ornithologists' Union at Cambridge, Massachusetts, in 1900. Elliot combined charity with clarity:

> And first among his most eminent characteristics was his love of truth, and he was constantly striving with all the force of his energetic nature to search it out and take its teaching to himself wherever he might find it, careless where it might lead him or what preconceived views or opinions it might overthrow or destroy. He believed with Carlyle that "there is no reliance for this world or any other but just the truth, there is no hope for the world but just so far as men find out and believe the truth and match their own lives to it." It was therefore in his search for truth and an attempt to apply the principles of physical science to psychical research that in 1880 he became affiliated with the Theosophical Society of India and was elected President of its American Board of Control, and was continued in that office for several years. He was much interested in the subject and investigated its principles and methods with his usual thoroughness, even visiting Europe in company with Madame Blavatsky and other prominent members of the sect, and his connection with this and kindred societies resulted in the production of several

publications such as *Biogen* and the *Daemon of Darwin*. But the knowledge that he gained of this interesting but peculiar doctrine was not of that satisfying character as to cause him to hold fast to its tenets, nor to enable him to retain his respect for its leaders, and although he gives no reasons for the action, yet in the memorandum in which he records his election as President in 1885 and his re-election in the following year, with characteristic frankness he states that he was expelled from the Society in 1889. Those of us who have little sympathy with the claims asserted by the disciples of Theosophy cannot but regard his expulsion from the Society as having conferred a greater honor upon him than his election to the Presidency, and can easily imagine the action he may have taken in the Council to cause such a result after he finally satisfied himself that the doctrine could not substantiate its claims. He detested shams of all kinds and hurled the full force of his invective against those who had proved themselves unworthy or who strove to appear entitled to more than was their due.

Elliot failed to mention that Coues's expulsion from the mystical order came after publication in 1889 of his article entitled "Madame Blavatsky's Famous Hoax."

A eulogy would have been required in that era for Coues regardless of how he spent the remainder of his life, for he was one of three American ornithologists who in 1883 called for a meeting of ornithologists in New York in September which resulted in formation of the American Ornithologists' Union. As it turned out, however, his greatest work in ornithology remained ahead. In 1903, Coues's fifth edition of *The Key to North American Birds* was published posthumously. It was the culmination of what had ranged from extensive revisions to complete rewriting through four previous editions beginning in 1872.

In the eulogy, Elliot referred to the *Key* as "a work that in its conception and the masterly manner in which it was carried out in all its details stands as one of the best if not *the* best bird book ever written." As a friend, Elliot might have been suspected of exaggerating. But he wasn't. For even today, three-quarters of a century later, Coues's *Key* can still be read profitably, particularly his 241-page introduction, which is a complete treatise on ornithology of that day.

Born in 1842 in Portsmouth, New Hampshire, Coues attended Gonzaga College in Washington, and then entered Columbia University, where he acquired a bachelor's degree. In 1862 he became a medical cadet in the U.S. Army. He served through the Civil War and remained in the service to become one of those saddlebag surgeons who accompanied the cavalry troops in the West in pursuit of Indians. He was an army doctor until 1881, when he objected to being reassigned to Fort Whipple, Arizona, and resigned his commission.

Two of Coues's better-known books, *Birds of the Northwest* (1874) and *Birds of the Colorado Valley* (1878), were products of his service with the army. His work from 1884 to 1891 as zoology editor of the *Century Dictionary* won him acclaim. J. A. Allen, a noted zoologist of the era, referred to Coues's 40,000 entries in the dictionary as "practically an encyclopedia of ornithology." Throughout the period he wrote hundreds of papers for ornithological journals. He also had publications and some renown as a mammalogist and herpetologist, but nothing in those fields approached his ornithological work.

Of especial interest to ornithologists is the fact that Coues was chairman of the American Ornithologists' Union committee that promulgated its Code of Nomenclature in 1886. From the Code Committee came the *Check List of North American Birds*, patterned after Coues's own volume by that name published in 1873. The *Check List*, which undergoes periodic revision, is published by the A.O.U. as the final authority on bird names, distribution, and systematics, with which ornithologists must either conform or furnish convincing evidence that an entry in the book is in error and in need of revision.

A scholar who was severe in imprinting upon himself the rigid code of discipline necessary to scientific thought, Coues never completely stamped out a broad streak of humanity in his character. His so-called "sparrow war," in which he engaged the prestigious Dr. T. M. Brewer, Boston physician and ornithologist, had many elements of near-comedy, and Coues seemed at least later to take a philosophical view of the long-running encounter. In the *Osprey*, an ornithological journal, of May 1897, Coues, an opponent to the introduction of the European House Sparrow (also known as English Sparrow) in America, told how he finally had won a debate with Dr. Brewer before the Nuttall Ornithological Club of Cambridge. He added:

> The most distinguished opponents I ever had were not ornithologists and never pretended to be such. I recollect two of them —Henry Ward Beecher and Henry Bergh. The latter, the founder of the noble Society for the Prevention of Cruelty to Animals, published a tirade against me, in which he called me a "murderer," and all sorts of dreadful things besides. Baird told me he thought it the finest piece of pure invective he ever read. Many

years afterwards I met Mr. Bergh for the first time, and became impressed with the same profound respect for his personal character that I had always felt for his humane life-work.

I have sometimes wondered if chagrin at defeat in the Sparrow War did not hasten Dr. Brewer's demise (January 23, 1880). The war practically ended with his death, though it was long before sentimentalists ceased to exhibit hysteria. I naturally lost all active interest in the subject when I had proven my case to the satisfaction of the public, and the Sparrow had proven his case—which was that he had come to stay. . . .

In the fifth edition of the *Key*, Coues had this, in part, to say of the House Sparrow:

Repeatedly imported since 1858, and especially in the sixties, during a craze which even affected some ornithologists, making people fancy that a granivorous conirostral species would rid us of insect-pests, this sturdy and invincible little bird has overrun the whole country, and proved a nuisance without a redeeming quality. The original offender in the case is said to have been one Deblois, of Portland, Me., in 1858; but the pernicious activity of Dr. T. M. Brewer affected the city fathers of Boston in 1868–69, and even the Smithsonian Institution at Washington, about the same years. New York had the sparrow-fever in 1860–64, and Philadelphia was not as slow as usual in catching the contagion, in 1869. There is no need to follow the sad record further. Well-informed persons denounced the bird without avail during the years when it might have been abated, but protest has long been futile, for the sparrows have had it all their own way, and can afford to laugh at legislatures, like rats, mice, cockroaches and other parasites of the human race which we must endure. This species, of all birds, naturally attaches itself most closely to man, and easily modifies its habits to suit such artificial surroundings; this ready yielding to conditions of environment, and profiting by them, makes it one of the creatures best fitted to survive in the struggle for existence under whatever conditions man may afford or enforce; hence it wins in every competition with native birds, and in this country has as yet developed no counteractive influences to restore a disturbed balance of forces, nor any check whatever upon its limitless increase. Its habits need not be noted, as they are already better known to every one than those of any native bird whatever, but few realize how many million dollars the bird has already cost us. Nest anywhere about buildings, also in trees, bushes, and vines, built of any rubbish, usually lined with feathers, and making a bulky, unsightly object amidst dirty surroundings; eggs indefinitely numerous, usually 5 to 7, about 0.90 × 0.60, dull whitish thickly marked with dark brown and neutral tints; several broods a year are raised, as the birds breed in and out of season.

One familiar with birds will note quickly that Coues worked in an era when "splitters" approached a zenith. The form and plumage of birds provided the major clues as to the relationship among species, and a slight variation in plumage might be seized upon as justification for naming a new species. Coues was among ornithologists who had accepted Darwin's theory with its implications of fluidity in speciation, but at the time he worked no general agreement upon the boundaries that separated existing species had been determined. The certainty that the Creator had shaped immutable models no longer could be relied upon. The whole area of classification was in flux. Coues's systematics varied considerably from the then recent model set by Baird. The order in which genera of birds appeared reflected a different way of looking at birds. Although Coues was sensitive to the proliferation of supposed species and warned against the trend, his list of North American species and subspecies totaled more than 900. A more conservative modern estimate by Dr. Ernst Mayr of the Museum of Comparative Zoology, Cambridge, Massachusetts, and Dr. Lester L. Short of the American Museum of Natural History places North American species at 607. The discrepancy may be accounted for in part by modern taxonomists, or classifiers, who are more interested in recognizing the extent to which birds are similar than in emphasizing minor differences.

Coues understood rather clearly that Darwinism had revolutionized natural history and that the work he and others were doing in the period likely would be transient. Part of his charm stems from that recognition. He is less autocratic than the older naturalists, for he lacks the conviction that he has ferreted out secrets from a design that has lasted since the day of creation. He understands Pontius Pilate's and Bacon's question: What is truth? Fortunately, he was able to cast his attitude in words understandable to the layman. The following excerpts from the *Key* reflect this attitude:

So rapid, indeed, has been the progress, and so radical the changes wrought during the last few years, that I doubt not this is the time to take our bearings anew and proceed with judicious conservatism. Neither do I doubt that just at this moment a new departure is imminent, hinging upon the establishment of the American Ornithologists' Union. It behooves us, therefore, to consider the question, not alone of where we stand to-day, but also, of whither we are tending; for we are certainly in a transition state, and not even the near future can as yet be accurately forecast. The pliability and elasticity of our trinomial system of nomenclature is very great; and the method lends itself so readily to the nicest discriminations of geographical races,—of the finest shades of variation in subspecific characters with climatic and other local conditions of environment, that our new toy may not impossibly prove a dangerous instrument, if it be not used with judgment and caution. We seem to be in danger of going too far, if not too fast, in this direction. It is not to cry "halt!"—for any advance is better than any standstill; but it is to urge prudence, caution, and circumspection, lest we be forced to recede ingloriously from an untenable position,—that these words are penned, with a serious sense of their necessity.

In the present unsettled and perplexing state of our nomenclature, when appeal to no "authority" or ultimate jurisdiction is possible, it is well to formulate and codify some canons of nomenclature by which to agree to abide. It is well to apply such canons rigidly, with thorough sifting of synonymy, no matter what precedents be disregarded, what innovations be caused. It is well to use trinomials for subspecific determinations. But it is not well to overdo the "variety business;" feather-splitting is no better than hair-splitting, and the liberties of the "American idea" must never degenerate into license. Our action in this regard must stop short of a point where an unfavorable reaction would be the inevitable result. . . .

In no department of natural history has the late revolution in biological thought been more effective than in remodeling, presumably for the better, the ideas underlying classification. In earlier days, when "species" were supposed to be independent creations, it was natural and almost inevitable to regard them as fixed facts in nature. A species was as actual and tangible as an individual, and the notion was, that, given any two specimens, it should be perfectly possible to decide whether they were of the same or different species, according to whether or not they answered the "specific characters" laid down for them. The same fancy vitiated all ideas upon the subject of genera, families, and higher groups. A "genus" was to be discovered in nature, just like a species; to be named and defined. Then species that answered the definition were "typical;" those that did not do so well were "sub-typical;" those that did worse, were "aberrant." A good deal was said of "types of structure," much as if living creatures were originally run into moulds, like casting type-metal, to receive some indelible stamp; while—to carry out my simile—it was supposed that by looking at some particular aspect of such an animal, as at the face of a printer's type, it could be determined in what box in the case the creature should be put; the boxes themselves being supposed to be arranged by Nature in some particular way to make them fit perfectly alongside each other by threes or fives, or in stars and circles, or what not. How much ingenuity was wasted in striving to put together such a Chinese puzzle as these fancies made of Nature's processes and results, I need not say; suffice it, that such views have become extinct, by the method of natural selection, and others, apparently better fitted to survive, are now in the struggle for existence. . . .

In Coues's day the bird-watcher had more than a life list on which he checked off the species of birds that he had seen. Instead, he had somewhere around the house a stack of skins removed from the birds he had shot. The efficient binocular that renders an undistorted form and reliable colors did not exist. Telescopes of the era were hardly portable. Indeed, nowhere in his discussion of birding does Coues suggest that a visual record of a bird might have any validity. Until quite recently, the rules that Coues implied were necessary to ordinary bird observations and were considered the only inviolable method of establishing the presence of a rare bird in an area in which it had not been seen before. One shot the bird and presented the skin as evidence. Development of accurate color cameras that are highly portable have changed these ground rules. One now may offer a color photograph as a sight record, provided definitive characteristics of the bird are clearly evident. The possibility of cheating with the camera is no greater than the possibility of cheating with a hand-displayed bird skin. Bird skins commonly were traded among birders— and persons who never went afield could buy bird skins from dealers.

In reading the following brief excerpts from Coues's extensive directions for field birders, one must remember that he was a sensitive person who actually had a great love for birds. The extent in which it varies from modern practices among birders, so many of whom are violently opposed to hunting, is a measure of the differing attitudes of 1900 and today:

> How many Birds of the Same Kind do you want?—*All you can get*—with some reasonable limitations; say fifty or a hundred of any but the most abundant and widely diffused species. You may often be provoked with your friend for speaking of some bird he shot, but did not bring you, because, he says, "Why, you've got one like that!" Birdskins are capital; capital unemployed may be useless, but can never be worthless. Birdskins are a medium of exchange among ornithologists the world over; they represent value,—money value and scientific value. If you have more of one kind than you can use, exchange with some one for species you lack; both parties to the transaction are equally benefited. Let me bring this matter under several heads. (a.) Your own "series" of skins of any species is incomplete until it contains at least one example of each sex, of every normal state of plumage, and every normal transition stage of plumage, and further illustrates at least the principal abnormal variations in size, form, and color to which the species may be subject; I will even add that every different faunal area the bird is known to inhabit should be represented by a specimen, particularly if there be anything exceptional in the geographical distribution of the species. Any additional specimens to all such are your *only* "duplicates," properly speaking. (b.) Birds vary so much in their size, form, and coloring, that a "specific character" can only be precisely determined from examination of a large number of specimens, shot at different times, in different places; still less can the "limits of variation" in these respects be settled without ample materials. (c.) The *rarity* of any bird is necessarily an arbitrary and fluctuating consideration, because in the nature of the case there can be no natural unit of comparison, nor standard of appreciation. It may be said, in general terms, no bird is actually "rare." With a few possible exceptions, as in the cases of birds occupying extraordinarily limited areas, like some of the birds of paradise, or about to become extinct, like the pied duck, enough birds of all kinds exist to overstock every public and private collection in the world, without sensible diminution of their numbers. "Rarity" or the reverse is only predicable upon the accidental (so to speak) circumstances that throw, or tend to throw, specimens into naturalists' hands. *Accessibility* is the variable element

in every case. The fulmar petrel is said (on what authority I know not) to exceed any other bird in its aggregate of individuals; how do the skins of that bird you have handled compare in number with specimens you have seen of the "rare" warbler of your own vicinity? All birds are common somewhere at some season; the point is, have collectors been there at the time? Moreover, even the arbitrary appreciation of "rarity" is fluctuating, and may change at any time; long sought and highly prized birds are liable to appear suddenly in great numbers in places that knew them not before; a single heavy "invoice" of a bird from some distant or little-explored region may at once stock the market, and depreciate the current value of the species to almost nothing. For example, Baird's bunting and Sprague's lark remained for thirty years among our special desiderata, only one specimen of the former and two or three of the latter being known. Yet they are two of the most abundant birds of Dakota, where in 1873 I took as many of both as I desired; and specimens enough have lately been secured to stock all the leading museums of this country and Europe. (d.) Some practical deductions are to be made from these premises. Your object is to make yourself acquainted with all the birds of your vicinity, and to preserve a complete suite of specimens of every species. Begin by shooting every bird you can, coupling this sad destruction, however, with the closest observations upon habits. You will very soon fill your series of a few kinds, that you find almost everywhere, almost daily. Then if you are in a region the ornithology of which is well known to the profession, at once stop killing these common birds—they are in every collection. You should not, as a rule, destroy any more robins, bluebirds, song-sparrows, and the like, than you want for yourself. Keep an eye on them, studying them always, but turn your actual pursuit into other channels, until in this way, gradually eliminating the undesirables, you exhaust the bird fauna as far as possible (you will not *quite* exhaust it—at least for many years). But if you are in a new or little-known locality, I had almost said the very reverse course is the best. The chances are that the most abundant and characteristic birds are "rare" in collections. Many a bird's range is quite restricted: you may happen to be just at its metropolis; seize the opportunity and get good store, yes, up to fifty or a hundred; all you can spare will be thankfully received by those who have none. Quite as likely, birds that are scarce just where you happen to be, are so only because you are on the edge of their habitat, and are plentiful in more accessible regions. But, rare or not, it is always a point to determine the exact geographical distribution of a species; and this is fixed best by having specimens to tell each its own tale, from as many different and widely separated localities as possible. This alone warrants procuring one or more specimens in every locality; the commonest bird acquires a certain value if it be captured away from its ordinary range. An Eastern bluebird (*Sialia sialis*) shot in California might be considered more valuable than the "rarest" bird of that State, and would certainly be worth a hundred Massachusetts skins; a varied thrush (*Turdus naevius*) killed in Massachusetts is worth a like number from Oregon. But let all your justifiable destruction of birds be tempered with mercy; your humanity will be continually shocked with the havoc you work, and should never permit you to take life wantonly. Never shoot a bird you do not fully intend to preserve, or to utilize in some proper way. Bird-life is too beautiful a thing to destroy to no purpose; too sacred a thing, like all life, to be sacrificed, unless the tribute is hallowed by worthiness of motive. "Not a sparrow falleth to the ground without His notice."

I should not neglect to speak particularly of the care to be taken to secure full suites of *females*. Most miscellaneous collections contain four or more males to every female,—a disproportion that should be as far reduced as possible. The occasion of the disparity is obvious: females are usually more shy and retiring in disposition, and consequently less frequently noticed, while their smaller size and plainer plumage, as a rule, further favor their eluding observation. The difference in coloring is greatest among those groups where the males are most richly clad, and the shyness of the mother birds is most marked during the breeding season, just when the males, full of song, and in their nuptial attire, become most conspicuous. It is often worth while to neglect the gay Benedicts, to trace out and secure the plainer but not less interesting females. This pursuit, moreover, often leads to discovery of the nests and eggs,—an important consideration. Although both sexes are generally found together when breeding, and mixing indiscriminately at other seasons, they often go in separate flocks, and often migrate independently of each other; in this case the males usually in advance. Towards the end of the passage of some warblers, for instance, we may get almost nothing but females, all our specimens of a few days before having been males. The notable exceptions to the rule of smaller size of the female are among rapacious birds and many waders, though in these last the disparity is not so marked. I only recall one instance, among American birds, of the female being more richly colored than the male—the phalaropes. When the sexes are notably different in adult life, the *young* of both sexes usually resemble the adult female, the young males gradually assuming their distinctive characters. When the adults of both sexes are alike, the young commonly differ from them.

In the same connection I wish to urge a point, the importance of which is often overlooked; it is our practical interpretation of the adage, "a bird in the hand is worth two in the bush." Always keep the first specimen you secure of a species till you get another; no matter how common the species, how poor the specimen, or how certain you may feel of getting other better ones, *keep it.* Your most reasonable calculations may come to naught, from a variety of circumstances, and *any* specimen is better than no specimen, on general principles. And in general, do not, if you can help it, discard any specimen *in the field.* No tyro can tell what will prove valuable and what not; while even the expert may regret to find that a point comes up which a specimen he injudiciously discarded might have determined. Let a collection be "weeded out," if at all, only after deliberate and mature examination, when the scientific results it affords have been elaborated by a competent ornithologist; and even then, the refuse (with certain limitations) had better be put where it will do *some* good, than be destroyed utterly. For instance, I myself once valued, and used, some Smithsonian "sweepings"; and I know very well what to do with specimens, *now*, to which I would not give house-room in my own cabinet. If forced to reduce bulk, owing to limited facilities for transportation in the field (as too often happens) throw away according to *size,* other things being equal. Given only so many cubic inches or feet, eliminate the few *large* birds which take up the space that would contain fifty or a hundred different little ones. If you have a fine large bald eagle or pelican, for instance, throw it away first, and follow it with your ducks, geese, etc. In this way, the bulk of a large miscellaneous collection may be reduced one half, perhaps, with very little depreciation of its actual value. The same principle may be extended to other collections in natural history (excepting fossils, which are always weighty, if not also bulky); very few birdskins, indeed, being as valuable contributions to science as, for example, a vial of miscellaneous insects that occupies no more room may prove to be.

The current decline among birds of prey is reflected in Coues's advice that included a "fine large bald eagle" among the bird skins to be thrown away first for the sake of saving space. One may be imprisoned today for owning a fine, or even decrepit, bald eagle.

Chapter XVIII

◆•◆

The Protectionists:
Brewster, Hornaday, and Co.

On 17 November 1873 the following letter was mailed to a half-dozen young men in Cambridge, Massachusetts:

> Dear Sir
> You are respectfully invited by the undersigned to meet them at the residence of Mr. Wm Brewster, next Monday evening at 7½ o'clock relative to forming an ornitholocal [*sic*] society.
> If you are desirous of becoming a member we will be happy to consult with you.
>
>

Signed R. Deane
H. A. Purdie
W. D. Scott
Wm Brewster

Of the four who signed the letter, perhaps not even William Brewster was conscious of the impact that this desire for organization, which seems to have been Brewster's, would have upon wildlife conservation in America. As events eventually were to prove, Brewster was a most improbable gladiator in what was to be a rough field indeed: the emergence of unified bands of Americans demanding a better deal for wildlife. The movement was to suffer from faltering beginnings, and occasionally it was so poorly organized that the bottom fell out, but somehow it bumbled through adversities. Perhaps its saving grace was that the issue was greater than the leaders it attracted.

It is odd that the first organization Brewster motivated was never itself to become seriously involved in saving wildlife. It was formed as an ornithologists' club with scientific study of birds as its sole objective. For two years before writing the letter, the signers, who were of college age, had each Monday visited the attic of Brewster's parents' home on Brattle Street at Sparks Street in Cambridge to dis-

WILLIAM BREWSTER (1851–1919), ornithologist and organizer, first president of the Massachusetts Audubon Society and a leader in spreading the Audubon movement to other states, founder of the Nuttall Ornithological Club, one of the oldest bird societies in America, and a founder of the American Ornithologists' Union. He was photographed at his camp in Maine on Lake Umbagog, the location where he gathered information for one of his books, *The Birds of Lake Umbagog*.

cuss a rare treasure that Brewster owned: Audubon's five-volume *Ornithological Biography*. At the first formal meeting on 24 November 1873, according to Brewster's journal, which seems to contain the only surviving minutes, "We enlarged the Bird Club, by the addition of four new members, elected officers, &c, and gave it the name of the 'Nuttall Orn. Club.'" Brewster, who was twenty-two years old, was elected president, and the other signers filled the officers' roll. The four new members were Francis Parkman Atkinson, Harry Balch Bailey, Ernest Ingersoll, and Walter Woodman. To protect itself against further immaturity, the club limited its lowest age bracket for membership to college freshman age. Through its history to date, the Nuttall Ornithological Club has limited its activities to publishing scientific tracts on birds and maintaining a camaraderie among elitists and professionals in birding. Until its hundredth anniversary in 1973, it remained a binocular brotherhood, excluding even those women who were more accomplished ornithologists than most members.

The Nuttall Club was a comfortable group of sixteen men when, on May 6, 1876, it issued volume 1, number 1, of the *Nuttall Ornithological Club Bulletin*, a twenty-eight-page journal with a hand-colored plate of the Brewster's warbler as a frontispiece. The printing bill was $60.55, but the number of copies the club received remains vague. It is possible that 300 copies were printed, for the number appears in connection with later issues of the quarterly. Because there were far more journal copies than there were members, the Nuttall Club placed the publication on sale through booksellers and actively sought subscribers at one dollar a year for the four-issue volumes. The subscription list that year rose to 270 names and for the next couple of years wavered in that vicinity. Apparently the club had saturated the ornithology market. Some of the subscribers were so poor that they paid on an installment plan of twenty-five cents, and a few applied for periods of grace on the grounds that they needed the journal but lacked the quarter at the moment.

The implications of *Bulletin* publication seemed to have escaped the general club member. A club whose members either lived in Cambridge or could get to Brewster's home regularly by trolley had gone national without acquiring national ambitions.

After the publication of the first issue of the *Bulletin*, the Nuttall Club members discovered that in choosing coeditors they had teamed an inexperienced person and an overpretentious person. By May, when the second issue should have been ready for the press, it appeared that the copy might never be assembled. At the May 20, 1876, meeting, the club made a decision that would affect the course of scientific publication for the next forty-five years. They chose as a third associate editor Joel Asaph Allen, thirty-eight-year-old head of the ornithology department at the Museum of Comparative Zoology. Allen had joined the club a few weeks earlier, about the time that it became serious about publishing the *Bulletin*, and the membership, who had hesitated to invite him because he was considerably older and more distinguished than they were, were delighted. In retrospect, their surprise that Allen would join was indicative of the naiveté of the members. The scent of publication is a spoor that naturalists always have pursued vigorously. Allen moved into the vacuum between his coeditors and made the *Bulletin* and *The Auk*, which succeeded it, outstanding journals. In addition to editing the ornithology journals for forty years, he edited twenty-two volumes of the *Bulletin of the American Museum of Natural History*. In 1885 he moved to the American Museum, where he was curator of birds and mammals, a post to which he devoted the remainder of his life.

The Nuttall membership found Allen uncommunicative after he became *Bulletin* editor. When he attended meetings, he said nothing. The practice of reading every paper at a meeting before it was published also ceased. He became somewhat of a mystery man to them. What they did not recognize was the fact that in spite of his talent as a writer and editor, Allen was a social recluse. He found it impossible to face a crowd, refused to speak in public. In fact, he had difficulty functioning in groups of more than five persons.

On February 10, 1883, Brewster wrote Ingersoll a letter in which he disclosed that "for some time" he had had in mind the organization of a club of superornithologists "who care enough about ornithology to do their share of the work." He suggested: "An American Ornithologists' Union, limited to, say, twelve members, could, I think, be made up in such a way as to be a very strong institution." Another ornithologist, Dr. Elliott Coues, had been thinking along similar but more expansive lines. Letters were sent out to ornithologists in 1883 under the combined sponsorship of Brewster, Coues, and Allen, inviting ornithologists to join the A.O.U.

Since Brewster was the perennial president of the Nuttall Club, Allen its editor, and Coues listed on the *Bulletin* as an associate editor, an entirely honorary position, it often has been said that the American Ornithologists' Union was a spin-off organization of Nuttall. Allen, in fact, often credited the Nuttall Club as originator of the A.O.U. The record as recalled by Ingersoll seems to differ from Allen's recollection. Ingersoll saw it as a Brewster spin-off, noting that the general membership of the Nuttall Club, then about fifteen persons, was kept in ignorance by Brewster and that invitation to A.O.U. membership was sent to only three or four of them. The principal link between the two organizations seems to have been negative: editor Allen moved to the A.O.U. and took the Nuttall Club's quarterly with him.

In *The Auk* issue of October 1884, the proceedings from the A.O.U. second annual meeting, held at the American Museum of Natural History in New York, included the following paragraph:

> Mr. Brewster called attention to the wholesale slaughter of birds, particularly terns, along our coast for millinery purposes, giving some startling statistics of this destruction, and moved the

appointment of a committee for the protection of North American birds and their eggs against wanton and indiscriminate destruction, the committee to consist of six, with power to increase its number, and to cooperate with other existing protective associations having similar objects in view. After earnest support of the motion by Messrs. Brewster, Chamberlain, Coues, Goss, Merriam and Sennett, it was unanimously adopted, and the following gentlemen were named as constituting the committee: Wm. Brewster, H. A. Purdie, George B. Grinnell, Eugene P. Bicknell, Wm. Dutcher and Frederic A. Ober.

One of the committee members, Dr. George Bird Grinnell, later was to make this report on results: "During the ensuing year this Committee did nothing."

The public was to hear more later, however, from three members of that committee: William Brewster, George Bird Grinnell, and William Dutcher. Through avenues other than the A.O.U. conservation committees, they were to make emotional impacts that stirred action among citizens who appreciated justice for wildlife more than scientific inquiries into its ecological problems. Another member of the committee, C. Hart Merriam, was to make substantial contributions to wildlife welfare through another medium.

A reorganized A.O.U. Committee for the Protection of North American Birds made the first organized public impact for bird preservation on February 26, 1886, when it published a lengthy report in *Science* magazine. In slightly altered form, it was issued as Bulletin No. 1 of the committee. It contained a model law for bird protection. In May 1886, the New York Legislature passed a bird law based largely upon the model. It was an early victory for bird protectionists.

The A.O.U. has continued through the years to supply scientific assessments of trends among bird populations and to scout out factors limiting success among many species. Despite their value, the reports are of a nature that seldom makes first-page news.

Simultaneously with the publication of the A.O.U. report, one of the committee members, Dr. George Bird Grinnell, editor of *Forest and Stream* magazine, launched the first major attempt to enroll citizens who were not necessarily naturalists in a nationwide organization dedicated to the protection of wildlife, principally birds. Grinnell was a naturalist of many accomplishments. Among other things, he mastered several Indian languages and lived for periods with Western tribes. He even had the capacity to admire Othniel C. Marsh, for whom he worked several seasons in the great boneyards of the

Far West. Possibly the Marsh admiration came from the "Red Cloud affair," in which Marsh fought for better treatment of the Oglala Sioux nation. Chief Red Cloud, a predecessor of Sitting Bull, convinced Marsh that the $400,000 supposedly spent annually on the Sioux nation produced nothing beyond a scanty supply of rotted meat and weevily flour, and that federal overseers pocketed most of the money. Marsh fought his way through the corrupt Grant administration and finally obtained an audience with President U. S. Grant. In the end, Marsh broke up the thievery carried out in the Department of Interior by what the press called "the Indian Ring" and forced their resignations. It was one of his most courageous and selfless acts.

Just before announcing the formation of a national group, which he called "The Audubon Society," Grinnell had returned from a visit with the Blackfeet Indians on their reservation in northwest Montana. While there he had discovered the "Land of the Walled-In Lakes," which through his perseverance would become Glacier National Park in 1895. But at the moment, he was engaged in an activity for which he had limited talent: organizing a viable, militant, nationwide group to protect birds.

As an editor, Grinnell seemed to have the idea that a membership of activisits could be built much as magazine circulation was amassed. He began the Audubon Society as an extralimital service of *Forest and Stream*. A year later, in February 1887, he launched a special publication, *Audubon Magazine*, to serve the membership. Membership was free. Support of the work would come from sales of the magazine.

To join the Audubon Society, one had merely to sign a pledge that he or she would support at least one of three objectives. Grinnell urged that the prospective member give consideration to signing a pledge covering all three objectives, but one objective was sufficient. The objectives were:

> To prevent as far as possible:
> (1) The killing of any wild bird not used for food.
> (2) The taking or destroying of the eggs or nests of any wild birds.
> (3) The wearing of the feathers of wild birds. Ostrich feathers, whether from wild or tame birds, and those of domestic fowls, are exempted.

As one may imagine, arguments soon developed over whether

wrenching plumes from tame ostriches raised for the trade or killing wild ostriches for their plumes could be justified in any terms other than commercial.

The Audubon Society of Grinnell collapsed of its own loose structure with the issuance of the January 1889 edition, which rounded out two years of publication. On its death, it had 48,862 members—or, rather, signatures to pledges which required nothing in the way of support. In the magazine's farewell, Grinnell explained that "we have no such subscription list as is fairly remunerative for the trouble and expense involved in the publication of the magazine. . . ."

Audubon Magazine published letters from such citizens as John Greenleaf Whittier, Henry Ward Beecher, and John Burroughs. Its pages carried popularized life histories of many bird species, emotional appeals against the killing of birds, special features for young readers, reports on life among the Indians, and some generalized adventure and fiction. Among the Society's directors was Celia Thaxter, poet laureate of the Isles of Shoals and then grande dame of American literature and a resident of Boston. For the first issue, February 1887, she wrote under the title "Woman's Heartlessness" an essay from which this excerpt is taken:

When the Audubon Society was first organized, it seemed a comparatively simple thing to awaken in the minds of all bird-wearing women a sense of what their "decoration" involved. We flattered ourselves that the tender and compassionate heart of woman would at once respond to the appeal for mercy, but after many months of effort we are obliged to acknowledge ourselves mistaken in our estimate of that universal compassion, that tender heart in which we believed. Not among the ignorant and uncultured so much as the educated and enlightened do we find the indifference and hardness that baffles and perplexes us. Not always, heaven be praised! but too often—I think I may say in two-thirds of the cases to which we appeal. One lady said to me, "I think there is a great deal of sentiment wasted on the birds. There are so many of them, they never will be missed, any more than mosquitoes! I shall put birds on my new bonnet." This was a fond and devoted mother, a cultivated and accomplished woman. It seemed a desperate case indeed, but still I strove with it. "Why do you give yourself so much trouble?" she asked. "They will soon go out of fashion and there will be an end of it." "That may be," I replied, "but fashion next year may order them back again, and how many women will have human feeling enough to refuse to wear them?" It was merely waste of breath, however, and she went her way, a charnel house of beaks and claws and bones and feathers and glass eyes upon her fatuous head. Another, mocking, says, "Why don't you try to save the little fishes in the sea?" and continues to walk the world with dozens of warblers' wings making her headgear hideous. Not one in fifty is found willing to remove at once the birds from her head, even if languidly she does acquiesce in the assertion that it is a cruel sin against nature to destroy them. "When these are worn out I am willing to promise not to buy any more," is what we hear, and we are thankful indeed for even so much grace; but, alas! birds never "wear out." And as their wearer does not carry a placard stating their history, that they were bought last year or perhaps given to her, and she does not intend to buy more, her economy goes on setting the bad example, or it may be her indolence is to blame—one is as fatal as the other. Occasionally, but too rarely, we meet a fine spirit, the fire of whose generous impulse consumes at once all selfish considerations, who recognizes the importance of her own responsibility, and whose action is swift as her thought to pluck out the murderous sign, and go forth free from its dishonor. And how refreshing is the sight of the birdless bonnet! The face beneath, no matter how plain it may be, seems to possess a gentle charm. She might have had birds, this woman, for they are cheap enough and plentiful enough, heaven knows! But she has them not, therefore she must wear within things infinitely precious, namely, good sense, good taste, good feeling. Heaven bless every woman who dares turn her back on Fashion and go about thus beautifully adorned!

As his Audubon effort was dying, Grinnell was among a dozen men invited to a dinner in December 1887 by Theodore Roosevelt. Roosevelt had returned the previous winter from his ranch on the Little Missouri River, departing just before a blizzard had wiped out most of the cattle he had overstocked on the harsh range. The total ranch experience had cost him $52,500 but had turned him into a physically tough character ready for a fling in New York politics that eventually would carry him to the White House. While no minutes of the dinner remain, it is believed to have occurred at the home of a Roosevelt sister, Corinne Robinson, at 422 Madison Avenue in New York City. The outcome of the dinner was the organization of the Boone and Crockett Club. Its goal was to do for larger mammals what the Audubon Society had set out to do for birds—halt commercial killing.

The club limited its membership to 100, and since it was founded by big-game hunters, its basic requirement was that any candidate for membership must be a sportsmen of high caliber who had killed in fair chase at least one specimen of three species of the larger game mammals of North America. The Boone and Crockett Club, which still thrives, received its early impetus from Roosevelt. Much of what it did in its early existence, especially for hoofed mammals, is indistinguishable from the public actions of Roosevelt, for his energy dominated the club.

In 1892, John Muir ceased his role as a lone voice crying from the western mountains and gave a nonprofit corporate image to that battle by organizing the Sierra Club. It continued as a landscape preserver through the decades and in the 1960s came down out of the mountains to engage in general environmental work on the East Coast as well.

In the chronology, it appears that William Brewster emerged again as a pivotal person in organized conservation. The impression, of course, is incorrect, for he continued actively with the American Ornithologists' Union and Nuttall Club throughout the intervening years. However, in 1896 he accepted an additional role as president of the first Audubon Society that was established on sound enough grounds to remain in existence today. In later years, Miss Minna B. Hall recalled the history of its founding:

> You may like to hear how the Audubon Society started. Mrs. Hemenway, then Harriet Lawrence, lived across the street from me here in Longwood. One day she came over with *The Boston Blue Book*. We marked the names of the ladies of fashion who would be likely to wear aigrettes on their hats or in their hair. We had heard that Snowy Egrets in the Florida Everglades were being exterminated by plume hunters who shot the old birds, leaving the young to starve on the nests. These plumes brought a high price in the market. We then sent out circulars asking the women to join a society for the protection of birds, especially the Egret. Some women joined and some who preferred to wear the feathers would not join. We then went to see Mr. William Brewster of Cambridge and asked him if he would be our President. He accepted and we had our first meeting at Mrs. Hemenway's house on Clarendon Street on February 10, 1896.

The success of the Massachusetts Audubon Society, which Brewster headed, led to establishment of several independent state Audubon societies before the turn of the century. Since birds were their concern and so many of their leaders were ornithologists, it became a custom for the various state Audubon societies to meet annually as sort of a subsidiary at the American Ornithologists' Union's annual meetings. It was not an ideal arrangement, as there were mixed feelings about Audubon goals among ornithologists. It was an era in which ornithologists studied birds by killing them. Optical equipment was too poor to provide reliable visual information, and besides, collecting birds with the gun was an ornithological tradition. Many ornithologists were convinced that if Audubon protection goals were achieved, their field days would end. Even the earlier but ineffective Audubon Society organized by Grinnell had alarmed many professional ornithologists. Oddly, that alarmed group included Brewster, who devoted the summer of 1886 gunning all the common birds in the Concord region so that he could have a complete skin collection. He advised friends that the season might provide them the last chance to collect before a law banned the practice. The dichotomy among the A.O.U. membership was illustrated by an anecdote related by T. Gilbert Pearson, who was to become the first secretary of a national Audubon coalition. He attended the A.O.U. meeting at the National Museum in Washington in 1902. He saw a young man outside the assembly hall handing out fliers to A.O.U. members as they emerged from a session. The young man handed one of the papers to an older man who asked him what message it contained. "It is a notice of a meeting of the Audubon societies to be held tomorrow night," the young man answered. "What are Audubon societies?" the older man asked. "Societies to protect birds," the younger man replied. The older man handed back the paper and said, "I am not interested. I do not protect birds. I kill them." Pearson learned that the young man was Harry G. Oberholser and the older man, Charles B. Cory, both prominent ornithologists.

Brewster and an active Massachusetts Audubon board devoted considerable effort toward coordinating activities of the independent state groups. In 1901 a national committee of state Audubon representatives was formed, and from it emerged on January 5, 1905, the National Association of Audubon Societies for the Protection of Wild Birds and Animals. William Dutcher of New York, a member of the first A.O.U. Bird Protection Committee, was named the first president of the association.

Among the early goals of the Audubon societies, after curbing the plume hunters and millinery trade, was the abolition of hunting wildlife for the meat market. This brought an unexpected reaction from William Brewster. In his "Adventures in Bird Protection," T. Gilbert Pearson gave but one sentence to the matter: "Mr. William Brewster, although in his day regarded as a stalwart game-protector, resigned as a director of the National Association of Audubon Societies in 1912 because I was advocating the passage of a bill pending in the Massachusetts Legislature to stop the sale of game." An explanation of Brewster's action does not now exist. He was a sportsman and active hunter, but so were most of the key men in the early Audubon movement. In fact, most of them opposed market hunting more on the grounds that it would deplete the resource for sportsmen than for humane reasons.

The national association gradually evolved into the present National Audubon Society, whose activities have expanded recently on an international basis.

Perhaps more typical of what the general public regards as "the Audubon attitude" was Dr. William T. Hornaday, director of the New York Zoological Park, which was operated by the New York Zoological Society, one of the early great forces in American conservation. Behind Dr. Hornaday was the president of the society, Dr. Henry Fairfield Osborn, who was not only a great naturalist but also the young confidant through whom Edward Drinker Cope tested much of his material before engaging Marsh in newspaper columns. Among other activities, Dr. Hornaday had been a leader in the Bison Society, which saved the remnant population of these Great Plains ungulates. The New York Zoological Society today remains one of the most active conservation organizations, with projects designed to save endangered species in North America and the rest of the world.

A respected naturalist, Dr. Hornaday was fifty-eight years old and had witnessed one of the most destructive periods of wildlife exploitation when he wrote *Our Vanishing Wild Life*. His position was considerably more extreme than that of his contemporaries. In many respects, he was a man ahead of his times. Certainly his view that wildlife belonged to all people and not just to those who might reduce it to possession was not a prevailing attitude. His preface to *Our Vanishing Wild Life* affords an insight to his views:

> The writing of this book has taught me many things. Beyond question, we are exterminating our finest species of mammals, birds and fishes *according to law!*

I am appalled by the mass of evidence proving that throughout the entire United States and Canada, in every state and province, the existing legal system for the preservation of wild life is fatally defective. There is not a single state in our country from which the killable game is not being rapidly and persistently shot to death, legally or illegally, very much more rapidly than it is breeding, with extermination for the most of it close in sight. This statement is not open to argument; for millions of men know that it is literally true. We are living in a fool's paradise.

The rage for wild-life slaughter is far more prevalent to-day throughout the world than it was in 1872, when the buffalo butchers paved the prairies of Texas and Colorado with festering carcasses. From one end of our continent to the other, there is a restless, resistless desire to "kill, *kill!*"

I have been shocked by the accumulation of evidence showing that all over our country and Canada fully nine-tenths of our protective laws have practically been dictated by the killers of the game, and that in all save a very few instances the hunters have been exceedingly careful to provide "open seasons" for slaughter, as long as any game remains to kill!

And yet, the game of North America does not belong wholly and exclusively to the men who kill! The other ninety-seven per cent of the People have vested rights in it, far exceeding those of the three per cent. Posterity has claims upon it that no honest man can ignore.

I am now going to ask both the true sportsman and the people who do not kill wild things to awake, and do their plain duty in protecting and preserving the game and other wild life which belongs partly to us, but chiefly to those who come after us. Can they be aroused, before it is too late?

The time to discuss tiresome academic theories regarding "bag limits" and different "open seasons" as being sufficient to preserve the game, has gone by! We have reached the point where the alternatives are *long closed seasons or a gameless continent;* and we must choose one or the other, speedily. A continent without wild life is like a forest with no leaves on the trees.

The great increase in the slaughter of song birds for food, by the negroes and poor whites of the South, has become an unbearable scourge to our migratory birds,—the very birds on which farmers north and south depend for protection from the insect hordes,—the very birds that are most near and dear to the people of the North. *Song-bird slaughter is growing and spreading,* with the decrease of the game birds! It is a matter that requires instant attention and stern repression. At the present moment it seems that the only remedy lies in federal protection for all migratory birds,—because so many states will not do their duty.

We are weary of witnessing the greed, selfishness and cruelty of "civilized" man toward the wild creatures of the earth. We are sick of tales of slaughter and pictures of carnage. It is time for a sweeping Reformation; and that is precisely what we now demand.

I have been a sportsman myself; but times have changed, and we must change also. When game was plentiful, I believed that it was right for men and boys to kill a limited amount of it for sport and for the table. But the old basis has been swept away by an Army of Destruction that now is almost beyond all control. We must awake, and arouse to the new situation, face it like men, and adjust our minds to the new conditions. The three million gunners of to-day must no longer expect or demand the same generous hunting privileges that were right for hunters fifty years ago, when game was fifty times as plentiful as it is now and there was only one killer for every fifty now in the field.

The fatalistic idea that bag-limit laws can save the game is to-day *the curse of all our game birds, mammals and fishes!* It is a fraud, a delusion and a snare. That miserable fetich has been worshipped much too long. Our game is being exterminated, everywhere, by blind insistence upon "open seasons," and solemn reliance upon "legal bag-limits." If a majority of the people of America feel that so long as there is any game alive there must be an annual two months or four months open season for its slaughter, then assuredly we soon will have a gameless continent.

The only thing that will save the game is by stopping the killing of it! In establishing and promulgating this principle, the cause of wild-life protection greatly needs three things: money, labor, and publicity. With the first, we can secure the second and third. But can we get it,—and *get it in time to save?*

As was true of most contemporary naturalists, Dr. Hornaday had but a vague idea of animal ecology. He regarded all predatory birds and mammals as vermin that should be exterminated. He wrote: "There are several species of birds that may at once be put under sentence of death for their destructiveness of useful birds, without any extenuating circumstances worth mentioning." One of these birds was the peregrine falcon, a bird now extirpated in the East by the chain reaction of hard pesticides. Several major conservation groups now are working to restore the bird. Weirdly, as he was writing, the predatory birds and mammals had been reduced severely both by agricultural practices and the gun. Dr. Hornaday knew this but exhorted conservationists to wipe them out even though he could report: "As a rule, the few predatory wild animals that remain are not slaughtering the birds to a serious extent; and for this we may well be thankful."

In what may be the most correct statement he ever made, Dr. Hornaday insisted: "Here is an inexorable law of Nature, to which there are no exceptions: *No wild species of bird, mammal, reptile or fish can withstand exploitation for commercial purposes.*"

The truth of that statement might have borne questioning in 1912, when the technology of hunting and catching the vast schools of ocean fishes or in hunting down the speedy blue whale and its rorqual relatives remained primitive. But its application to most terrestrial species was evident then, and further technological developments in hunting methods have proved it totally today.

In the battle to save wildlife, literally thousands of organizations have arisen and disappeared, most leaving no traces. Indeed, so many survive today and so many new ones are being organized that the National Wildlife Federation annually produces a directory of organizations which, if it were a telephone directory, would be large enough to serve a medium-sized city. While the directory identifies most state and federal bureaus that deal with wildlife problems, it hits only the high spots among private agencies, listing primarily those that have been in existence long enough to have achieved a few goals. The federation, organized in 1936, was a sportsmen's club response to inadequate enforcement of game laws and poor administration of game policies. As it matured, it became a broad conservation organization, and one now finds it teamed with diverse groups in fighting such issues as the overexploitation of whales.

The often crude efforts of the early conservationists must be measured in the context of their times. America was undergoing population expansion, the Indian was being displaced in the West, new industries were burgeoning, and the eastern farm was dying. Americans were experiencing cultural shock as old ways were replaced by new. Railroad networks were connecting all communities into a communications web, and for the first time what may have been seen as a local problem finally became identified as a national problem.

Almost a symptom of cultural shock was the common conception, even among conservationists, that many wildlife declines could be blamed upon the hunting activities of recent immigrants, especially those from the Mediterranean area. In the South, they found blacks exceptionally exploitive of wildlife. Overlooked was the fact that many of those who were blamed as exploiters were themselves so exploited by the economy that they had no time to kill wildlife.

Well-intentioned persons created wildlife refuges of a half acre or less, almost as though they expected wildlife to flock behind the protective wording of signs nailed to tree trunks. Bird protectors were killing eagles, hawks, owls, and other predators without giving a thought to the fact that these creatures who live at the top of the food chain were the most endangered. For the most part, predators had suffered disastrous declines, because the wild populations on which they feed were disappearing. Meanwhile, the average citizen was quite confident that oppressed birds and mammals would "go somewhere else" and continue living. The concept that most environments already shelter as many members of a species as can live there had not emerged. It was even argued by some citizens that the Carolina paroquets were migrating to Australia. At the time, the paroquets were being extirpated through agricultural practices that eliminated their food, through being shot as agricultural pests, and through being captured as cage birds. Most persons, including conservationists, did not understand that each species native to a wild landscape has several requirements that must be met or it cannot survive. A minor change in the environment which removes or lessens any one of the basic requirements can mean death to a species, or more probably to several species. The identification of these requirements, which are so crucial to wildlife survival, had barely begun.

Chapter XIX

The Conservationists: Roosevelt and Nature Scribes

In 1887 the new Division of Economic Ornithology and mammalogy of the U.S. Department of Agriculture issued its first annual report. It contained the following passage, embodying a most unusual attitude for the period:

> On the 23d of June, 1885, the legislature of Pennsylvania passed an act known as the "scalp act," ostensibly "for the benefit of agriculture," which provides a bounty of 50 cents each on Hawks, Owls, Weasels, and Minks killed within the limits of the State, and a fee of 20 cents to the notary or justice taking the affidavit.
>
> By virtue of this act about $90,000 has been paid in bounties during the year and a half that has elapsed since the law went into effect. This represents the destruction of at least 128,571 of the above-mentioned animals, most of which were Hawks and Owls.
>
> Granting that five thousand chickens are killed annually in Pennsylvania by Hawks and Owls, and that they are worth 25 cents each (a liberal estimate in view of the fact that a large proportion of them are killed when very young), the total loss would be $1,250, and the poultry killed in a year and a half would be worth $1,875. Hence it appears that during the past eighteen months the State of Pennsylvania has expended $90,000 to save its farmers a loss of $1,875. But this estimate by no means represents the actual loss to the farmer and taxpayer of the State. It is within bounds to say that in the course of a year every Hawk and Owl destroys at least one thousand mice, or their equivalent in insects, and that each mouse or its equivalent so destroyed would cause the farmer a loss of 2 cents per annum. Therefore, omitting all reference to the enormous increase in the numbers of these noxious animals when nature's means of holding

them in check has been removed, the lowest possible estimate of the value to the farmer of each Hawk, Owl, and Weasel would be $20 a year, or $30 in a year and a half.

Hence, in addition to the $90,000 actually expended by the State in destroying 128,571 of its benefactors, it has incurred a loss to its agricultural interests of at least $3,857,130, or a total loss of $3,947,130 in a year and a half, which is at the rate of $2,631,420 per annum! In other words, the State has thrown away $2,105 for every dollar saved! And even this does not represent fairly the full loss, for the slaughter of such a vast number of predaceous birds and mammals is almost certain to be followed by a correspondingly enormous increase in the numbers of mice and insects formerly held in check by them, and it will take many years to restore the balance thus blindly destroyed through ignorance of the economic relations of our common birds and mammals.

A knowledge of the food-habits of our common birds and mammals would benefit every intelligent farmer to the extent of many dollars each year, and occasionally would save him the loss of an entire crop. It would save certain States many thousands of dollars which they now throw away in bounties, and would add millions of dollars to the proceeds derived from our agricultural industries.

Hence it becomes the duty of the division to attempt to educate the farming classes in the truths of economic ornithology and mammalogy.

The author of the report, Dr. C. Hart Merriam, exaggerated a bit. Not every hawk and owl destroys a thousand mice a year; some prefer other provender and ignore mice. The report, however, was on the right track in attacking bounties, which at best are a useless waste of taxes. In addition, it was a rather fearless endorsement of predatory birds, which were unpopular creatures then and destined to remain so for another half-century.

In addition to providing the citizens with unexpected information on the nation's wildlife, Dr. Merriam sought the cooperation of farmers, ranchers, ornithologists, and mammalogists—indeed, every citizen—in amassing biological facts about birds and mammals. He gave detailed directions on, among other things, how to preserve the stomach contents of freshly killed animals and gave directions on methods of shipping the material to him in Washington. He asked for observations on the migrations of birds and mammals.

The flurry of activities within the Division of Economic Ornithology and Mammalogy was supported by a total budget of $10,000, and Dr. Merriam, a new man on the job, was expanding the federal interest in the welfare of wildlife, which up to that point had been nil.

A year earlier he had become the first economic ornithologist employed by' the federal government. He resigned the private practice of medicine in New York to accept the post. Since there was no administrative provision for such a position, he had been assigned to the Division of Economic Entomology, a rather new bureau assigned to study injurious insects. The total federal support for ornithology that year was $5,000, and Congress expected Merriam to organize an office as well as to pay salaries. The following year, Merriam had succeeded in separating his activities from entomology and had himself named chief of a new Division of Economic Ornithology and Mammalogy. A short time later, he was heading the U.S. Biological Survey, the predecessor of the present U.S. Fish and Wildlife Service. From 1885 to 1910, when he resigned to continue wildlife research, Dr. Merriam was a great constructive force within the government in the battle to save American wildlife. His most solid achievements in the field came with the Theodore Roosevelt administration, but he had worked tirelessly through preceding administrations to build the foundation that made quick progress possible. In 1903 he suggested that Pelican Island, off the Florida coast, be sanctioned as a new type of government reservation: a national wildlife refuge. President Roosevelt approved his proposal, and Merriam assigned the first federal wildlife agent as protector of the birds there. The pelicans deserted the island almost immediately and did not return for some thirty years, but a precedent had been set. It was to grow into a great network of refuges protecting wetlands primarily for migrating waterfowl.

While still a practicing physician, Dr. Merriam was among the small band of naturalists who founded the Linnaean Society of New York on March 7, 1879. He was elected the first president of that now prestigious organization. Two years before accepting the federal appointment, he had written an extensive monograph entitled *The Vertebrates of the Adirondack Region*, a tome still readable even within today's greater knowledge of the creatures. As a student he had accompanied Cope of the Cope-Marsh skirmish as a biologist of the famed Hayden Survey. He later was to serve as president of the American Ornithologists' Union and was active with the Boone and Crockett Club as well as other organizations.

The murder of Guy Bradley, an Audubon warden at the Lake

Cuthbert rookery in what now is the Everglades National Park, perhaps was indicative of the problems surrounding early wildlife protection. It at least illustrated the general public apathy that often existed in areas where wildlife abounded. Bradley was shot by plume hunters as he boarded their boat near Cape Sable to search for plumes. Although there was general knowledge, or at least deep suspicion, concerning the malefactors, nothing was done to punish them.

In fact, until the Lacey Act of 1894 ended the practice, little was done to prevent hunting in the national parks. The public attitude toward Yellowstone, for instance, was quite different than it is today. The idea of declaring an area a wildlife refuge was generally considered unnecessary and perhaps an infringement upon the rights of free citizens. A progenitor within our clan, Henry Sheldon Reynolds, a naturalist and oftimes natural history professor, spent part of July and most of August 1883 in Yellowstone. At the time he was a silver assayer for the Hecla Mining Company at the mines near the now defunct Glendale, Montana. He and his family had joined a wagon-and-buggy train of families from the Dillon-Glendale-Twin Bridges area and trekked down by Virginia City to enter the park. It was twelve years after the park had been created. His journal relates how the travelers lived on "swan steaks," which were the breast muscles of the trumpeter swan, which eventually was reduced almost to extirpation. At the first eruption of one of the irregular geysers, the vacationers dashed off to witness it in such a hurry that they left the Canada geese roasting on spits over an open fire and the supper was ruined. It is obvious from remarks in the journal that they were living off the land, as though Yellowstone Park were a grocery store; and that their attitude was not unusual for others seemed to be doing the same.

It was long after wildlife had declined into low levels that anyone gave serious consideration to creating a public sanctuary. The idea of dedicating an area solely for the use of wildlife seems to have occurred in California. That sanctuary now is in the heart of Oakland and is known as Lake Merritt. Samuel Merritt of Oakland bought the land, then lying outside the city, in 1852 and created the lake by damming a slough. Senator Edward Thompson introduced a bill to make the lake a waterfowl sanctuary in the 1869–70 session of the California Legislature, and it was passed March 18, 1870, according to the California Senate Journal. Oddly, there seems to have been no public notice of the creation of the sanctuary, and the history of its origin, beyond the Senate record, remains vague.

The assassination of President William McKinley at the Pan-

American Exposition in Buffalo, New York, September 6, 1901, resulted in a second naturalist attaining the White House. Thomas
Jefferson, whose *Notes on Virginia* contained early natural history
reports, has been regarded as the first naturalist president. His argument with the famous French naturalist the Comte de Buffon over
whether New World creatures were merely degenerate or dwarfed
forms of Old World cousins should have qualified Jefferson for the
honor. To settle the matter, Jefferson had a moose collected in Vermont and sent its skeleton to Buffon. The moose happens to be the
world's largest member of the deer family, so the French genius of
natural history, who had no American experience, became more careful in his transatlantic interpretations.

The new naturalist in the White House was Theodore Roosevelt.
Undoubtedly a more knowledgeable naturalist than Jefferson, Roosevelt also was far more vocal. The Comte de Buffon would have gotten far more than a moose skeleton from Roosevelt. He could have
depended upon receiving a verbal comeuppance of vigor.

Modern historians have made it rather clear that much of the work
Roosevelt did in conservation fields, particularly the national forest
projects done with Gifford Pinchot, were not as radical in the economic sense as many citizens of that era supposed. They were saving
the forests, not as playgrounds, as many persons today suppose, but
as timber reservations for the use of industry. In fact, they were saving the timber barons from the barons' own greed, which was destroying the resource on which they thrived. The conservation
achievements of Roosevelt are often belittled today, but to endorse
such a position one would have to overlook the Governors' Conference which Roosevelt convened in 1908. The conference remains one
of the landmarks in conservation history. It provided the first great
stocktaking of American resources, and many of its predictions regarding the potential exhaustion of nonrenewable resources finally are
approaching reality. If it failed in any aspect, it was in the matter of a
timetable: the more pessimistic participants expected the well to go
dry much faster.

Roosevelt not only invented the word *conservation* as a symbol to
describe the wise use of resources while preserving them, but also
was an active conservator as well as a field naturalist. He set aside 148
million acres of timberland, established more than fifty wildlife refuges, doubled the number of national parks, and created a new cate-
gory of park, which he named national monument, and set up sixteen
of them, including the Grand Canyon. It was an impressive score.

As a naturalist, Roosevelt wrote several books, some of whose titles rather carefully shielded much of the natural history content. Among them were *African Game Trails, Through the Brazilian Wilderness, Hunting Trips of a Ranchman,* and *Outdoor Pastimes of an American Hunter.* He also wrote natural history papers for magazines, and it is in this field that naturalists most often recall him.

The most notable of these papers were "Men Who Misinterpret Nature," published in *Everybody's Magazine* in June 1907, and "Nature Fakers," published in *Everybody's* in September 1907. Roosevelt was in the White House at the time of publication, and the nature and content of the articles created national comment, much of it unfavorable.

One needs a bit of background to understand how Roosevelt got involved in the field of nature story criticism, which then was in vogue. Roosevelt's friend John Burroughs got him embroiled in the dispute. In 1903, Burroughs wrote for *The Atlantic* a story entitled "Real and Sham Natural History." In it he denounced Charles G. D. Roberts, Canadian poet and nature writer, and the extremely prolific William J. Long, a Stamford, Connecticut, Congregational minister, who was performing for wildlife a service somewhat similar to what Parson Weems did for George Washington: using the subject as a center for moralizing myths. In the article, Burroughs attacked Ernest Thompson Seton, wildlife artist and author, as the founder of what he considered a shaky school of nature writing and referred to Seton's popular wildlife book *Wild Animals I Have Known* as deserving the title: *Wild Animals I ALONE Have Known.*

Although more tolerant of Seton than Burroughs was, Roosevelt agreed with Burroughs's estimate of Roberts and, particularly, Long. He and Burroughs discussed the subject both by correspondence and in person on a trip to Yellowstone.

As occasionally happens, Burroughs's attack on Seton had a spin-off of great value to natural history. Seton was a much sounder naturalist than Burroughs had assessed him as being. While it may have been true that Roberts and Long were copying the Seton format of fictionalizing natural history observations, they were remiss in their natural history background and Seton was not. There perhaps was a streak of envy involved in Burroughs's attack, for Seton was a successful writer in the nature field and more than a contemporary of Burroughs; he was indeed a serious competitor.

Seton later gave this version of his first postpublication exchange with Burroughs in his autobiography, *Trail of an Artist-Naturalist:*

Then a curious event took place. Andrew Carnegie was giving a dinner to the fifty outstanding New York writers. Hamlin Garland and Clarence Stedman, among the number, called at my New York apartment that night, so we could go together.

Hamlin's first question was: "What are you going to do about Uncle John's attack?"

"Nothing at all," I replied.

"What! Nothing!"

"No, nothing. The attack is a sufficient answer to itself."

"Well," said Garland, and Stedman agreed: "That is all very well as a general attitude; and would do now, if Uncle John were a nobody. But there is no question that Burroughs has a seat on Mount Olympus, and what he says goes around the world. Some one must reply—the attack is so unjust and so untrue. How would you like me to reply?"

"For yourself, Hamlin, do as you please. Authorized by me, not one word. I am going to sit tight, do nothing, and win."

So we talked in the car till we came to Carnegie's house on Fifth Avenue at Ninety-first Street. We entered the big reception room, paid our respects to Mr. and Mrs. Carnegie. Then, in a far corner, I saw a group of three men in earnest discussion. All three had hair as white as snow. They were Mark Twain, William Dean Howells, and John Burroughs. I learned afterward they were talking about me.

I turned to Garland and said: "Now, Hamlin, watch your uncle, and learn a lesson on 'how to win a battle.' "

I walked over to the group—all old acquaintances—and said cheerily: "How do, everybody." Howells and Mark shook hands with me cordially. Burroughs turned his back, and began to study a small picture on the wall. But I followed him up and said: "Here, Uncle John, don't try to pull that stuff on me."

Howells, timid and gentle, was fearful of a scene, so fled away. Mark Twain cocked up his head in a comical way, and prepared to enjoy it.

Burroughs knew he was cornered. He turned red and stammered: "Now, see here, Seton, you are not holding that up against me personally?"

"Holding what?" I said with subterfuge.

"Oh, well!" he said. "You know—"

"Know what?" I answered.

"You know I roasted you in *The Atlantic Monthly*."

"You did?" I replied with an affectation of great surprise.

He went on: "There was nothing personal in it, it was purely an academic analysis."

"You amaze me," I answered. Just then Carnegie came over and took me by the arm: "I want you to meet some people over here," he said, and led me to another group.

I took advantage of the opportunity to say: "Mr. Carnegie, where am I placed at the table?" He pointed to the extreme east. "Where is John Burroughs?" He pointed to the extreme west. I said: "No, no! you place us together, and you'll see some fun."

"By George," he said, "that's a sporty proposition. I will!" He changed the place cards, so Burroughs and I sat side by side. And, believe me, I was conscious of the fact that every one near by was watching and listening to us.

Burroughs looked unhappy and terribly nervous, but I assumed the mastery and talked with academic aloofness. Part of our dialogue ran thus:

"Mr. Burroughs, did you ever make a special study of wolves?"

"No."

"Did you ever hunt wolves?"

"No."

"Did you ever photograph or draw wolves in a zoo?"

"No."

"Did you ever skin or dissect a wolf?"

"No."

"Did you ever live in wolf country?"

"No."

"Did you ever see a wild wolf?"

"No."

"Then, by what rule of logic are you equipped to judge me, who have done all of these things hundreds of times?"

Burroughs turned very red. He was much flustered, and exclaimed: "Well, there are fundamental principles of interpretation and observation that apply to all animals alike."

One other shot I fired into him. "Of course," I said, "it is all right to criticize me. I am used to it. I am public property. But why did you attack that innocent young child of nature, W. J. Long [whom I knew nothing about]? He is telling the truth sincerely as he sees it. Now he is crushed and broken, sitting desolate on the edge of his grave. Mr. Burroughs, if you hear of a terrible tragedy in that boy's home in the near future, you can lay it to only one cause—the blame will be wholly yours."

Poor old John broke down and wept. The fact that I did not

know anything at all about Long or what he had written, did not have any real bearing.

Seton was to get a mild back-of-the-hand from Roosevelt when the President finally went public with his ideas concerning his fellow naturalists who lived by the pen. Oddly, Roosevelt's brush at Seton came three years after Burroughs had made a semi-apology to Seton in another *Atlantic* piece in which he commented:

THE OLD BULL'S LAST FIGHT, by Ernest Thompson Seton, was Plate XXIX in his *Life Histories of Northern Animals*. Seton's drawings ranged from cartoons to rather elaborate and exact renditions, particularly of mammals. Seton had a flair for the dramatic that, combined with his arrogant egotism, made his acceptance difficult for other naturalists. His fictionalized lives of mammals often were criticized. The old bull drawing overdoes a natural situation a bit, since aged bison usually are too short of breath for such heroic struggles, and it has a sense of endlessness that exaggerates the normal pack size.

Some are nature students, dryly scientific, some are senti-
mental, some are sensational and a few are altogether admirable.
Mr. Thompson Seton, as an artist and raconteur, ranks by far the
highest in this field; he is truly delightful.

Seton not only was talented but also was rather vain. His autobiography reeks of self-adulation. By reading between the lines, one
readily understands that he felt grossly underappreciated, or at least
that others' regard for him fell far short of his own. The Burroughs-
Roosevelt criticisms led him to produce his outstanding work, *The
Lives of Game Animals*. The Seton pen, whether employed in art or
writing, always was highly sensitive to cash register trends. His books
portraying the lives of animals within a fiction frame had been what
one might call best sellers today. He was convinced that a serious
work presented in a scientific format would be a dismal seller at best.
He and his publisher considered a first printing of 2,000 copies as
the break-even point for a publication. Seton was certain that there
were not 2,000 readers of English who would invest in a serious work
such as the *Lives*. But he was bitter about the criticisms and determined to produce a work that would vindicate his honor. He and his
publishers, Doubleday, Page and Company, worked out an agreement
by which 177 copies of the work would be printed as a deluxe edition, with the provision that a regular edition would be published in
the indeterminate future if there were public response. Seton expected to complete the work, which finally consisted of four volumes,
in three years. It eventually required eight years, with Seton abandon-
ing all other publication plans, declining lecture bids, giving up vaca-
tions, and devoting his entire effort to the work. In the preface to
volume 4, Seton gloats a bit, justifiably as it turned out. He gives the
background that spurred the effort:

In 1904, owing to attacks on the reliability of my animal stories
as natural history, I was induced to offer a sample of my serious
scientific work.

President Theodore Roosevelt had always been my friend and
backer, and about this time he urged me to publish my observations. He said: "People do not dream of how many facts you
have back of your stories." Although I was far from ready, it
seemed wise to respond; so, in 1909, I published a preliminary of
the present work, as *Life Histories of Northern Animals*.

This had the effect foretold by many friends—it silenced my critics.

And as a guarantee of the work's authenticity, he writes:

Nevertheless, the Biological Survey, the National Museum, and the American Museum have given me every help and every encouragement. The eminent men whose names are listed in the "Acknowledgments" have freely and cheerfully given me their best information and the benefit of their lifelong training as naturalists.

This, in effect, guarantees the authenticity of all facts submitted—a guarantee that, in its fullness and force, has never before been equalled in a popular natural history.

In *Trail of an Artist-Naturalist*, he reports in what is almost modesty for him:

I set to work to do so; and after three or four years got out my scientific work, *Life Histories of Northern Animals*, in two quarto volumes. This was acclaimed as a masterpiece. For this I was awarded the Camp-Fire gold medal, for the most valuable contribution to popular natural history of the year. It was, however, merely the prodrome of my *Lives of Game Animals*, which came out ten years later in four large quarto volumes, and for which I got the Burroughs Medal and the Elliot Gold Medal of the National Institute of Science. This is the highest recognition offered in America, and effectively silenced all my critics. Every scientific library in America today points to *Seton's Lives*, as the last word and best authority on the subject.

The *Lives* was the first great popular work on mammalogy since John Bachman collaborated with the Audubons. The work was republished as eight volumes in 1953, a tribute to its lasting value. If there is a professional mammalogist working today in the American field who has not read at least portions of the *Lives*, he or she probably would claim to have. What's more important, he or she undoubtedly uses some of the field techniques suggested by Seton, although perhaps unknowingly.

Roosevelt obviously had no knowledge that Seton would turn out a classic mammalogy when he decided he no longer would remain silent concerning nature writers. Even though he treated Seton with some respect in his comments, his description of what he did not appreciate was broad enough to encompass Seton's work. After all, Burroughs was essentially correct in crediting Seton as the original type, whom offenders were copying.

Edward B. Clark, Washington correspondent for the *Chicago Evening Post*, precipitated Roosevelt's first criticism of nature writers. Clark, who was an amateur naturalist and frequent hiking companion of Roosevelt, had a discussion with the President one spring evening at the White House. Roosevelt voiced considerable disapproval of Long, Roberts, and Jack London, whose hairy-chested scrivening on Alaska was commercially viable. The next day Clark paraphrased Roosevelt's remarks and showed him a copy. Roosevelt felt that Clark had not covered the field thoroughly and added about one-third to the manuscript in his own handwriting on White House stationery. Clark submitted the piece to *Everybody's Magazine* under his own by-line as an interview with the President and gave it the title "Roosevelt on Nature-Fakirs." A champion for simplified English spelling, one of the skills which he never mastered, Roosevelt in the ensuing debate insisted upon spelling the derisive terms as "nature fakers."

In *The Works of Theodore Roosevelt*, a twenty-two-volume compendium of his writings, the President accepted responsibility for the following portion of Clark's "interview," which appears in a section of volume 5 classified as "Papers on Natural History":

Men Who Misinterpret Nature

I DON'T believe for a minute that some of these men who are writing nature stories and putting the word "truth" prominently in their prefaces know the heart of the wild things. Neither do I believe that certain men who, while they may say nothing specifically about truth, do claim attention as realists because of their animal stories, have succeeded in learning the real secrets of the life of the wilderness. They don't know, or if they do know, they indulge in the wildest exaggeration under the mistaken notion that they are strengthening their stories.

As for the matter of giving these books to the children for the purpose of teaching them the facts of natural history—why, it's an outrage. If these stories were written as fables, published as fables, and put into the children's hands as fables, all would be well and good. As it is, they are read and believed because the writer not only says they are true, but lays stress upon his pledge.

There is no more reason why the children of the country should be taught a false natural history than why they should be taught a false physical geography.

Dropping the matter of the school-books for a moment, take the stories of some of the nature writers who wish to be known as realists. Realism is truth. A writer like Stewart Edward White is true to nature; he knows the forest and the mountain and the desert; he puts down what he sees; and he sees the truth. But certain others either have not seen at all, or they have seen superficially. Nature-writing with them is no labor of love. Their readers, in the main persons who have never lived apart from the paved streets, take the wildest flights of the imagination of these "realists" as an inspired word from the gospel of nature. It is false teaching.

Take the chapter from Jack London's "White Fang" that tells the story of a fight between the great northern wolf, White Fang, and a bulldog. Reading this, I can't believe that Mr. London knows much about the wolves, and I am certain that he knows nothing about their fighting, or as a realist he would not tell this tale. Here is a great wolf of the northern breed; its strength is such that with one stroke it can hamstring a horse or gut a steer, and yet it is represented as ripping and slashing with "long, tearing strokes" again and again and again a bulldog not much more than a third its size, and the bulldog, which should be in ribbons, keeps on fighting without having suffered any appreciable injury. This thing is the very sublimity of absurdity. In such a fight the chance for the dog would be only one in a thousand, its victory being possible only through getting a throat grip the instant that the fight started. This kind of realism is a closet product.

In the same book London describes a great dog-wolf being torn in pieces by a lucivee, a northern lynx. This is about as sensible as to describe a tom cat tearing in pieces a thirty-pound fighting bull-terrier. Nobody who really knew anything about either a lynx or a wolf would write such nonsense. Now, I don't want to be misunderstood. If the stories of these writers were written in the spirit that inspired Mowgli and we were told tales like those of the animals at the Council Rock, of their deliberations and their something more than human conclusions, we should know that we were getting the very essence of fable, and we should be content to read, enjoy, and accept them as fables. We don't in the least mind impossibilities in avowed fairy-tales; and Bagheera and Baloo and Kaa are simply delightful variants of

Prince Charming and Jack the Slayer of Giants. But when such fables are written by a make-believe realist, the matter assumes an entirely different complexion. Men who have visited the haunts of the wild beasts, who have seen them, and have learned at least something of their ways, resent such gross falsifying of nature's records.

William J. Long is perhaps the worst of these nature-writing offenders. It is his stories, I am told, that have been put, in part, into many of the public schools of the country in order that from them the children may get the truths of wild-animal life.

Take Mr. Long's story of "Wayeeses, the White Wolf." Here is what the writer says in his preface to the story: "Every incident in this wolf's life, from his grasshopper hunting to the cunning caribou chase, and from the den in the rocks to the meeting of wolf and children on the storm-swept barrens, is minutely true to fact, and is based squarely upon my own observation and that of my Indians."

As a matter of fact, the story of Wayeeses is filled with the wildest improbabilities and a few mathematical impossibilities. If Mr. Long wants us to believe his story of the killing of the caribou fawn by the wolf in the way that he says it was done, he must produce eye-witnesses and affidavits. I don't believe the thing occurred. Nothing except a shark or an alligator will attempt to kill by a bite behind the shoulder. There is no less vulnerable point of attack; an animal might be bitten there in a confused scuffle, of course, or seized in his jump so as to throw him; but no man who knows anything of the habits of wolves or even of fighting dogs would dream of describing this as the place to kill with one bite. I have seen scores of animals that have been killed by wolves; the killing or crippling bites were always in the throat, flank, or ham. Mr. George Shiras, who has seen not scores but hundreds of such carcasses, tells me that the death wounds or disabling wounds were invariably in the throat or the flank, except when the animal was first hamstrung.

If Mr. Long's wolf killed the caribou fawn by a bite through the heart, as the writer asserts, the wolf either turned a somersault—or pretty near it—or else got his head upside down under the fore legs of the fawn, a sufficiently difficult performance. Wayeeses would have to do this before he could get the whole breast of the animal in his mouth in order to crush it and bite through to the heart. It is very unlikely that any wolf outside of a book would be fool enough to attempt a thing like this even with a fawn caribou, when the killing could be done far more surely in so many easier ways.

But the absurdity of this story is as nothing to the story of the killing of a bull caribou by the same wolf, using the same method. "A terrific rush, a quick snap under the stag's chest just behind the fore legs where the heart lay; then the big wolf leaped aside and sat down quietly again to watch."

Mr. Long has Wayeeses, after tearing the caribou's heart, hold himself "with tremendous will-power from rushing in headlong and driving the game, which might run for miles if too hard pressed."

Now here Mr. Long is not thinking of anything he has ever seen, but has a confused memory of what he has heard or read of gut-wounded animals. A caribou with such a hurt may go on for a long distance before it drops, and it is wise not to follow it too closely, because if not followed it will often lie down, and in an hour or so will become too stiff to get up. But it would seem that even Mr. Long might know, what a child should know, that no caribou and no land mammal of any kind lives after the heart is pierced as he describes; whether followed or not, the caribou would fall in a few jumps. This, however, is the least of the absurdities of the story. That Wayeeses tore the heart of the bull caribou in the way that Mr. Long describes is a mathematical impossibility. The wolf's jaw would not gape right; the skin and the chest walls with all the protective bone and tissue could not possibly be crushed in; the teeth of the wolf could not pierce through them to the heart, for no wolf's teeth are long enough for the job, nor are the teeth of any other carnivorous land mammal. By no possibility could a wolf or any other flesh-eating land mammal perform such a feat. It would need the tusks of a walrus. Mr. Long actually cannot know the length of a wolf's fang; let him measure one, and then measure what the length would have to be to do the thing he describes; and then let him avow his story a pleasing fable. He will get a clear idea of just what the feat would be if he will hang a grapefruit in the middle of a keg of flour, and then see whether a big dog could bite through the keg into the grapefruit; it would be a parallel performance to the one he describes when he makes his picturebook wolf bite into the heart of a bull caribou.

As a sort of a climax of absurdity to this "true story of Wayeeses," Mr. Long draws a picture of this wilderness wolf, savage from tip to tip, doing for some lost children the kindly service of leading them home through the forest. Now let me repeat that this would be all right if the story were avowedly a fairy-tale, like Kipling's "Jungle Book." But it is grotesque to claim literal truthfulness for such a tissue of absurdities.

I wonder sometimes as I read the lynx stories of Mr. Long if this wilderness tramper ever saw a lynx to know it at all in any real sense. He has several stories of the lynx. They vary little in their grotesque inaccuracy. Take the story of "Upweekis the Shadow," which has place in a little book that I am told is used as one of the supplementary readers from which American school-children are expected to get accurate knowledge of wilderness ways. There are all kinds of absurdities in this lynx "study." In one place, for instance, Mr. Long describes a number of lynxes gathered around the nearly eaten carcass of a caribou, while a menagerie of smaller beasts, including a pine-marten, circulates freely among them. Now, of course, a marten would circulate among a company of lynxes just about as long as a mouse would circulate among a company of cats. But the most comic feature of Mr. Long's lynx article is his account of various desperate encounters he had with the animal, which he evidently regards as a monster dangerous to man.

We are told by the writer that a lone lynx made him exceedingly "uncomfortable" for half an afternoon. The animal "dogged" him hour after hour through the wilderness. He tells of making double time for four miles in order to reach camp before night should fall and give the lynx the advantage. Mr. Long declares that he had an encounter with the lynx before he succeeded in driving it from the trail. In reality, any one is in just as much danger of being attacked by a domestic cat when walking through his own garden as Mr. Long was of being attacked by this lynx of the northern wilderness.

Once more let me say that if the fairy-tale mark were put on the stories of these writers, criticism would pass. Apparently, however, they wish to be known as teachers, or possibly they have a feeling of pride that springs from the belief that their readers will think of them as of those who have tramped the wilds and met nature in its gentleness and in its fierceness face to face.

Some of the writers who at times offend, at other times do excellent work. Mr. Thompson Seton has made interesting observations of fact, and much of his fiction has a real value. But he should make it clear that it *is* fiction, and not fact.

Many of the nature stories of Charles G. D. Roberts are avowedly fairy-tales, and no one is deceived by them. When such is the case, we all owe a debt to Mr. Roberts, for he is a charming writer and he loves the wilderness. But even Mr. Roberts fails to consult possibilities in some of his stories.

The lynx seems to have an unholy fascination for these realists, and Mr. Roberts has succumbed to it. I wish he had learned a little of the real lynx, as distinguished from the Mr. Long lynx, before he wrote the story called "On the Night Trail."

It's a big lynx that weighs over forty pounds. A fifty-pound lynx is a giant among the American species. An ordinary lucivee is about the size of a big Rocky Mountain bobcat. I have seen a light-weight dog, a cross between a bull-terrier and a collie, take a full-grown, able-bodied lynx out of a hole, though this is a rather exceptional feat. When the lynx is hard pressed and gets into a good place it will turn and fight just as a domestic cat will fight in the same circumstances, but it won't fight on its own initiative. In a hole it can usually stand off a good dog, but in the open any big fighting dog will kill it. I have known two ordinary foxhounds to kill a lucivee; several times I have seen a Rocky Mountain lynx, or bobcat, killed by a pack of half a dozen or more hounds and terriers, and in no case did the struggle last over a few seconds, the lynx being killed so quickly that it had no time to leave a serious mark on any one of its numerous foes.

Now in this "Night-Trail" story of Mr. Roberts a man catches a lynx in a trap, ties it up, puts it into a bag, and, swinging it over his shoulder, starts through the woods with his burden. On his way the man is attacked by eight wolves that form themselves in a crescent at his front. He is armed with an axe and as well as he can he fights off his wolf assailants. In the crisis, in order to give the lynx a chance for its life and perhaps a chance to create "an effective diversion in his own favor," the man slashes the sack open, cuts the lynx's bonds, and sets it free.

The lynx, according to Mr. Roberts, goes into the fray with the wolves with a sort of savage exultation. Several of the wolves receive slashes which send them yelping out of the battle. Now the thing is so utterly ridiculous that any man who knows both the wolf and the lynx loses patience. Real wolves would have made shreds of a real lynx within a twinkling of the time they closed in to the attack. The animal of the story would have stood no more chance with the eight wolves than a house cat would stand in a fight with eight bull-terriers.

In one of the books that I understand is used as a supplementary reader is a story of "the caribou school." It is difficult to discuss this story with patience. The writer, Mr. Long, vouches for the truth of everything in the book by saying that the sketches are the result "of many years' personal observation in woods and fields." He tells of finding half a dozen mother caribou and nearly twice as many little ones gathered together in a natural opening surrounded by dense underbrush—and this was their schoolroom. Then there follows a description of the mother caribou's method of teaching manners to the young, of giving them lessons in jumping; and of impressing upon them the necessity of following the leader. Mr. Long allows little for instinct. He says: "It was true kindergarten teaching, for under the guise of a frolic the calves were being taught a needful lesson." Such a tale, which the school-children receive stamped with the word "truth," should need no comment; and it is rather startling to think of any school authorities accepting it.

The preservation of the useful and beautiful animal and bird life of the country depends largely upon creating in the young an interest in the life of the woods and fields. If the child mind is fed with stories that are false to nature, the children will go to the haunts of the animal only to meet with disappointment. The result will be disbelief, and the death of interest. The men who misinterpret nature and replace facts with fiction, undo the work of those who in the love of nature interpret it aright.

Three months later in *Everybody's Magazine,* the President published an extended but less interesting piece, which he entitled "Nature-Fakers." The title and his frequent use of the hyphenated word put it into the language.

Roosevelt, whose flamboyance as well as progressive political opinions kept him a controversial person, did not escape scot-free in the uproar that followed his pronouncements on nature literature. He was condemned in the press for using the nation's highest office to attack private citizens. Cartoonists depicted wildlife fleeing before a menacing Roosevelt, armed to his prominent teeth.

Perhaps the most devastating attack was the Reverend Long's open letter to Roosevelt published in newspapers across the nation. In it, he said:

Who is he to write, "I don't believe that some of these nature-writers know the heart of wild things"? I find after carefully reading two of his big books that every time he gets near the heart of a wild thing he invariably puts a bullet through it.

Or perhaps even worse was a poem printed in the *New York Sun:*

> Hail, blustering statesman, butcher of big game,
> Less President than Prince in pride of will,
> Whose pastime is the princely sport, to kill,
> Whose murderous feats unnumbered fools acclaim!

Chapter XX

Painting Feathers: Fuertes

A knowledge of birds disqualifies one as a critic of the art of Louis Agassiz Fuertes.

A field ornithologist familiar with the behavior of birds usually is amazed by the reality that Fuertes captured with brush or pen. The ornithologist sees the Fuertes bird poised, ready to commit itself to some action typical of its species. Perhaps it is that closely defining phrase "typical of its species" that the ornithologist appreciates most, for Fuertes knew and portrayed birds, not in a general way, but within the context of each species' behavior pattern. But the essential element that captures the ornithologist's admiration is that a Fuertes bird is a true bird. It is not a feathered human. It is not some indefinable creature capable of folkloric action. It is a bird, in appearance, in attitude, in structure—totally avian in all aspects.

Curators of art museums, however, usually find Fuertes less exciting. If the Fuertes painting has a message, the curator has missed it. He sees nothing dynamic, possibly since the dynamism that exists requires the viewer's own experiences for recognition. The curator would prefer an Audubon flock, swirling through a design that convinces the uninitiated.

Perhaps Fuertes came nearest to fulfilling artistic expectations in his penciled field sketches. With a few strokes of the pencil, he records an attitude, a behavior, a position of the bird in flight or at rest. To some extent, they remind one of the economy involved in the few Oriental brush strokes that amazingly become fighting stallions. But, once again, such sketches speak fully only to those who know the message.

His birds of Ethiopia portraits, which may be his best work, were progressing so splendidly that one wonders what Fuertes might have accomplished if he had been a more careful automobile driver. It must remain speculation, however, for on August 22, 1927, at fifty-three years of age, Fuertes drove around a hay-wagon and met a rail-

RAPTOR-AND-PREY pencil sketch by Louis Agassiz Fuertes was taken from the Massachusetts Audubon Society's collection of Fuertes originals. Fuertes made many field sketches, usually less detailed than this example, in which he recorded natural poses of birds. The sketch suggests a goshawk holding a robin, although the bill has a notched tooth more typical of a falcon. However, Fuertes knew that the essence of a bird came through in a drawing as the sum of just such details as this—and the reader can be assured that it was corrected in the finished painting.

road train at Potter's Crossing, near Unadilla, New York, and was killed instantly. Remarkably, a collection of Ethiopian paintings which he had been showing an editor was thrown clear of the wreckage.

The accident closed thirty years during which Fuertes was the most prolific as well as most admired bird artist in America. Fuertes had painted everything from small cards to be tucked into baking soda boxes to illustrations for monumental state bird books. He worked in an era when the printing of color plates was being perfected. As a result, his illustrations were available to millions of Americans. As a matter of fact, he was the first bird painter since Audubon to make the medium his full-time work, and he was more successful than

Audubon in that he was a recognized illustrator before he was graduated from Cornell and during the remainder of his life always had more commissions than he could fill.

Wherever one might rank Fuertes as an artist, naturalists have always recognized him as a truly great naturalist. He fulfilled the exacting restrictions of the trade: the exact color and quality of the feather, the precise proportions to all parts of the anatomy, the rendition of a portrait that would serve identification better than a mounted specimen or a study skin. For Fuertes imparted the illusion of life, and he knew the living bird thoroughly. Those who suppose that the same thing might be done with a camera need to review Fuertes's plates and color photos.

Born in Ithaca, New York, where he kept a home all his life, Fuertes began painting birds seriously at the age of fourteen, without any formal training. His father, who was born in Puerto Rico and had become a faculty member at Cornell University, saw no future in bird painting. So Fuertes enrolled in 1893 at Cornell as an architecture student.

As a sophomore, Fuertes traveled to Washington, D.C., with the Cornell Glee Club. There he was introduced to Dr. Elliott Coues, then a leading American ornithologist, by a nephew of Coues who also was a member of the glee club. Coues was so impressed by Fuertes's illustrations that he arranged for an exhibition of fifty of them at the American Ornithologists' Union's meeting in Washington in 1895. The following year, Coues arranged for Fuertes to accompany a collection of his work to the A.O.U. convention in Cambridge, Massachusetts.

The association with Coues was most fortunate. The ornithologist arranged for Fuertes to illustrate a children's book, *Citizen Bird*, on which he was collaborating. Coues also provided useful criticism of Fuertes's work as long as he lived. A typical comment from Coues appeared in a letter of November 1896, in which he said:

> As I think I told you in New York, I will accept all the pictures you showed us, with two exceptions of the nuthatch and the hummingbird, which I should like to have you do over again. Put the nuthatch in the most characteristic attitude, head downward on a perpendicular tree trunk, with a full rounded breast, and bill pointing horizontally out to right or left. Take the framework away from the hummingbirds, set the female better on the nest, and draw the bills thinner.
>
> And in general, *keep your accessories down*. What we want is

the *bird*, with least possible scenery, stage setting, framework or background of any description. You will remember that even in the cases of those very fine pictures of the summer warbler and the yellow-rump, the *foliage* about them somewhat interfered with the effect. Be always careful about this. . . .

In other words, Coues was advising Fuertes to trim away the art and concentrate upon the illustration. It was good advice in that it made Fuertes the most desired illustrator in the business.

In another letter, Coues advises:

I heartily approve this lot, with no criticism except in one case. You must do the turnstone over again. It is good, but not up to your present mark; for you have relapsed into your early crudeness about the belly and legs. I noticed in your early drawings that you had not learned to handle these parts. Now you have gotten the plover on its legs just right, and you must remodel the turnstone to make it stand as the plover does. At present the turnstone has got its legs pulled out about an inch too far. It would pass muster with ordinary drawings, but it is not up to your mark, and you must either fit it with a new pair of legs, or draw another altogether. You see how solicitous I am that nothing whatever shall appear in these drawings to detract from your highest standard of excellence.

Coues himself was a competent sketcher of bird parts and included many of his own drawings in his famous *Key to North American Birds,* the great fifth edition of which was to contain more than 200 wash drawings by Fuertes, many as full-page illustrations. Coues was to perform another service for Fuertes at a critical point in the young artist's life. Fuertes's father was convinced that no one could earn a living painting birds. Coues wrote the following letter to Fuertes's *mother* on March 29, 1897, as Fuertes neared the time for graduation from Cornell:

My dear Mrs. Fuertes:—

I am naturally much pleased to receive your letter. We "understand."

I fully believe Louis is too sensible and honest a character to be spoiled by what has been said, or I would have refrained from giving him in public even his just dues. His letter to me today contains some expressions that I like, regarding his absorbing interest in his work, which he says is the last thing he thinks of at night, etc. That is what I should expect, if he is on the right track, and there seems to be no danger of turning his head while it is so full of what he wants and intends to do. Then there is a naiveté about his apology for not thanking me more properly—he has been too busy, he says, with "a mixture of examinations, laboratory reports, and bird-painting." That is delightful!

I am sure that real genius can never be stayed or thwarted—the most we can do is to guide it a little, in its modes of expression. This I have tried to do in the present case. I saw his *possibilities,* two years ago, when he had not then drawn a single picture quite fit to print, and undertook to discipline him into the necessary technique. The result thus far is fully up to my expectations—yet I regard it as only a beginning.

If the present series of 111 pictures turn out as I expect, I can probably secure him a contract worth several thousand dollars cash. Both fame and fortune seem to be within his grasp, if I can guide him along the way now opened. I have had the handling of a good many boys who wanted to do this or that in science, but had no means, and I have uniformly told them that the *first* thing was to secure means of livelihood, which they could not hope for in science at the outset; and to come to me again, in the matter of ornithology, *when* they had become self-supporting in some "practical" trade, business or other occupation. With Louis it is different. If things turn out as I expect, the thousand dollars or so he will put in his pocket for this work is very little in comparison with what he will be able to earn soon. He should be independent of the world from the start; if his work goes on as it should, he could command more than a *fair* price for the productions of his pencil and brush. I have sometimes fancied his father was not altogether pleased, or even satisfied, and imagined he had other plans for his son's future. But if Louis' gifts be what I believe them, he will never make anything of himself, except along the lines of their exercise and development—never attain to more than "respectable mediocrity" (which for me means dead failure) in any other direction. I weighed my words in the Osprey, in saying that this country has not before seen Louis' equal in the *possibilities* of zoological art (I did not say actualities, as yet; good as his pictures already are, I regard them as indicative only of what he may attain to, if he keeps on as he has begun).

I hope he is not getting hurried or worried about his present press of work. It is urgent, to be sure, as we are printing the text of the book rapidly, and shall be done before he gets all his pictures made to go with it. But I wish you would see that he does not over work. Far better let the work wait a little, than have a single picture in it that shows signs of haste or carelessness. Every one should be as good as he can possibly make it, and he must take his own time.

As soon as he has finished with this contract, and graduated from college, I hope he will be able to take a long rest, go off in the woods, and get fresh inspiration from contact with nature. Do you know, I can see a difference between the pictures he makes of birds he knows alive, and those he has only dead specimens of to work from? I should like to have him turned loose for the summer, with his field glasses, pencils and sketch book. There is nothing like it, for the ends we have in view.

I should like to hear from you further, and probably also Mr. Fuertes may wish to write, as the probable shaping of a gifted young man's career is of course of the utmost importance.

Mrs. Coues thanks you for your kind message, and joins me in cordial regards.

Very sincerely yours,
(Signed) Elliott Coues

The Coues letter may have cast the deciding vote in the family decision regarding Fuertes's future. Fuertes's father was not unduly cautious; the nation was in one of its periodic depressions, and no one had made a living, in good times or bad, at painting birds within his lifetime.

In July 1897, a month after graduation from Cornell, Fuertes came under the influence of a second mentor, Abbott H. Thayer, a famous animal painter of the period. Fuertes already had illustrated three books while finishing studies at Cornell, a success greater than an artist of his young years might expect. Thayer was not only a painter but also a naturalist. He had a theory that the color patterns of most animals served as camouflage. He considered the most outlandish color splashes on animals as concealing coloration under the light conditions common to their habitats. Thayer painted creatures that blended into the environment, as wild animals indeed do, often producing a picture that could qualify as a puzzle. Thayer met Fuertes at the A.O.U. meeting in Cambridge and invited him to travel to the Thayer summer home in Dublin, New Hampshire, for study. In a letter to Fuertes, Thayer said: "I omitted to say (what I suppose is, however, obvious) that of course the pleasure of teaching you would be the only form of pay that I could accept."

The Fuertes-Thayer friendship continued to Thayer's death. Fuertes was to recall the beginning thus:

As unexpectedly and as providentially as was the aid and advice of Coues in the material and scientific side of the work, came almost simultaneously an invaluable opportunity to study the much harder and even more exacting work of painting. Mr. Abbott H. Thayer, one of America's greatest painters, who is also a most keen and efficient naturalist—the one person in the world best able to help and criticize—volunteered his help, and a year of priceless study with him was the outcome.

It is amazing that Thayer remained associated with Fuertes so long, since the nature of Fuertes's commercial commitments forced him to violate many of the basic effects that Thayer strove for. Indeed, many of Fuertes's excellent illustrations have no background against which protective coloration might be demonstrated. He chose instead the Coues injunction that the bird's the thing.

Thayer's theories did serve Fuertes in World War I. The bird artist assisted the United States government's camouflage efforts on military equipment.

Dr. Frank M. Chapman of the American Museum of Natural History, whose *Handbook of Birds of Eastern North America* was perhaps the most popular field guide of the day, was a confidant of Fuertes. Among other things, Fuertes was a consistent contributor to *Bird-Lore*, a forerunner to *Audubon Magazine*, which Chapman edited for many years. Fuertes also did illustrations for later editions of Chapman's *Handbook*. After Fuertes's death Chapman wrote:

With growing regret Fuertes found that his work as an illustrator left him small time for the development of his art as a painter of birds in their haunts, and with the conclusion of the series of plates for the *Birds of Massachusetts*, on which he was engaged at the time of his death, he had determined to accept no more large commissions of this nature.

Dr. Arthur A. Allen, a famed ornithologist at Cornell and longtime friend of Fuertes, described the artist's work habits thus:

His was an artistic temperament, however, and days would pass without his being able to do a thing, to be suddenly followed by an inspiration that would enable him to nearly complete five or six birds in a single day. And this inspiration might last for a week or more, during which time he would turn out an immense amount of work.

Rivaling Fuertes's talent for bird portraiture was his talent for attaching himself to scientific expeditions, which provided him with a cosmopolitan view most valuable to a naturalist. He traveled to the Bering Sea, Alberta, Saskatchewan, the Gulf of St. Lawrence, California, Nevada, Texas, Minnesota, Florida, the Bahamas, Mexico, Colombia, and Ethiopia. It was an era in which railroads and steamships had attained maximum efficiency and the automobile was adding to human mobility.

Travel gave Fuertes an intimate knowledge of a broad spectrum of birds, far more than was available to the generations that preceded him. Chapman was impressed by Fuertes's familiarity with birds and his capacity to describe them in words as well as colors. Words, however, were not Fuertes's principal medium. He was too busy with brush and pen. In *Bird-Lore*, Chapman included the following paragraphs in a Fuertes obituary:

SNOW GEESE is an unpublished painting by Louis Agassiz Fuertes now owned by a private collector. Snow geese are grazing birds, particularly fond of salt marsh grasses.

For depth of appreciation and expression of pure sentiment I do not recall anything in the literature of ornithology that exceeds Fuertes' description of the call of the Tinamou (*Crypturus*). William Brewster was deeply affected by the soft, wailing notes of this bird, and his emotions were almost equally stirred by Fuertes' tribute to them. It reads:

"In the tropics, as in more familiar scenes, the bird-songs of the fields are frank, pastoral, and prevalent. With us, the Meadowlark, Field Sparrow, Vesper and Song Sparrows pipe often and openly, and, from May to October, their notes are almost constantly in the air. But the forest birds are more reluctant singers, and their rare notes are all mystery, romance, and reclusive shyness. The Field Sparrow will sit on a dock-stalk and sing, looking you in the eyes; the Veery will quietly fade away when your presence is discovered. . . .

"But, enter the forest, and all is of another world. For a long time, perhaps, as you make your way through the heavy hush of its darkened ways, no sound strikes the ear but the drip of water from spongy moss-clumps or broad leaves. You feel yourself to be the only animate thing in your universe. All at once, perhaps far off through the forest, perhaps close behind you, you hear the strangely moving whinny of a Tinamou. I think no sound I have ever heard has more deeply reached into me and taken hold. Whether it is the intensity of feeling that a deep, silent forest always imposes; the velvet smoothness of the wailing call; the dramatic crescendo and diminuendo that exactly parallels its minor cadence up and down a small scale; something, perhaps the combination of all these, makes one feel as if he had been caught with his soul naked in his hands, when, in the midst of his subdued and chastened revery, this spirit-voice takes the words from his tongue and expresses too perfectly all the mystery, romance, and tragedy that the struggling, parasite-ridden forest diffuses through its damp shade. No vocal expression could more wonderfully convey this intangible, subduing, pervasive quality of silence; a paradox, perhaps, but not out of place with this bird of mystery."

A few interesting anecdotes from his travels with Fuertes were included by Chapman. He recalled:

Equally trying, but of a wholly different kind, was an experience that illustrated Fuertes' tact and good nature, invaluable assets to the traveler, particularly in southern countries.

We had stopped at a little inn in the heart of the Andes to prepare some specimens secured during the preceding day's journey. The one room was lighted by a single door and this was darkened by a group of natives intently watching Fuertes skinning and drawing birds. With unfailing patience Fuertes would ask them to move and always they quickly obeyed, only to crowd back again as their curiosity overcame their desire to oblige. Finally they became so fascinated by Fuertes' work and by the man himself that when, after several hours' labor he started for the field, they all declared their intention of accompanying him! Did Fuertes protest? not a word! He cordially welcomed them and then, heading for a near-by marsh, plunged in and left a row of wondering men standing on its border, or, as he expressed it, he "combed them out."

Fuertes' value in the field was not restricted to his cheerful comradeship and his skill as an artist. He was a keen, tireless, and persistent collector and a stimulating scientific associate. In the Canadian Rockies it was Fuertes who discovered the nests of Ptarmigan and Pipit that appear in the American Museum's Arctic-Alpine Group. In Mexico it was Fuertes who in the field recognized as new the Oriole subsequently named for him, and in the dense subtropical forests of the Colombian Andes he secured specimens and identified the notes of birds which no other member of our party saw.

Nor did he confine his activities to science and art, to preserving birds as well as to painting them. Always he did more than his share of the work incident to travel and life in the open. He was an experienced woodsman, a good packer, a capital cook, a master hand with tools, who could mend anything, and in adversity and sickness no mother could have been more tender.

So one might continue to enumerate the qualities for which Fuertes was beloved and still fail to convey a realization of the rare personal charm which made his mere presence a source of joyous possibilities. To those whose lives were enriched by his friendship the world will never be the same again.

After several years of association with Cornell as a sort of unofficial distinguished alumnus in residence at Ithaca, Fuertes finally was invited to join the faculty. He accepted. Dr. Allen described the result:

Fuertes was not an orator—his manner of speaking and frequent digressions often made it difficult for students to take notes on his lectures—but so vivid was his personality, so original his vocabulary, so humorous his metaphors and so warm his human sympathy, that notes were never necessary. Students left the classroom inspired. They remembered everything he said and discussed it among themselves as though it had been a baseball game. It was not study to them; it was recreation. Those who have heard Fuertes on the formal lecture platform have occasionally been disappointed, for whenever he felt constrained, he did not indulge in those flights of metaphors that made his informal discourse so delightful. But with students he always felt at home; he was one of them and one with them, and they responded with the best that was in them.

Chapter XXI

------◆◆------

The Land Above All:
Leopold

Aldo Leopold began his career in wildlife management as an ardent exterminator of wolves and mountain lions, but grew in wisdom until near the end of his career he was arguing for sanctuaries for predators and reintroduction of wolves into areas where they had been exterminated.

Leopold's essential goal remained the same throughout his career: the establishment of healthy, huntable deer herds. As he explained in his masterwork, *A Sand County Almanac:* "I thought that because fewer wolves meant more deer, that no wolves would mean a hunters' paradise." He was to learn that nature does not work according to such simplified maxims.

Leopold died from a heart attack on April 21, 1948, while fighting a grass fire that threatened his sand county farm in Wisconsin. A week earlier the Oxford University Press had accepted for publication his *Almanac*, a volume he had completed seven years earlier but for which he had not been able to find a publisher. The book was an almost instant success. To this day, it remains the clearest and perhaps most poetic expression of what the ultimate goal of ecology might be. Leopold termed that ultimate a "land ethic."

Although one must read the entire *Almanac* to experience truly the message Leopold transmitted, its essence is expressed quite clearly in two sentences from the essay "The Land Ethic": "A thing is right when it tends to preserve the integrity, stability and beauty of the biotic community. It is wrong when it tends otherwise."

In more material terms, he couched the message in the introduction to the *Almanac* in these words:

But wherever the truth may lie, this much is crystal-clear: our bigger-and-better society is now like a hypochrondriac, so obsessed with its own economic health as to have lost the capacity to remain healthy. The whole world is so greedy for more bathtubs that it has lost the stability necessary to build them, or even to turn off the tap. Nothing could be more salutary at this stage than a little healthy contempt for a plethora of material blessings.

The symbolic bathtubs and loss of stability in American culture are more understandable to Americans today than they were in 1949 when the first edition of the *Almanac* appeared. And part of the reason that they are understandable rests within the covers of the *Almanac*, a volume that has been studied by almost every active conservationist in our time.

The *Almanac* has often been described as a modern *Walden*, which within limits it may be. A more accurate description would have it a more poetic and knowledgeable version of George Perkins Marsh's *Man and Nature*. What in Marsh's time could be visualized had in Leopold's time become reality.

The thinking of Aldo Leopold and his disciples has become so commonplace in natural history today that one must understand the background from which it evolved in order to appreciate his contribution.

At the time of Leopold's birth, January 11, 1887, the American attitude toward nature had reached a zenith of unreality. The average American still was fighting the wilderness, but for the most part the wilderness no longer existed. The nation had become industrialized and was laced together by railroad networks. The bison, once the greatest mass of ungulates the world had ever known, were reduced to a remnant. Market hunting of wildlife thrived, where there remained enough targets to sustain the industry. The timber barons had slashed away much of the American forests. Leopold, who was born and spent his early life in Burlington, Iowa, on a farm overlooking the Mississippi River, was later to recall that his father was concerned about the decline of waterfowl and had adopted a then Spartan self-restriction against shooting the birds in spring migration. Such destructive practices as spring shooting of waterfowl, which reduces the capital stock of birds at a time that they are returning north to breed, not only were considered sporting but also were unrecognized as detrimental. Indeed, Leopold was in his thirties when the practice was halted in April 1920 by a U.S. Supreme Court decision that upheld the right of a federal agent, Ray P. Holland, to arrest the attorney general of Missouri, who was duck hunting in the spring as a well-publicized challenge to the Federal Migratory Bird Treaty of 1918. The attorney general considered the treaty an illegal restraint upon the citizens' rights.

The almost unrestricted war against wildlife and nature was headed toward a respite, but not without resistance from adults who had matured in an era in which humans were free to make any decision by axe, plow, or gun. It was not until 1894 that the pioneering Park Protection Act passed by Congress halted hunting in the national parks.

The Federal Bureau of Forestry was created in 1891, when Leopold was four years old, but it was an underfunded agency whose existence was largely theoretical until a few years later, when Theodore Roosevelt became president and named Gifford Pinchot to create and head the U.S. Forest Service. The Forest Service was to become important in Leopold's early career, for he was among the young men who prepared for the new profession of forestry at the Yale School of Forestry founded by Pinchot. It was as a professional forester for the U.S. Forest Service that Leopold made his first studies of wildlife management in the Southwest.

The concerned conservationists at the turn of the century recognized the extent of man's abuse of nature but lacked a clear concept of what should be done to correct it. Most efforts moved along the lines proposed by Dr. William T. Hornaday, namely, to pass laws that might have given wildlife some protection if enforced, to wage war on the natural predators, and to restock animals and fish with no real knowledge of whether the land and water where they were being planted could support them. The conservationists' program was inadequate, especially when applied within a culture based upon total exploitation of the environment.

The Roosevelt years had focused public attention upon conservation problems, and indeed some programs were working rather well at the federal administrative level when Leopold received a degree in forestry at Yale in 1909 and joined the Forest Service in the New Mexico–Arizona Territories. Perhaps the most successful federal program involved the control of hunting for waterfowl, although the breeding grounds of these birds were being destroyed by agricultural expansion in the pothole country of the United States and Canadian high plains. Songbirds had begun recovering, too, largely because the federal government had halted the plumage trade and the Audubon societies had succeeded through publicity in involving the average citizen in the protection of the birds in his or her backyard. Otherwise, the conservation programs of the era were largely in shambles, misdirected in content, philosophy, and effectiveness.

When New Mexico and Arizona were admitted to the Union in 1912, those sparsely settled states lacked governmental structures and funds for wildlife protection. The U.S. Forest Service entered an agreement with the states through which forest rangers were deputized as state game wardens. It was through this arrangement that Leopold became involved with wildlife work. In June 1915, he was assigned full time to organizing game and fish work in the service's Southwest District. The Forest Service lacked both a federal mandate and experience in wildlife matters. Leopold was its first specialist in the field, and he was a forester rather than a wildlife biologist. He immediately went to work on his first publication on wildlife management, a mimeographed "Game and Fish Handbook" for rangers in the Southwest District.

In carrying out his wildlife duties for the Forest Service, Leopold became a public speaker, secretary of the New Mexico Game Protective Association, and editor of the association's quarterly bulletin, *The Pine Cone*, which he founded. *The Pine Cone* was filled with exhortations to the public to wipe out wolves. Leopold was also active in working out coalitions among sportsmen, cattle grazers, chambers of commerce, and other commercial interests, all aimed at creating a rapid expansion of deer herds in the Southwest to attract hunters from the East and their dollars. For his services, Leopold won the W. T. Hornaday Gold Medal from the Permanent Wildlife Protection Fund and a special commendation from Theodore Roosevelt.

Ironic as it may seem in relation to his more mature philosophy, Leopold resigned from the Forest Service in 1918 to become secretary of the Albuquerque Chamber of Commerce. After a year, he returned to the service and began research on soil erosion and watershed management in the Southwest. The work took him into the Gila National Forest, and his enthusiasm for that particular roadless area was instrumental in having it designated by the service as a wilderness area in 1924, one of the first official wilderness units in the nation.

Leopold progressed in the service. In 1924 he was sent to Wisconsin, where he was second in command at the U.S. Forest Products Laboratory in Madison. This was a research facility where wood chips and chemicals were whipped into wallboard and the like, with recipes being distributed to industries. It was a challenging institution to chemists but not much to a naturalist.

In 1928, Leopold received an offer from the Sporting Arms and Ammunition Manufacturers' Institute to conduct game surveys of the north central states. Leopold resigned from the Forest Service to take the assignment. The move had two significant results: in 1931 he published from the SAAM work his *Report on a Game Survey of the North Central States,* and he had cut himself off from dependable employment when the nation entered its worst depression with the stock market crash of October 1929.

With a wife and five children to support, Leopold had letterheads printed identifying him as a "consulting forester" and sought commissions in a depression market. He also used his time to write a book, which he had tinkered with in differing forms. It was published by Charles Scribner's Sons in 1933 under the title *Game Management*. Under his by-line, Leopold identified himself as consulting forester because the profession of wildlife manager, which the book itself was to create, was then unknown. *Game Management* placed the solution to wildlife problems on a sound ecological basis for the first time. Leopold advised that to increase a wildlife species, one had to study the animal's life history, learn what its needs were, and alter the landscape to meet those needs. The crucial key to success lay in determining what necessary factor or factors were in short supply. Leopold referred to the shortage as the "limiting factor." The limiting factor might be the lack of shelter necessary for reproduction and escape from predators, as for example, the lack of standing dead trees that raccoons could use for dens. Or it might be an intermittent water supply that failed at critical periods in an animal's life cycle. Or it might be the lack of sufficient palatable food, either year round or on a seasonal basis. For instance, an area might supply sufficient food, or even an overabundance, through the spring, summer, and autumn, but if there were insufficient alternate food sources to tide the species over the winter, it would surely disappear.

Most ranges, Leopold argued, produced more animals than the existing habitat could support. The then prevalent practice of stocking additional animals on the range was more than a waste of money. Not only may the stocked population be expected to die, but also its competition with residents of the species and its pressure upon the existing resources might be and often are detrimental rather than helpful. To increase game, he said, the wildlife manager need only improve the range and correct the limiting factor and nature would provide the population expansion.

Game Management was such a fundamental and imaginative text that it has remained a basic work in the wildlife management field for more than forty years, an unusual span for a textbook. It is amazing for its clarity as well as for the fact that Leopold avoided mentioning in it his inspired conception of nature, which appears in the *Almanac*, parts of which he already had written. He did not, for instance, warn students of the deer problems with which he was familiar and which were to plague him throughout his career.

It was Leopold's misfortune not only to have a fetish about increasing the nation's deer herds but also to have it at an awkward period in the history of those ungulates. At the time of his birth, the nation's forests were in a state of ruin. Deer are particularly adapted to forest cycles. In the absence of forests, deer, especially the white-tailed deer in the East, almost disappeared. During Leopold's boyhood, the restoration of deer was a sportsman's goal in almost every state east of the Rockies. The effort had limited success, for deer cannot thrive on treeless cultivated fields. As mechanized farming in the West brought a decline to farming on the rocky glaciated fields of the northeast and north central states, the land reverted to trees. Regenerating forests, crowded with small succulent trees on which deer browse, are the ideal deer habitat.

There is a saying that ranks almost as a proverb, that men tend to live forty years behind their times. Although Leopold was often avant-garde in his thinking in regard to wildlife, in his special interest of deer restoration he remained old-fashioned. The idea that deer must be protected with unusual tenderness in order to survive, which applied to deer living under the adverse habitat conditions that existed around 1900, died hard in his mind and in the minds of sportsmen. Leopold failed to grasp his own basic principle; namely, that when the limiting factor, in the deer's case a shortage of tender twigs, is corrected, a species will expand its population. In sprouting new forests, nature provided deer with a bonanza.

In two regions, and under quite different circumstances, Leopold found himself working to expand deer herds without realizing that the problem he should have been dealing with was an irruption of deer beyond the limits of the environment to support them.

In the Southwest, Leopold as a young man had gone along with the cattlemen, deer hunters, and sheepmen in a campaign to extirpate wolves. The effort eradicated wolves, but at the same time destroyed a healthy balance among deer, wolves, and forests. In that region the deer populations already had reached the maximum density that the forests could support. The hunting pressure from wolves kept the deer within bounds. When the wolf disappeared, deer expanded drastically and began destroying the forests.

In Wisconsin, Leopold was late in recognizing the abundance that nature had bestowed upon deer. The animals were thriving in numbers beyond the eventual ability of the landscape to support them. Leopold at first worked with those who were stimulating the overproduction. By the time he recognized what was happening, he found that he had created a public opinion structure toward deer preservation that he could not overcome.

One of the most appealing essays in the *Almanac* bears the ungrammatical title "Thinking Like a Mountain." In it he discloses his mistaken thinking in regard to wolves and the deer of the Southwest.

Thinking Like a Mountain*

A deep chesty bawl echoes from rimrock to rimrock, rolls down the mountain, and fades into the far blackness of the night. It is an outburst of wild defiant sorrow, and of contempt for all the adversities of the world.

Every living thing (and perhaps many a dead one as well) pays heed to that call. To the deer it is a reminder of the way of all flesh, to the pine a forecast of midnight scuffles and of blood upon the snow, to the coyote a promise of gleanings to come, to the cowman a threat of red ink at the bank, to the hunter a challenge of fang against bullet. Yet behind these obvious and immediate hopes and fears there lies a deeper meaning, known only to the mountain itself. Only the mountain has lived long enough to listen objectively to the howl of a wolf.

Those unable to decipher the hidden meaning know nevertheless that it is there, for it is felt in all wolf country, and distinguishes that country from all other land. It tingles in the spine of all who hear wolves by night, or who scan their tracks by day. Even without sight or sound of wolf, it is implicit in a hundred small events: the midnight whinny of a pack horse, the rattle of rolling rocks, the bound of a fleeing deer, the way shadows lie under the spruces. Only the ineducable tyro can fail to sense the presence or absence of wolves, or the fact that mountains have a secret opinion about them.

My own conviction on this score dates from the day I saw a wolf die. We were eating lunch on a high rimrock, at the foot of which a turbulent river elbowed its way. We saw what we thought was a doe fording the torrent, her breast awash in white water. When she climbed the bank toward us and shook out her tail, we realized our error: it was a wolf. A half-dozen others, evidently grown pups, sprang from the willows and all joined in a welcoming mêlée of wagging tails and playful maulings. What was literally a pile of wolves writhed and tumbled in the center of an open flat at the foot of our rimrock.

In those days we had never heard of passing up a chance to kill a wolf. In a second we were pumping lead into the pack, but with more excitement than accuracy: how to aim a steep down-hill shot is always confusing. When our rifles were empty, the old wolf was down, and a pup was dragging a leg into impassable slide-rocks.

We reached the old wolf in time to watch a fierce green fire dying in her eyes. I realized then, and have known ever since, that there was something new to me in those eyes—something known only to her and to the mountain. I was young then, and full of trigger-itch; I thought that because fewer wolves meant more deer, that no wolves would mean hunters' paradise. But after seeing the green fire die, I sensed that neither the wolf nor the mountain agreed with such a view.

*   *   *

Since then I have lived to see state after state extirpate its wolves. I have watched the face of many a newly wolfless mountain, and seen the south-facing slopes wrinkle with a maze of new deer trails. I have seen every edible bush and seedling browsed, first to anaemic desuetude, and then to death. I have seen every edible tree defoliated to the height of a saddlehorn. Such a mountain looks as if someone had given God a new pruning shears, and forbidden Him all other exercise. In the end the starved bones of the hoped-for deer herd, dead of its own too-much, bleach with the bones of the dead sage, or molder under the high-lined junipers.

I now suspect that just as a deer herd lives in mortal fear of its wolves, so does a mountain live in mortal fear of its deer. And perhaps with better cause, for while a buck pulled down by wolves can be replaced in two or three years, a range pulled down by too many deer may fail of replacement in as many decades.

So also with cows. The cowman who cleans his range of wolves does not realize that he is taking over the wolf's job of trimming the herd to fit the range. He has not learned to think like a mountain. Hence we have dustbowls, and rivers washing the future into the sea.

*   *   *

We all strive for safety, prosperity, comfort, long life, and dullness. The deer strives with his supple legs, the cowman with trap and poison, the statesman with pen, the most of us with machines, votes, and dollars, but it all comes to the same thing: peace in our time. A measure of success in this is all well enough, and perhaps is a requisite to objective thinking, but too much safety seems to yield only danger in the long run. Perhaps this is behind Thoreau's dictum: In wildness is the salvation of the world. Perhaps this is the hidden meaning in the howl of the wolf, long known among mountains, but seldom perceived among men.

During his years as a consultant to the Sporting Arms and Ammunition Manufacturers, Leopold worked to establish wildlife management courses in the north central universities and to revolutionize thinking among fish and game administrators. At both he was a success. As a phase of the work he delivered a course of lectures at the University of Wisconsin, and in August 1933 the Wisconsin Alumni Research Foundation underwrote a chair of game management to which he was appointed. He spent the remainder of his years on the university faculty but remained highly visible publicly, taking part in campaigns to improve wildlife management practices of the state, and working with the Franklin Roosevelt New Deal in hopes of phasing surplus croplands and such depression programs as the Civilian Conservation Corps into effective units that would benefit wildlife. He soon found that Washington's primary interest was in employing the unemployed, and that whether wildlife benefited had a low priority. In fact, his experiences with the federal government, both as employee and consultant, disillusioned him to the extent that he felt that state governments, closer to the problems, offered the only hope of organizing an effective wildlife program. Later, his work with the states convinced him that the future of wildlife lay with the farmers and landowners. As for them, he noted that they were loathe to do anything for wildlife's benefit unless it had a profit angle.

The Leopold crusade within the north central states was more successful than he considered it. For example, Missouri at the time Leopold began his survey had an antiquated wildlife system that perhaps was typical of the average state. The legislature regulated wildlife and set the hunting and fishing seasons to accommodate political pressures. Game wardens too often were relatives of county officials and by no means tireless servants. About the only persons ever arrested for game-law infractions were strangers. One could sit on the back porch on a hot summer night and listen to the staccato blasts as natives dynamited fish in the river. In the few counties where deer remained, they usually were hunted at night by jacklight, often as not by the game warden himself. The authorities involved with fish and game were mostly political appointees who had no knowledge of biology or game management. The condition of wildlife stocks within the state was either unknown or only vaguely perceived. A campaign in the early thirties, based largely upon Leopold's findings and the discontent of those who recognized the situation, resulted in the formation of a nonpolitical regulatory commission, which replaced the legislature in wildlife administration fields. It appointed vigilant wardens whose habit of arresting politicians and substantial citizens for game-law violations soon convinced the more backward and recalcitrant citizens that game regulations should be obeyed. More importantly, the commission hired biologists who immediately applied Leopold's principle that the way to game abundance lay in improving the habitat.

The *Almanac* represents the culmination of Leopold's thinking about nature. He had arrived at the stage where he no longer spoke of animals as "game," and indeed even his earlier volume, *Game Management*, while as oriented toward exploitation as its title suggests, had a content that led to referring to workers in the field as "wildlife" managers. In general, wildlife management has not yet attained a broadness that would benefit all animals, although there is a growing trend among citizens to demand such all-inclusiveness. Neither, for that matter, has Leopold's message of the oneness of man, nature, and the land attained more than lip service. In the *Almanac*, one learns why the ethic had not achieved its goal and what may be the limiting factor on its destiny.

The Ethical Sequence*

This extension of ethics, so far studied only by philosophers, is actually a process in ecological evolution. Its sequences may be described in ecological as well as in philosophical terms. An ethic, ecologically, is a limitation on freedom of action in the struggle for existence. An ethic, philosophically, is a differentiation of social from anti-social conduct. These are two definitions of one thing. The thing has its origin in the tendency of interdependent individuals or groups to evolve modes of co-operation. The ecologist

* "The Ethical Sequence," "The Community Concept," "The Ecological Conscience," and "The Land Pyramid" are excerpted from "The Land Ethic," from *A Sand County Almanac with other essays on conservation from Round River* by Aldo Leopold. Copyright © 1949, 1953, 1966 by Oxford University Press, Inc. Reprinted by permission. Pages 217–220, 222–223, 224–225, and 235–236.

calls these symbioses. Politics and economics are advanced symbioses in which the original free-for-all competition has been replaced, in part, by co-operative mechanisms with an ethical content.

The complexity of co-operative mechanisms has increased with population density, and with the efficiency of tools. It was simpler, for example, to define the anti-social uses of sticks and stones in the days of the mastodons than of bullets and billboards in the age of motors.

The first ethics dealt with the relation between individuals; the Mosaic Decalogue is an example. Later accretions dealt with the relation between the individual and society. The Golden Rule tries to integrate the individual to society; democracy to integrate social organization to the individual.

There is as yet no ethic dealing with man's relation to land and to the animals and plants which grow upon it. Land, like Odysseus' slave-girls, is still property. The land-relation is still strictly economic, entailing privileges but not obligations.

The extension of ethics to this third element in human environment is, if I read the evidence correctly, an evolutionary possibility and an ecological necessity. It is the third step in sequence. The first two have already been taken. Individual thinkers since the days of Ezekiel and Isaiah have asserted that the despoliation of land is not only inexpedient but wrong. Society, however, has not yet affirmed their belief. I regard the present conservation movement as the embryo of such an affirmation.

An ethic may be regarded as a mode of guidance for meeting ecological situations so new or intricate, or involving such deferred reactions, that the path of social expediency is not discernible to the average individual. Animal instincts are modes of guidance for the individual in meeting such situations. Ethics are possibly a kind of community instinct in-the-making.

The Community Concept

All ethics so far evolved rest upon a single premise: that the individual is a member of a community of interdependent parts. His instincts prompt him to compete for his place in that community, but his ethics prompt him also to co-operate (perhaps in order that there may be a place to compete for).

The land ethic simply enlarges the boundaries of the community to include soils, waters, plants, and animals, or collectively: the land.

This sounds simple: do we not already sing our love for and obligation to the land of the free and the home of the brave? Yes, but just what and whom do we love? Certainly not the soil, which we are sending helter-skelter downriver. Certainly not the waters, which we assume have no function except to turn turbines, float barges, and carry off sewage. Certainly not the plants, of which we exterminate whole communities without batting an eye. Certainly not the animals, of which we have already extirpated many of the largest and most beautiful species. A land ethic of course cannot prevent the alteration, management, and use of these "resources," but it does affirm their right to continued existence, and, at least in spots, their continued existence in a natural state.

In short, a land ethic changes the role of *Homo sapiens* from conqueror of the land-community to plain member and citizen of it. It implies respect for his fellow-members, and also respect for the community as such.

In human history, we have learned (I hope) that the conqueror role is eventually self-defeating. Why? Because it is implicit in such a role that the conqueror knows, *ex cathedra*, just what makes the community clock tick, and just what and who is valuable, and what and who is worthless, in community life. It always turns out that he knows neither, and this is why his conquests eventually defeat themselves.

In the biotic community, a parallel situation exists. Abraham knew exactly what the land was for: it was to drip milk and honey into Abraham's mouth. At the present moment, the assurance with which we regard this assumption is inverse to the degree of our education.

The ordinary citizen today assumes that science knows what makes the community clock tick; the scientist is equally sure that he does not. He knows that the biotic mechanism is so complex that its workings may never be fully understood. . . .

The Ecological Conscience

Conservation is a state of harmony between men and land. Despite nearly a century of propaganda, conservation still proceeds at a snail's pace; progress still consists largely of letterhead pieties and convention oratory. On the back forty we still slip two steps backward for each forward stride.

The usual answer to this dilemma is "more conservation education." No one will debate this, but is it certain that only the *volume* of education needs stepping up? Is something lacking in the *content* as well?

It is difficult to give a fair summary of its content in brief form, but, as I understand it, the content is substantially this: obey the law, vote right, join some organizations, and practice what conservation is profitable on your own land; the government will do the rest.

Is not this formula too easy to accomplish anything worthwhile? It defines no right or wrong, assigns no obligation, calls for no sacrifice, implies no change in the current philosophy of values. In respect of land-use, it urges only enlightened self-interest. Just how far will such education take us? An example will perhaps yield a partial answer.

By 1930 it had become clear to all except the ecologically blind that southwestern Wisconsin's topsoil was slipping seaward. In 1933 the farmers were told that if they would adopt certain remedial practices for five years, the public would donate CCC labor to install them, plus the necessary machinery and materials. The offer was widely accepted, but the practices were widely forgotten when the five-year contract period was up. The farmers continued only those practices that yielded an immediate and visible economic gain for themselves. . . .

The puzzling aspect of such situations is that the existence of obligations over and above self-interest is taken for granted in such rural community enterprises as the betterment of roads, schools, churches, and baseball teams. Their existence is not taken for granted, nor as yet seriously discussed, in bettering the behavior of the water that falls on the land, or in the preserving of the beauty or diversity of the farm landscape. Land-use ethics are still governed wholly by economic self-interest, just as social ethics were a century ago.

To sum up: we asked the farmer to do what he conveniently could to save his soil, and he has done just that, and only that. The farmer who clears the woods off a 75 percent slope, turns his cows into the clearing, and dumps its rainfall, rocks, and soil into the community creek, is still (if otherwise decent) a respected member of society. If he puts lime on his fields and plants his crops on contour, he is still entitled to all the privileges and emoluments of his Soil Conservation District. The District is a beautiful piece of social machinery, but it is coughing along on two cylinders because we have been too timid, and too anxious for quick success, to tell the farmer the true magnitude of his obligations. Obligations have no meaning without conscience, and the problem we face is the extension of the social conscience from people to land.

No important change in ethics was ever accomplished without an internal change in our intellectual emphasis, loyalties, affections, and convictions. The proof that conservation has not yet touched these foundations of conduct lies in the fact that philosophy and religion have not yet heard of it. In our attempt to make conservation easy, we have made it trivial. . . .

The Land Pyramid

The combined evidence of history and ecology seems to support one general deduction: the less violent the man-made changes, the greater the probability of successful readjustment in the pyramid. Violence, in turn, varies with human population density; a dense population requires a more violent conversion. In this respect, North America has a better chance for permanence than Europe, if she can contrive to limit her density.

This deduction runs counter to our current philosophy, which assumes that because a small increase in density enriched human life, that an indefinite increase will enrich it indefinitely. Ecology knows of no density relationship that holds for indefinitely wide limits. All gains from density are subject to a law of diminishing returns.

Whatever may be the equation for men and land, it is improbable that we as yet know all its terms. Recent discoveries in mineral and vitamin nutrition reveal unsuspected dependencies in the up-circuit: incredibly minute quantities of certain substances determine the value of soils to plants, of plants to animals. What of the down-circuit? What of the vanishing species, the preservation of which we now regard as an esthetic luxury? They helped build the soil; in what unsuspected ways may they be essential to its maintenance? Professor Weaver proposes that we use prairie flowers to reflocculate the wasting soils of the dusty bowl; who knows for what purpose cranes and condors, otters and grizzlies may some day be used?

Chapter XXII

Visualizing Invisible Death: Carson

Rachel Carson's challenge was to convince the public that a certain substance, which became invisible after application and which at the time had assumed great economic importance, was harmful to higher organisms and should be banned.

To suggest publicly that DDT and related chlorinated hydrocarbons should be abolished from the marketplace was an act that required immense innocence or great courage. Since World War II these chemical compounds had been regarded by the public as miraculous. During the war, DDT had reduced the exposure of the military in the Southwest Pacific to malaria through its use against mosquitoes. In the European theater, DDT had protected armies against the body lice and fleas that had spread typhus among soldiers since antiquity. At home, consumers had become accustomed to unblemished apples and wormless cherries, and farmers raised unexpectedly bountiful crops as a result of hard pesticides. The cotton belt of the Southeast, facing possible bankruptcy through ascendency of its old adversary, the boll weevil, embraced chlorinated hydrocarbons as a path to fiscal salvation.

Despite the widespread use of DDT, there was no evidence of any human dropping dead as a result of it. Naturalists had pointed out that birds frequently disappeared from an area after an application of DDT. But lawns were not littered with bird bodies, and the public was unfamiliar with the vast sweep of death that goes through bird population even under normal conditions without telltale evidence. Fish often were killed quite promptly after an application of DDT on a watershed. But even such pesticides as rotenone, an insecticide generally harmless to warm-blooded organisms, killed fish. Fish kills were accepted as resulting from "improper" application of the new pesticides.

Although the new pesticides were acclaimed for their long-lasting qualities, it was assumed that there was a limit to their longevity. It was known that while the material might remain active for weeks in a field or forest, it eventually disappeared. The route by which it disappeared was unknown. Laboratory workers could report honestly that analysis of water samples usually showed little or no DDT content. Soil samples might show very little in relation to the poundage of pesticides that had been applied. Most supposed that chlorinated hydrocarbons broke down after exposure to sunlight, or that nature detoxified them in time, as it disposed of so many other pesticides.

The eventual explanation of what was happening to make DDT disappear was a bit shocking: the material is fat-soluble, and organisms, including man, were withdrawing it from the more visible environment through storing it in their fatty tissues.

To overcome massive public indifference to the use of hard pesticides was less of a challenge than to confront important interests whose profits and livelihoods were tied intimately to continued use of chlorinated hydrocarbons. While collecting data for her book *Silent Spring*, Miss Carson received a request from Dr. Clarence Cottam, distinguished field biologist and director of the Welder Wildlife Foundation, that she appear on a pesticide panel being organized by the National Audubon Society. In declining, Miss Carson explained: "But, as you know, the whole thing is so explosive and the pressures on the other side so powerful and enormous, that I feel it far wiser to keep my own council insofar as I can until I am ready to launch my attack as a whole."

Miss Carson knew from the experiences of others that her "attack as a whole" would bring drastic reaction from entrenched interests who could use everything from ridicule to an array of supposed scientific findings that defended DDT. In top echelons, these interests had the ability to enlist the best publicists of Madison Avenue in a counterattack. But equally devastating would be the ridicule of farmers, gardeners, and other operators at the grass-root level, who had confidence in the Agriculture Extension Service and pesticide-marketing institutions. After all, the U.S. Department of Agriculture thoroughly endorsed DDT and other hard pesticides and was ready to defend the material. But one did not have to be an agricultural tycoon to benefit from the new pesticides. The suburbanite with a ten-by-twelve-foot plot was growing delicate flowers that in the past insects would have chewed to the ground. He or she was familiar with the wonders of pesticides as recited in home gardening magazines. Besides, any busybody who proposed canceling hard pesticides was little more than a subversive, who would turn the next backyard barbecue into a mosquito-harried debacle. Almost all the data that Miss Carson had assembled for the book that would be named *Silent Spring* had already appeared in print. Generally it had appeared in obscure scientific journals or in conservation organs not readily available to the general public. The data also had appeared in a form not easily understood by lay readers, or addressed to a problem not high on most persons' list of priorities, such as DDT's effect upon bird communities.

As she explained in the preface to *Silent Spring*, Miss Carson became involved in the pesticide controversy through a letter that she received from Mrs. Olga Owens Huckins, retired book editor of the *Boston Post*, who sent her a detailed account of the devastation on the Huckins's property after an aerial spraying of Duxbury, Massachusetts, by a mosquito-control plane. Miss Carson earlier had read scientific reports regarding chlorinated hydrocarbons and decided to do something to inform the public about the negative side of hard pesticides.

Although Miss Carson was a superb writer, and her *The Sea Around Us*, published in 1950, had set a new record by the number of weeks that it remained at the top of the best-seller lists, she found that she could not interest the leading popular magazines in an article warning the public about pesticides. One magazine famed for its research laboratory, which supposedly tested all products advertised within its pages, rejected the piece with an editor's explanation that the scientist in charge of the laboratory doubted that her data could be substantiated. In the end, she found herself in the position of either being silenced or being forced to write a book. She wrote the book.

A landmark in natural history, *Silent Spring* was published in 1962. The volume almost immediately became a best seller in every nation where English is a primary language. In the next couple of years translations sold in France, Germany, Italy, Denmark, Sweden, Norway, Finland, Holland, Spain, Brazil, Iceland, Japan, Portugal, Yugoslavia, and Israel. The combined readership made her the best-known American woman naturalist in history, and possibly made her the most honored naturalist of her era.

Although she lived to accept almost every important medal granted by American conservation and science organizations, her work on *Silent Spring* developed into a race against time. Hampered by arthritis and frequently disabled by annoying eye irritations, she discovered near the end of the four years of research and writing that went into *Silent Spring* that she suffered bone cancer.

Miss Carson's death from cancer on April 14, 1964, prompted a response from opponents that may have established a new low mark in ineptness. The opponents suggested that Miss Carson had written the book in bitterness because she thought that pesticides had contributed to her fatal illness. This was not only a measure of crassness but also a most ill-advised move. If there was anything that the pesticide industry did not need at the time, it was an implication further linking in the public mind a connection between pesticides and cancer. The most rabid opponents hardly could have done the pesticide industry greater disservice.

Miss Carson achieved great naturalist status with publication of her classic, *The Sea Around Us*. Actually, an earlier book, *Under the Sea-Wind*, published in 1941, would have qualified her for the honor, even though the volume failed to attain the best-seller list as her later volumes did. As a marine zoologist, Miss Carson had every right to be proud of *The Edge of the Sea*, published in 1955, in which she turned what might have been another handbook into literary brilliance.

Naturalists, and indeed writers in other fields, seldom are the best judges of the quality of their work. Miss Carson may have been an exception. When she realized that death might be near, she chose from all her lines the concluding chapter of her lesser-known book, *The Edge of the Sea*, as a reading for her funeral. Entitled "The Enduring Sea," it goes:*

Now I hear the sea sounds about me; the night high tide is rising, swirling with a confused rush of waters against the rocks below my study window. Fog has come into the bay from the open sea, and it lies over water and over the land's edge, seeping back into the spruces and stealing softly among the juniper and the bayberry. The restive waters, the cold wet breadth of the fog, are of a world in which man is an uneasy trespasser; he punctuates the night with the complaining groan and grunt of a foghorn, sensing the power and menace of the sea.

Hearing the rising tide, I think how it is pressing also against other shores I know—rising on a southern beach where there is no fog, but a moon edging all the waves with silver and touching the wet sands with lambent sheen, and on a still more distant shore sending its streaming currents against the moonlit pinnacles and the dark caves of the coral rock.

Then in my thoughts these shores, so different in their nature and in the inhabitants they support, are made one by the unifying touch of the sea. For the differences I sense in this particular instant of time that is mine are but the differences of a moment, determined by our place in the stream of time and in the long rhythms of the sea. Once this rocky coast beneath me was a plain of sand; then the sea rose and found a new shore line. And again

* Reprinted from *The Edge of the Sea*, by Rachel Carson, copyright © 1955 by the Houghton Mifflin Co., Boston, by permission. Pages 249–250.

in some shadowy future the surf will have ground these rocks to sand and will have returned the coast to its earlier state. And so in my mind's eye these coastal forms merge and blend in a shifting, kaleidoscopic pattern in which there is no finality, no ultimate and fixed reality—earth becoming fluid as the sea itself.

On all these shores there are echoes of past and future: of the flow of time, obliterating yet containing all that has gone before; of the sea's eternal rhythms—the tides, the beat of surf, the pressing rivers of the currents—shaping, changing, dominating; of the stream of life, flowing as inexorably as any ocean current, from past to unknown future. For as the shore configuration changes in the flow of time, the pattern of life changes, never static, never quite the same from year to year. Whenever the sea builds a new coast, waves of living creatures surge against it, seeking a foothold, establishing their colonies. And so we come to perceive life as a force as tangible as any of the physical realities of the sea, a force strong and purposeful, as incapable of being crushed or diverted from its ends as the rising tide.

Contemplating the teeming life of the shore, we have an uneasy sense of the communication of some universal truth that lies just beyond our grasp. What is the message signaled by the hordes of diatoms, flashing their microscopic lights in the night sea? What truth is expressed by the legions of the barnacles, whitening the rocks with their habitations, each small creature within finding the necessities of its existence in the sweep of the surf? And what is the meaning of so tiny a being as the transparent wisp of protoplasm that is a sea lace, existing for some reason inscrutable to us— a reason that demands its presence by the trillion amid the rocks and weeds of the shore? The meaning haunts and ever eludes us, and in its very pursuit we approach the ultimate mystery of Life itself.

The instantaneous success of *Silent Spring* puzzled many naturalists. The research findings, the field observations of naturalists, hunters, and ordinary citizens—all had been made public. The mass of data, both verified and unverified, was far greater than that which appeared in the book. Miss Carson wisely limited her selections to verified data that could be defended. The choices required a firm base of biological knowledge. It was this background that enabled Miss Carson to reorganize existing material, judge its scientific worth, and reduce the mass of research data into terms understandable to the public. Her literary skill gave the ignored data the smashing impact that it previously had lacked.

Another obstacle Miss Carson had to overcome in *Silent Spring* was the belief held by many scientists and most laymen that the world was too massive a system for the puny disturbances of man to have any lasting effect upon it. If not a tenet of science, such an outlook was prevalent among scientists in the years when Miss Carson entered the discipline. Unquestionably there were sincere critics who felt that Miss Carson had exaggerated beyond bounds, because of their belief that the world ecosystem could decompose any substance before it became a serious threat. *Time* magazine in its review of *Silent Spring* reflected the philosophy. The writer quoted Miss Carson's words: "It is not possible to add pesticides to water anywhere without threatening the purity of water everywhere." The writer commented: "It takes only a moment of reflection to show that this is nonsense." Yet the record shows that DDT has pervaded the world's oceans and can be found in polar ice!

In her review of factors leading to the widespread pesticide abuse that she condemned, Miss Carson gained a new perspective on science. In the final paragraph of the last chapter, "The Other Road," in *Silent Spring*, she reports:

> The "control of nature" is a phrase conceived in arrogance, born of the Neanderthal age of biology and philosophy, when it was supposed that nature exists for the convenience of man. The concepts and practices of applied entomology for the most part date from that Stone Age of science. It is our alarming misfortune that so primitive a science has armed itself with the most modern and terrible weapons, and that in turning them against the insects it has also turned them against the earth.

Perhaps Miss Carson's ultimate disillusionment came after publication of *Silent Spring*. Although her major encouragement and data came from research physicians, particularly those in public health fields, Miss Carson was to discover that when controversy engulfed *Silent Spring*, the American Medical Association through its *AMA News* of November 26, 1962, advised physicians concerned about the issue to resolve their doubts by writing to the National Agricultural Chemicals Association for its "information kit." The NACA, of course, is the marketing organization for chemical pesticides and, regardless of what virtues it may have, hardly could be expected to present unbiased views.

The turning point in the controversy came on May 15, 1963, when the President's Science Advisory Committee issued its report entitled *Use of Pesticides*. In it was this statement:

Public literature and the experiences of panel members indicate that, until the publication of *Silent Spring* by Rachel Carson, people were generally unaware of the toxicity of pesticides. The government should present this information to the public in a way that will make it aware of the dangers while recognizing the value of pesticides.

In its May 24, 1963, edition of *Science,* the journal of the American Association for the Advancement of Science, the association commented:

The long awaited pesticides report of the President's Science Advisory Committee (PSAC) was issued last week, and, though it is a temperate document, even in tone, and carefully balanced in its assessment of risks versus benefits, it adds up to a fairly thorough-going vindication of Rachel Carson's *Silent Spring* thesis.

The PSAC report had been critical of industry and government agencies, especially the U.S. Department of Agriculture. It furnished the necessary confirmation of Miss Carson's allegations. From that point, the general public was to have a different and more sensible attitude toward the roles of industry and the government agencies, which supposedly shielded the public from harm.

A superficial acquaintance with Miss Carson might have led one to rank her among the less likely persons to write a book which she herself recognized would cast her into the vortex of bitter controversy. From her childhood in Springdale, Pennsylvania, where she was born May 27, 1907, up to the publication date of *Silent Spring*, Miss Carson had been known as a most reserved person. At the age of ten, she had written a story that she sold to *St. Nicholas* magazine for ten dollars. Although it is not unusual for a writer to be using a pen at an early age—indeed the talent seems always to be present and often emerges early—writing seriously for publication may indicate a social withdrawal, leading one who wishes to be expressive to choose written rather than oral paths. Through her school days, including the freshman year at the Pennsylvania College for Women (now Chatham College), her goal was to be a writer. In her sophomore year, however, she came under the influence of Mary Skinker, an exceptional teacher of biology, and from then on writing became a secondary goal. On graduation from Chatham in 1928, she entered the graduate school at Johns Hopkins University, where she received a master's degree in zoology. After teaching zoology at the University of Maryland, Miss Carson became a writer for the U.S. Bureau of Fisheries at $19.25 a week. The nation was in the depths of a depression, and such federal positions were highly desired. On August 17, 1936, she qualified for a permanent Civil Service appointment in the Fisheries Bureau at $2,000 a year. She was among the first women employed by the bureau at higher than clerical rank. After the Bureau of Fisheries and the Biological Survey were combined in 1940 to form the new U.S. Fish and Wildlife Service, Miss Carson progressed rapidly in the service and became its chief editor in 1949, a positon she held until she resigned from the service in 1952.

Although she had published *Under the Sea-Wind*, the volume came out one month before the Pearl Harbor attack and the public missed it while preoccupied by war matters. The book sold fewer than 1,600 copies in six years. An artistic success and highly regarded by many persons with an interest in natural history, *Sea-Wind* did not destroy her anonymity.

Publication of *The Sea Around Us* in 1950 brought her financial success, and the public demand to meet her forced her to make public appearances and take speaking engagements. She disliked such exposure, and the experience failed to dissolve her basic shyness. Paul Brooks, who was editor-in-chief at Houghton Mifflin, and was associated with Miss Carson in publication of both *The Edge of the Sea* and *Silent Spring*, perhaps best has described her as "a very private person."

A quiet, unassuming woman, Miss Carson seems to have lived a life completely devoid of anything that would provide a personal anecdote. Opponents who would not have hesitated to make a personal attack on her had to be satisfied with implications that she was a little old lady whose misguided and faulty statements were upsetting a public that should know better than to accept them. Although a rather attractive woman, she never had married. She perhaps had an exaggerated sense of duty to her family. She remained a loyal helper to her mother, who not only was dependent upon her and lived to advanced age but also became an invalid. When a sister died, she reared two nieces. Later, one niece died and Miss Carson adopted her five-year-old son, Roger. They were experiences that she apparently found satisfying, for there is no hint in what few letters have become public that she felt burdened.

The breadth of her view of natural history and a rather astute perception of the cultural acceptance of pesticides appear in the chapter entitled "The Obligation to Endure," a dissertation that gave readers the background that made the remainder of *Silent Spring* understandable to laymen:*

The history of life on earth has been a history of interaction between living things and their surroundings. To a large extent, the physical form and the habits of the earth's vegetation and its animal life have been molded by the environment. Considering the whole span of earthly time, the opposite effect, in which life actually modifies its surroundings, has been relatively slight. Only within the moment of time represented by the present century has one species—man—acquired significant power to alter the nature of his world.

During the past quarter century this power has not only increased to one of disturbing magnitude but it has changed in character. The most alarming of all man's assaults upon the environment is the contamination of air, earth, rivers, and sea with dangerous and even lethal materials. This pollution is for the most part irrecoverable; the chain of evil it initiates not only in the world that must support life but in living tissues is for the most part irreversible. In this now universal contamination of the environment, chemicals are the sinister and little-recognized partners of radiation in changing the very nature of the world—the very nature of its life. Strontium 90, released through nuclear explosions into the air, comes to earth in rain or drifts down as fallout, lodges in soil, enters into the grass or corn or wheat grown there, and in time takes up its abode in the bones of a human being, there to remain until his death. Similarly, chemicals sprayed on croplands or forests or gardens lie long in soil, entering into living organisms, passing from one to another in a chain of poisoning and death. Or they pass mysteriously by underground streams until they emerge and, through the alchemy of air and sunlight, combine into new forms that kill vegetation, sicken cattle, and work unknown harm on those who drink from once pure wells. As Albert Schweitzer has said, "Man can hardly even recognize the devils of his own creation."

It took hundreds of millions of years to produce the life that now inhabits the earth—eons of time in which that developing and

* Reprinted from *Silent Spring*, by Rachel Carson, copyright © 1962 by the Houghton Mifflin Co., Boston, by permission. Pages 5–13.

evolving and diversifying life reached a state of adjustment and balance with its surroundings. The environment, rigorously shaping and directing the life it supported, contained elements that were hostile as well as supporting. Certain rocks gave out dangerous radiation; even within the light of the sun, from which all life draws its energy, there were short-wave radiations with power to injure. Given time—time not in years but in millennia—life adjusts, and a balance has been reached. For time is the essential ingredient; but in the modern world there is no time.

The rapidity of change and the speed with which new situations are created follow the impetuous and heedless pace of man rather than the deliberate pace of nature. Radiation is no longer merely the background radiation of rocks, the bombardment of cosmic rays, the ultraviolet of the sun that have existed before there was any life on earth; radiation is now the unnatural creation of man's tampering with the atom. The chemicals to which life is asked to make its adjustment are no longer merely the calcium and silica and copper and all the rest of the minerals washed out of the rocks and carried in rivers to the sea; they are the synthetic creations of man's inventive mind, brewed in his laboratories, and having no counterparts in nature.

To adjust to these chemicals would require time on the scale that is nature's; it would require not merely the years of a man's life but the life of generations. And even this, were it by some miracle possible, would be futile, for the new chemicals come from our laboratories in an endless stream; almost five hundred annually find their way into actual use in the United States alone. The figure is staggering and its implications are not easily grasped —500 new chemicals to which the bodies of men and animals are required somehow to adapt each year, chemicals totally outside the limits of biologic experience.

Among them are many that are used in man's war against nature. Since the mid-1940s over 200 basic chemicals have been created for use in killing insects, weeds, rodents, and other organisms described in the modern vernacular as "pests"; and they are sold under several thousand different brand names.

These sprays, dusts, and aerosols are now applied almost universally to farms, gardens, forests, and homes—nonselective chemicals that have the power to kill every insect, the "good" and the "bad," to still the song of birds and the leaping of fish in the streams, to coat the leaves with a deadly film, and to linger on in soil—all this though the intended target may be only a few weeds or insects. Can anyone believe it is possible to lay down such a barrage of poisons on the surface of the earth without making it unfit for all life? They should not be called "insecticides," but "biocides."

The whole process of spraying seems caught up in an endless spiral. Since DDT was released for civilian use, a process of escalation has been going on in which ever more toxic materials must be found. This has happened because insects, in a triumphant vindication of Darwin's principle of the survival of the fittest, have evolved super races immune to the particular insecticide used, hence a deadlier one has always to be developed—and then a deadlier one than that. It has happened also because, for reasons to be described later, destructive insects often undergo a "flare-back," or resurgence, after spraying, in numbers greater than before. Thus the chemical war is never won, and all life is caught in its violent crossfire.

Along with the possibility of the extinction of mankind by nuclear war, the central problem of our age has therefore become the contamination of man's total environment with such substances of incredible potential for harm—substances that accumulate in the tissues of plants and animals and even penetrate the germ cells to shatter or alter the very material of heredity upon which the shape of the future depends.

Some would-be architects of our future look toward a time when it will be possible to alter the human germ plasm by design. But we may easily be doing so now by inadvertence, for many chemicals, like radiation, bring about gene mutations. It is ironic to think that man might determine his own future by something so seemingly trivial as the choice of an insect spray.

All this has been risked—for what? Future historians may well be amazed by our distorted sense of proportion. How could intelligent beings seek to control a few unwanted species by a method that contaminated the entire environment and brought the threat of disease and death even to their own kind? Yet this is precisely what we have done. We have done it, moreover, for reasons that collapse the moment we examine them. We are told that the enormous and expanding use of pesticides is necessary to maintain farm production. Yet is our real problem not one of *overproduction?* Our farms, despite measures to remove acreages from production and to pay farmers *not* to produce, have yielded such a staggering excess of crops that the American taxpayer in 1962 is paying out more than one billion dollars a year as the total carrying cost of the surplus-food storage program. And is the situation helped when one branch of the Agriculture Department tries to reduce production while another states, as it did in 1958, "It is believed generally that reduction of crop acreages under provisions of the Soil Bank will stimulate interest in use of chemicals to obtain maximum production on the land retained in crops."

All this is not to say there is no insect problem and no need of control. I am saying, rather, that control must be geared to realities, not to mythical situations, and that the methods employed must be such that they do not destroy us along with the insects.

The problem whose attempted solution has brought such a train of disaster in its wake is an accompaniment of our modern way of life. Long before the age of man, insects inhabited the earth—a group of extraordinarily varied and adaptable beings. Over the course of time since man's advent, a small percentage of the more than half a million species of insects have come into conflict with human welfare in two principal ways: as competitors for the food supply and as carriers of human disease.

Disease-carrying insects become important where human beings are crowded together, especially under conditions where sanitation is poor, as in time of natural disaster or war or in situations of extreme poverty and deprivation. Then control of some sort becomes necessary. It is a sobering fact, however, as we shall presently see, that the method of massive chemical control has had only limited success, and also threatens to worsen the very conditions it is intended to curb.

Under primitive agricultural conditions the farmer had few insect problems. These arose with the intensification of agriculture —the devotion of immense acreages to a single crop. Such a system set the stage for explosive increases in specific insect populations. Single-crop farming does not take advantage of the principles by which nature works; it is agriculture as an engineer might conceive it to be. Nature has introduced great variety into the landscape, but man has displayed a passion for simplifying it. Thus he undoes the built-in checks and balances by which nature holds the species within bounds. One important natural check is a limit on the amount of suitable habitat for each species. Obviously then, an insect that lives on wheat can build up its population to much higher levels on a farm devoted to wheat than on one in which wheat is intermingled with other crops to which the insect is not adapted.

The same thing happens in other situations. A generation or more ago, the towns of large areas of the United States lined their streets with the noble elm tree. Now the beauty they hopefully created is threatened with complete destruction as disease sweeps through the elms, carried by a beetle that would have only limited chance to build up large populations and to spread from tree to tree if the elms were only occasional trees in a richly diversified planting.

Another factor in the modern insect problem is one that must be viewed against a background of geologic and human history: the spreading of thousands of different kinds of organisms from their native homes to invade new territories. This worldwide migration has been studied and graphically described by the British ecologist Charles Elton in his recent book *The Ecology of Invasions*. During the Cretaceous Period, some hundred million years ago, flooding seas cut many land bridges between continents and living things found themselves confined in what Elton calls "colossal separate nature reserves." There, isolated from others of their kind, they developed many new species. When some of the land masses were joined again, about 15 million years ago, these species began to move out into new territories—a movement that is not only still in progress but is now receiving considerable assistance from man.

The importation of plants is the primary agent in the modern spread of species, for animals have almost invariably gone along with the plants, quarantine being a comparatively recent and not completely effective innovation. The United States Office of Plant Introduction alone has introduced almost 200,000 species and varieties of plants from all over the world. Nearly half of the 180 or so major insect enemies of plants in the United States are accidental imports from abroad, and most of them have come as hitchhikers on plants.

In new territory, out of reach of the restraining hand of the natural enemies that kept down its numbers in its native land, an invading plant or animal is able to become enormously abundant. Thus it is no accident that our most troublesome insects are introduced species.

These invasions, both the naturally occurring and those dependent on human assistance, are likely to continue indefinitely. Quarantine and massive chemical campaigns are only extremely expensive ways of buying time. We are faced, according to Dr. Elton, "with a life-and-death need not just to find new technological means of suppressing this plant or that animal"; instead we need the basic knowledge of animal populations and their relations to their surroundings that will "promote an even balance and damp down the explosive power of outbreaks and new invasions."

Much of the necessary knowledge is now available but we do not use it. We train ecologists in our universities and even employ them in our governmental agencies but we seldom take their advice. We allow the chemical death rain to fall as though there were no alternative, whereas in fact there are many, and our ingenuity could soon discover many more if given opportunity.

Have we fallen into a mesmerized state that makes us accept as inevitable that which is inferior or detrimental, as though having lost the will or the vision to demand that which is good? Such thinking, in the words of the ecologist Paul Shepard, "idealizes life with only its head out of water, inches above the limits of toleration of the corruption of its own environment. . . . Why should we tolerate a diet of weak poisons, a home in insipid surroundings, a circle of acquaintances who are not quite our enemies, the noise of motors with just enough relief to prevent insanity? Who would want to live in a world which is just not quite fatal?"

Yet such a world is pressed upon us. The crusade to create a chemically sterile, insect-free world seems to have engendered a fanatic zeal on the part of many specialists and most of the so-called control agencies. On every hand there is evidence that those engaged in spraying operations exercise a ruthless power. "The regulatory entomologists . . . function as prosecutor, judge and jury, tax assessor and collector and sheriff to enforce their own orders," said Connecticut entomologist Neely Turner. The most flagrant abuses go unchecked in both state and federal agencies.

It is not my contention that chemical insecticides must never be used. I do contend that we have put poisonous and biologically potent chemicals indiscriminately into the hands of persons largely or wholly ignorant of their potentials for harm. We have subjected enormous numbers of people to contact with these poisons, without their consent and often without their knowledge. If the Bill of Rights contains no guarantee that a citizen shall be secure against lethal poisons distributed either by private individuals or by public officials, it is surely only because our forefathers, despite their considerable wisdom and foresight, could conceive of no such problem.

I contend, furthermore, that we have allowed these chemicals to be used with little or no advance investigation of their effect

on soil, water, wildlife, and man himself. Future generations are
unlikely to condone our lack of prudent concern for the integrity
of the natural world that supports all life.

There is still very limited awareness of the nature of the threat.
This is an era of specialists, each of whom sees his own problem
and is unaware of or intolerant of the larger frame into which
it fits. It is also an era dominated by industry, in which the
right to make a dollar at whatever cost is seldom challenged.
When the public protests, confronted with some obvious evidence
of damaging results of pesticide applications, it is fed little tran-
quilizing pills of half truth. We urgently need an end to these
false assurances, to the sugar coating of unpalatable facts. It is the
public that is being asked to assume the risks that the insect con-
trollers calculate. The public must decide whether it wishes to
continue on the present road, and it can do so only when in full
possession of the facts. In the words of Jean Rostand, "The obligation to endure gives us the right to know."

The urgency to produce food is now greater than it was in Miss
Carson's period, which she correctly pictured as a culture in which
farmers were paid not to farm and to leave their acres fallow. The
counterproductiveness of hard pesticides that she details, however, remains valid. She not only would be but indeed *was* the first to recognize that an argument based on the idea that man must submit to
dangerous poisons in order to stave off starvation is specious. Reduced
to such a dilemma, mankind has but a choice of how to die. The choice
is rather to find alternatives. Those who maintain there are no alternatives might be characterized as technicians, and pessimistic ones, rather
than scientists.

From the perspective of a decade later, it is apparent that Miss
Carson was conservative in most of her material and comments. The
situation was worse than she depicted. There were several environ-
mentally destructive substances on the market which she did not mention. Indeed, the potential of some still was not recognized. Among
the unrecognized was polychlorinated biphenyls, commonly known as
PCBs, an all-pervading contaminant that has been in industrial use for
more than forty years. One of the modern American dictionaries,
copyrighted in 1969, failed to record the term or abbreviation *PCBs,*
and to check the spelling of the chemical one must resort to conservation or environmental magazines.

The controversy that followed publication of *Silent Spring* alerted
the public to many pesticide hazards. As with most publications, the

book was condemned or approved most vociferously by those who had never read it. But the controversy undoubtedly did more to spread the word than the book itself did, despite its enormous success in bookstores.

However, the agricultural establishment and its congressional supporters moved with surprising inertia as demands for banning DDT built. The substance was not proscribed by the Environmental Protection Agency until 1973, largely through legal delays—and the fact that through most of the period there was no legal agency of the scope of the EPA, which came into existence on December 2, 1970. The truth is that by the time DDT received official scorn it had declined in effectiveness, as Miss Carson predicted. The more persistent pests had evolved into immune forms that could live with DDT. It had reached the point of limited returns and no longer was held in high esteem by the agricultural establishment.

Since the DDT victory, the EPA has continued reviewing the effects of hard pesticides and in 1974 removed aldrin and dieldrin from the market. In 1975 it began proceedings against heptachlor and chlordane.

The vigilance that Miss Carson found lacking in the pesticide situation has been restored to some extent through the creation of such agencies as the federal Environmental Protection Agency and state counterparts. Creation of these units can be traced directly to *Silent Spring* and the furor it stimulated. So far the activity of those who call themselves "ecologists" has prevented the new agencies from drifting, either by congressional or executive fiat or through indifference, into the neglect that characterized earlier agencies that the public supposed were watching its interests.